*The Reading Method* is the documented account of perhaps the most revolutionary long-range experiment ever attempted in the history of language teaching. From reports, articles, addresses, texts, programs, outlines, announcements, correspondence, records, test forms, student papers, staff minutes, course materials, and raw data sheets, Otto F. Bond has written the final report of thirty years of experimental teaching of a second language at the learning level. There is in the history of language teaching no record of a similar experiment on such a scale and over such a long period of time.

*The Reading Method* presents chronologically the details of organization and administration; the obstacles, problems, solutions, principles, and practices that lie behind a way of second-language teaching which has been familiar to all teachers and students of foreign languages since the middle 1920's.

It is the record of experiments in the use of audio-visual material, the role of oral-aural experience, the effects of intensive versus extensive reading, and of every problem and pedogogical variable encountered in thirty years of methodological experiment. With the publication of *The Reading Method* the dearth of concrete and objective evidence needed to evaluate this uniformly successful method is at an end.

OTTO F. BOND *is William Rainey Harper Professor Emeritus of French in the College of the University of Chicago, and author or co-author of a dozen standard language texts and reference books. Mr. Bond is a Chevalier of the Legion of Honor.*

# THE READING METHOD

# THE READING METHOD

*An Experiment in College French*

## BY OTTO F. BOND

*The University of Chicago*

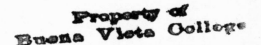

THE UNIVERSITY OF CHICAGO PRESS

THE UNIVERSITY OF CHICAGO PRESS, CHICAGO 37
Cambridge University Press, London, N.W. 1, England

TO

*Julia Hopkins Bond*

# FOREWORD

AN EXPERIMENT in the teaching of a foreign language began in the autumn of 1920 in the Laboratory Schools of the University of Chicago. In 1950 it was still going on in the College.

For thirty years the teaching of elementary French has been under continuous scrutiny, measurement, and revision. Although in certain areas there remain unsolved, perhaps unsolvable, questions, some basic principles, an outline, an established chronological order of trainings, effective materials and techniques, and a tested philosophy have come out of this long stage of trial and error and constitute what may be called a *method*.

This book is the history and the testimonial of that method. If the popular conception of the so-called "Reading Method" differs from the description of it given herein, perhaps the latter may serve to correct the former. A correction is long past due.

Previous to the beginning of this experiment, the author, who assumes the major responsibility for the development of the method, had taught French for six years by the "Grammar-Translation" method, followed by six years of fanatic devotion to the Müster-schule brand of the "Direct Method," topped off with a three-year experience with the "Army French" of World War I.

During this last period, the lamentable inefficiency in all language skills that was shown by the forty thousand soldier-students in the forty-two Army French schools under his direction in the Southern War Department convinced him that reforms in foreign language teaching in the American educational setting were needed. Anyone could see that something was wrong, and no one denied that something could and should be done about it. That is the background of the author's interest and participation in this educational experiment.

Many persons have shared in this work. Twenty-two full-time instructors, approximately seven thousand college students who completed in thirty years more than twenty thousand quarter-courses in first-year and second-year French, and a thousand graduate students who studied elementary French for graduate reading requirements have made their contribution to its progress and to its *matériel*. It is underwritten by a long and varied classroom experience. Its findings are bedded upon hard lessons, the impersonal evidence of statistical analysis and objective measurement, and patient trial and error. They were not handed down upon tablets of stone.

Sandburg has said that you cannot lay hands upon a language. Neither can you with ease or certainty lay hands upon its learning processes. Furthermore, in language investigation, the human subjects are complex, variable, unpredictable, uncontrollable, and, unlike laboratory guinea pigs, must be left in a negotiable state for further educational growth. One cannot conduct a language experiment, of course, with the thoroughness of scientific research. Classroom conditions are not laboratory conditions. But that does not mean that one must reject an objective or laboratory approach to language-teaching problems. There is a reasonable compromise possible. We tried to find it and to maintain it.

Most teachers have moments of doubt about the necessity or the value of certain details, procedures, or aspects of their teaching. We noted such doubts, recorded them on paper, stated our reactions as fully and as impartially as we could, and discussed them with our colleagues. Decisions were usually based upon joint experience and opinion. If we failed to obtain a crystal-clear judgment, we at least came to know better the nature and the limitations of our job and to sense the need or the possibilities of its improvement. At all times, we preferred the question mark to the exclamation point. We were, and we still are, unsatisfied. The horizon recedes as one approaches it.

In the preparation of this book, the author has utilized the accumulated files of three decades of documentation: class lists, student personal and study records, outside reading reports and summaries, questionnaires, the minutes of staff conferences, staff reports, data on progress and achievement tests, the forms and results of quarterly and comprehensive examinations, placement and admissions data, requisitions, accounts, schedules, programs, syllabi, lists, files of tests, indexes, announcements, catalogues, blueprints, audio-visual material, textbooks, editorial files, reprints of articles and addresses by the staff and others, survey and committee reports, personal correspondence, official communications, etc., *ad nauseam*. Little of importance transpired without a record. Some sixty thousand pieces of documentation have been consulted.

But the complete story is not there. There are imponderables and incommensurables that defy graphs, statistics, percentages, and coefficients of correlation. And there are many things seen and heard that are not so well remembered. Voices have been stilled and hands stayed. People have gone their separate ways. If, then, opinion and conviction take over at times and dogmatism creeps in, the author begs the reader to recall that, as with Mrs. Miniver, it is difficult to dissociate one's self from the center of the universe.

It has been a long and arduous task, although pleasant and rewarding, at least in retrospect. It has been particularly rewarding in the contacts which it has afforded with that perennial enigma, Youth, as well as with members of the teaching profession in the University of Chicago and abroad.

One cannot repay in a Foreword one's indebtedness to the many persons who, consciously or unconsciously, have contributed to one's work through their voice, action, or printed words. Their anonymity here implies on the part of the author no lack of appreciation and gratitude. There are those, however, without whose timely aid and sympathetic encouragement the continuance of our experimentation would not have been possible. Of these, the author would mention with special gratitude President Emeritus Ernest H. Wilkins, of Oberlin College, formerly dean of the Colleges of the University of Chicago; the late Henry C. Morrison, professor of education and superintendent of the Laboratory Schools of the University of Chicago; Chauncey S. Boucher, professor of American history and formerly dean of the College of Arts, Literature, and Science; William A. Nitze, professor emeritus of Romance languages and literatures of the University of Chicago; Dr. Michael West, formerly principal of Teachers' College, Dacca, India; the late Robert D. Cole, professor of education in the University of Pennsylvania; and F. Champion Ward, present dean of the College, the University of Chicago.

Sharing intimately in the undertaking are the author's colleagues, past and present, on the French staff,[1] and his co-workers, the late John C. Ransmeier in Spanish and Peter Hagboldt in German, both of whom left unfinished the task so well begun. Their interest in the problems of second-language learning, their zeal in experimentation, and their teamwork have remained a valued part of the traditions of the College staff. Besides the author, only one member of the original staff of 1920–23 remains: Professor Durbin Rowland, who has contributed no small part to the development and success of the Reading Method and to our *esprit de corps*.

A final acknowledgment, long overdue, goes to an unwitting benefactor whom we never knew in person, the late Professor Dickinson S. Miller, of Harvard University. In an article in the *New Republic*, June, 1921, he wrote the words that were adopted as a slogan for this language investigation: *The economical use of means aimed at an end firmly fixed*. That has been our intention, if not our practice.

O. F. B.

UNIVERSITY OF CHICAGO

# TABLE OF CONTENTS

# THE LURE OF LANGUAGE

Human language is *terra incognita*, despite its antiquity and the more than eight thousand years that have passed since its first written forms marked the beginning of a new ethnic era in the history of civilization. Man is still exploring its mystery, slowly and laboriously uncovering minute truths concerning its origins, its ultimate nature, its manifestations and use. Simple enough for a child to master, yet so complicated that its ways defy mature analysis, it challenges the mind as do few other human phenomena.

Not the least of its mysteries are the ways of its learning processes, particularly in the case of a language which, for the learner, is not his mother-tongue. As a school activity, the learning of a second language appears on the surface as a simple exercise of the intellect and of the will. But that is not so. Its problems, at unexpected turns, bring one sharply into contact with the whole complex of man in his universe.

It is this complexity and perplexity of language that make its exploration fascinating.[1] Beginning, say, with Comenius in the seventeenth century, we see a continuous succession of explorers into this distinctly human activity. The pygmy structure of theory and facts built up by them marks a prodigious effort that confronts a modern worker in the field with the question of the worth of his own possible accomplishment. He would perhaps feel less hesitant were he faced with fewer unknowns and a more enduring medium.

If one questions the need for studying the ways and means of language learning, one may consider, for example, the practical aspects of the teaching and learning of a second language in Britain's colonial empire; or the cultural and social advantages sought by millions of students of French, Spanish, or German in the schools of the Orient and of the Occident or the uncounted men and women in

1

business, industry, and the professions who, for one reason or another, seek to know a foreign language; or the growing import of languages in the centers of world affairs. More and more the learning of foreign languages becomes incumbent upon civilized man. As international barriers weaken or fall, his need for extending his means of communication grows. The language problem has become acute.

In the United States it came into sharp professional focus in the two decades *entre deux guerres.* In one year, 1925, a thoroughgoing survey[2] of our school systems showed for 10,483 public and 1,341 private and secondary schools and 293 colleges an enrolment in French, German, and Spanish in the secondary schools of 850,114 pupils, and for both secondary schools and colleges, an enrolment of well over 1,000,000. There were many more, for the survey represented only 90 per cent of the public school population, 54 per cent of the private schools, and less than 50 per cent of the colleges. Furthermore, it did not include private learners, home-study students, and data on other than the three foreign languages mentioned.

A million second-language learners in the educational network of the United States in a given year—what an immense consumption of human energy, what an incalculable expenditure of time, at what an enormous private and public cost! And this expenditure of energy, time, and money affected not only the learner but the teacher, the tutor, the administrator, and the taxable body of citizenry. Surely, any inquiry into language learning, however modest its results, if honestly conducted, would be a justifiable line of research.

How effective was this effort? What use was made of the language proficiency? How permanent was the proficiency? These are vital questions, asked then, as now, by parents, teachers, superintendents, trustees, fiscal agencies—and by the student. The tendency here, as elsewhere in the curriculum, is to evaluate the language experience in finite terms: earning capacity, clock hours, academic credits, employment, postschool use. As well try to evaluate likewise one's friendships, family life, social impulses, aesthetic and ethical experiences, or recreation. The main values of language learning are not mensurable solely in units of cost, time, calories, credits, or jobs. Life is not just an expense ledger, with language proficiency in one column or the other.

Nonetheless, questions of effectiveness of training, economy in learning, language use and permanency, and their like, are pertinent questions, deserving of serious answers, if the latter can be found.

Between 1920 and 1940, language teachers, psychologists, educators, lexicographers, methodologists, and graduate students joined in a frontal attack upon these issues with unprecedented enthusiasm and vigor and with far-reaching effects. To quote Professor Fife:

> The epoch which began in 1924 with the initiation of the Modern Language Study and reached a certain conclusion in 1942, made contributions of historical importance in the sharpening of objectives, the establishment of the priority of the reading objective for practical and cultural utility, and the development of standardized tests of achievement. It also laid the foundation for integrating cultural studies in foreign areas with the attainment of language competence. It thus created an atmosphere which, reinforced by the war experience, may now develop more rapidly into realistic programs under the pressure of increased international interest. The most important contribution of the decades chronicled in the three volumes of the *Analytical Bibliography* has been the recognition of the necessity for basing objectives and methods on the results of sound experimentation.[3]

It was perhaps the world war of 1914–18, with its antedating of so much that was thought fixed and stable, its need for new techniques, its emphasis on achievement, its tremendous expansion in living, the renaissance of interest in foreign cultures that followed it, and the surge toward liberal education, that gave impetus to the movement. Enrolments soared; schoolrooms overflowed. Language study became a universal "must." For the language teachers it was a chance to recoup the loss of morale suffered in the experiences of "war French" and to turn the page.

Then came the searching, sobering, impersonal evaluation of the whole structure of language teaching and learning in our American and Canadian schools, the results of which fill the eighteen volumes of the *Modern Language Study*, the last of which appeared in September, 1934, seven years after the appearance of the initial report and eleven years after the organization of the study. It was a costly labor, involving more than sixty major collaborators and three hundred thousand dollars. Perhaps no survey in a single field in education has ever approximated it in scope, organization, thoroughness, achievement, and influence.

These eighteen volumes are more than a huge compendium of

bibliographical and historical matter and an analysis of existent conditions of enrolment, course organization, teacher-training, and achievement. They include statistical and interpretive reports on the wholesale administration of batteries of objective achievement tests in reading, vocabulary, and grammar; a laboratory study of eye-movements in silent reading; compilations of range-frequency lists in French, German, and Spanish, necessitating the counting of millions of words of running discourse; idiom lists similarly compiled for the three languages cited; prognosis tests and their interpretation; and a score of special studies dealing with such matters as the influence of foreign language learning upon training in English, the reliabilities of certain language tests, new testing techniques, class sectioning and class size in relation to achievement, the layering of frequency lists into minimum basic vocabularies, relative attainment by different methods of instruction, syntax frequency counts, etc. They form a colossal monument of 5,592 pages dedicated to the lure of language.

It would be not unreasonable to expect only a mild flurry of investigative activity in the years following. Not so. Volume I of the Canadian committee's report[4] contains 340 pages of annotated bibliography of modern writings on the subject. The foreign language methodologies of Handschin[5] and Cole[6] provide literally thousands of references to books, articles, journals, pamphlets, and theses dealing with language learning. The teacher's handbook by T. E. Oliver[7] is a bibliographical reference list that fills 706 large pages, covering every conceivable angle of the topic. The first volume of Coleman's *Analytical Bibliography* abstracts 572 titles appearing in 1927–32, unrecorded in the works mentioned above. The second volume, covering 1932–37, summarizes 1,125 publications; and the third and last volume abstracts an additional 853 publications appearing in 1937–42, having excluded, because of costs, some 200 articles and publications dealing with foreign language teaching abroad. Altogether, these three bibliographies list 2,550 separate works treating second-language learning, approximately 2,000 of which appeared *after* the last published volume of the *Modern Language Study*. The present-day explorer in foreign language teaching does not set out without compass and chart!

And yet, relatively only a few teachers were actively engaged in serious language experimentation.[8] In 1932, 1,000 inquiries brought 403 responses, of which 95 indicated research in progress. A similar inquiry in 1933 addressed to 3,000 teachers brought 179 responses and 67 indications of investigations. A third survey in 1936 of 5,500 teachers met with 907 responses showing 207 studies under way.[9] Here is but a very small cross-section of the 12,000 foreign language teachers in the United States.

Aims, material, and methods continued to hold first place in interest—45 per cent of the activity in 1932–42. Curricular problems were in second place. State and city syllabi showed little real change. Syllabi committees and school boards move forward like the siege towers of Caesar—with precaution and facing in all directions. In textbooks there was more evidence of reform and progress, particularly in graded offerings for early reading. As for grammars, despite the blandishments of the prefaces in respect to the reading objective, textually they kept to the status quo. A very definite and heartening trend, however, showed in testing techniques, objective rating, and the standardization of materials for course evaluation. There were increasing evidences also of a conjunction between the educational psychologist and the foreign language teacher in the working-out of practical problems of the classroom.

In England, in Canada, in Japan, in the United States, in India, researchers were busy measuring the units of work in the learning of a foreign word, gauging the readability of books, drawing up and testing minimum word lists, defining and grading idioms, counting the frequency of syntactical phenomena, photographing the production of speech sounds and rhythms, investigating audio-visual aids to language learning, preparing graded readers, constructing and standardizing language proficiency tests—in short, reducing the percentage of the unknown, the percentage of error, the percentage of failure, for the millions of language learners of the future, trying "to take hold of a language, and mark it with signs for its remembrance."

## CHAPTER I

# ANALYZING THE JOB

## 1. *The Theory of Uniqueness*

IT IS sometimes asserted that foreign language learning differs so much from the learning of other subjects in the curriculum and makes such a unique contribution to a liberal education that special consideration by the administrator is not only desirable but imperative. In this belief, the language teacher tends to become oversensitive in regard to criticism or change, whether either originates within or outside his professional group. Being somewhat conservative, he dislikes the thought of having to tailor his course to the cloth at hand. As a result, the language course is often unrealistic and the teacher dissatisfied. The foreign language journals attest the fact.

The issue can be reduced to this: Is it possible to construct and implement a course that can be adjusted to local pupil and curricular requirements; that will be effective as either a terminal or a foundation course; that will be generalized, yet personalized; and that will yield a high degree of proficiency with reasonable permanence? Such a course would ask for no curricular favors and would be ready at any time to show incontrovertible evidence of its achievement. That is the issue, oversimplified no doubt, and the challenge.

Most of the problems of such a course would be common to courses in other subject matters. There is no lack of authoritative opinion on that point.

West[1] has identified the techniques of foreign language teaching with those of teaching English. The interrelations of the science, the language-arts, and the expression-type subjects in the common-school curriculum have been pointed out by Morrison.[2] Hagboldt[3] has set forth clearly and with rare brevity the basic principles of language learning, many of which are basic to all learning. And Coleman,[4] in his report on the teaching of modern foreign languages in the United States, has presented teachers and administrators with the hard facts of reality.

But of fundamental consideration in teaching languages, as in teaching anything else, is the student, viewed as an individual and as a member of a group. It would be well to "learn" him before trying to teach him.[5]

To do that is not so simple as it sounds. Four major attempts were made in the course of our experimentation: (1) an investigation into the causes of language failure, based on 125 cases in a single year, 1921–22; (2) a survey in 1923 of the time-load of 450 elementary French and Spanish students; (3) an investigation in 1924 of the distribution of student time and voluntary reading for 1,786 autumn registrants in the College; and (4) an analysis of student personal data collected between 1923 and 1928 from 938 registrants in elementary French courses.

Through these four investigations made during the formative years of our course, we learned who our students were, what they wanted, their working conditions, their attitudes toward language study, why they succeeded or failed, their reactions to changing programs and procedures, and their individual and relative achievement in learning a foreign language. We also discovered that the problems of language teaching are, by and large, the problems of all teaching and that they can be solved by methods found in the laboratory, the factory, the club, and the studio. They are not unique.

## 2. Who Are the Students?

In an institution like the University of Chicago, located in a great city, operating on a quarter system, complicated in its structure and policies, and attracting a heterogeneous student body, it is very difficult to conduct a pedagogical experiment. Students have a maddening way of appearing and disappearing in a course of study without giving reasons or records. As a result, student data are frequently incomplete.

Such was the case with the 1930 survey of student personal records. We used the personal record form reproduced in Appendix III (p. 310), selecting for analysis all the cards on file for registrants in elementary French (French 1ABC)[6] in the five-year period 1923–28. The file was begun in 1922; it now contains over five thousand entries. In spite of some incompleteness of information, we were able to gather a very useful body of facts for the determination of directions, objectives, and techniques.

Placement and continuity are two of the more vexing problems for the language teacher. The survey revealed that, of 918 students in the elementary French course, only 26 per cent took the full three-quarter sequence in regular order, that is, 1A in the autumn, 1B in the winter, and 1C in the spring. Sixty-two per cent took fractions of the sequence (as: 1A, 1AB, 1AC, 1B, 1BC, 1C),[7] and 12 per cent dropped out without completing the work of one quarter.

Of the 566 registrants who did not take the complete sequence, 34 per cent satisfied the language requirement through promotion (1A to 1C) or advanced standing (1BC, 1C), but 66 per cent stopped short of validation (1A, 1AB, 1B), at least within the limits of the investigation. It is likely that most of the latter never resumed the study and should be added to the wastage represented by the 113 students who dropped the course without even a quarter's credit.

Withdrawals, broken continuity, and piecemeal accreditation are particularly serious matters[8] in a foreign language course, where the mastery of both skill and content is expected. It seemed clear from the survey that only one out of four registrants in first-year French progressed regularly from the beginning to the end of the course. Could anything be done to increase the number of continuations and completions?

Another disturbing problem in a language course is the presence of students differing in college experience and maturity. As an instance, in the group surveyed, 57.5 per cent were Freshmen; 22.2 per cent, Sophomores; 8.5 per cent, Juniors; 5.1 per cent, Seniors; 2.4 per cent, graduate students; and 4.3 per cent, unclassified. How to fit a single language course to such a disparate clientele was a perplexing question. It was also a question that had to be answered in the interests of the student.

What happened to the Freshmen registrants? Fifty per cent (266) completed the three-quarter sequence in regular order (ABC); 41.2 per cent showed broken continuity; and 8.8 per cent dropped out without completing one quarter's work. At that, the Freshman group made the best showing, since it registered 60 per cent of the total number of completions, although it composed only 57.5 per cent of the total number of French 1 registrants.

The break in Freshman continuation occurred more frequently at the end of 1B (41.2 per cent) as compared with 1A (18.4 per cent), suggesting that the second quarter was the critical point in the sequence. Changes in chronology, content, and procedures in 1B might prevent some of this loss, although no doubt there were other than studial factors involved.

The nature, amount, and recency of previous language experience are also factors to be considered in course planning. The 1930 survey revealed that the foreign language "barrier" no longer existed as such for nearly two-thirds (62.6 per cent) of the 918 registrants in French 1. The percentage was probably higher, for the records were often incomplete on this point. In the matter of the French language, 15 per cent had had from one to eight semesters in high school or one or two semesters in college, with 64 per cent of the cases in the one-year high-school bracket. For the latter, previous experience was of questionable value.

Time has not changed wastage. In 1945 an analysis of 167 applicants for college placement in French showed that 16 per cent had had only one year of the language in high school. The entire group failed on the standard American Council on Education Cooperative French test and were held to the language requirement. Again, in September, 1947, 13 per cent of the 194 applicants had had only one year of French; 84.6 per cent failed on the standard test. Since 62 per cent of this group had graduated from high school in June of that year, the recency factor could not be invoked in their favor. In the present as in the past,[9] one year of French in high school is of doubtful continuation value.

Since 15 per cent of the first-year French registrants already had some experience with the language, it was desirable to know the kind and quality of that instruction for course planning and student counseling. Unfortunately, the survey failed to supply reliable data on these points, owing to lack of uniformity in interpreting the questions on the record card and to the confusion of methods and texts in the schools after the Coleman report of 1926. However, from an inspection of the cards, it was obvious that procedures, methods, and texts varied widely. Here, then, was another area for salvage operations.

The study preferences of the language registrant tend to influence his objectives, participation, and attainment in the course; they, too, were analyzed in the survey. Of 483 registrants in French 1, the study preferences of 56.6 per cent were in the humanities; 23.8 per cent in the social sciences; and 19.6 per cent in the biological and physical sciences. Approximately twenty years later, the order is in reverse and humanities are at the bottom of the scale. Economics, politics, technological advancement, and international affairs influence the common-school curriculum, in which foreign language study is a variable and *not* a constant. The given moment prescribes and limits. Has second-language learning a "core" value that is not subject to educational market conditions? If it has, should it not be guaranteed against time and circumstance in the curriculum?

The more formal aspects of student personnel have been presented up to this point. There are informal, personal matters that may point up success or failure in language study, such as age, foreign parentage, physical handicaps, and attitude toward the study of English or of the foreign language. The survey brought out some interesting facts in regard to them.

The average age for the 164 students who completed 1A was nineteen years, with 65 per cent of the group in the eighteen- to nineteen-year range. Ages ranged from sixteen to thirty-eight for the total group.

Approximately 28 per cent of 1,006 student cases analyzed were of foreign parentage and came into French 1 with a foreign language background or inheritance to be reckoned with as an asset or a liability. Twenty nationalities were represented, the Balto-Slavic group ranking first, with the Germanic, Scandinavian, Romanic, and oriental groups following in ranking order.

Thirty per cent of 918 cases showed the presence of a physical defect that might have some bearing upon their success or failure in a language course. Most serious were the 48 cases of defective hearing or speech.

Seventy-one students expressed a positive dislike for the study of English. Fifty-one declared that they found the study of a foreign language unduly difficult for them; they supported their opinion with fifty-two different reasons, including trouble with English grammar, poor memory, a dislike for foreign languages, and oral-aural difficulties. Sixty-two had begun the study of a foreign language and then dropped it; they gave personal reasons (such as illness, dislike, want of interest, and parental pressure) in 40 per cent of the cases, and administrative causes (schedule changes, requirements, leaving school, etc.) in the remaining 60 per cent. Fifty-two students had avoided all foreign language study in their preparatory training.

There is no point in continuing with this analysis. The reader who has taught a foreign language course will already have recognized his own experiences and problems. We merely substantiated through this survey what everyone knows. In the last twenty years of our experiment there has been little change in these conditions. As far as the College of the University of Chicago is concerned, the situation is normal and constant.

For most students entering college the over-all time-load quickly becomes a most important factor in achievement, aiding or nullifying the best-planned program. To find out what the study conditions were for our language students, a survey was made (1923) of the time-load of 450 registrants in the autumn quarter of French, German, and Spanish 1ABC, checking time spent in preparing assignments, outside employment, transportation, and campus and off-campus activities.

The results showed an average over-all time-load of 63.5 hours per week, of which 50.5 hours were spent in class and in the preparation of lessons. The remainder was spent in transportation (range, 1.2–4.6 hours), remunerative employment (range, 5.6–9.0 hours), and activities (range, 4.5–5.0 hours). The weekly time-load in French averaged 5 hours in class and $8\frac{1}{2}$ hours in preparation. German required 10 hours in preparation. A section of 25 students in French 1A averaged 50.5 hours per week in study and class activities, and 16.8 hours in nonstudy activities, or a total weekly time-load of 67.3 hours.

The extremes revealed by the survey demonstrated a need for equalization and setting up a standard norm for course time requirements, with machinery for its enforcement. Obviously, the language staff could not proceed with maximum effectiveness unless it knew the fair amount of time at its disposal and the working conditions of its students, for course failures are too often only *time-management* failures. The staff was interested in obtaining a low incidence of failure.

Consequently, in the winter of 1924, a college-wide survey[10] was made of the time distribution of the 3,053 students registered in the preceding autumn quarter. Of the 1,989 questionnaires returned, 1,786 were analyzed and tabulated. Fifty-eight per cent represented students in the College of Arts.

For those carrying a normal program, i.e., three courses, the mean time per week per course was 12 hours, or an average weekly study-load of 36 hours. Women required less time than men. Juniors spent least time, and Freshmen most. In the three-major group, 16.8 per cent spent less than 10 hours per week per course; 25.7 per cent spent more than 25 hours. Only 18.2 per cent of the cases showed a perfect correlation between what the student actually spent and the time he thought he should spend on a single course. He thought 13 hours would be a fair demand, on the average. The faculty thought differently; in 197 returns to a special questionnaire, it indicated an expectancy of 24–60 hours, with a median range of 40–45 hours for a three-course program, or an average of approximately 15 hours per week per course in a normal program.

A year later, with the survey *Report* in hand, the faculty settled for a 42–45-hour study-week, or normally a 2 to 1 ratio of preparation and classwork. This ratio became the time base of our experiment; with our 5-hour week, the over-all time-load for French 1 was standardized at 15 hours until 1930.

We needed to know how the student used his "surplus" time, since nonstudy activities often have a more direct bearing upon academic achievement than does the study-load. The survey gave us the following answers, expressed in averages for three-major students in the undergraduate colleges:

1. *Serious reading.*—Of 1,492 cases, 11.4 per cent reported no time devoted to serious reading; 10.8 per cent reported 1 hour; 20.1 per cent, 2 hours; and 16 per cent, 3 hours. The average was approximately 3 hours per week.

2. *Gainful employment.*—Thirty-one per cent spent between 10 and 15 hours per week in outside work. Two-thirds of the men and one-third of the women in the total group answering (1,373 cases) were earning part or all of their college expenses.

3. *Transportation.*—662 students (42.5 per cent) spent 5–10 hours weekly in commuting; 208 of them were also gainfully employed, and 291 had home duties in excess of 5 week hours.

4. *Dramatics.*—64 students participated in dramatics, spending an average of 5–10 hours per week on training; the same group gave 30–35 hours to their three-major program.

5. *Social affairs.*—Of the fraternity-club group (467 members), the average member spent 20–25 hours per week on outside activities and social affairs. Other students averaged 15–20 hours. Less than 35 hours were spent on a normal three-major program by 48.4 per cent of the group, compared to 30.7 per cent for the nonfraternity-club group. On purely social affairs (teas, dances, receptions), 64.5 of the men (706) and 44.7 per cent of the women (713) spent from 1 to 5 hours per week.

6. *Athletics.*—745 college Freshmen and Sophomores were regularly enrolled in gymnasium classes. Of the total group, 57.1 per cent indicated 2 or more hours spent weekly as spectators at athletic contests, and 50.4 per cent reported an average of 1–5 hours per week spent on indoor games (cards, chess, checkers, etc.).

7. *Amusements.*—Motion pictures accounted for an average of 2 hours per week for 34.4 per cent of 1,464 students. The theater, lectures, and concerts accounted for a similar expenditure of time for 58.8 per cent (1,487 cases).

8. *Religious activities.*—36.4 per cent of the total group spent 2–4 hours in religious activities; on the other hand, 33 per cent of the men and 29.3 per cent of the women gave no time to religious meetings or work.

Overparticipation in nonstudy activities, and not participation, is the real hazard. Concern could be felt for the 719 men and 688 women who *averaged* three nonstudy connections, or for the 109 men and 62 women who reported more time spent on outside matters than on their courses, or for that third of the total group that reported living under strain because of "lack of time." Apparently from 20 to 25 per cent of all the undergraduates reporting (1,786) spent as much time on gainful employment, home duties, nonstudy activities, and organized social affairs as they devoted to a normal load of three-major courses and serious reading. It was reasonable to suppose that this condition extended to the registrants in our elementary language classes.

Here, in the data reported above, was M, our average student, the middle man in a thousand. He could be described somewhat as follows: a Freshman, without previous acquaintance with French, but with some foreign language experience in high school, probably two years of Latin; about nineteen years old, of American birth and parentage, without relevant physical handicaps; not disliking the formal study of English and not considering the study of foreign languages unduly difficult for him. He had not begun a foreign language course in high school and then dropped it with loss of credit.

M preferred the humanities, with a leaning toward English or history. He was taking French because he wanted to, and not because he had to. By one combination or another of the three quarters in French 1, he would successfully clear 1C. He would spend from 12 to 13 hours per week on the course and 36 hours or so on his three-major program, with 2 hours per week for serious reading.

He was earning part (or all) of his expenses, and commuted between his home and the university. He attended few social affairs, belonged to no fraternal organization, spent 2 hours a week at concerts, lectures, or plays; attended gymnasium classes regularly and weekly athletic contests; and averaged about three nonstudy connections. Altogether, his autumn quarter time-load averaged from 55 to 60 hours per week. He no doubt complained of "lack of time."

Student M should be the main target of our experimentation, of course; but there were also the exceptional students, good and bad, and the extreme cases in one classification or another; we were interested in them, too. Could the ends be played *with* the middle, at the same time? That is, could we serve the individual while serving the group? To be able to answer that question, we needed to know what the student wanted.

### 3. *What Do the Students Want?*

There was little usable information about what students wanted with a foreign language. Books on foreign language methodology, journal articles, conference and survey reports, and random addresses gave (and still give) many reasons why people should study a foreign language, but it was invariably the language teacher who was speaking. We decided to let the student speak for himself.

On the personal record form used in the 1930 survey, the student was asked: "Why are you studying French?" The question was asked on the first day of the course, before course or teacher could influence the answer. We received 1,014 responses, of which 57 per cent came from Freshmen, 11.8 per cent from Sophomores, and the residue from Juniors, Seniors, graduate students, and unclassified students.

Three hundred and thirty-two (32.7 per cent) were following a personal desire; they did not explain further. One hundred and fifty-nine (15.7 per cent) said they wanted French for business, professional, and teaching purposes. Under "professional" purposes they listed architecture, art, chemistry, dancing, diplomacy, drama, economics, engineering, history, journalism, linguistics, law, library science, literary work, military service, music, political science, secretarial work, sociology, and translating. Literary, cultural, and travel values were cited by 25 per cent. Academic requirements (medicine, law, Ph.B.) accounted for 23.6 per cent of the registrants; they were the "compulsory" cases.

Apparently, three-fourths of the student personnel in French 1 were there of their own free will. That fact seemed to indicate the necessity for "personalized" instruction, if interest were to be maintained and satisfactory end-products guaranteed. A prefabricated or prerequisite type of course, such as the usual college beginning French course, would result in too much disappointment, mediocrity, and wastage. The thought that three out of four of our students could drop French without serious academic consequences was, to say the least, disconcerting. What did they want from French 1? Had they any preferences?

Again, the survey furnished an answer. Of the four language skills, reading rated highest (32.2 per cent). Taken in combination with writing or speaking, it appeared in 70 per cent of the responses. Speaking, with a single rating of 11.3 per cent, was mentioned in only 50 per cent of the 1,009 cases. No check was made on aural skill, in the belief that it would be corollary to "speaking." Writing rated less than 1 per cent, appearing in only 16 per cent of the responses. Another 16 per cent expressed no preferences. Since the survey covered 1923–28, previous to the Coleman report (1929) and still in the bloom period of the "Direct Method," the student preference for *reading* was quite significant.

An interesting comparison is afforded by two surveys made later at the instigation of the writer: the Stephens College survey in 1938 and Miss Emerson's survey for the Illinois Junior College Association in 1940, both subsequent to the Coleman report and during the controversial period of the so-called "Reading Method."

In the Stephens survey the reasons for studying French were narrowed down to seven specific statements to be checked by the student. The results for 174 beginners are given in Table 1.

TABLE 1

Per cent

1. To satisfy later academic requirements............... 63
2. To satisfy a need in a chosen field of study........... 43
3. To use in travel................................... 39
4. To read and appreciate French literature............. 33
5. To be able to recognize French phrases seen (in reading, menus, etc.) and heard (movies)..................... 82
6. To develop an understanding of the French nation, people, and culture............................... 24
7. To prepare for advanced work in French............ 7
8. Other reasons than those specified.................. 1

Senior college and university requirements evidently weighed heavily in the decisions at Stephens, as did the absurd but human reaction to French frills in novels, menus, and movies. More significant is the recognition of personal values, a laudable desire to get something more than credits.

Miss Emerson, using a questionnaire form similar to the form in the Chicago survey, except for the addition of aural comprehension to the other skills, classified 367 responses under (1) practical reasons, (2) cultural reasons, and (3) language *per se*. Fifty-eight per cent listed practical reasons (travel, academic requirements, research, foreign service, fashion designing, commerce, art, music, library work, journalism, etc.); 10.6 per cent, cultural reasons (such as "understanding and acquisition of culture"; "to round out a liberal education"); and 29.1 per cent, an interest in the language for itself.

The preferences in skills show a shifting toward the spoken language, already under the influence of the European war. Sixty-five per cent gave speaking first or second place; 36.5 per cent, first place. Sixty per cent named reading as their first or second choice; 37.4 per cent, first choice. Aural comprehension was the first or second choice of 46 per cent. Writing was preferred by only 16 per cent.

It is doubtful whether the students saw a connection between oral ability and aural comprehension, or else they thought of "speaking" as "reading aloud" or "pronouncing." The terms needed definition. The little interest in writing reflects meaningfully upon current classroom practices. One is impressed by the well-defined views of these junior college students of Metropolitan Chicago. It would be interesting to know whether they got what they wanted.

Now that we knew why student M was with us and what he wanted of us, we could proceed to map out a course accordingly.

A course, however, involves credits, credits demand grades, and grades imply criteria for making judgments. There is something back of an A grade or an F grade other than ranking on a test. If the staff intended to bring the greatest good to the greatest number, it should know what makes a language student "good" or "bad." Grades are results, not causes. If one knew *why* some students get A and others get F, one might be able, by better planning, guidance, or motivation, to augment the number of the one and to diminish the number of the other.

## 4. *Behind the F Grade*

We began by looking for the real cause behind the F Grade. Because the real reason is usually personal and extraneous to the course, it often escapes the notice of the instructor, particularly in an urban university where student-instructor contacts are few and superficial. Consequently, at the end of the fourth, seventh, and eleventh weeks of each of the three quarters of French 1, special case reports on exceptional and delinquent students were made by each instructor. The reports were based on the information given on the personal record forms referred to above, supplemented by classroom observation and conferences between instructor and student.

The following examples illustrate the nature and form of these case reports:

*LZ.*—French 1C, sec. *a*. College of Arts. From V.H.S., Arkansas, 1921. American. Cultural background wanting; life in Arkansas lumber camps. Slow mentality, lazy, inaccurate, aimless, without method. Bored. In college for sake of city amusements and fraternity life. Parvenu; recently inherited half-million dollars in oil-land leases.

*AX.*—French 1B, sec. *b*. College of Arts. From H.P.H.S., Chicago, 1920. American, age seventeen. Capable, intelligent, retentive. Will not heed warnings; does not study. Not seriously interested in college work. Member of six social, literary, and fraternal organizations. Takes female leads in two dramatic productions. Outside work as drugstore clerk, 40 hours per week, in order to pay hockey expenses.

During 1921–22, five instructors submitted forty-five quarter and mid-quarter reports, indicating that 125 students in French and Spanish 1ABC had received the quarter grade of F. From the causes of failure assigned in the case histories, the following classified list was drawn up; the figure in parentheses shows the frequency of the particular cause:

1. *Preparation.*—Inadequate general preparation (25), inadequate course preparation (28), inadequate English preparation (24), no previous foreign language experience (14), delayed or broken continuation in the sequence (9), deficient language sense (13). Total counts: 113.

2. *Attendance.*—Late registration (6), excessive absences (30). Total counts: 36.

3. *Health.*—Poor health (5), illness (12), nervousness (8), worry and homesickness (5), defective hearing (7), defective speech (5). Total counts: 42.

4. *Mental habits.*—Inattentiveness in class (6), nonobservance of language technicalities (7), inaccuracy (8), incoherence in thought and expression (3), dependence (7), lack of initiative (5), laziness (26), superficiality (20), tendency to bluff (11), tendency to "sponge" (10), ineffective study habits (26), erratic study habits (32), incorrect attitude toward language study (32). Total counts: 193.

5. *Personality.*—Obstructive egotism (13), pedagogical resistance (9), diffidence (7), lack of confidence (1), lack of aggressiveness (4), irresolution (2). Total counts: 36.

6. *Mentality.*—Immaturity (15), poor comprehension or obtuseness (20), slow learner (20), defective memory (9), defective mentality (14), student over-age (6). Total counts: 84.

7. *Interests.*—Student activities (10), social activities (28), athletic activities (9), gainful employment (37), family problems (15), transfer of interest (15). Total counts: 114.

The six causes listed under *preparation* are common in the reports. Three of them are no doubt loosely used, i.e., "inadequate general preparation (including "want of background"), "no previous foreign language experience," and "deficient language sense." The lack of previous experience in a foreign language is a questionable cause of failure, although the 1930 survey showed that, of 52 cases, the average took only two quarters of the year sequence, with the grade of C. The terms "want of background" and "deficient language sense" were rather vague, hiding a more definite reason for failure not isolated by the instructor making the report.

There is in these reports the recurring statement that the student knows little or no English grammar. It is no doubt true. And it would doubtless be an advantage in the learning of the foreign language if the student had acquired linguistic sense through a thorough study of his mother-tongue. However, a great many people have learned a language who have had little or no proficiency in any kind of grammar. Indeed, a great many people learned to use both the spoken and the written forms of a language long before grammar had been formulated and made a subject of study in the schools.

The problem is to recognize the fact of the limitation and to adapt method and technique accordingly. That we had not solved this problem by 1928, at least in respect to the students who "disliked" the study of English, is shown by the fact that, out of 71 cases registered in French 1, 13 failed, 12 dropped out of the course in progress, and 12 did not continue beyond 1A—a loss of 52 per cent of the personnel of the group. The student who disliked the study of English was a bad risk.

One understands the failures (18.3 per cent) ascribed to inadequate language preparation, when one considers that a student could be admitted to French 1C (third quarter) on the basis of one Carnegie unit of high-school French, regardless of its nature, quality, or recency. We were not always able to locate misfits by the fourth week of the quarter or to get them removed, when once located; as a consequence, they received a terminal grade of F.

In 1930, the University of Wisconsin, through the untiring efforts of Professor F. D. Cheydleur, initiated foreign language placement tests. Between 1930 and 1943, over 8,300 students validated their credits by means of placement tests, resulting in 1,300 promotions (16 per cent) and about 300 demotions (4 per cent). But not until 1946 were we able in the College to get rid of this nuisance product of the credit system, by instituting placement tests in the foreign languages, having tried without success remedial sections, sectioning for ability, and staggered schedules.

Language failure for *attendance* causes is universal and perennial. Oral-aural skill cannot be had normally by absenting one's self from classroom practice. In 1921–22, when attendance in class was enforced officially, 5.8 per cent of the counts brought against the 125 students who failed in French 1 and Spanish 1 were for late registration or excessive absences. Ten years later, a special check on attendance in 23 sections of elementary (1ABC) and intermediate (2AB) French, German, and Spanish during the last three full weeks of the winter quarter, which is the critical mid-point of the sequence, revealed that absenteeism in German amounted to 11.7 per cent of maximum possible attendance; in French, to 17.6 per cent; and in Spanish, to 21.0 per cent. From one-ninth to one-fifth of the available class time was not being used—an effect of the "freedom clause" of the New Plan. Again, in June, 1941, of 68 students who took the French 1 comprehensive examination, 24 were totally unknown to the staff or did not attend class in the spring quarter. Eighteen of them failed in the examination. In 1950, absenteeism was still the commonest single cause of language failure. As any teacher of art, music, English writing, or a sport well knows, it takes regular, continuous practice under supervision to get satisfactory results. Any other system is but shadow boxing.

*Health* causes constituted 6.8 per cent of the counts contributing to failure in the 1922 survey. Nearly 1 out of 10 students in the group and 30 per cent of the 918 students checked in the 1930 survey were under one or more physical handicaps, some of which were particularly serious from the special viewpoint of language learning. Cases of harelip, lisp, stammer, loss of uvula, adenoidal growths, faulty native articulation, deafness, myopia, partial blindness, etc., are real language barriers needing early detection and sympathetic and careful handling if they are not to cause failure in the language course.

The fourth group of causes, *mental habits*, received more attention in the reports than any other group, totaling 31.2 per cent of the 618 counts. Whether they were really more prevalent, or were more noticeable in the classroom, or whether instructors react more readily and with more assurance to them than to other causes is a question.

They are closely connected with the causes listed under *interests*. The latter are often at the root of the so-called "mental" habits, which may be not so much habitual as temporary effects of a lack of interest. In the writer's opinion, such is the case of "inattentiveness in class," "incorrect attitude toward language study," and "laziness." The prominence of the latter count (26 cases) makes closer analysis advisable. Much that is ascribed to "laziness" may be due to transferred interest, drowsiness for lack of sleep or because of poor ventilation in the classroom, poor or erratic study habits, discouragement, or some emotional disturbance affecting the will to work.

The label "incorrect attitude toward language study" includes the enforced study of the subject, personal distaste for language in particular or in general, an exclusive interest in one aspect of language, and false or misleading conceptions of the nature and usefulness of second-language learning. These are potentially harmful attitudes in the early stages of a language course.

To these borderline liabilities one may add the risks incurred by those students who consider foreign language study unduly difficult or by those who began the study of a foreign language in high school and dropped it short of a credit point. In the 1930 survey, 51 students who thought language study particularly difficult averaged only 1.8 quarters in the French sequence and 1.9 grade points (C to C—) per course. In the second category, 62 students averaged 1.85 quarters per student and 2.6 grade points (B— to C) per quarter.

"Nonobservance of language technicalities" refers to inattention to accents, elisions, liaison, case endings, agreements, prepositional usage, and kindred "minor" (*sic*) details too unimportant to notice or to practice. Reliance on such aids as interlineation, verb "wheels," word lists, homework, vocabularies, etc., are included under "dependence." "Tendency to sponge" covers such causes as cheating, borrowing, copying, "leaning," misuse of text in blackboard drill, use of translations, prompting. "Superficiality" includes low standards of accomplishment.

The causes of failure listed under *personality* are fairly easy to recognize. "Obstructive egotism" includes cynicism, conceit, and superciliousness. "Pedagogical resistance" denotes refusal to follow advice, neglect of cautions, or wilful nonobservance of instructional details.

The most hopeless group of causes from either an educational or an economical point of view is the group listed under *mentality*. They are, of course, serious charges that call for well-considered and substantiated judgments.

The item of "student over-age" reflects a common belief among language teachers that fixation of speech habits in adult learners makes the acquisition of a second language difficult and sometimes impossible. The belief is erroneous.

In the Baird survey (1930) of achievement in first-year French in the College during 1927–30, in order to find the relation between student age and performance, a study was made of 164 students for whom there were available their age at the beginning of the sequence and their scores in vocabulary, grammar, and reading on the American Council on Education (A.C.E.) French test, administered at the end of 1A, autumn quarter. The scores used in the correlation were the total scores.

The age range was sixteen to thirty-eight, with the mid-interval at nineteen. The A.C.E. test scores ranged from 15 to 120 out of a maximum possible total of 153, with the mid-interval at 55–60. The coefficient of correlation obtained was — .04, a wholly negative showing. Test medians were as follows: vocabulary, 25.8; grammar, 12.3; reading, 13.1. The national norms were 23.8 in vocabulary, 12.4 in grammar, and 12.5 in reading, on a basis of one college semester. The attainment in 1A (one quarter), therefore, compared very favorably with the national achievement in one semester. Age seemed to have little to do with performance, at least in the three skills measured. We discontinued the practice of indicating "over-age" as a cause of failure.[11]

The Baird survey revealed also that 57.7 per cent of the F grades reported in French 1A were incurred by students in the age range sixteen to nineteen, whereas only 25 per cent were incurred by students in the age range twenty to twenty-five, and 17.3 per cent by those in the twenty-six to thirty-five age range. The 168 cases checked were noncontinuants, i.e., students who completed 1A but who did not take 1B or 1C within the three-year period covered by the survey. This showing for the older students adds further support to the correlational data cited above.

The seventh group of causes of failure, i.e., *interests*, are difficult to discover and to correct, because they are distinctly personal and must be learned by confessional means. Their prevalence (18.5 per cent) ranks them second only to the causes that are grouped under *mental habits* and equal to those listed under *preparation*. Qualitatively and quantitatively, under the demands of present-day living, they are important determinants of success and failure.

By "student activities" are meant all local campus activities, such as participation in dramatic, literary, musical, artistic, political, charitable, religious, and studial (for Honors, prizes, scholarships) endeavors. Included under "social activities" are those connected with fraternities, women's clubs, social organizations, and student boards. "Family problems" include transportation (often serious in a large city, where so many students live at home, sometimes at great distances from the campus), household duties, maintenance of a family, care or support of sick or indigent members of the family, family interference, incompatibility in the home life, financial burdens, etc.

The transferral by the student of his interest in the language course to another subject, curricular or not, always casts a shadow over his language teacher. It sometimes incites the teacher to emulate the *jongleur* of Notre-Dame or to utter laments or threats of reprisal; and yet the cause is usually beyond the teacher's control. The loss or lack of interest in the language course may be rotative, in the case of the overloaded student, or may happen at the birth of some new, unsuspected interest, or be a result of a newly found direction for what he considers his lifework. This new direction may be extra-curricular, as in art, dramatics, music, social work, the radio, crafts, business, etc., or it may be simply the necessity of earning a living. In the contest between a job and French, the winner is not hard to choose.

The grand total of 618 counts brought against this group of 125 students who failed in elementary French and Spanish courses in a single year raises two questions: (1) What *can* the college do to lessen the causes of failure? and (2) What *should* the college do, once the answer to the first question is found? The second question is construed as one of educational economy; the first, as a matter of administrative powers and controls.

To arrive at even a general opinion from the survey data, it would be necessary to regroup the forty-five causes according to (A) those which the college cannot correct, (B) those which the college can correct but which it would be uneconomical to attempt to correct, and (C) those which are within the province or duty of the college to try to correct. The regroupings would be as follows:

*Group A.*—Inadequate general preparation, inadequate course preparation, inadequate preparation in English, lack of previous foreign language experience, delayed continuation in 1ABC, deficient language sense, late registration, poor health, illness, nervousness, worry, homesickness, defective hearing or speech, lack of initiative or of aggressiveness, poor comprehension (obtuseness), mental slowness, defective memory, defective mentality, over-age (?), family problems. Total: 269 counts.

*Group B.*—Inattentiveness in class, nonobservance of language technicalities, dependence, laziness, superficiality, tendency to bluff or to sponge, erratic study habits, incorrect attitude toward language study, obstructive egotism, pedagogical resistance, immaturity. Total: 173 counts.

*Group C.*—Excessive absences, inaccuracy, incoherence in thought or expression, ineffective study habits, diffidence, lack of confidence, irresolution, extra-curricular activities, outside employment, transfer of interest. Total: 176 counts.

Group A contributed 44 per cent of the counts; Groups B and C, about 28 per cent each. Groups A and B combined accounted for 72 per cent of the total number of counts. Only 28 per cent, as listed under Group C, were clearly within the province and the duty of the College to try to correct.

In respect to the conduct of our language experiment, there were three general conclusions to be drawn from this investigation: (1) many of the language failures in 1921–22 were beyond administrative and instructional controls; (2) there was urgent need for prompt and rational action in such cases; and (3) procedural adjustments should be made in our language courses which would tend to reduce or to eliminate wastage by failure.

We saw the necessity of laying out a language course with stop-walk-go controls that would lessen the chance of accidents, allow for pedestrian traffic, and permit through traffic at either normal or accelerated speed. That much we could do for the betterment of the conditions learned through the survey. For the staff, in the future, no student would be a "bad" student solely because of a letter grade of F received in an examination, and nothing more.

By 1950, administrative and educational changes in the College had made less frequent many of the causes of failure that we had noted three decades before.

Selective admission, prognosis tests, Freshman Week routines, placement tests, flexible study programs, accelerated (and decelerated) programs leading to the Bachelor's degree, comprehensive examinations, objective measurement of proficiencies, centralized accrediting methods, voluntary class attendance, abolition of unitary entrance requirements and course equivalents, dual College and divisional status, withdrawal of the university from major competitive athletics, obligatory dormitory residence for eleventh- and twelfth-grade registrants, a student health service, a faculty-advisory system, specialized personnel service, and extensive changes in the structure of the College curriculum, with Honors and preceptorial opportunities for the ambitious and capable student—all these have done much to correct the deficiencies of twenty-five years ago. However, changes bring new problems, and students still fail, as they did in 1921.

While these changes were being made, we continued to experiment with the instructional details and policies of our elementary language courses, selecting, testing, analyzing, rearranging their components, objectives, and methods, in our determination to lower the mortality rate, reward superior achievement, and give students $Q^1$, M, and $Q^3$ an equal chance.

Thinking about them was not sufficient. Between 1920 and 1927, for example, two instructors wrote a total of 140 reports (including 14 special reports with tabulations, graphs, and listings) for French 1ABC, in which they analyzed 700 cases of A and F students out of 2,455 course registrants and discussed aims, materials, procedures, and outcomes, quarter by quarter. On the fourth, seventh, and tenth weeks of every quarter they reported on the state of the course. Their colleagues in Spanish and German did likewise.

In 1922, we posited a course of action and set about its implementation. Three years later, method and course had taken form. By 1927, we had accumulated a body of critical data as a basis for the analyses of 1928–32. And, by 1940, French 1ABC and the Reading Method were firmly grounded realities with highly predictable outcomes. It had taken twenty years of trial, analysis, and revision to arrive at the goal.

Little progress would have been made, very likely, without our course reports. Their *raison d'être* is explained best in the words of

H. C. Morrison, in his final memorandum (February, 1927) to the staffs of the experimental Junior College:

There are two ways in which one may look at the teaching process. One way is to work at it as a purely amateur and traditional kind of task, varying from good to bad in accordance with the teacher's interest, industry, and insight. The other way is to look at it, like any other scientific procedure, as a systematic process in which the teacher has clearly in mind exactly the objectives which he expects to obtain in the learning of his students, has a justifiable teaching procedure, observes the results which he is getting, consistently inquires why the results are what they are, intelligently modifies his procedure, and so on. Now there is no possible scientific procedure apart from observing, recording, and drawing inferences. Hence the reporting is valuable as much for the training it gives the teacher as for the record which it constitutes.

If a teacher at the end of three months' work can file at best only a perfunctory and inadequate statement of what he has been doing, it is pretty good evidence that in reality he does not know what he has been doing—at least not in any analytical sense. His teaching may or may not have been stimulating and effective.

A *good* report does not necessarily mean the record of a series of test results. Such a report is a good one only in case the test results themselves are significant in the presence of the teaching situation which has been described. In brief, facts are seldom of any particular interest unless there goes with the facts a convincing argument showing why the facts are what they are.

Acute and intelligent observation of what is going on in the classroom and in the experiences of the students usually gives us the most significant kind of material we can find. . . . Nevertheless the observations must be accurate, they must record facts within the competency of the observer, and the statements must be just inferences from the facts rather than dogmatic statements. Such expressions as "I am fully convinced," "It goes without saying," "It stands to reason," "Our work has been better than ever before," "I am greatly pleased over the outcome of this quarter's work," have no place in a proper report, unless the record also shows *why* the instructor is convinced, and *why* it stands to reason, and *why* there is ground for satisfaction in the quarter's work.

These four paragraphs in the Morrison memorandum will also serve here as a clear statement of the prevailing spirit and philosophy of this investigation into the teaching of a second language.

## CHAPTER II

# THE EVOLUTION OF A METHOD

## 1. *Genesis*

IN THE spring of 1920 the General Faculty of the University of Chicago approved the transfer of the first-year courses in French and Spanish from the College of Arts to the School of Education to administer experimentally as subjects in secondary education. The two courses formed part of the newly constituted Junior College, attached to the University High School and, as one of the Laboratory Schools, placed under the direction of Professor Henry C. Morrison. This was the first step toward the New College, officially proclaimed ten years later.

It was an unusual opportunity for language investigation. There were no staff organization, academic hierarchy, predetermined policies, or commitments of any sort. A concentration of responsibility and authority in one person (the superintendent of the Laboratory Schools), freedom and encouragement to explore, and a readiness to co-operate characterized the new administration. The staff was new to itself and to the university. Its members did not hold the same educational views or follow the same linguistic methods. There was no physical plant, no office space, no equipment, no budget, no provision for service. Three dilapidated rooms in a sinking, ramshackle, wooden, one-story building, housing campus student publications and the bakery, overrun with cockroaches, and permeated with the scent of cinnamon rolls, were the classrooms.

The schedule was simple: three staggered sections of French and Spanish 1A, 1B, and 1C in a five-day week.

There was one unpromising condition: credit for the year sequence would be withheld until a fourth major (2A) given by the Department of Romance Languages in the College of Arts should be successfully completed.

The writer, accustomed to charting his course in advance of sailing, asked questions: Was he to choose method and material with French 2A in mind? Would the students be under high-school or university regulations in matters of attendance, discipline, authority, grading, reporting, homework, etc.? Would any *realia* be available? Or would there be funds for their purchase or for the maintenance of a French "center" with newspapers, journals, books? What were the section limits? What kind of students would the courses attract? What was the value of the courses as a degree requirement? What were the admission restrictions, etc.?

The answers were cautious and tinged with negativism. The instructor was free as to material and methods, while remaining tethered (like *maître* Séguin's goat) to French 2A. The students, although of college status, would in respect to the course be under high-school regulations. There were no *realia*, no "center," no allocated funds. Sections would be limited (!) to 35 students; registration would be unrestricted, one unit of preparation admitting to 1C without challenge; and the degree requirement would be four majors, the fourth being 2A, a course that was *not* of an experimental nature.

The terrain was rugged, but interesting; the air, bracing. We called the first classes to order in October, 1920.

## 2. *First Trial Course, 1920–21*

At the end of the autumn quarter, Mr. Morrison called for a report covering (*a*) a description of the course, showing the method and technique used; (*b*) the initial and final registration, discussing in a classified manner the students who dropped out during the quarter and their reasons for doing so; and (*c*) the objectives aimed at for the quarter and the success in attaining those objectives.

The following condensed report presents the data called for:

I. *General plan* (*1A*).—Study of the sounds of French, using phonetic symbols, occupied exclusively the first two weeks (10 hours) and continued intermittently through the quarter. An analysis of grammar, developed naturally as the forms were encountered in reading, and utilized solely for purposes of comprehending the printed or spoken word, began the third week and continued thereafter. Practice in accurate translation from French to English, looking toward independent reading. Home reading assignments. Practice in aural comprehension (oral reading, anecdotes, simple dictation) and in oral production (oral reading, pronunciation practice).

II. *Techniques.*—(1) Phonetics: demonstration of the formation of speech sounds, using International Phonetic Association symbols and charts, followed by choral and individual drill. Some transcription into phonetic characters. Comparison with other languages. Correction of errors in oral reading. (2) Grammar: classroom analysis of text; phonetic explanations of grammar (Bovée); home assignment of specific points for analysis in the reading text. Recognition study of irregular verbs, using the two-conjugation theory, followed by recall on verb blanks. (3) Translation: from home assignments, sight, review passages, from oral presentation, and of transposed material. (4) Aural comprehension: telling of anecdotes followed by written check, part conduct of recitations, comments in French, oral reading of assigned practice passages, dictation of simple known material, choral repetition. (5) Oral practice: individual and choral reading, paradigms, difficult words, set phrases, phonetic analysis.

III. *Materials.*—Bovée, *Carte phonétique*, and mimeographed material. Berthon, *Première grammaire française* (Dent), with mimeographed summaries. Bierman and Frank, *Conversational French Reader* (Allyn & Bacon); Méras, *Le premier livre* (American Book Co.) The Berthon text was used for reference, the Bierman text serving as a basis for the class work. Forty-five selections were read intensively. The Méras text was used for home extensive reading. Total coverage: approximately 270 pages.

IV. *Registration.*—In three sections, there were 80 registrants; 15 dropped out en route, and 7 failed. Of the 15 drops, 12 were men and 3 were women; of the 7 failures, 3 were men and 4 were women. Thirty-three of the 80 registrants were of foreign extraction (Polish, Russian, Lithuanian, Austrian, Czech, German, Swedish, Italian, Hawaiian, Filipino, Chinese). Thirty-six per cent had gainful employment, ranging from two to six hours daily. Of the 22 drops and failures, 6 were ascribed to overload through employment, 2 to late transferral, 4 to racial handicaps, 3 to bluffing, and 7 to wrong attitudes. Section overcrowding entered into 12 cases. Common to all was an acceptance of low standards ("sufficient to pass is enough").

V. *Attainment of objectives.*—The objectives were (*a*) comprehension of the printed word, (*b*) comprehension of the spoken word, and (*c*) a correct pronunciation. Attainment in *a* and *b* was measured by progress tests and by a final examination; attainment in *c* was a matter of the instructor's opinion. The final grade was based on an average of progress test and final examination grades, and not on daily recitation marks.

In this report, the first of twenty-one final reports to be filed by the instructor during the succeeding seven years, one already discerns the separation of the active and passive phases of language learning, the analytical approach to grammar for reading comprehension purposes, the emphasis on an increased reading experience of both intensive and extensive types, the postponement of speech and writing training, the continuous attention to the spoken word, and the concern for the individual learner that were to become the hallmark of the Reading Method.

The techniques employed were for the most part those to be found in the textbooks and classrooms of the time, particularly in the tradition of the oral method. There were no tests of the objective type, like the American Council tests, and consequently there were no standards for comparison. One had to trust to the professional judgment and integrity of the teacher. In that connection, consider the concluding remarks in the report in question:

I believe that the students who completed the course satisfactorily are un-usually well equipped for independent work. The evidence secured from class exercises and minor tests have shown a progressive capacity for learning the language in the phases studied beyond any point known to me in my teaching experience. However, the winter will prove the soundness of the impression, and will determine the value of separating the passive and active phases of lan-guage study, at least for the adult beginner. It is hoped to prove by experience that more and better work can be accomplished thus and that it can be of en-during quality.

Among the recommendations were adequate housing, more co-operation between student and instructor, the early elimination of the noncollege type of student, the concentration of personnel work on the American-born male student as the worst language offender, an investigation into the outside activities of college students, and a more closely knit departmental organization.

An immediate result of the report was an administration request for detailed information on course personnel who dropped out while the course was in progress or who received an F. It was further re-quested that a mid-quarter report be made upon students of low standing, with recommendations (drop, probation, etc.). It was hoped that probation might result in some salvage, but later reports were to prove the hope unfounded. The usual cause of failure was outside the language course.

The final report for the winter quarter, 1921, presented a changing picture from the preceding quarter. The trial balloon had run into cross-currents, some of our own making and some due to the direction set by fourth-quarter (2A) requirements:

I. *Objectives.*—The understanding of written French of moderate difficulty; the ability to converse in simple French; the ability to write simple French; the ability to understand spoken French of moderate difficulty; increased accuracy in pronunciation; and a knowledge of the elements of formal French grammar.

II. *Methods.*—(1) Understanding of written French: through translation of assigned reading, practice in sight reading, extensive (outside) reading, translation by the instructor of difficult passages, special attention to idioms, tense usages, and special grammatical topics (pronoun order, use of the subjunctive, conditional sentences). (2) Conversational ability: question-and-answer on reading text, part reading of plays, indirect questions, practice in types of questions, common phrases. (3) Composition ability: formal exercises, drills on special grammatical topics, occasional résumés of material read outside the classroom, sight translation, and dictation. (4) Aural comprehension: dictation of known material, translation of material heard but not seen, telling of anecdotes, short talks in French on related material, and conversational practice. (5) Pronunciation: class and individual practice and correction, oral reading; use of phonetics in correction or in demonstration only. (6) Grammar: review of grammar covering the work of the autumn quarter, special topics, and text analysis.

III. *Materials.*—Bierman and Frank, *Conversational French Reader* (text completed, 65 pp.). Méras, *Le premier livre:* lessons 1–60 (oral and written exercises, 151 pp.). *Le Petit Journal* (Doubleday), issues from December 1, 1920, to March 1, 1921 (24 pp.), for sight and prepared reading. Labiche, *Le Voyage de M. Perrichon* (Ginn), Acts I–III (60 pp.), as assigned reading. Berthon, *Grammaire française* (Dent), as a reference grammar (158 pp., including review of autumn quarter's work). Verb blanks and special mimeographed material on topical grammar.

IV. *Registration.*—In two sections of 1B: 45 registrations, 45 completions, no drops, 38 satisfactory grades, 7 failures (15.5 per cent). All failures were by American-born students. Percentage of C and C— grades: autumn, 36.0 per cent; winter, 52.6 per cent. Six of the 7 failures had received warnings in the preceding quarter. Outside activities, work and social, were on the increase.

V. *Attainment.*—The greatest growth was in the understanding of the printed word; the least, in the ability to understand the spoken word. The latter was due mainly to the emphasis on composition and to the importance attached to composition by the average student. The single-phase approach of the autumn quarter resulted also in an "unusual facility in the translating of English to French." Weakness in pronunciation, wherever found in the autumn, persisted into the winter quarter.

French 1B was caught upon three horns of a dilemma: (1) the low correlation between entrance credits and actual proficiency; (2) the seesaw type of instability typical of language courses which try to develop active and passive skills at the same time and *below* the level of adjustment to reading and aural comprehension; and (3) the special requirements of a compulsory fourth-quarter course toward which 1B must be pointed. The necessity for adapting unsuitable material to new methods, the lack of adequate equipment and housing, and the absence of an official advisory system added to the other difficulties. Nevertheless, we moved into the spring quarter determined to weld the reproduction and recognition abilities into a satisfactory whole.

The final report for the spring quarter, 1921, has been lost. The following information has been pieced together from scattered memoranda in the files; it indicates a fairly successful conclusion to the year:

I. *Objectives.*—Comprehension of spoken and written French of increasing difficulty; the ability to use simple French in speech and informal writing; an accurate knowledge of the elements of grammar, and accuracy in applying it through retranslation.

II. *Methods.*—Grammatical exercises, oral and written, following the traditional order of presentation. Some free theme-writing, prepared or sight. Summaries of common errors found in themes. Brief phonetic review. Reading material subject to questionnaires, translation, oral summaries, and vocabulary drill. Study and practice of 50 common idioms. Limited amount of extensive reading, subject to brief reports in English. French the language of the classroom half the total time. Coverage: 450 pages, of which 250 were in the reading text.

III. *Materials.*—Buffum, *French Short Stories* (Holt), in full. Carnahan, *Review French Grammar* (Holt), in full. Nitze and Wilkins, *Handbook of French Phonetics* (Holt), exercises. *Le Petit Journal* (Doubleday-Page), six issues.

IV. *Registration.*—In four sections of 1C there were 91 registrations, a shrinkage in total registration of 6 from the 1B initial registration, and of 42 from the initial registration in Autumn 1A. Of the 91 registrants, 84 completed the course with 78 passing grades (92.8 per cent), and 6 failed. They earned an average of three grade points (B−) per student.

Actually, the year's shrinkage was less than indicated. The registrar failed to remove early changes from the rolls, and an unwarranted reliance was placed upon "card" or initial registration in computing the totals. However, the matter of annual shrinkage was one to be noted in the future.

What was the *bilan* for the year? Had we learned anything from the experiment with French 1 that could be followed up profitably in 1921–22? A few facts and conclusions emerged from the confusion of the year sharply enough to warrant further attention.

First, it would be difficult to develop a highly productive language course within the time limits and rigid conditions set by the faculty of the university. Much more attention to instructional detail, chronological order, checking, and continuation analysis would be needed than was usually spent upon a Freshman language course.

Note what the faculty had prescribed:

It is recommended that college French and Spanish begin with the courses now designated as French 4 (2A) and Spanish 4 (2A). The future designation of a point at which senior college French and Spanish ought to begin will develop as experience accumulates under the plan proposed [*Minutes,* April 10, 1920];

and, further, in the *Circular of Information* (June, 1921):

By a vote of the Faculty the University has discontinued the giving of instruction in elementary French and Spanish in the College department. Students who enter without any previous knowledge of these languages may prepare themselves for the courses numbered 4 (2A) in French or in Spanish by taking a *special one-year course of Junior College grade provided in the University High School.* [The italics are the writer's.] Students who have had one year of regular high school instruction take course 3 (1C) in the Junior College department of the University High School [p. 178].

French 1ABC, therefore, was quite circumscribed. It was an elementary course of junior college grade offered in the University High School, without degree credit, to prepare for another course *not* of senior college grade given in the university, which could not be counted in a principal or secondary sequence. The fourth course (2A) not only served as a check upon 1ABC, but credit for the latter, by action of the department, was to be withheld until French 2A should be "completed commendably." And, finally, since a student with one unit of entrance credit in French could enter 1C, the first two quarters (1AB) had an official, if not an actual, parity with one high-school year of the language.

Do these or similar restrictions of thirty years ago rest with the birch rod in the educational museum, or are they still in force here and there in the colleges of 1950?

The hazards of French 1 appear more plainly in a letter addressed to the writer by Professor Algernon Coleman, dated August 12, 1920, before the experiment began, in which he sets forth the *expectancy* for students entering French 4 (2A):

If you add to the grammatical material contained in Part I, Fraser and Squair (*Complete French Grammar*), the current forms of the current irregular verbs, coupled with additional drill in the use of the more important phenomena, you will have excellent preparation for French 4 so far as that item is concerned. At the end of your year, your better students should be able to understand what you say to them in French on the topics taken from your reading and grammar work; they should be able to reply briefly but with fair readiness to your questions in that language, and to relate simply the stories or incidents you read and practice, whether called on to do it orally or in writing.

They should know how all French sounds are made, and be able to use intelligently the phonetic symbols, both for reading and to indicate at the board how the various spellings are transcribed. They should know and be able to apply the common usage in regard to liaison and elision, and they should have read and worked over carefully some 200 or 300 pages of reading matter—worked over orally with the aim of assimilating a basic vocabulary and of possessing with fair thoroughness the everyday idioms. Naturally the written exercises should supplement and intensify the oral study of the passages chosen, and students should be able to reproduce accurately in English the more difficult passages.

It would be desirable, of course, to work over thus all the reading material, but with students of college age, who are going to do not more than one or two years—most of them—we have to sacrifice something here to the exigencies of the conditions. Such students can do more in the way of learning grammatical material as such than the high school beginners can, so it is my principle to utilize this power, but to supplement it and reinforce it by all the oral practice and vocabulary practice and idiom practice that my ingenuity and the time available will allow.

I say nothing above about methods. My own practice is to engraft on the grammar and reading the chief principles of the direct approach, keeping in mind the age and preparation of the class and the length of time they will probably be in French classes. Contrary to the wholehearted direct adherents, my oral work is intensified and enlarged from the end of the first quarter on, rather than from the first day, though necessarily it is always considered important. . . .

The experiment you're going to undertake is a very interesting one. I hope you will keep a record of what you do in the various classes, with the notion that it may be useful as a document.

Nine years later, the readers of the Coleman report on *The Teaching of Modern Foreign Languages in the United States* will find quite a different prescription for a beginning French class, based this time on the data gathered in the investigations by the *Modern Language Study*.

Not until 1927 was French 1 to become officially independent of the fourth major, although 2A had to be revised in 1923 because of the 50 per cent continuation from French 1. It is apparent from the above quotations that any new approach to language learning would have to be cut out of an old suit instead of from new cloth. That was our principal dilemma.

A second result of the first experimental year was an outline for French 1[1] that was comparable with the Coleman prescription and that could serve as a base line for the projection of a second trial course. The outline was supplemented by a day-by-day program and a battery of 23 tests; it follows in brief:

*French 1A.*—Ability to pronounce French with a fair degree of accuracy; to translate simple French; to understand simple spoken French; and to recognize structural forms and elementary syntax. Tests: (1) pronunciation, (2) translation, (3) dictation, (4) regular and common irregular verbs, (5) grammar recognition, (6) aural comprehension, sight and prepared.

*French 1B.*—Accurate pronunciation; aural comprehension of more difficult French; formal grammar and syntax; ability to translate more difficult French; oral and written composition; planned vocabulary-building and sentence expansion. Tests: (1) pronunciation, (2) sight dictation, (3) grammar analysis, (4) sight translation, (5) sight composition, (6) oral composition, (7) irregular verbs and idioms, (8) vocabulary expansion, (9) reading comprehension (sight).

*French 1C.*—Accurate pronunciation; aural comprehension of normal spoken French; a knowledge of the principles of French phonetics; a review of grammar; and the ability to translate fairly difficult French. Tests: (1) pronunciation, (2) sight dictation, (3) sight composition, (4) oral composition, (5) irregular verbs and idioms, (6) phonetics, (7) translation from French to English, (8) reading comprehension.

It was important that we keep a careful watch upon the established bounds for French 1 and check all new departures. The daily program for each quarter was made out three months in advance. Each of the 26 progress tests and the three final examinations were subject to time checks, grade distributions, and sometimes to analyses of errors. Whenever the point system of determining grades could not be satisfactorily applied, we relied on personal judgment. Copies of all tests, graphs, and analyses were sent to the superintendent's office, to be taken up later in conferences. The latter served to equalize our judgments and to establish a common body of criteria.

Since the tests were for teaching purposes and not often for grading purposes, they were not announced in advance. It was assumed that when a test is announced, it ceases to be a test, creates a wholly undesirable attitude and condition, and places the instructor in the position of covering up, ostrich-like, what he wants or should want to find out.

A third outcome of the trial year was a list of "problems" for immediate (!) consideration. It is not difficult to comprehend their importance to the experiment; it *is* difficult to understand why some of them are still unsolved. The list follows, as reported (the comments in brackets are the writer's).

1. Adequate housing and equipment. [A standard plaint.]
2. Departmental unity. [To avoid duplication of work.]
3. Reduction of class size. [Limits were 30–35.]
4. A phonetic laboratory. [Classroom practice is insufficient.]
5. Special sections. [For slow learners, one-unit entrants.]
6. Collection and analysis of student data. [Time-load and the causes for A and F grades.]
7. Representation in faculty bodies dealing with Freshmen. [Allocation to the high school made administrative action in the case of College students difficult.]
8. Definition of relationship. [In high school and College.]
9. Power to act in accrediting students at registration.
10. A policy toward student dishonesty, absenteeism, gainful employment, and the nine-letter grading system. [The university used A, A−, B, B−, C, C−, D, E, F in grading.]

We were looking for those ideal conditions which, once found, invariably generate a new set of problems for another set of experimenters. But they seemed highly desirable then.

For a final evaluation of attainment in French 1ABC, we needed to know about the work of continuants in French 2A. We therefore checked the records for 2A in the summer and autumn quarters, 1921, in the office of the recorder. Of the 77 students who completed 1C in the trial sequence, 56 registered subsequently in 2A. Five students postponed continuation, and 16 were out of residence. Forty-three registered in the autumn sections of 2A, where they formed 43.5 per cent of the enrolment. They earned 47.5 per cent of the grades above C− (passing), 46 per cent of the honor grades (A, A−, B), and incurred only one failure.

Three-fourths of the group lost from one to two points in passing through the fourth course. Their gains in reading and aural comprehension had been made at some expense of the ability to write French, which was a prime requisite in 2A. The deficiency would have to be corrected, but without sacrificing the gains, if that were possible.

A definite lowering of the mortality rate for elementary French was another product of the trial year. Previous to the beginning of the experiment, in 1919–20, in the College course there were 125 grades below C— (passing) and 47 drops, totaling 172 unsatisfactory grades, or 26 per cent of the total number (660) of quarter registrants. In 1920–21, in the experimental course, there were 38 grades below C—, and 35 drops, or a total of 73 unsatisfactory cases, which was 18 per cent of the total enrolment of 404 quarter students. The comparison involved 26 sections of the course given in the College of Arts and 18 sections of French 1ABC in the Junior College. In three sections of 1A in 1919, the rate rose to 33 per cent; in five others, the rate was half the enrolment. No doubt, some of this loss was caused directly by postwar conditions.

Through failures and drops, French 1ABC suffered a shrinkage of 36.9 per cent between the beginning and end of the year. In 1919–20, the shrinkage was 27.5 per cent. An amount of shrinkage is normal in first-year courses, and there are sometimes many causes involved. In 1920–21 there were still postwar conditions, no screening of applicants, a new policy of eliminating the unfit as early as possible in the course, changes in the nature and conditions of French 1, and a general decline in college registration. Nevertheless, shrinkage was a factor that should be watched. It has, in a way, barometric significance.

### 3. *Second Trial Course, 1921–22*

In the autumn of 1921, there were five sections of French 1A and three sections of 1C. Students successfully completing autumn 1C normally went into 2A in the Senior College in the winter quarter, making way for winter registrants in 1A, who continued with 1B in the spring and 1C in the following autumn. This system of staggering courses was favorable to forward and backward movement of students within the sequence according to their demonstrated ability, but it had various disadvantages, such as broken continuation in the colleges, shifting programs and schedules, changes in materials, and difficulty in staffing. The system was maintained until 1933, nevertheless, as a necessary evil.

For present purposes, details of course organization and administration and all other pertinent data are derived from the quarterly staff final reports to the superintendent and from the student records that pertain to "straight" sequences, i.e., autumn 1A, winter 1B, and spring 1C. They are more fully representative of what we were trying to accomplish than the "staggered" sequences, although for the over-all data, i.e., registration, grades, demotions, promotions, and continuation, both types of sequences must be considered, since the official records make no distinctions between them. Actually, the staggered sequences usually followed the straight sequences in general pattern, although occasionally the autumn 1C course introduced an innovation.

Such was the case in the autumn of 1921. All registrants for French 1C, i.e., students offering one high-school unit in the language, reviewing, or repeating the course because of previous failure, were required to take four preliminary tests, namely, pronunciation, grammar, dictation, and translation from French to English. The tests were given during the third week of the quarter. The results were compared with classwork and the information on the personal record cards; and recommendations, with case histories and test distributions, were sent to the director at the end of the fourth week. Recommendations took two forms: demotion to 1A (autumn) or 1B (winter) or probation for three weeks, subject to reconsideration and report to the director and the dean of the College at the end of the seventh week of the quarter.

Although the tests lacked objectivity in form (they paralleled ones used in 1B), they served fairly well to screen out the more flagrantly unfit and to soften the impact of a collision between a credit and a proficiency. As a matter of record, they were the first "placement" tests with administrative sanction and powers in the university.[2]

A fifth preliminary test was administered to all 1A registrants in the third week of the quarter as an English discrimination test in order to locate those students in need of remedial grammar and to test the reliability of one of the causes of language failure commonly mentioned in staff reports.

The student was asked to identify in a compound-complex sentence an adverb, an adjective, an indirect object, a preposition, a relative pronoun, a phrase, a clause, a case of agreement, an auxiliary verb, and a generic article. He was also asked to correct the following sentence: "The man and his wife knows that their son saw you and I last week"; to define certain terms used in phonetics (vowel, consonant); and to name the organs of speech.

The results were disturbing. Of 46 students, 9 failed to identify a clause; only 10 indicated correctly a relative pronoun; 10 could not identify a case of agreement; 14 failed to find an auxiliary verb; not one identified a generic article; and 6 thought "you and I" correct as used. Except for a premedical student, all the examinees failed in the phonetic part.

The staff was saddened and frustrated; the students remained cheerful and optimistic. Director Morrison opined that a foreign language could be learned by an illiterate person quite ignorant of generic articles and auxiliary verbs *per se*. The only valuable result of the experience was a common agreement that a minimum of use of grammatical terminology was a desideratum in teaching a foreign language at the beginning level.[3] The test was not repeated.

The preliminary tests showed that 50 per cent of the 1C registrants were inadequately prepared for the course. The average one-year high-school course clearly did not equal 1AB as organized.

The work of the autumn, 1921, quarter is described in a final report that covers two sections of 1A and one section of 1C, as follows:

I. *Objectives.*—French 1A: unchanged from autumn, 1920. French 1C: The ability to write simple French; a fair knowledge of grammar and phonetics; practice in the translation of difficult French. It was not possible to carry out the spring 1C program in the autumn section.

II. *Materials.*—French 1A: 20 specially prepared lessons in recognition grammar;[4] conjugation of 10 model irregular verbs; Méras and Roth, *Elementary French Reader* (in full); *Le Petit Journal* (read sparingly). French 1C: Carnahan, *Review French Grammar* (in full); Nitze and Wilkins, *Handbook of French Phonetics* (exercises in Part II; Daudet, *Choix de contes*, and Maupassant, *Huit contes choisis; Le Petit Journal* (six issues). Total reading: 250 pages.

III. *Methods.*—French 1A: Sounds of the language taught without the use of phonetic symbols, using the nearest English equivalent as a starting point and indicating the difference for the French sound, and giving corrective directions. Fundamentals of the grammar taught so as to make possible reading and translation from the French by the third week of the quarter. Practice in the understanding of spoken French by means of dictation, translation of oral material, and question and answer. Uninterrupted drill on regular and irregular verb forms. No oral or written composition. French 1C: the traditional grammar-translation method, largely as prescribed by the textbooks used. It was impractical to attempt anything different under the circumstances.

IV. *Results.*—French 1A: 33 per cent of the 39 completions were unsatisfactory (6 drops, 3 failures, 4 provisional or incomplete grades); 60 per cent of the grades were in the honor range (A, A−, B). French 1C: Of the initial registration of 26, 6 dropped after the preliminary tests, and 5 failed in the course work; total loss, 42 per cent.

V. *Recommendations.*—(1) A departmental reading collection and reading lists. (2) Office conditions that would offer privacy for student conferences. (3) Transfer of phonetic instruction from classroom to laboratory for both advanced and retarded students. (4) An adjustment in equating one unit of preparation. (5) A central record file of every student registering in a Junior College language course. (6) Preparation of adequate tests for placement and for accrediting.

The heavy loss in these sections was typical of all our language courses. Insufficient preparation for 1C was not the main cause; the student time-load was the main factor, as demonstrated by the following abstracts of cases taken from one section of 1C in the autumn quarter:

*MC.*—38 week-hours as night usher at the Tivoli theater; lieutenant in M.S. Cavalry School; 50 per cent failing.

*NE.*—40 week-hours as drug clerk; member of 6 organizations, including Blackfriars (men's dramatic society), in which he plays leads; 60 per cent failing.

*GO.*—20 week-hours as auto mechanic; 80 per cent failing.

*PO.*—12 week-hours as salesman; fraternity pledge; football practice (later a gridiron star); 80 per cent failing.

*LA.*—45 week-hours as office clerk; football squad. Dropped.

*CL.*—20 week-hours in Y.M.C.A. boy's work. Warned.

*SU.*—18 week-hours as waiter in University Commons. Honor work.

*RE.*—28 week-hours as music student. Honor work.

*SE.*—24 week-hours in downtown movie orchestra. Dropped.

*DA.*—15 week-hours in clerical work, plus Saturday employment.

*CO.*—technical worker (hours unknown); 50 per cent failing.

*GR.*—college tutoring (hours unknown). Dropped.

Fifty per cent of the students in this section were engaged in an average of more than 20 hours per week in gainful employment. All were carrying normal loads of three major courses for which 45–52 hours per week were expected for preparation and recitation. There were capable students in this group, but their work was suffering because of fatigue, dispersal of interest, and shortening of the periods of preparation. The influence of the latter showed particularly in oral-aural skills; in a fourth-week aural comprehension test, only one-third of this section made a passing grade of C— or better.

There was no improvement in the 1B sections in the winter. Eighteen students worked a total of 455 week-hours, or an average of 28.5 hours; five failed on the fourth-week tests and dropped the course, and four were placed on probation. Fraternity initiations lasting two weeks cut down the quality of the work for many others. On the other hand, there were eleven exceptional (A) students, all without previous contact with French. One worked 24 week-hours and carried six courses; another was earning all his expenses and maintaining an A record in all his courses. There was grist of both sorts for the quarterly reports.

The following final report for the winter quarter, 1922, covers one section of 1A and two sections of 1B, with 42 completions:

I. *Work of the course.*—French 1A: as indicated for the preceding quarter. Slight use of French in instruction. Coverage: 155 pages. French 1B: Twenty lessons of a composition grammar; correction of pronunciation with aid of phonetic transcription; dictation and practice in oral reading; aural comprehension; sight translation; continued study of irregular verbs; two reports on collateral reading. Reading and translation of Smith and Greenleaf, *Elementary French Reader;* Labiche, *Le Voyage de M. Perrichon; Le Petit Journal* (4 issues). Total reading: 350 pages.

II. *Personnel.*—There were few transfers or newcomers in 1B; almost all were continuants from 1A. Work slumped during the fourth, fifth, and sixth weeks because of fraternity initiations, the Washington Prom, and Portfolio (dramatics). Students co-operative and uncomplaining, with lively interest in all phases of the work; several did extra reading on their own initiative.

III. *Results.*—Only 3 failures out of 42 grades. Thirteen students received B or better; 11 received B—; 15 received C or C—. Composition work in 1B was least satisfactory (as could be expected from 1A training).

IV. *Comment.*—(1) Opportunity to interview in private the C— cases would improve the situation. [The "office" was a headquarters room for everyone and everything.] (2) The 850-page reading objective could be raised to 1,000 pages by means of a reading collection and reading lists. (3) Revision of materials used in 1A and 1B would provide more reading time. (4) More evidence available this quarter that one-unit placement needs adjustment downward.

Chronological order is important in any learning process. We began to experiment in shifting about the various phases of language learning within the framework of French 1. In the first trial year the shifts were limited to 1A. In the second year, 1B was the target, as the greatly condensed outline for 1B in the winter quarter of 1922 (Table 2) illustrates. There were fifty-five 50-minute periods spaced

TABLE 2

FRENCH 1B OUTLINE, WINTER, 1922*

| Periods | Assignments | Tests |
|---|---|---|
| 1–20.... | Records, preliminaries (1)<br>Grammar: articles, nouns, adjectives, adverbs, partitive (8)<br>Irregular verbs, supplemented by S & G drills, Part III, sight (5)<br>Phonetic theory, and S & G, pp. 1–16, with all exercises (5)<br>Pretests (1) | Grammar, irreg. verbs, phonetics, dictation |
| 21–40... | Grammar: pronouns, verbs, etc. (10)<br>Reading and composition, from S & G; including *Deux amis, La dernière classe, Mon Oncle Jules* at sight (6-pp. assignments) (10) | Composition, grammar theory, translation, oral composition |
| 41–55... | *Le Voyage de M. Perrichon,* with all oral and written drills (10)<br>*Le Petit Journal,* reading and discussion, with résumés (5) | Pronunciation, phonetics, oral composition, written composition, translation, dictation |

* Texts: S & G = Smith and Greenleaf, *Elementary French Reader* (Holt). Grammar: 18 mimeographed, experimental lessons. Labiche, *Le Voyage de M. Perrichon* (Allyn & Bacon). *Le Petit Journal* (Doubleday-Page).

through 11 weeks. Batteries of tests, as indicated, were given at the end of the fourth, seventh, and eleventh weeks, corresponding to the dates of the reports to the director. (The numbers in parentheses refer to the number of periods devoted to the assignments.)

The course was heavily weighted with grammar and translation, with considerable emphasis on oral and written composition, but it was not an out-and-out grammar-translation course. It was a hybrid, with strong characteristics of the reading course that was to develop from it later. Already, reading was the focal activity of 30 out of the 55 assignments.

The 1B pretests indicated in the preceding outline were in reading comprehension, translation, and dictation. They were administered in a single 50-minute period. The reading test consisted of an excerpt from a folk tale to be read in 5 minutes, and 20 questions in French to be answered in English in the same amount of time. The translation test, an anecdote 250 words in length, was allowed 15 minutes for reading and written translation. The dictation was a passage of 100 words to be read at a rate below normal, with one repetition; the credits were weighted. Five minutes were allowed for final revision of the three tests.

Within 2 days, readjustments which were thought advisable were completed and the administrative officers notified. The practice was successful and was extended to all the foreign language courses in the Junior College and was retained until the New Plan (1932). By preventing language failure at the source, higher efficiency resulted, wastage decreased, and student-instructor relations were improved.

Spring, 1922, results were much better than in the preceding year, partly because of the pretesting in 1B and autumn 1C and partly because of the prepared day-by-day programs. The following condensation of a report on one section of 1B and two sections of 1C represents the general situation:

I. *Work of the course.*—French 1B: little change from the winter course; total reading, 325 pages. French 1C; with one exception, unchanged from spring 1921. A compromise course with French 2A in mind. One innovation: a system of voluntary (extensive) reading, for which 9 periods were allowed in the program for student reports and conferences. The material, selected by the student, was in the field of his interest. The amount read averaged 209 pages per student, bringing the average total amount read during the quarter to 667 pages, including the grammar text, or 473 pages in reading text only.

II. *Student personnel.*—Fifty per cent of 1B personnel was composed of students who had failed to pass 1C pretests. French 1C had 23 continuants from 1B, and 6 new one-unit entrants. The usual "spring slump" and an increased time-load reduced considerably the general achievement.

III. *Results.*—There were 4 failures in the 41 grades reported, all of them occurring in 1B. In 1C there were no grades below C—; 4 students received A, and 13 were in the honors range (A–B). Twenty-five of the 29 students in 1C indicated their intention to continue in 2A in the autumn.

IV. *Recommendations.*—(1) Better facilities for student conferences. (2) A departmental reading collection open to class personnel. (3) Reading lists for guidance in selecting extensive reading material. (4) Bulletin boards. (5) Visual material for informal talks on cultural matters. (6) Phonetic laboratory to supplement the classroom. (7) Action in the matter of excessive absenteeism. [How perennial!] (8) Revision of personal record forms.

All but the sixth of these recommendations were in effect six months later; the sixth was held up because of costs.

A survey of the continuation records of students completing French and Spanish 1ABC in the two-year period 1920–22 was made in April, 1922. Three hundred and forty-eight students had registered for French 1A, 290 for 1B, and 288 for 1C. These figures do not indicate straight continuations, i.e., 1ABC in a given year; they include broken or lapsed continuations, new registrants in 1B or 1C, and review or repeat cases.

These interquarter shifts made it hard to gauge what was being accomplished. For example, 85 of the 121 registrants in autumn 1A finished the course with credit. The loss of 36 registrants was due to withdrawals (13), final failure (7), absence from the final quarterly examinations (11), change in schedule (1), and erroneous inclusion in the final roll (4). Only 70 of the 85 students who completed 1A with credit were among the 92 students registered in winter 1B; there was no knowledge of the intentions of the missing 15 students. Twenty-two registrants were new and unschooled in the work of 1A. The total spring registration in 1C was 81, of which only 54 represented winter 1B completions. Four 1B completions were not in residence, and 2 others postponed continuation. Twenty-seven of the 1C students were new entrants in the sequence, unacquainted with either 1A or 1B. In sum, of the original 121 starters in the autumn, less than 50 per cent were in at the finish in the spring. That proved to be normal expectancy.

How much of this loss was preventable, it was impossible to determine. There was some reason to think that half the cases could have been prevented. The heavy concentration of loss in the autumn quarter indicated a logical point for remedial action. Another indication was the advisability of self-contained, unitary, quarter-courses that would form a sort of staircase sequence more easily adjustable to demotion, promotion, and irregularities in continuation.

In the Senior College, French 2A (winter, 1922) had 44 completions, 55 per cent of which were Junior College continuants. The latter earned 61.5 per cent of the honor grades and incurred no failures. In the same quarter, 23 continuants from 1920–21 who had taken 2A in the autumn completed 2B, earning 48.4 per cent of the honor grades and no failures. They constituted 35 per cent of the 2B enrolment. Six promotional cases that involved "skips" from 1C to

2B resulted in honor grades in the advanced course. Promotion became a regular practice from then on.

Two experiments that were to play a very important part in the development of the Reading Method marked the end of this second trial course, namely, the practice of correlated reading as part of the reading program for 1C and the formation of a departmental reading collection.

Previous to the spring quarter, author and subject index cards were made for several works in each of seventeen library classifications selected from the general catalogue of the University Library. Before indexing, the staff examined the books as to their makeup, edition, publication date, nature of the contents, authoritativeness, and readability from a foreign language viewpoint. Although superficial, the examination provided a degree of insurance. From these cards, the student made out a regular call-slip and drew the book from the library under its regulations. The author card served also as charge card and a record of the number of calls.

Nine reading conference hours[5] were scheduled during a 4-week period in 1C; classwork was suspended on these days. The conference hour was spent in discussing reports, helping in making further selections, translating troublesome passages, interpreting, furnishing background information, and interesting the student in related material. The report form was simple: a $3 \times 5$ ruled card indicating author, title, name of the student, date, amount read to date, and brief answers to four questions, namely, subject matter of the report, a summarizing statement, a quotation or statement of the most interesting point, and a statement as to whether the reader liked or disliked the material (and for what reason).

The system of reportage, through the written form and the oral discussion, afforded a fairly reliable check upon the reader's understanding and appreciation of what he had read, without being too time-consuming or burdensome. The group discussions were a stimulus to everyone in the class.

The minimum amount set for the 9 reports was 100 pages; the amount actually read by the 28 students in the experimental groups was 5,912 pages, an average of 208.6 pages per student. The material ranged through nearly all the classifications. The ratio of fiction to nonfiction was approximately 3 to 1. A brief sampling of the data will illustrate the unusual nature of this first-year reading experience:

*LE.*—Interested in criminal law; read 162 pages of Zola, *L'Affaire Dreyfus* and references in the *Encyclopédie.*

*GI.*—Interested in amateur radio; read 60 pages of articles in *L'Illustration.*

*WH.*—Interested in inorganic chemistry; read 321 pages concerning selenium, radium, and magnesium.

*PC.*—Interested in dramatics; read 211 pages in Beaumarchais, *Le Barbier de Séville* and Coquelin, *L'Art de dire le monologue.*

*PI.*—Interested in music; read 168 pages of biography and operatic summaries, including *L'Arlésienne* and *Thaïs.*

*CO.*—Interested in government; read 200 pages in Barthélemy, *Le Gouvernement de France* and Roche, *Quand serons-nous en France?*

*FA.*—Interested in literature; read 747 pages of short stories, novels, and plays, including Assolant, *Récits de la vieille France,* and A. France, *L'Etui de nacre* and *Crainquebille.*

Unfortunately, at that time, we had no objective means for measuring language abilities and have therefore no index of the skill which these readers must have possessed.

The enthusiasm of the students was astonishing; they neglected other courses, slighted regular assignments, requested suggestions for summer reading, and inquired about further possibilities of language study here and abroad. The experiment demonstrated a way of increasing reading beyond the capacity of the classroom and an excellent means of stimulating genuine interest. Correlated reading became a regular part of third-quarter routine from 1922 to the present. As conditions and material allowed, extensive reading was pushed back into 1B and finally into 1A, becoming the one continuous activity in the whole sequence.

A second result of the trial procedure was the creation of a departmental reading collection, one of the recommendations of earlier staff reports. In a special report to the director, attention had been called to the status of Junior College language students,[6] which presented obstacles to normal library service and to the lack of funds and facilities that would enable the language department to provide the type of service needed, e.g., access to open shelves, privilege of longer loans and repeated renewals, freedom from penalties and fines for overdue books, and consultation of books during and between class periods. Such a collection, it was argued, would promote a greater amount of outside reading and at an earlier stage; would foster more genuine interest in language study; could contribute to a broader knowledge of French culture; and would provide students and staff with easily accessible reference material.

The report brought about the transfer of French and Spanish books that did not deal with education from the library of the School of Education to the office of the Junior College Romance languages staff. The action was rather embarrassing; the books had been given to the library by a "founding father" who was not too puritanical in his tastes for French fiction. After screening, we had a revolving bookcase full of fusty volumes, none of which could be read before the middle of 1C, and few of which held any appeal for college youth of even three decades ago. But the collection was a beginning. In ten years the revolving bookcase grew into a fairly representative collection of 2,000 volumes, upon which our elementary courses came more and more to depend, making possible the high attainment in reading that is detailed in a later chapter.[7]

Two recommendations made in the staff reports during the year were acted upon favorably by the faculties, namely, a college-wide investigation into the causes of failure[8] and a readjustment of the rating policy in respect to one unit of foreign language presented for admission to the College. Henceforth one-unit entrants were to be admitted "regularly to 1B or, on approval, to 1C, the approval to be based on evidence submitted by the Department." The ruling went into effect in June, 1922.

### 4. *Third Trial Course, 1922–23*

From an organizational viewpoint the year opened auspiciously. The members of the French and Spanish staffs[9] now formed a department, with chairman, examiner, and a budget. Space had been provided for office, files, and the newly created reading collection. Registration for 1A had been reduced from limits of 30–35 to a maximum of 30; but for the present 1C remained unchanged. One-unit entrants were placed in 1B instead of 1C, as formerly, with promotion and fee adjustments possible for deserving cases at the end of the fourth week. The staff could now turn to less material matters.

It lost no time in submitting the following list of subjects it wished

to investigate to Superintendent Morrison and Director Judd of the
School of Education for their approval:

1. Development of a technique of extensive reading to be applied at all levels
   of French and Spanish 1.
2. Organization and administration of a model library for Junior College foreign language courses.
3. Development of a system of personal, study, and reading records as an aid
   in course administration and instruction.
4. Causes of language failure, with special reference to failure attributed to
   outside employment, lack of previous language training, lack of ability in
   English and over-age.
5. The achievement of students who offer only one unit of a foreign language
   for admission.
6. Pretesting, pretests, and results of their application in order to determine
   placement in a language sequence.
7. Development of a technique of instruction for students exhibiting slow
   assimilation or poor study methods in the 1A courses, with the use of
   special sections.
8. The nature and value of phonetic instruction, with practical means of
   application, e.g., laboratory, recordings, charts, graded texts, etc.
9. Development of effective reading material for all levels of the elementary
   language course: its nature and use.
10. The teaching of composition: nature, place in the program, and means of
    objective measurement.
11. Means for the stimulation and retention of interest in foreign language
    courses at the beginning level.
12. Oral work: nature, place, and function in the first-year language sequence.

Commissioned to proceed with any of the projects that interested
it, the staff impatiently and enthusiastically adopted all twelve.
Since then, staffs have come and gone, and several of the projects are
still unfinished business, especially items 4, 6, and 12. But the list
remains as a statement of objectives toward which the staff worked
for thirty years. That determined and concerted effort, supported
and encouraged by an interested administration, failed to produce a
wholly satisfactory solution for some of these familiar problems of
foreign language teaching is but another proof that the effective
teaching of a second language is a tough and resistant assignment.

According to the autumn final report, the placing of one-unit
entrants in 1B did not solve the problem fully; at the end of the
fourth week, 7 of the 14 cases were demoted to 1A. The remaining
cases barely justified retention in 1B. Because of the lack of selective

admission and of intelligence tests, it was not possible to know how representative of high-school training such cases as the following were:

*RH.*—One year, W.H.H.S., Cincinnati. No knowledge of texts studied, topics covered, or irregular verbs. Transferred from 2A to 1C to 1B to 1A.

*LH.*—One year, ———— University, Atlanta. Grammar not completed; no oral practice; little translation (55 pp.); two teachers in one year.

*RH.*—One year, H.T.H.S., Chicago. Grammar (100 pp.); oral method reader (60 pp.); no past tenses or irregular verbs; two teachers in one year.

*ZC.*—One year, L.H.S., Chicago. Only text was Méras, *Le premier livre.* [Equivalent to first half of 1A.]

*EL.*—One year, T.T.L.S., Chicago. (Honor entrance scholar.) Direct method, singing, games, playlets; no irregular verbs, no subjunctive forms. Reading limited to *Le premier livre.*

Until placement tests replaced entrance credits in 1946 for admission to College language courses, we continued to have maladjustments of this kind. The worthless admission credit is a great source of unhappiness, injustice, and wastage.

The following condensation of an autumn, 1922, report, covering two sections of 1A and one section of 1B, describes the first stage of the third trial course:

I. *Programs.*—French 1A centered upon the ability to read and to understand simple spoken French. The early reading of Méras, *Petits contes de France,* and Lavisse, *Histoire de France: Cours élémentaire,* was facilitated by the use of a specially prepared analytical grammar (20 lessons). Insistence upon ready and accurate pronunciation of isolated units. No practice in conversation or formal composition. Recognition knowledge of 65 irregular verbs, with some recall practice, using verb blanks. Tests as previously. Finals were mainly *oral.* Total reading: 240 pages. French 1B did not differ materially from the 1921–22 program. Smith and Greenleaf, *An Elementary French Reader,* and Labiche, *Le Voyage de M. Perrichon.* Specially prepared review grammar material (20 lessons). *Le Petit Journal* (3 issues). Total reading: 250 pages.

II. *Results.*—Fifty per cent of the 62 final grades were in the honors range. Only 6 students failed to receive credit, including 3 cases of provisional grades. One student read 1,962 pages (*Lectures faciles, Mythes et légendes, La Mare au Diable, Quatre-vingt-treize, La Sœur du soleil, Les trois mousquetaires*) during the last seven weeks of French 1A. He had no previous experience with the language.

III. *Remarks.*—Because of the reading of 100 pages in excess of the amount read in 1A previously and of the new treatment of the verb, reading and comprehension tests regularly used in 1A failed to measure fully the attainment of the better students; new tests will be necessary. It is quite clear that 65 type verbs can be learned effectively in the initial quarter without undue hardship or interference with other phases of study, but the procedures cannot be the traditional ones.[10]

There are four important points in this report, namely, the first instance of extensive reading in 1A, the presentation in 1A of grammar "for reading only," a comprehensive study of irregular verbs for the purpose of early reading, and the emphasis upon the ability to comprehend the spoken language. Henceforth these four practices become fixed characteristics of the Reading Method. As one instructor concluded in his report: "If there is anything outstanding in the performance of the autumn quarter, it is the feeling and the proof that we are nearing, though perhaps slowly, a not unattainable ideal of a first-year French course at the college level, economical, effective, and flexible, yet definite and stable."

A second attempt to reward the exceptional student met with success. At the beginning of the autumn quarter, three students who had completed 1C the preceding spring were allowed to skip 2A and register for 2B. Each one had done grade A work in 1ABC, had read extensively 1,000 pages of ungraded material in excess of requirements, and already possessed the proficiency obtainable (we thought) in the course skipped. They completed 2B with credit, but at the C grade level. The instructor in charge explained that she did not approve of "skipping" courses.

A fourth student (HW), promoted from 1A to 1C the following quarter and completing 2A in the spring with top-ranking honors, was promoted again over 2BC to French 11 (advanced grammar) the next autumn. He was the student for whom 1,962 pages were reported in 1A. The 1A–1C skip did not happen often. As the sequence became more unified, the omission of 1B became less advisable, and the 1A–1C skip was discontinued in favor of the 1B–2A and 1C–2B combinations. They were a partial solution for the problem of the "forgotten quartile."

The work of the winter quarter, 1923, is described in the following final report covering two sections in 1B and one section of 1C:

I. *Programs.*—French 1B: little change from previous procedures. The increase in extensive reading planned was canceled for lack of facilities, lists, and time. No free composition, due to illness of the instructor. Same texts as before, including the experimental review grammar material. Total reading: 300 pages, intensively.

II. *Results.*—Fifty-one of the 62 registrants completed their course, 11 in the honors range and 10 with the grade of F. Their grade-point average was 1.8, less than a C. There were 11 provisional grades for incomplete work, of which only 3 were credit marks. Of the 10 failures, 6 were ascribed mainly to slow learning, and 4 to low standards and poor study habits. Five of the provisional grades were due to illness. The generally low quality of student personnel was supplemented by an epidemic of influenza, causing excessive absenteeism. Student HW read an additional 2,448 pages in winter 1C, bringing his total to 6,900 pages, or over two million words read in two quarters!

III. *Remarks.*—New and more detailed reading report forms and new study and personal record forms are being prepared. Reading lists have been requested of other university departments to facilitate correlated reading in the spring. A bulletin board service attracted much attention; clippings and foreign periodicals, prints, postcards, current news items concerning France added interest and cultural values to the classroom instruction. Standardized tests are badly needed.

In matters of general policy, the staff adopted extensive reading in 1A and 1B as regular procedure, discontinued pretests in 1B, omitted the D grade in final reports, abolished "allowed" cuts, agreed to give only one-half credit in cases of excessive or unexcused absenteeism, began the practice of removing inactives from class lists before the final roll, and outlawed the prevailing traditional practice of tutoring one another's students.

The survey of the causes of failure and the custom of reporting deficient and exceptional students three times per quarter influenced the action of the faculties in passing the following resolutions, in February, 1923:

(1) That the students in the Colleges be limited by a process of selective admission and selective retention to the number that can be taught effectively in view of the facilities of the University and its major purposes of instruction and research.

(2) That, if possible, beginning with the Autumn quarter, 1923, students shall be admitted by selection on the basis of evidence of (*a*) adequate mentality; (*b*) seriousness of purpose; (*c*) intellectual interests and attainments; and (*d*) intellectual promise.

A joint committee of administrative officers of the university, chairmaned by Professor Morrison, made a study of conditions and practices relating to the subject and reported to the faculties in October, 1923. The report was adopted and placed in effect in October, 1924. The change in policies so affected our experimentation that we were obliged to consider the first four years as a period apart from the succeeding years.

To the four points in the second resolution, the committee added a fifth, i.e., an acceptable health certificate pending report of a physical examination by the university health officer. A sixth point recommended by the Junior College language staff was not adopted, namely, a requirement that applicants for admission be able to finance the first two quarters without the need for remunerative employment. The recommendation was made a point of advice to be given at the time of application for admission. Headway had been made toward the reduction of college failures.

In the spring quarter a section of French 2A was intrusted temporarily to the Junior College staff, giving it an opportunity to compare at first hand the achievement of 1ABC and 2A. A few changes were made in the second-year course: less time to phonetics, reduction of grammar to 10 lessons in Part II of the Fraser and Squair *Grammar*, the inclusion of free themes, and a minimum requirement of 300 pages in extensive reading. Inasmuch as most of the 25 registrants had passed through 1C, we had a chance to observe 1ABC and two-unit students in competition in the same course and section.

The results are summarized in the following spring report covering the work of 26 students in 1C and 26 in French 2A:

I. *Programs.*—French 1C: Read Daudet, *Lettres de mon moulin* and Daniels, *Contes de la France contemporaine;* total, 168 pages, excluding drills. Completed Carnahan, *French Review Grammar*. Total coverage intensively: 283 pages. Extensive reading, reported weekly for last 8 weeks, totaled 5,835 pages, or an average of 265 pages per student. Average of intensive and extensive reading combined, 548 pages.

French 2A: [The work followed the catalogue announcement, except for the changes indicated above.] Intensive study, oral and written, of France, *Le Livre de mon ami*, and Augier-Sandeau, *Le Gendre de M. Poirier*, supplemented by lessons 40–50 in the Fraser and Squair grammar; total coverage, 281 pages. Extensive reading of 14,044 pages, averaging 562 pages for each of the 25 active enrolees. The total study and reading experience was therefore 706 pages per student, on the average. The ability to write free themes was exceptional and led to the discontinuance of formal grammar study during the last weeks of the quarter.

II. *Results.*—There were no failures in either 1C or 2A. The grade distribution was as follows: A (4), A— (11), B (10), B— (11), C (8), C— (3), Provisional (2). Seventy-six per cent of the 2A students received honor grades. The students averaged 3.7 points (approximately B).

III. *Remarks.*—(1) "The spirit of work in 2A was remarkable. Several members became absorbedly interested in using their reading ability in French to the profit of their other studies; a few changed minor sequences in other subjects to French; others, without solicitation, studied French works in mathematics, aeronautics, biology, art, literature, etc. I can account for this spirit only on the grounds that they had already formed in 1B and 1C the habit of using the language to further their own ends. French 2A was for them not so much another course in language as it was a course in language *use;* they had replaced learning how by doing."

(2) "I am convinced that a first-year course that visualizes as its main aim from the *first day* the use of the language for the individual needs of the student, and proceeds simply and directly . . . to make a tool of the language, will meet with enthusiastic success on the part of the students . . . and that this usefulness will have a longer duration and will be more productive in a practical way. . . . It is becoming obvious that the two-year college course is too long by two quarters. . . ."

(3) In spite of restrictions raising the minimum requirement in extensive reading to 250 pages for 1C, requiring the instructor's approval of reading programs, and insisting upon more thorough reportage, more reading was done per capita than in any previous quarter. There were also more cases of correlated reading.

(4) All 1C students intended to complete the language requirements (2A) in the autumn. Fifty per cent of the 2A students planned to complete the second-year sequence.

Four of the 15 cases of exceptional students analyzed in this report are summarized below:

*YM, YM.*—French 1ABC. These twins were energetic, of high intelligence, quick perception and regular study habits, and accurate and painstaking. Each read over 250 pages of contemporary short stories and reported over 40 detailed analyses on special forms, in addition to regular reading reports.

*AC.*—French 1ABC. Quiet, industrious, dependable, alert, accurate, independent thinker. Main interest in mathematics. At the end of 1C, she changed her minor sequence to French and registered for 2ABC. Employed as stenographer and filing clerk. She read 401 pages of literary criticism and plays illustrative of the development of the French drama.

*HW.*—French 1A/1C/2A. Tireless worker, exceptionally quick and accurate, retentive, sound judgment, high standards, co-operative. Primary interest is law. Has a straight A record. Total outside reading for three quarters: 10,741 pages, mainly in the French novel. He also reported 23 special analyses of short stories. Granted the privilege of absenting himself two days a week from classwork. Recommended for further promotion in the autumn.

We now had a history of 12 promotions over a quarter-course in 1ABC and 2A, all of which had been successful. There were three other types of rewards for exceptional students in current use, namely, the privilege of not attending class one or more days per week, the substitution of special study topics for routine assignments, and the substitution of free themes for set retranslation exercises. Freedom from class attendance usually entailed more extensive reading as approved by the instructor.[11] The special topics included analyses of short stories to be submitted on special forms at reading conference hours. These rewards were sparingly bestowed and were much appreciated.

TABLE 3

| Week and Day | | Assignment* | Class Activity |
|---|---|---|---|
| 1 | Mon...... | Student records; course outlined | |
| | Tues...... | RVG, chap. i, Supplement, pp.8–12 | Test: irregular verbs |
| | Wed...... | RVG, chap. i, all exercises | Board work, dictation |
| | Thur..... | RVG, chap. ii, all exercises | Board and aural drill |
| | Fri....... | CO ("Les Prisonniers"), chap. i | Oral work; test: articles |
| 2 | Mon...... | LM ("L'Installation"), chap. i | Oral-aural; transfers |
| | Tues...... | LM (same), chap. ii | Composition correction |
| | Wed...... | RVG, chap. iii, complete | Drills; test: idioms |
| | Thur..... | RVG, chap. iv, complete | Board and dictation |
| | Fri....... | RVG, chaps. i–iv (review), "Prisonniers," chap. ii | Drills; test: articles |
| 3 | Mon...... | RVG, chap. v, complete | Oral recitation; verbs |
| | Tues...... | LM ("L'Installation"), chap. iii | Analysis: tenses and usage |
| | Wed...... | RVG, chap. vi, complete | Test: tense usage |
| | Thur..... | LM ("Le Sous-préfet aux champs"), chap. i | *Explication orale* |
| | Fri....... | RVG, chap. vii, complete; numbers quiz | Oral and written drill |
| 4 | Mon...... | LM ("Le Sous-préfet"), drills | Oral; test: translation |
| | Tues...... | RVG, chap. viii, complete; begin extensive reading; reading lists | Board work; test: auxiliary verb usage |
| | Wed...... | RVG, chap. ix, complete | Oral-aural; test: irregular verbs |
| | Thur..... | RVG, review chaps. v–ix | Test: grammar usage |
| | Fri....... | Extensive reading conference, 1 | Discussion of reports |

* Abbreviations: RVG (*Review French Grammar*), LM (*Lettres de mon moulin*), CO (*Contes de la France contemporaine*).

In order to make the various types of adjustment in the student personnel of 1ABC which have been described, it was necessary to have a work schedule laid out in advance for an entire quarter. It was in outline form, like the excerpt from the spring, 1923, schedule for French 1C shown in Table 3.

Lacking the American Council on Education standardized tests developed later by the *Modern Language Study*, we had to rely upon homemade materials for measuring attainment. As has been stated previously, the tests were rarely longer than 15 minutes, usually objective in type, and always unannounced. The course schedules were not issued to the students; they knew the past but not the future. The frequency of the tests (there were 16 in 1C) is explained by the necessity of knowing as soon and as precisely as possible what was going on, not only for the purposes of the experiment, but also to control demotions and promotions and to deal with the one-unit situation. The sequence was unquestionably "tight"; it was necessary to squeeze out as much guesswork as possible, especially with the materials in use. The perfect tooling of a scientifically planned language course[12] was for us only a deferred hope.

The final examination in 1C consisted of (1) a passage of 200 words from *L'Elixir du révérend père Gaucher* to be translated; (2) the first two sentences of the passage to be dictated; (3) the first sentence to be transcribed into phonetic symbols; (4) a questionnaire that required a knowledge of the whole story, to be answered in French; and (5) two passages in composition, the first based on the story by Daudet, and the second in the form of a free theme. The time limit was 50 minutes. The test was cast in the traditional mold and applied to the specific work of the quarter; it was not much more than a test of progress in a prescribed course.

An incident during the quarter has a bearing upon the question of vocabulary acquisition through extensive reading. Student HW, who read 10,741 pages in 1A, 1C, and 2A (he skipped 1B), was placed in a small room that had only a transom window and a chair with a writing arm. He was given a tablet of paper and some pencils and was asked to write all the French words that he could recall, spelling them as accurately as he could. He was not to leave the room until he could no longer think of a new word.

HW was in the room about four hours, and wrote 1,304 French words, excluding duplicates, with very few misspellings. He listed the grammatical variables, ordinal and cardinal numbers from 1 to 20 and by tens to 100, the days of the week, months, seasons, primary colors, points of the compass, dimensional terms, grammatical nomenclature, and lists of connectives, prepositions, adverbs, and common regular and irregular verbs. About 75 per cent of the words were content words, often directly traceable to specific readings. In many instances he resorted to antonyms, homonyms, synonyms, word groups, derivatives, cognates, and physical and ideological associations; at other times, he developed categories (as trees, minerals, parts of the body, etc.). It was an extraordinary display of word power evoked by the unaided memory and made possible only through quantitative reading in addition to classroom assignments.

Two new extensive reading procedures were tried out: a revised report slip with a sheet of instructions and an analytical report sheet for short stories.

The slip was 4 × 6 inches in size, printed on thin stock, and provided space for the following information: (*recto*) author, title, student's name, course, date, amount being reported, total amount read to date, subject of the material reported upon, what was liked or disliked about the material, and the beginning of a brief summary; (*verso*) end of the summary and a quotation of the most interesting or most valuable point. The instruction sheet offered advice for making out the form, as follows:

1. Under "like or dislike" the answer may vary from slip to slip. Give your own reaction, not some critic's. Avoid generalizations, as "interesting," "silly," "increases the vocabulary," etc.

2. State in definite terms some literary value, referring to style, characterization, development, etc. Avoid meaningless or perfunctory answers.

3. In summarizing, confine yourself to the space provided. That means brevity, the essentials, the significant.

4. The quotation must be in French. Make it significant in relation to the original text. Not just any sentence will answer the purpose. Think before you select it and be ready to justify its selection in the conference hour.

The mimeographed analytical form for reporting short stories listed 114 points relating to vocabulary, form, theme, style, structure, content, mood, and characterization, e.g., (*vocabulary*) slang, daily, period, allusions, pedantic; (*form*) fable, allegory, dramatic, fantasy; (*theme*) morbid, trite, novel, moralizing; (*style*) sentimental, impressionistic, didactic, intimate; (*plot*) plausible, slow, tedious, melodramatic, intricate, simple. After each characteristic a space was provided for a check mark. The use of the check list was discontinued after three quarters; the students tired of making marks instead of phrases and preferred the regular report slips. But meantime we had obtained some evidence that quantitative outside reading could lead to an understanding and appreciation of literary values at the same time, even in a first-year French course. Had the experiment continued, we might have found a statistical answer to the question sometimes raised as to proof of the quality, as well as the quantity, of extensive reading.

The practice of correlated reading raised a small but at times annoying problem: the selection of the material. If the student were to read what he wanted to read and if what he wanted to read was expository material in nonliterary fields, it was essential that the selection of material be such that he would find the reading interesting, purposeful, and worth while, or he would soon turn to less desirable but less exacting matter. Since the student was usually unacquainted with French contributions to the special field, it fell to the staff to make the selection for him. Few instructors felt qualified to pass upon material outside their language specialty, despite their exposure to the cultural radiation of university training. We therefore appealed directly to the heads of fifteen College departments, asking for bibliographical help, saying in part:

> To make our experiment successful, there must be sufficient material in the libraries adapted to the linguistic level of the student and of profit to him in the earlier stages of the special subject selected for reading. The Romance Languages department of the College needs and desires the active co-operation of the other departments in the selection of such material, and in the purchase of the books if they are not available at present. . . . Such assistance will put new meaning into the present foreign language reading requirement, and will make possible a correlation of studies that should impart a renewed and genuine interest in both subjects, to their mutual advantage.

Fourteen of the fifteen departments responded with enthusiasm; the fifteenth (chemistry) thought the French contribution negligible (!). By June, 1923, we had a list of 60 titles, expertly chosen, representing art, sociology, philosophy, psychology, political science, history, physics, mathematics, geology, geography, zoölogy, anatomy, botany, and physiology. Some of the titles were as follows:

LECOMTE, G. *L'Art impressioniste.*
RAMBAUD, A. *Histoire de la civilisation française.*
LACOMBE, P. *Petite histoire du peuple français.*
BERNARD, C. *La Médecine expérimentale.*
VALLÉRY-RADOT. *La Vie de Pasteur.*
POINCARÉ, H. *L'Avenir de la science.*
DRUDE, O. *Manuel de géographie bontanique,* trans. POIRAULT.
DE MARTONNE, E. *Abrégé de géographie physique.*

FAYOL, H. *Administration industrielle et générale.*
CAMBON, V. *L'Industrie organisée.*
————. *La Science française.* 2 vols.

The full list showed two errors common to such attempts at integration, namely, the prevalence of current and temporary writings and the inclusion of works intended to meet the requirements of certain advanced courses in a specialized field. We soon discovered that the students preferred general or fundamental works to more specialized readings for a Senior College course, especially if they had not yet completed the prerequisite courses.

In integrated reading there is always the danger of exceeding the limits of the student's knowledge of the special subject, thereby doubling the difficulty of the undertaking. In the above list, for example, the Fayol item was probably beyond the comprehension of a Junior College student who intended to major in business administration. There is also the chance that required readings for a course may change with the calendar, forcing changes in reading lists and book reserves. A minor annoyance is the recommendation of a book known to its proponent only from his graduate study notes.

During the third trial year there were four experimental groups in third-quarter extensive reading. Two of the lines of experimentation were to determine a suitable time allowance for the feature and to find a satisfactory minimum amount to set for the students. The net results pointed to an allowance of 10 conference days and a minimum requirement of 250 pages.

In Group A, 28 students were assigned a minimum of 100 pages covering 9 conference hours. They read 5,912 pages, which was 3,112 pages in excess of requirements, or an average per student of 211 pages. Thirty-nine students in Group B, with a minimum requirement of 200 pages for 10 conference hours, read 10,677 pages, an excess of 2,877 pages, or an average of 274 pages per student. Group C, with 18 students and a requirement of 200 pages per student for 6 conference hours, read 6,606 pages, in excess by 3,006 pages, or an average of 367 pages per student. Group D, with a minimum of 250 pages for 8 conference hours, read 5,835 pages, an excess of 335 pages, or an average of 265 pages for the 22 students in the group. In sum, four groups totaling 107 third-quarter students reported 29,030 pages of extensive reading over 33 conference hours, or an average of

271 pages per student. This amount was in excess of the minimum requirements by 9,330 pages—a surprising display of interest and ability on the part of language beginners! For without *both interest and ability* they could not and would not have read 29,000 pages of ungraded French texts in less than one college quarter.

These readers did not confine themselves to literature. They read in nineteen classifications, taxing the ingenuity of the staff and the resources of the reading collection. As an illustration, they read 10,462 pages in the novel, 5,795 pages in the short story, 3,804 pages in the drama, 1,683 pages in history, 1,071 pages in the medical

TABLE 4

| Case No. | Course | Reading in French 1C |
|---|---|---|
| 1...... | Law | Zola, *L'Affaire Dreyfus* |
| 2...... | Physics | *Larousse mensuel*, articles on radio |
| 3...... | Chemistry | *Larousse mensuel*, rare elements |
| 4...... | Elocution | Coquelin, *L'Art de dire le monologue* |
| 5...... | Music | Romain-Rolland, *Musiciens d'aujourd'hui* |
| 6...... | Political science | Barthélemy, *Le Gouvernement de France* |
| 7...... | Philosophy | France, *Le Puits de Sainte-Claire* |
| 8...... | History | Funck-Brentano, *Légendes et archives de la Bastille* |
| 9...... | Bacteriology | Valléry-Radot, *La Vie de Pasteur* |
| 10...... | History | Lavisse and Rambaud, *Histoire générale* |
| 11...... | Drama (history) | Dondo, *Pathelin, et d'autres pièces* |
| 12...... | Political economy | Bazin, *Le Blé qui lève* |

sciences, 1,745 pages in general science, 805 pages in folklore, 745 pages in travel, 381 pages in philosophy, 912 pages in the arts, and 718 pages in the political sciences.

Many of them availed themselves of the opportunity to make their reading in French aid in the work of other courses, as the partial list of integrated reading given in Table 4 illustrates.

As was said previously, the lack or inaccessibility of suitable material in many of the scientific fields often barred the student from doing integrated reading. The most accessible form of scientific reading material is the journal, but the French scientific journals are, as a rule, much too specialized to be appreciated by junior college students. They are more liable to discourage than to encourage voluntary reading. We rarely recommended them. Manuals in the natural

sciences were avoided altogether, because they have little to contribute in vocabulary or in style and are usually devoid of interest.

## 5. *Balance Sheet for 1920–23*

Success in a way of teaching a subject is sometimes predicated upon registration figures, gains in continuation, grade averages, and little else. "What is the percentage of withdrawals?" "What is the annual shrinkage?" "How many do you fail?" "How many of your students continue the study of French, and how well do they do?" Such questions are more easily asked than answered. They drive one to statistics, but statistics can be misleading and inconclusive. There are so many influences that condition the answers and that are not subject to the laws of numbers.

For instance, between 1920 and 1923 there were 1,144 student course completions in French 1, distributed as follows: 455 in 1A, 390 in 1B, and 299 in 1C. It would appear that the shrinkage for the year amounted to 34 per cent. If that were really so, the situation would be serious. But we are not dealing with one set of students. They come and go at the quarter intervals, disappear to reappear later, or drop out of school permanently. Changes such as demotions, promotions, cancellation of sections, changes in the time schedule, etc., upset statistical counts. In fact, the staff identified 18 different factors in explanation of the 34 per cent shrinkage, but the combinations responsible for any particular segment of the triennium could not be isolated with certainty. The total number of completions for each of the three years was as follows: 404 in 1920–21; 382 in 1921–22; and 358 in 1922–23. The *annual* shrinkage was only 5 per cent.

Registration figures are unreliable for comparative data. Even completion figures may be inaccurate. In the final rolls for 1920–21 appear the names of 34 students who dropped the course at the fourth week; in 1921–22, there were 26 such cases; in 1922–23, 18 cases. Still, in 1951, final rolls are sprinkled with academic "ghosts," the names of students alive only in a statistical sense, some of whom disappeared even before registrations closed.

Most of the shrinkage in completions appeared in 1A and 1B, but primarily in 1A. That would indicate that the causes were largely outside the course of study. Direct continuation from 1A to 1C was on the increase. But it was reasonable to suppose that some part in the general shrinkage was due to the nature of French 1. What that part may have been, the staff attempted to explain in its June, 1923, report:

1. Reduction of the number of 1A sections changed the percentage ratio of morning to afternoon hours, affecting the enrolment of students gainfully employed in the afternoon.

2. Placement according to proved ability instead of entrance credits discouraged registration on the part of students for whom French 1 was an elective.

3. We were still labeled "high-school" courses in some official announcements.

4. Our omission of D (pass without credit) and E (conditional) grades, our testing program, our disregard of lesson learning, and our personnel activities were not popular with undergraduates.

5. Oriental students were excused from modern foreign language requirements by action of the faculties, autumn, 1922. In 1921, we had 21 registrants; in 1922, only 3.

6. A postwar decline in French and Spanish registration had set in, following a resumption of the study of German, outlawed during the world war.

7. French 1C so overlapped 2A that the impression had gained ground among underclassmen that our language courses were needlessly difficult.

8. Senior College students who wanted a reading knowledge of French only were beginning to drop out of the sequence at the end of 1B, thinking that they were secure against failure in the graduate reading examinations.

No doubt the sort of thing that was going on in 1ABC was not popular with Freshman undergraduates. We were not anxious that it be a "popular" course. Eventually, the substantial students would come its way, and the sequence would settle down to a reasonably constant ratio of registration, completion, and continuation. Of course, that never happened; depressions, world politics, wars, and internal changes in the university saw to that.

In June, 1924, the writer made a survey of French and Spanish grades earned in 1ABC from 1920 to 1924 inclusive. It is convenient to quote from that report, although it covers one year beyond the term of the present discussion.

For the two languages, there were 2,676 quarter grades, of which 85.8 per cent were passing (C—) or above. The total number of grade points was 6,166, or an average of 2.59 points (B—) per student completion. The loss by failure amounted to an annual average of 14.2 per cent.

In French alone, 82.3 per cent of the 576 completions in 1A received a grade of C— or better, and averaged 2.74 grade points for the whole group. The loss by failure was 17.7 per cent. In French 1B, 457 students received 1,109 grade points, an average of 2.71 points per student (B—). The percentage of passing grades was 90.4; of failures, 9.6. French 1C had 370 completions, of which 90.5 per cent received the grade of C— or better. The average for the group was 2.82 grade points, approximately B—.

Apparently, French 1A saw more failures than either 1B or 1C, but the lowest average quality of work was done in 1B. If one compares the 2.74 grade-point average for 1A, normally composed of students without previous experience in French, with the 2.82 grade-point average for 1C, which included in its personnel many one-unit entrants, one cannot give the latter too much credit for their share in the achievement of 1C.

The percentages of failure in 1B and 1C were not excessive, but the percentage of 17.7 in 1A, almost twice that of either of the other two quarters, was disturbing, in spite of what had been learned from the inquiry into the causes of failure and the students' use of their time. Many of the possible causes were known; the reports to Superintendent Morrison phrased and rephrased them. Good excuses were not lacking. There was some consolation in the fact that the percentage of failures for the whole sequence had been lowered by approximately 6 per cent from the percentage for 1919–20, the year preceding our administration of the course. Nevertheless, however one looked at it, the 1A percentage of F grades was too high. The conduct and organization of the course and outside conditions adversely affecting the quality of its work would have to be re-examined.

Eventually, the 2-1-1 ratio of failures was broken.

The search for evidence of the achievement in 1ABC during the trial period led to the more advanced French courses in the College of Arts, Literature, and Science. The purpose of the investigation was (1) to ascertain how many of the 1C finalists went on to the required credit course 2A and to further study of the language; (2) to secure evidence concerning the effectiveness of the methods used in 1ABC, in so far as grades obtained in subsequent courses constituted valid evidence; (3) to compare the attainment in 1C with attainment in later courses in the case of 1C continuants; (4) to learn the extent of the check in 2A upon the proficiencies acquired in 1ABC; and (5) to test the claim that 1ABC was equivalent to two high-school years in achievement. The results of the survey could seriously affect the second phase of the experiment.

The survey was made in May, 1923. The first students to complete 1C were in the spring quarter, 1921. Except for a few cases of promotion, they were the only ones eligible for continuation into courses beyond 2ABC. For continuation data in 2A, only four groups were available, namely, spring and autumn, 1921, and spring and autumn, 1922. The data were taken from the instructor's grade reports in the Bureau of Records, the records of the Home-Study Department, and student personal records in our files.

In this period, 383 students completed French 2A. Forty per cent (153) were continuants from 1C. Of the 222 eligible continuants, 47 were not in residence temporarily or permanently, 12 had been promoted over 2A to a more advanced course, and 3 had earned credit for 2A by means of correspondence-study courses. The 1C segment of French 2A enrollees earned 417 grade points, or 44 per cent of the total number. Junior College continuants had made a satisfactory showing in a fourth major course. They earned 41 per cent of the honor grades (A, A−, B), and incurred 21.7 per cent of the unsatisfactory grades (D, E, F, and Provisional). Comprising two-fifths of the membership of 2A, they had incurred only one-fifth of the poor grades. One student received the conditional grade of E, subsequently raised to a pass (D). None incurred an F grade. The evidence seemed to prove that the 1ABC-trained student, on the average, was as good as, or better than, the two-unit students with whom he was in competition in 2A.

The grade-point average for the 222 students who completed 1C was 3.1 points (B); for the 163 continuants who completed 2A, it was 2.8 points; for the 63 who completed 2B, 3.5 points; for the 35 completing 2C, 3.9 points (A−); and for the 14 who completed upper Senior College courses, 4.0 points (A−). Only 127 of the Junior College students who completed 2A were eligible for continuation beyond that point during the period studied. This fact, with the fact that 2A satisfied the language requirement, explains largely the drop in continuation figures for the higher courses. That 50 per cent of the eligible students went on to a sixth major (2C) could be considered proof of their interest and efficiency.

Forty-five per cent of those who completed 2C registered in Senior College courses, as follows: Exercices oraux (1), Modern French Grammar (9), Cours de style (5), Théâtre de Molière (4), Corneille et Racine (3), Survey of French Drama (5), Survey of French Novel (5), Practical Phonetics (1). The 14 students averaged 4.0 grade points (B) per student course.

There were 12 cases of promotion during the three-year period, i.e., 8 from 1C to 2B; 1 from 1C to 2C; 1 from 1C to French 11 (Modern French Grammar); and 2 from 2A to 2C (when 2A was under Junior College administration). The 12 students averaged 3.1 grade points per course, although the Senior College instructors did not look with favor upon the practice of "skipping" courses. Prerequisites are the sacred cows of college faculties.

There were four general conclusions to be drawn from this survey: (1) continuation from 1C to 2A was very satisfactory; (2) if 2A were modified in favor of more reading and oral-aural practice and less grammatical theory, more continuation might result; (3) the postponement of formal grammar to the *end* of 1C, with more oral training and free themes in 1B, would raise the average achievement for continuants in 2A; and (4) there was in 1ABC the foundation for a satisfactory one-year terminal college French course. We could now proceed to refinements.

The course and method had been adapted to extension courses by correspondence in 1922–23.[13] The method had been paralleled in Spanish since the beginning of the experiment, and German had been added in 1922. The three trial years had been profitable and instructive years.

## CHAPTER III

# ECONOMIES AND REFINEMENTS

## 1. *Major Administrative Changes, 1923–32*[1]

IN THE ten years following the end of the third trial course, a number of far-reaching administrative changes in the University of Chicago occurred which necessitated shifts and adjustments in the elementary language courses.

In the spring of 1925, the university changed its grading system, dropping the minus-letter values (A—, B—, C—) and the provisional grade E. A year later a readjustment of entrance unit equivalents led to the abolition of the fourth language-major requirement, leaving French, German, and Spanish 1ABC in the status of a terminal course.

The following year (1927), the Junior College modern foreign language courses, which had been administered since 1920 as an experimental unit in the Laboratory Schools of the School of Education, were officially transferred to the jurisdiction of the College of Arts, Literature, and Science and became a department of modern languages. In the autumn, the six majors of instruction, i.e., 1ABC and 2ABC, were reduced to five majors and the administration of 2A and 2B was intrusted to the newly formed Modern Language Department.

In 1932, the New College Plan incorporating the last two years of high school with the first two years of college and necessitating a reorganization of the college curriculum was approved by the University Senate. With the reorganization came an advisory system, comprehensive examinations, the publication of syllabi, and other changes of a more or less untried nature. It was no longer easy to check the results of our courses with past performance.

Most of the changes in French 1ABC between 1923 and 1932 were aimed at making the course more economical of time and labor for both student and instructor, at effecting refinements of procedures and materials, and at determining the best possible chronological order for the development of the various skills. It was also a period of more objective evaluation, due to the appearance of the American Council on Education language tests and of long-term studies dealing, in general, with the relation of reading to language learning. With the publication of textbooks and materials made to our own specifications and tried out in our courses, we became better equipped to attain our objectives. Of special value to us were the findings and the word and idiom lists of the Modern Foreign Language Study, in the program of which we had been unable to take active part but which had used liberally our data, outlines, and resources. For every language teacher in the country it was an exciting period, a time of conflict in ideologies the echoes of which still sound in this second postwar period, although less loudly than a decade ago.

Before considering in detail the developments in our experimental course, it will be useful to examine its outline, a product of the three trial years discussed in the previous chapter.[2] There will be few radical changes in its main lines in later years; revision will be in minor ways, of value only in the aggregate. The outline (Table 5) will serve also to guide the reader through the intricacies of further discussions. The brief summary of the conditions affecting the course and its aims which prefaces the outline, provides the necessary setting.

## 2. Basic Outline. I (1924)

*Conditions.*—French 1ABC is a sequence of three quarter-courses, or majors, consisting of 36 weeks of five 50-minute periods each. The university foreign language requirement is "four majors in one language" and is met by the successful completion of French 2A. Full credit for the four majors is granted only when they are taken during the first half of the student's undergraduate program. Until the fourth major has been credited, course credits for 1ABC have no value toward a degree. They carry only half-credit for upper-class students.

It is recommended that 1ABC be taken in consecutive quarters (normally autumn, winter, and spring). Students who enter with one unit of credit in French begin with 1B or, with the approval of the departmental examiner, with 1C. Right is reserved to place the student according to his demonstrated ability to use the language. The decision is made after personal conference, inspection of the student's personal record card and admission record, examination by pretests, and classroom achievement during the first two weeks of the quarter. Changes in placement are cleared through the proper deans and the office of the registrar. All placements are open to further revision at the end of the fourth week. Case reports on exceptional and deficient students are made at the fourth, seventh, and twelfth weeks of the quarter to the superintendent of the Laboratory Schools of the School of Education.

TABLE 5

OUTLINE OF FRENCH 1ABC*

| Feature | French 1A | French 1B | French 1C |
|---|---|---|---|
| Primary object | Comprehension of easy French, written and spoken | Reproduction of easy French, written and spoken | Comprehension and reproduction of more difficult French |
| Grammar | Analysis of the language structure for comprehension only (Bond, *Introduction to the Study of French*) | Analysis continued with beginning of speech and writing (Bond, *Introduction to Composition*) | Formal grammar as a corrective review (Carnahan, *French Review Grammar*) |
| Composition | No English-French composition: occasional theme or résumé based on reading | Oral and written composition, with "direct" exercises on texts, résumés, themes, and sentence expansion (Bond, *Introduction to Composition*) | Formal composition, English-French translation; "direct" exercises (Carnahan, *French Review Grammar*) |
| Reading | Intensive, starting 2d week (200 pp.); extensive, with reports, starting 7th week (50 pp.); topic: French history and geography (Méras and Roth, *Petits contes de France;* Lavisse, *Histoire de France*) | Intensive, with some translation and questionnaires (200 pp.); extensive, with reports beginning 8th week (100 pp.); topic: French people, customs, folklore, daily life (Daudet, *Le Petit Chose;* Labiche, *Le Voyage de M. Perrichon*) | Intensive, with little translation and questionnaires (150–200 pp.); extensive, with reports, beginning 4th week (250 pp.); topic: French arts, literature, science (Daudet, *Lettres de mon moulin;* Daniels, *Contes de la France contemporaine*) |
| Translation | Daily, beginning 2d week, oral and written, prepared and sight | As for 1A, but not daily and with more sight translation | Very limited use of translation from French to English |
| Pronunciation | Foundation drill by phonetic method without aid of I.P.A. symbols; concert and individual practice daily; analysis of personal problems | Practice with aid of I.P.A. symbols; phonetic theory; analysis of personal problems | Brief phonetic review; oral reading and phenomena of connected speech (Nitze and Wilkins, *French Phonetics*) |

* All page quantities are for actual textual matter, exclusive of exercise material.

TABLE 5—*Continued*

| Feature | French 1A | French 1B | French 1C |
|---|---|---|---|
| Oral-aural practice | Daily practice in understanding material related by instructor; use of simple questions; some dictation of simple known material | Aural comprehension and oral composition; questionnaires; dictation of familiar material | Story-telling by instructor, checked by oral or written résumés by students; unrestricted dictation; instructional use of French |
| Vocabulary | Recognition, tested = 1,000 words; no organized effort to secure reproductive vocabulary (New York Society for the Experimental Study of Education list) | Recognition total of 2,000 words, tested; reproduction total = 500–800 words; vocabulary-building (list as in 1A) | Recognition total of approx. 3,000–4,000 words, according to type and amount of extensive reading; reproduction total of 1,000 words; vocabulary-building (list as in 1A) |
| Idioms | No organized study of idioms; some attention to prepositional compounds | Reproduction total of 25–50 commonest idioms; recognition total of approx. 100 (Wilkins list, *Le Petit Journal, Supplement,* April 1, 1923) | Reproduction total of 60–80, as listed in Carnahan, *Review Grammar;* recognition total of approx. 200 (Wilkins list) |
| Verbs | Recognition knowledge by 3d week of all regular verb forms; by 7th week of 20 commonest irregular verbs; recognition and formal reproduction of 42 irregular verbs by end of quarter | Formal review of all regular and 42 irregular verbs; use in oral and written composition (1A list) | Further review, with drills, of 42 irregular verbs and their compounds, as listed in Carnahan, *French Review Grammar* |
| Testing | Minor progress tests, followed by needed retesting; major achievement tests on separate abilities, 4th, 7th, and 11th weeks; final examination | Pretesting for placement; major and minor tests as for 1A; final examination | As for French 1B |
| Motivation | Bulletin board displays: news items, postcards, cartoons, prints, posters, circulars, travel and study information; class presentation of topical matter | Bulletin board; use of *Le Petit Journal* in sight reading; reading lists and promotional discussions; promotion for excellent work to 1C | Bulletin board; use of *Le Petit Journal* as in 1B; reading lists and special extensive reading assignments; limited exemption from class attendance and promotion to advanced courses for exceptional students |

*Aims.*—(1) To economize material, time, and effort for student and instructor. (2) To develop as early as possible the ability to read French, and to make it the primary aim, placing second the ability to understand spoken French. (3) To encourage and reward individual excellence and yet insure a common body of instruction that will allow successful continuation study. (4) To enable the student to realize that the study of French can contribute to his well-being. (5) To provide the student with independent means of using French as a tool in the pursuit of his own interests.

Would this outline stand up under the test of the classroom? Was it flexible enough to adjust to the changing policies of the College? How valid were its timing and its distribution of the phases of language learning? Was it suitable for both terminal and preparatory training? What would be the results of its application, the measure of the skills obtained by its use? To find the answers, we set aside the next four years (1924–27) of the seven-year plan as a period of checking, comprehensive surveys, and internal adjustments in the sequence.

### 3. On the Record, 1923–24

What happened is easily discernible from the reports. Nine reports per year by each instructor left not a worth-while grain of information in concealment.

In French 1A (autumn, 1923) the extensive reading was stepped up from 50 to 100 pages, with reports on the prepared forms. Free composition was attempted, relying on transfer from reading. It was not successful; structural details had failed to register sufficiently for recall. The staff concluded that "free composition at this early stage should be based on practice with simple, fundamental units of expression, or patterns, without reference to grammatical principles or other analysis." Since such a procedure would require special techniques and materials, it was postponed. It has not yet been tried.

In 1B (autumn) the program was changed twice to meet the needs of one-unit entrants who were not able to follow the course as outlined. A study of one section of 1B, taken from a final report, illustrates the seriousness of this problem:

Of 23 registrants, 3 had studied only regular verb forms; 2 knew nothing of the subjunctive and conditional tenses and their use; only 1 had a formal command of the 42 irregular type verbs known to 1A students; 4 had never translated English to French; 3 had not heard a spoken French word; 6 had delayed continuation for a year or more; 2 who were foreign born were barely intelligible in English; only 5 had read more than 100 pages. . . .

It was the old situation of the round peg and the square hole. Whatever we did, we had to consider round and square pegs at the same time.

In 1B (winter, 1924), which was a continuation of 1A in the autumn, 55 per cent of the students received honor grades, and only 7.2 per cent failed. This was the highest percentage of honor grades and the lowest percentage of failure for 1B since the beginning of the experiment. The staff investigated the causes and came to the following conclusions:

The significance . . . seems to be as follows: (a) a better administrative system, due to the gathering and constant use of personal records, the maintenance of student-instructor contacts, prompt and adequate placement of registrants, promotions and demotions at mid-term and between quarters, and a known policy of holding ability, and not quantity, as a measure of progress; (b) a more closely knit organization of the courses, flexible and yet definitely pointed at realizable objectives; (c) an improvement in methods tending to develop student initiative, mainly through extensive reading and free composition, with reforms in the presentation of grammatical, phonetic, and syntactical matter. It seems reasonable to believe that we shall be able eventually to reduce the percentage of failure to a negligible figure which will be a product of chance, beyond our control. . . .

That statement includes the principal factors contributing to the success of French 1 as they were to be substantiated by the experience of the next decade.

There were a few minor changes in 1B from the 1924 outline, i.e., no formal grammar, more informal composition (résumés, portraits, free themes), an increase in intensive reading to 297 pages, a minimum requirement of 200 pages in extensive reading, and increased practice in vocabulary-building. But these changes had significant results, as the following quotations from the reports indicate:

No grammar was used in the 1B sections. The exercises in the intensive reading texts were "direct," and whatever grammatical principles were called to the attention of the class evolved from the substitution and manipulation drills in the Labiche and Daudet texts. The analytical grammar in 1A, plus a considerable reading experience, made synthetic drills merely a matter of observation. In fact, a correlation between amount of reading done and composition ability is clearly and undeniably present.

In French 1C the composition work covered the retranslation exercises illustrating the rules in the Carnahan grammar, and the more direct exercises of the Daudet text. . . . I tried to break down somewhat the formal attitude of these students, trained for the most part on a year of high-school grammar, but the attempt succeeded in only a few cases. They had apparently lost the power, if ever possessed, of self-expression in French. . . . They were inferior, as a group, to a majority of the 1B students in the ability to express themselves in the language.

The free themes in 1B are convincing proof that composition can be taught without grammar and that self-expression that springs from the experience of the student is attainable in a crowded classroom and in a course in which . . . equal attention is paid to all phases of comprehension, as well.

The amount and accuracy, as well as the quality, of the reading done in and out of class seem to bear a direct relation to the highest and lowest ability in oral and written expression. . . .

The Spanish and German staffs concurred in this last statement, from their own experiences.[3] There were many cases of close correlation between reading and composition ability in 1B like the following, taken from a winter report:

*BO.*—Read 210 pp., too specialized, graded A—; composition, B—.
*BY.*—Read 202 pp., reports inaccurate, graded C; composition, C—.
*DA.*—Read 212 pp., daily-life vocabulary, graded A; composition, A—.
*IR.*—Read 209 pp., technical matter, graded B; composition, B—.
*MC.*—Read 154 pp., general vocabulary, graded A; composition, A—.
*MO.*—Read 308 pp., *Sans famille*, graded A—; composition A—.

The composition grades were obtained on final tests; the grade assigned to extensive reading, however, was approximated according to the degree of accuracy in the reading reports. We lacked the standard tests that made later correlations possible. We were sure, nevertheless, that a close relationship existed between extensive reading and other proficiencies.

The minimum requirement for 1B was 200 pages, double that for 1B the preceding year. Yet 46 students in two sections read a total of 10,711 pages, or an average of 233 pages per student. In the same quarter, 23 students in one section of 1C averaged 300 pages per student. The combined reading of the 69 students was distributed as follows: novel (6,888 pp.), drama (4,520), short story (1,436), literary criticism (974), biography (708), physics (604), chemistry (425), geography (404), zoölogy (321), anatomy (286), and in smaller amounts in descending order: philosophy, history, art, folklore, geology, political science, and mathematics.

In reply to the question "State why you like or dislike correlated reading?" asked of the 27 students who read in correlation with another subject, the following reasons for liking it were given:

1. Gain different views and attitudes (12 cases).
2. Material inaccessible in translation, or better in the original form (5 cases).
3. Get recent scientific knowledge (3 cases).
4. Practical application of language ability (2 cases).
5. Offers a comparison of peoples (2 cases).

On the negative side, three thought the material dull; three complained of time wasted in getting suitable material, and one thought it limited his vocabulary. Twenty-two suggestions were made for improving the feature; they concerned mainly library regulations and the accessibility of materials.

As examples of the use made of this reading: one student who read 100 pages of source material on Paraguay made a class report for History E-15 (South America); a second, who read 244 pages in invertebratology used the material for reference in Zoölogy 16 and as a term paper to absolve the requirements in English 3; a third read 218 pages of the *Vie de Pasteur* and wrote a term paper on the "Development of Immunization" for English 3; and a fourth read 210 pages on religious art in France in the thirteenth century for weekly reading reports in English 28 (Chaucer's *Canterbury Tales*). Here was proof that French 1 was reaching down to the individual student.

French 1C in the spring broke with several precedents. Two sections numbering 45 students made a record of 2.5 per cent failure and 44.4 per cent honor grades, and averaged 3.31 grade points (B—) per student. According to reports made during the investigation into the use of students' time,[4] the two hours estimated as needed for course preparation were not being fully used. We were not overworking our students, by their own statement.

Consequently, we made the following experimental changes in the outline for 1C at the beginning of the quarter: (1) the replacement of *Lettres de mon moulin* by *Les Misérables* (Scribner's); (2) the postponement of formal grammar and composition (Carnahan text) until the last six weeks of the quarter; (3) an increase in the reading minimum to 300 pages; (4) the elimination of phonetic review and the use of script; (5) the omission of formal, daily verb drill; (6) the omission of unit grammar tests; and (7) the requirement of B or better on a special test in pronunciation for a passing grade in 1C.

The change in reading text to one using an *explication de texte* method was ill advised. Part of the class hour in 1A, half of the hour in 1B, and all of the hour in 1C would have to be conducted in the foreign language if results were to be satisfactory. The staff queried the future use of the method.

The elimination of the usual phonetic review and the postponement of grammar also proved unsatisfactory in practice. The incidental correction of pronunciation in the class recitation was not sufficient to correct even the more obvious mistakes, and the student's interest in acquiring a correct pronunciation apparently declined in direct proportion to his acquisition of reading skill. Grammar had been deferred in the hope that informal composition, plus increased reading, would create a reserve of language use that, when submitted to the discipline of formal grammar, would result in a high attainment in oral and written expression. That was not the case in the spring 1C sections. The reports indicated a variety of possible reasons:

1. Practice writing was not begun early enough in 1A.

2. In the winter quarter, the exercises in the reading texts consumed too much time at the expense of free composition.

3. The deferment of grammar to the last half of the course did not allow review and retesting.

4. Oral practice, emphasized in 1B, was slighted in 1C in order to provide time for the formal written drill.

5. With only four days a week for classroom practice (the fifth was used for reading conferences) and with reading skill as the primary aim, the ability to "talk French" as another objective of the course was "asking too much."

6. The standard of ability to write French was too high, unless the staff was willing to compromise on other aims.

Under the circumstances, it was an instance of overreaching, due, no doubt, to ambitions for 1ABC and downward pressure from 2A. The condition, of course, is typical of curricular situations where the upper-level courses become rigid and unalterable. Changes in the lower-level courses must be kept within the prescribed limits. This is one of the main deterrents to productive experimentation in second-language learning. It was twenty years before French 1 became a free and independent course.

One instructor in 1C made an interesting observation concerning speech-and-writing ability at the end of the sequence:

Extensive reading builds up the active vocabulary very slowly, almost imperceptibly. The student who gets the gist of a page easily is unable to name a dozen new words or expressions when the page is finished. This may be natural enough, but one cannot write or say something without words. This quarter, the students were hampered by a lack of vocabulary when it came to writing and speaking French. With the increased ability to read, the recognition word stock crowded out the active vocabulary, cognizance of the single word diminishing with the increase in reading power. . . .[5]

The woods had replaced the trees. In so far as words were concerned, reading and writing in our present procedures were somewhat antagonistic. What we failed to see was that "free" speech and writing is like "free" reading; both develop by doing, by trial and error through quantitative experience, and not by means of codes.

This quarter marked the last attempt for ten years to apply the Morrisonian philosophy of "teach-test-reteach" to French 1. It had been applied only to the formal grammar instruction in 1C. The more pupil activity replaced teacher activity, the less applicable was the unit testing procedure. Free composition, like informal discourse, cannot be blocked out in units. Even grammar, the science of language, as studied in 1ABC, did not show reliable indexes of mastery under the unit system. At no one particular time did the members of a class know how to identify or to use certain French parts of speech. To test, teach, retest, and reteach the forms of French grammar by units of instruction not only would consume too much time but was counter to the theory of learning to read by reading and to our special interest in the personalizing of the learning process.[6]

Correlation in the spring sections of 1C was more general and more fruitful than in the winter quarter. The students approved of the practice, with few exceptions, and for reasons like those stated above. Disapproval arose from difficulty in getting suitable material or from lack of co-operation of instructors in other courses who were not interested in integration.[7] Thirty-one of the 44 third-quarter students correlated their reading with another course; the manner in which they did it is illustrated by the following cases:

[1] Read 101 pages of Binet-Simon, *La Mesure du développement de l'intelligence chez les jeunes enfants,* for Education 7 (tests and measurements).

[2] Read 285 pages in Troost, *Précis de chimie* for Chemistry 6 (qualitative analysis).

[3] Read 327 pages of Funck-Brentano, *Archives et légendes de la Bastille,* for History 3b (Europe, 1789–1914).

[4] Read 197 pages in Hugo, *Quatre-vingt-treize,* for History C6 (Napoleon and the French Revolution).

[5] Read 238 pages of Valléry-Radot, *Vie de Pasteur,* for Chemistry 8 (quantitative analysis).

[6] Read 120 pages of Gide and Rist, *Histoire des doctrines économiques,* for economics (general course).

[7] Read 413 pages of Molière, Beaumarchais, Marivaux, and Sardou for English 40 (introduction to English literature).

[8] Read 268 pages of Schinz, *Œuvres de Rousseau,* for Philosophy 4 (ethics).

As in the winter quarter, the spring reading spread into 18 library classifications: novel (5,707 pp.), drama (4,101), short story (1,198), history (1,040), biography (829), literary criticism (815), chemistry (530), physics (479), political economy (346), geography (310), philosophy (286), education (244), anatomy (164), political science (112), geology (104), folklore (45), sociology (36), zoölogy (34). The total amount was 16,531 pages read by 44 students, or an average of 376 pages per student. The range was from 101 to 1,022 pages. All the material was subject to written reports and conferences. It was an astonishing performance.

Two special reports closed the year: a report on registrations and credits during 1920–24, the results of which have been presented above,[8] and a report on the use made of the reading collection in 1923–24.[9]

According to the latter, there were 256 titles shelved in the old-fashioned revolving bookcase in the staff quarters; 106 were French, 92 Spanish, and 58 German. The collection, inherited from the School of Education library, was not planned for use in elementary language classes and was not particularly attractive. Two hundred and sixteen of the titles circulated during the year, accounting for 958 separate calls and about one-fourth of the extensive reading. In French, 92 of the 106 titles were in circulation and received 360 calls, an average of 4 calls per title. The balance of the reading material was obtained from the University Libraries, from the branches of the Chicago Public Library, from staff members, and through private purchase.

From a librarian's viewpoint, the most remarkable thing about this service was that, in spite of the accessibility of the books and the ease of the transaction of getting and returning loans without attendants or fines for overdue items, there was a loss of only three books on a basis of 1,000 calls.

The teacher's viewpoint is best described by the following quotation from an instructor's final report:

New acquisitions are taken into the classroom and discussed for a few minutes. Occasionally, time is taken to discuss the relationship of a group of writers, the tenets of a literary movement, the contribution of certain scientists, the treatment of a certain theme or way of life. These discussions, *with the books in hand,* never fail to stimulate a demand. . . .

There is not an hour in the school day . . . when one or more students cannot be seen poring over the books on the shelves. As a result, we have been asked countless questions, have listened to criticisms and indulged in arguments pertaining to men, movements, and art. Further, I have been called upon to suggest books for private purchase, booksellers, editions, and bindings and to approve of lists submitted as the beginnings of a private French book collection. One student has started a set of Hugo, another of Anatole France, and a third of *Jean Christophe.* This service is one of the enjoyable features of a departmental "reading-room."

In future building plans for the Junior College, provision should be made for an adequately equipped departmental reading-room which would form a *locus* for the activities of the department. Here would be housed the reading collection on wall shelves, with chairs and library tables where the students might comfortably examine the books and make out their reading reports. Such a room could serve as a consultation room, a language clubroom, and a meeting place for committees [!]. It should have a collection of wall maps, a display case, a bulletin board, and provision for the use of projection apparatus. It should be in suite arrangement with classrooms, offices, and the language laboratory. [*Note:* There was such a room three years later.]

Our practice in allowing students to skip courses had not been officially approved and was a matter of some annoyance to the accrediting officers of the university. Approval came in April, 1924, by the following action of the College Board:

Students of special proficiency registered in Romance 1 or 2 (French 1A, 1B) . . . may be promoted within any quarter to Romance 2 or 3 (1B, 1C) as the case may be, upon recommendation of the instructor and with the approval of his dean. In any such case the University Recorder shall promptly be notified of the transfer. The student so promoted shall be credited with the advanced major in which he attains a grade at the end of the quarter, but he shall not be credited with the major in which he was first registered.[10]

Our analysis of over a thousand cases of exceptional students had borne fruit. Henceforth, a proficient student could change from 1A to 1B in the autumn, move into 1C in the winter, and complete the fourth major (2A) in the spring, with official sanction. The "stop-and-go" course was at last a reality. But there was a hidden catch, as we soon found out. According to the new ruling, a student so promoted would have to take another quarter-course, since the language requirement stipulated "four majors in one language" and not "the fourth major." Promotion, then, brought no saving of time or effort. The time-serving, fee-paying, and classroom-sitting would continue as always. Mediocrity would have its rewards, and superiority its penalties. But in the realm of inner satisfactions a gain had been made.

### 4. *In the Groove, 1924–25*[11]

In the autumn of 1924 we undertook to introduce extensive reading earlier in 1A and to practice "directed" oral composition after the seventh week without the use of formal grammar. This was to be done as a supplementary activity without any change in the outline. It meant more emphasis upon accuracy in pronunciation and in reading and more dictation, vocalization, and the recall of verb forms.

Judging from the quarterly reports, achievement in oral and written expression far exceeded that of any pevious 1A course. It still lacked, however, the precision and direction to be had from the use of a well-ordered "sentence-expansion" procedure.

The students read the Méras text parallel with the study of the analytical grammar[12] after the second week, completed the grammar and began reading the Lavisse text extensively by the end of the fourth week, and practiced the recall of 43 irregular-type verbs. In many cases they did supplementary reading of their own choice after the seventh week. The classes covered 475 pages of reading text, of which 170 were of a cultural nature, read extensively.

Of the 52 students completing the two sections of 1A, 44.3 per cent received honor grades, 11.5 failed, 9.6 were given provisional grades, and 23.1 were promoted over 1B to 1C in the winter or the spring. No student reported having spent more than 15 week-hours on the course.

The 45 credit students read a total of 8,933 pages extensively, or an average of approximately 200 pages each. Thirty-six students read in excess of the minimum by an average of 105 pages. Individual reading ranged from 21 to 1,097 pages. The latter score was made by the only student in the two sections who had had French previously.

The character of this voluntary reading in the first quarter may be estimated from the following list (the number of pages read is in parentheses):

Audoux, *Marie-Claire* (258); Daudet, *Contes* (49), *La belle Nivernaise* (130); Mérimée, *Colomba* (193), *Carmen* (67), *Contes* (40); Maupassant, *Contes* (43); Labiche, *La Poudre aux yeux* (402), *Moi* (75); Balzac, *Contes* (81); Dumas, *Comte de Monte-Cristo* (130); Malot, *Sans famille* (637); France, *Le Livre de mon ami* (49), *Abeille* (146), *La Comédie de celui qui épousa une femme muette* (64); Bruno, *Le Tour de France* (71); Sand, *La Mare au Diable;* and Erckmann-Chatrian, *Waterlou, Le Conscrit de 1813.*

Estimating the contents of the average page at 300 words, the 36 students who read in excess of the requirement averaged 187,000 French words seen during the *first ten weeks* of the course. What power latent in the visualization of 187,000 French words seen at the very beginning of the course of study! Even though many of them were imperfectly comprehended, one cannot deny that once seen is better than never seen. Even their inner vocalization, properly harnessed, could work wonders for the advocate of oral proficiency. Progress had been made toward the acquisition of language "feeling" that more formal instruction could not have produced in so short a time, at such an early stage, and with such personal satisfaction. Already words were assuming the color and meaning that only rapid, continuous reading *without deciphering* can give.

How fluently and accurately could these beginners read sight material? An attempt was made to secure a reliable answer to this question during the tenth week of 1A. Under supervision, 17 students read a passage of 3,200 words at sight from Lavisse, *Histoire de France: Cours moyen* (Heath). They averaged 128 words a minute, with understanding of the material read which was checked by a 60-item questionnaire. They were allowed to use the end-vocabulary, which slowed down the average time in four cases, where a misunderstanding of directions led to looking up every word. The test was not perfect, but it gave us an estimate of what was going on in the first stage of our experiment.

We were curious also as to the rate of growth of the reading ability in an individual. An observant, mature, painstakingly accurate student without previous experience in French, Miss W—— H——, offered to log her reading for six weeks beginning with the first day of the quarter. The material was Méras and Roth, *Petits contes de France*, a reader intended to follow the use of an elementary grammar in a first-year course. On the second day, Miss W—— H—— read one page in 30 minutes; on the sixteenth day she averaged one page in 11 minutes; and on the thirtieth day, one page in 7 minutes, in spite of the increasing difficulty of the selections ("Marie Antoinette," "Napoléon Bonaparte"). She then read 70 pages of a treatise on physiological chemistry (Bernard, *Leçons de physiologie*)!

How would the reading of foreign language translations of known material in English affect rate and accuracy in learning to read the foreign language? Peter Hagboldt[13] tried to find an answer by taking two sections of German 1A, judged to be about equal in native intelligence, and using known material in translation for extensive reading in the one and unknown material in the other. The experimental group read in translation from the Bible, *Julius Caesar*, *The Talisman*, *Hamlet*, *Mill on the Floss*, and *Robinson Crusoe*. At the end of the ninth week, both groups were tested in sight translation from Hauff, *Zwerg Nase*, using a text without a vocabulary and in German letters. After 30 minutes of silent reading, the students were asked to answer 16 questions on the first 11 pages.

The average speed per hour for the 17 students who had *not* read translations was 21.8 pages, with an average of 12 questions answered, with 13.7 per cent of error. The 11 students who read translations averaged 24.8 pages per hour, with 15 questions answered and a percentage of 0.79 in error. The advantage was apparently with the experimental group, particularly in accuracy of understanding. However, inadequate controls, the absence of intelligence quotients for the two groups, disparities in vocabulary coverage, and certain subjective factors (guidance sessions, etc.) lessened considerably the validity of the test.

Several independent studies were made in the autumn quarter in respect to a possible correlation between amount of extensive reading and the skills tested in the final examinations. In one study a comparison was made for a section of French 1A in which 18 students read 3,841 pages, or an average of 213.4 pages per student, in excess by 123.6 pages of the minimum requirement. Table 6 sums the results for the upper and lower thirds of the class.

In this study, as in previous ones of the kind, the staff could see only general evidence of a relationship; beyond that it could only theorize.[14] But the fact that promotional cases, for which an A rating was required, were invariably found in the upper bracket of the amounts of extensive reading done by the sections was evidence enough for our purposes. In 1A, as an example, 7 promotional cases averaged 471.2 pages; in Spanish 1B (winter), 8 students who were recommended for promotion averaged 499 pages; and in German 1B, 12 students averaged 1,260 pages of extensive reading.[15] The

TABLE 6*

| Case | Amount of Reading (Pp.) | Dictation Test | Aural Test | Vocabulary (Per Cent) | Irreg. Verbs | Reading Comprehension |
|---|---|---|---|---|---|---|
| RU....... | 1,097 | Very good | A | 90 | Very good | A— (3d) |
| BA....... | 329 | Good | A | 90 | Very good | A (1st) |
| TO....... | 294 | Weak | B | 94 | Failed | B (5th) |
| BE....... | 209 | Excellent | A | 98 | Excellent | A (1st) |
| HE....... | 264 | Fair | A— | 98 | Fair | A— (3d) |
| MO....... | 202 | Fair | A | 99 | Good | A (1st) |
| [Middle third omitted; lower third follows.] | | | | | | |
| UL....... | 125 | Poor | F | 80 | Poor | F (abs.) |
| BU....... | 123 | Very weak | C | 50 | Failed | F (12th) |
| FA....... | 116 | Very poor | F | 90 | Failed | B (7th) |
| FR....... | 104 | Good | A | 70 | Very good | A— (4th) |
| DO....... | 101 | Very poor | F | 70 | Failed | F (abs.) |
| CA....... | 21 | Very poor | B | 93 | Failed | C— (10th) |

*Explanation of tests:* Dictation (passage from *Deux amis*); aural comprehension (anecdote, with question and answer); vocabulary (350 words in Méras text); irregular verbs (43 type verbs); reading comprehension (sight reading of *Deux amis*, and a two-page English summary). The numbers in parentheses in the last column show the final ranking order of the student.

high German average was due in part to the presence of a number of German-Americans in the group and in part to the special attention paid to prospective A students—an example of what can happen when the exceptional student gets as much attention as the deficient student usually receives.

The winter 1925 report states that 7.7 per cent of the 1B completions, who were continuants from 1A in the autumn, failed and that 42.3 per cent received honor grades. Three of the four students given provisional grades in the autumn failed in 1B; the fourth withdrew from college. The staff decided to discontinue the practice of giving provisional grades in 1A.

Instructors are often tenacious about retaining their A students in the belief that the "skimming-off" process lowers the morale and the achievement of the others left in the class. We repeatedly found the reverse to be true. After we had removed from 1A by promotion to 1C the nine top-ranking students, the remaining students speeded up their efforts and produced five more cases for promotion from 1B to 2A. Furthermore, six 1B students organized themselves into a guided-grammar study group during the last four weeks of the quarter, in order to attain the rank necessary for promotion from 1C in the spring to 2B the following autumn. Five of the six succeeded in obtaining the promotion.

An incident occurred in 1A and 1B that led to the later application of our methods to the training of graduate students for the reading requirement in foreign languages. Miss H—— A——, who completed 1A in the autumn, had included in her extensive reading a technical work on nutrition. In January, 1925, she applied for and passed the French reading examination for the doctorate. Again, in February, Miss W—— H——, who was reading Bernard's *La Médecine expérimentale* for 1B, took and passed the same examination. If these two students could satisfy the reading requirement by means of French 1A plus some specialized reading, why should others be required to register and serve time for one year of the language? A trial one-quarter course in the summer of 1926, entitled 101G, was the answer.[16]

Minimum reading requirements were removed from 1B in the winter quarter. The result was more reading done by more students than ever before. Fifty-one students reported 26,127 pages, an average of 512.3 pages per student. Twenty-one read above the average. The highest score was 1,419 pages; the lowest, 251 pages. Again, the correlation between amount of reading and achievement in the final tests was striking for the upper and lower quartiles. The eight honor students read over 725 pages each; the six F students, with one exception, read less than 300 pages each.

It should be noted in this connection that neither the quantity nor the quality of extensive reading ever entered into the computation of a final grade in any of the courses, although there were times when the staff was perilously close to instituting a system of penalties.

In one of the reports in the winter quarter appeared the first sign of a new problem, peculiar to a reading approach:

The extensive reading feature is an excellent ally, but it is not without its dangers. It becomes more apparent yearly that it is the most valuable thing we do. It is also becoming apparent that it has to be handled with care and submitted to some control, otherwise the student mistakes a slight comprehension ability for a real skill. Guidance in selecting material, personal conferences, occasional reports to the class, tests, close inspection of the report slips, and awareness on the part of the instructor are all necessary safeguards.

The catapulting effect of our reading "approach" in 1AB no doubt led some students to mistake the reading "adaptation" for genuine ability.[17] Even members of the staff sometimes confused one stage with the other.

By the end of the spring quarter, French 1C had changed considerably in personnel from autumn 1A. Fourteen students had been promoted; 12 had dropped out after failure; and a number of one-unit entrants had been added, bringing the total for the two sections to 39 students. Failures in 1C amounted to 4.9 per cent; honor grades, to 56.3 per cent.

For the three quarters, honor percentages were as follows: 1A, 44.3; 1B, 42.3; and 1C, 56.3. Failure percentages were: 1A, 7.2; 1B, 7.7; and 1C, 4.9. Twenty-eight students in all had been recommended for promotion; their achievement is included in a continuation report summarized in a later chapter.[18]

Past recommendations on the subject of the minus distinctions in the College nine-point grading system brought about a revision (June, 1925) of the system by faculty action. Henceforth we were to follow a five-letter system as follows: A, Excellent (6 points); B, Good (4 points); C, Fair (2 points); D, Poor (no points); F, Failure (−2 points). This change put the C− and D grades into one compartment (D) and abolished the nuisance grade E (conditional). Because of these changes, comparisons involving grades or grade points incurred in 1920–25 could not be carried further than the spring quarter, 1925.

The extensive reading average for the spring quarter 1C was 645 pages, the highest amount at that level in five years. The reading-rate test (Maupassant, *Deux amis*) showed an average rate for 37 students of 77–80 words per minute, with full comprehension. Approximately 42 per cent of the 23,862 pages read were integrated with a personal interest or a college course, as illustrated in the following cases:[19]

*SA.*—Read 1,304 pages in French comedy from Beaumarchais to Anatole France for class discussions in English 40 (modern comedy).

*CI.*—Read 556 pages from Mathiez and Dayot for material for themes in History 3 (modern European).

*WO.*—Read 325 pages in Corneille and Racine for a term paper, "Comparison of the *Medea* in Latin, Greek, and French," for Latin 17 and Greek 5 (drama).

*RY.*—Read 964 pages from Dayot and Aulard for themes in History 3 (modern European).

*MU.*—Read 425 pages from Taine for use in recitations in English (history of poetry).

*EN.*—Read 101 pages from Valléry-Radot, *Vie de Pasteur*, for recitations in zoölogy (basic course).

*CA.*—Read 472 pages from Taine and Stapfer for term paper, "What Kind of Man was Shakespeare?" in English 41 (Shakespeare).

From a purposeless, barrier-type college course without any very apparent relation to the student's existence, French 1 (in the words of an instructor) "has become an effective tool and a key for the unlocking of new facts and new impressions . . . the logical and economical necessity attached to the one hundred and fiftieth lesson."

Because of the work factor involved in the progressive increases of outside reading from 1921 onward, one might expect to find a mounting percentage of failures and a decreasing number of honor grades in the succeeding years. What actually happened was the reverse. Failures dropped steadily from 15.5 per cent in 1920–21 to 13.4 in 1921–22 (when extensive reading began); 10.3 in 1922–23; 11.6 in 1923–24; and 9.8 in 1924–25. These percentages include losses from *all* causes, i.e., failure, drops, and provisional grades. As the percentage of failures grew smaller, the percentage of honor grades grew larger: 33.3 per cent in 1920–21; 36.4 in 1921–22; 35.5 in 1922–23; 39.6 in 1923–24; and 47.6 in 1924–25.

Meantime, the extensive reading average increased from 208.6 pages per student in 1921–22 to 645 pages per student in spring, 1925. Yet the loss in student personnel shrank by only 3.6 per cent, and the honor grades increased by 11.2 per cent! Was this not another proof of the saving power of extensive reading? The full explanation of these two trends, of course, is not as simple as that, but the staff was agreed that increased reading experience had much to do with these shifts.[20]

The last survey of continuation records was made in the summer,

1925. Changes in accrediting, placement, recording, and marking
made further continuation studies impracticable.

Two members of the French staff[21] checked the final report sheets
of 13 Senior College instructors who had taught the 75 sections of
French 2 from 1920 to 1925. French 2 was a standardized second-
year course such as could be found in the majority of colleges at that
time. Its nature can be inferred (with due allowances for catalogue
statements) from the official University *Announcements:*

*104 (2A). Intermediate French.*—Grammar review. Considerable use of
French in class. Short themes based on reading. The *New Fraser and Squair;*
Coleman, *Intermediate French;* Nitze and Wilkins, *Handbook of French Phonetics.*
Class and collateral reading of about 200 pages from two or more of these texts:
Thiers, *Bonaparte en Égypte;* Sandeau, *Mademoiselle de la Seiglière;* Lamartine,
*Jeanne d'Arc;* Augier and Sandeau, *Le Gendre de M. Poirier;* Bazin, *Les Oberlé*
or *Le Blé qui lève;* France, *Le Livre de mon ami.* Prerequisite: two years of high
school French, or one year of college French.

*105 (2B). Advanced French.*—A reading course conducted largely in French.
Weekly written themes based on the readings. Special study of idioms and tense
uses. Class and collateral reading of about 350 pages from three or more of these
texts: Hugo, *Les Misérables;* Pailleron, *Le Monde où l'on s'ennuie;* France, *Le
Crime de Sylvestre Bonnard;* Taine, *Les Origines de la France contemporaine;*
Loti, *Le Pêcheur d'Islande;* Bornier, *La Fille de Roland;* Mérimée, selected
stories; Canfield, *French Lyrics.* Prerequisite: two and one-half years of high
school French, or four quarters of college French.

*106 (2C). Advanced French.*—Conducted in French. Careful reading of more
difficult modern texts, with increased attention to their character as literature.
Weekly summaries based on the reading. Continued study of idioms. Class and
collateral reading of about 500 pages from three or more of these texts: Rostand,
*Les Romanesques* or *Cyrano de Bergerac;* Renan, *Ma sœur Henriette;* Musset,
*Trois comédies;* Michelet, *Histoire de France;* France, *Crainquebille;* Canfield,
*French Lyrics.* Prerequisite: three years of high school French, or five quarters
(or three semesters) of college French.

The investigators checked the records of 1,553 students who had
completed one or more courses in this second-year sequence. Of this
number, 30.2 per cent (469) were Junior College continuants; the
others (1,084) were high-school or college students who had met the
prerequisites. The Junior College continuants won 1,493 grade
points, or 33.8 per cent of the total of 4,415 points. The average
number of points per Junior College continuant was 3.18, or slightly
more than B— in the grade scale. For the non–Junior College con-

tinuants the average was 2.69 points, or slighty less than B—. The difference of 0.49 points was in favor of the College continuants.

The Junior College group received 44.4 per cent of the honor grades, compared with 35.2 per cent for the non-College continuants, a difference of 9.2 per cent, again in favor of the former. Only seven-tenths of 1 per cent of the F grades was incurred by the College continuants: two E grades (conditional) subsequently raised to C, and one straight F grade.

One failure in five years of continuation study out of 469 students, including regular and promotional cases, in such a second-year course as described above was for us an encouraging piece of evidence as to the efficacy of French 1.

If one considers the nature of the staffing of the 75 sections of French 2, the evidence becomes even more heartening. In 2A, 33 sections had been taught by 13 different instructors: 2 regular staff members above the rank of instructor, 1 substitute instructor, and 10 graduate students. French 2B had been taught by 2 regular staff members and 4 graduate students. The 20 sections of 2C had been taught by 11 different persons: 6 graduate students, 2 substitutes from the Senior College staff, and 3 staff men from the lower college.[22]

How much has this situation changed in the American college during the last twenty-five years?

The Modern Foreign Language Study announced (March, 1925) its purpose and program of investigation,[23] and Professor Coleman, as special investigator, invited our co-operation. Regretfully, the staff was obliged to decline active participation beyond exchanges of correspondence, informal reports, trial runs of testing materials, and local conferences. The decision was forced by the critical stage of our own experiment, which required the full time and attention of the staff.

However, during the next two years we were able to render some slight service to the Study, through conferences with the Canadian investigator, Professor R. Keith Hicks, for his special report on our method;[24] a trial run of the *Iowa Placement Examination—FT1* in October, 1925; copies of French 1 programs and data for 1924–25 for the first and second experiments in teaching reading, conducted at the University of Iowa by Professor C. E. Young in 1925–27;[25] trial runs and analyses of the *American Council French Test—F10* in November, 1926, and March, 1927; and similar trials of experimental forms of the American Council French, German, and Spanish *Silent Reading Tests* in March, 1926. Indirectly, too, we served through Professor Morrison's *Practice of Teaching in the Secondary School,* in which our conception of second-language teaching was made known to participants in the Study investigations.[26]

Any account of the development of the Reading Method would be incomplete without a mention of the fortnightly staff conferences. The minutes are filled with discussions of perennial problems of teaching, such as criteria for grading, what to do about absenteeism, the value of the daily recitation, the curse of the "get-by" attitude, means of promoting and demoting students, advice to give on how best to study a language,[27] the problem of placement, the interpretation of data, etc.—problems the solution of which, even when found, changed with time and circumstance. Hundreds of man-hours went into these discussions, now helpful, now futile, but always essential.

The one question that recurs again and again in the minutes is the one of the standard for a passing grade.[28] In the minutes for March 12, 1925, one finds this entry:

If the instructor is satisfied that the student has definitely learned to *read,* then a grade of C. If the instructor is satisfied that the student has definitely learned to read and, in addition, has shown a definite *inclination to read generously* in extensive reading, then a mark of B. If the student has exhibited these qualities and has also exhibited conspicuous excellence in *both attitude and attainment,* then a mark of A. ... The essential point is to be able finally to abandon this year a passing grade based upon average performance in the daily lesson and not upon evidence of attainment. ... The issue is a grade founded upon definitely recognized attainments and not upon an average of classroom performance. ... Again, do we feel that we can trust the student as having acquired a certain definite capacity which is his and which he will carry with him? ...[29] [The italics are in the minutes.]

Again, in the minutes for January 6, 1926, one meets the same question, and Professor Morrison is quoted as saying:

I have been closing up the sixth-week reports and have the following comments to make. ... I note particularly your list of get-by students. ... I think these people should be jumped on the very first thing as soon as they turn up under these conditions and given the choice at once of either getting down to business or getting out. I can think of very few injustices to students which go to the root of things more definitely than this sort of destruction of their volitional development. . . .

Three months before, in the minutes for October 30, 1925, the staff secretary had recorded:

The daily grade is more or less futile. If it is used as the basis of promotion, there is a good deal of danger, for such grades stand for the *performance* of the day and not for actual *learning*. . . . This year, in making up the class records, members of the department should not allow the consideration of daily performance in class to influence the final mark. One should make it the rule rather to pass no one who has not given abundant evidence that he *can and will use the foreign language as anticipated*. . . . The kind of future work which the student can be trusted to do, therefore, is a highly important consideration. . . .

And so the argument went back and forth, just as it does in our schools and colleges today, subject to all sorts of pressure from the eligibility board of the Department of Physical Education up to the Scholarship Committee, and in spite of the abandonment of educational principles to the inexpert judgment of uneducated and often ineducable youth.

Such sessions at regular intervals acted upon the experiment as a sort of governor, keeping it from blowing up or running down. By such means we were better able to keep our eyes upon the ball. It is not easy to proceed directly from theory to practice in the classroom.[30]

## 5. *Round and Round, 1925–27*

The student who was interested only in "getting by" was the top problem for the new year, 1925–26.[31] It was necessary that we either find a way of making him proficient or get rid of him. Thanks to a well-functioning "underground" that relayed from quarter to quarter the word that a passing grade in French 1 was fully adequate protection against failure in 2A, his number was increasing rapidly and threatened a premature end to our essay in planned proficiency.

A special drive against this type of educational parasite was launched in the autumn 1A sections. By June, 1925, the "floater" population had been reduced, but not exterminated. It may be that control measures are all that one can hope for. An idea of what the crusade meant to one instructor may be learned from a series of excerpts from his reports.

Out of 54 students in 1A, all Freshmen but one, he listed 10 students as "deficient,"

... because of indifference to instructions and neglect of the work of the course, both due (according to recent confessions) to a belief that they could "get by" by cramming in the latter part of the course and by passing the final examination. In all cases, reports were made to the deans, and personal conferences were held and are being followed up. . . .

Four weeks later, at the end of the quarter, 3 of the 10 students were among the list of failures, analyzed as follows:

*KE.*—Unable to recoup. Dean insisted on her retention. Joined the "Quadranglers" (sorority-type club), although below passing in three courses. Not a serious student; out for social *réclame*.

*CL.*—Otis IQ, 116. Reticent; would not discuss his work; claimed no outside employment; warned repeatedly. Impression is that he is not frank and does not tell the truth about his work and study habits. Loafs around campus. Unconcerned.

*CO.*—Otis IQ, 121. Failed Latin in high school (1 yr.); had 5 quarters of French (U.H.S.). Unable to read French; unwilling to do extensive reading. Good-natured, lazy, indifferent.

A fourth student received a B, with the comment: "Called his bluff; scholarship material." Of the 6 others, the instructor wrote:

... These cases constituted my "problems" for the quarter. A constant watch was kept over them; they were counseled and aided as each individual needed, with frequent or regular conferences. . . . Nearly every case warranted an extension of time until the fourth week, or earlier in case of incorrect attitude, of winter 1B. . . . At the beginning of next quarter (winter, 1926), they will be called into conference, and the situation be made clear to them: either satisfaction of the work upon which they are conditioned before the end of the fourth week, or F and a return to 1A. . . .

Three failures, six conditional cases on probation, and one satisfactory student (B) in the suspect group: that was the score at the beginning of the winter quarter. At the end of the spring quarter, his final report summarizes the results as shown in Table 7.

Four of the ten idlers in 1A had been salvaged by the untiring efforts of the harassed instructor, who gave "from one to two hours per day to personnel work," although one of the students (MA) was a poor risk for continuation work in 2A. The others had not responded to his efforts. The following year the staff adopted the policy advocated by Professor Morrison and cited in the minutes for January, 1926.

The achievement in extensive reading for 1925–26, in two sections of French 1 in direct continuation under the same instructor, is summarized in Table 8. The reading in autumn 1A was less than in the autumn of the preceding year, but it was better in quality of material read. It was done without conferences or assignments and represented *voluntary* activity, since the requirement was met by the

TABLE 7

| Case | Autumn 1A | Winter 1B | Spring 1C |
|------|-----------|-----------|-----------|
| AR........ | C | Prov. (C) | C |
| CO........ | Prov. (F) | Prov. (C) | Dropped |
| KE........ | Prov. (F) | Dropped | ............ |
| MA....... | Prov. (C) | B | C (low) |
| PI........ | Prov. (C) | C | Dropped |
| BU........ | Prov. (C) | C | B |
| CL........ | Dropped | * | * |
| JO........ | Prov. (C) | F | ............ |
| KL........ | C | Dropped | ............ |
| MK....... | B | A | B |

* CL took 1A, winter, grade C; 1B, spring, grade B; did not take 1C.

TABLE 8

| Item | 1A | 1B | 1C |
|------|-----|-----|-----|
| Number of students reporting... | 50 | 37 | 32 |
| Total pages read.............. | 10,889 | 17,704 | 28,353 |
| Average of pages per student... | 217.6 | 478.5 | 886.0 |
| Minimum amount required..... | 115 | 350 | 500 |
| Lowest score................. | 68 | 228 | 530 |
| Highest score................ | 1,085 | 993 | 1,537 |

Méras text. The total reading experience, intensive and extensive, of these two sections averaged 564 pages per student, or close to 170,000 words of running discourse.

In the winter the extensive reading in 1B was directed experimentally toward a specific end, such as the novel, the drama, the short story, or the literature of the nineteenth century, with the purpose of correcting haphazard, unbalanced, or aimless reading and of covering some of the material read in French 2. In order to do this, the reading conference was made an individual and not a classroom affair, program talks were given in the classroom, and reading lists for special programs (development of the novel, the historical

novel, the short story, French comedy, etc.) were distributed to the
students.

The results of these procedures are seen in the incredible average of
886 pages per student in spring 1C. Every one of the 32 students met
the 500-page requirement, and one-third of them read 1,000 pages
or more. In fact, more than 12,000 pages were read *in excess* of the
minimum requirement. With one exception, all students who were
promoted during the year were great readers, the majority of them
belonging to what we called the "Mille" group, or those who read a
thousand pages per quarter.[32]

The reading list for these two 1C sections numbered 188 titles.
The range of their difficulty and value can be seen from the following:

France, *Le Livre de mon ami;* Rostand, *Cyrano de Bergerac;* Maurois, *Ariel;*
Loti, *Jérusalem;* Mâle, *L'Art français et l'art allemand au moyen âge;*
Renan, *Vie de Jésus;* Picard, *Théâtre;* Maeterlinck, *Théâtre;* France, *Vie
de Jeanne d'Arc;* Walle, *Argentine;* Loti, *Ramuntcho;* Poincaré, *Valeur de la
science;* Pérochon, *Nène;* Hugo, *Notre-Dame de Paris;* Jusserand, *Shakespeare en
France;* Daudet, *Tartarin de Tarascon;* Reinach, *Histoire des religions;* Saint-
Pierre, *Paul et Virginie;* Dumas, *Comte de Monte-Cristo;* de Launay, *Science
géologique;* Balzac, *Eugénie Grandet.*

All these books were read in French editions, without footnotes or
end-vocabularies. It is certainly not a publisher's approved list for
elementary courses, or such a list as one may find in a college catalogue announcement of a first-year course.

Three comments should be made about this reading achievement:
(1) only one A student was represented in the group, eleven of the
twelve exceptional students having been promoted: (2) the excessive
amount read above the requirement is *voluntary* reading, evidence of
the *will* to read; and (3) the nature and range of the books read show
the exercise of a personal choice that can be found only when the
ability to read has become fluent enough to convey pleasure and
profit to the reader.[33] One does not read such books voluntarily unless he has passed the stage of transverbalization, nor does he read
them unless he gets more for his pains than half-ideas of meaning.
This is the sort of proficiency that should mark the termination of a
reading course.

In view of what has been said previously about integrated reading and the co-operation of college departments in recognizing the usefulness of a foreign language proficiency, the following excerpt from an instructor's report is worth noting:

Correlation was better done and with more profit to the students than in other quarters. There is an increasing amount of co-operation on the part of other departments in the university in suggesting suitable titles, either through reading lists or in conferences with the students. In addition, they are encouraging the use of reading in foreign languages for themes, reports, and term papers. There are still gaps in departmental practices, but, in general, correlated reading is being encouraged in one way or another.

If the full bearing of this paragraph in a routine report were realized in every American college and university, the position of foreign languages in the scheme of general education would be improved and assured against circumstance. What powerful auxiliaries: *savoir* and *vouloir!*

Progress was being made in the revision and publication of materials built to the specifications of French 1 and already in use, especially the analytical grammar[34] used as an introduction to reading in 1A. The intensive reading texts used in 1A were, of course, not planned for the use to which they were put. Even the Méras text (*Petits contes de France*), designed for first-year students, contained 1,976 different words, only 62 per cent of which were within the first 2,000 words of the Vander Beke *French Word Book*, and 10 per cent of which were not in the frequency list at all.[35]

For 1B, we had a phonetic manual in print and a set of phonograph recordings based on the text,[36] suitable for use at any stage of the sequence. The manual had been in trial form since 1922. But the reading material was still problematic. In 1926 we were using Rambaud, *Civilisation française* (Holt), an all-French cultural reader, quite out of bounds in respect to vocabulary. It was selected because it obliged the student to stay within the French language; to define, discuss, and retell without reference to an English vocabulary; and to acquire a body of cultural information. But it was a hazardous leap from *Petits contes*, and not the progressive ascent in reading difficulty that we wanted. For the speech-and-writing program we filled in with De Sauzé, *Contes gais*, since the long-planned sentence-expansion text[37] had not materialized.

Materials for 1C were unchanged, except for a new type of review grammar and composition text[38] to replace the Carnahan text. The De Sauzé edition of *Jean Valjean* (Scribner's) was used instead of a cultural anthology in preparation as the third volume in a series of anthologies[39] which would cover the whole cultural program and intensive reading of the first year. The series was a grandiose scheme that was cut short later by the findings of the Modern Language Study and the word and idiom counts. Only the first and third volumes were published.

The textbook plays a prominent part in a classroom-conducted experiment. It can easily defeat a purpose for which it was not originally planned.[40] A great deal of staff time in conference was spent in selecting and adapting texts, and more time was spent in the classroom in trying to change conditions induced or maintained by the use of materials which were not suited to our particular purposes. Early in our experiment, we realized that if we were to get the tools we needed, we would probably have to make them ourselves[41] and then find a publisher.

In October, 1925, the University of Chicago Press agreed to publish a group of experimental materials—grammars, readers, manuals, blanks, forms—in French, Spanish, and German for our local use. Since then, the Press has continued to make available specialized materials for use with the Reading Method.[42] The first French text was ready in July, 1926; the first German text in 1927; and the first Spanish text in 1929.

Added to the work of textbook construction was the task of making progress and achievement tests and of revising the forms, for nothing brings out criticism as well as a test prepared by a member of the staff. Revisions were a standing order. But what we needed most was a set of standard tests, so that we could measure individual and group progress from quarter to quarter and from year to year. Not until the publication of the American Council on Education tests in vocabulary, grammar, and reading[43] did we possess such invaluable aids.

In its first *Bulletin* (September, 1925), the Modern Language Study had stated the desirability of standard, objective-type tests. The preliminary A.C.E. forms were tested in December and were being administered in January, "primarily for the purpose of establishing norms and testing the tests themselves" but also to provide material for studies such as the following, quoted from the committee's *Report of Progress:* ". . . Comparative achievement in classes in which extensive reading is practised and in classes that read less and do more formal linguistic work. (If classes such as those of Bond and Hagboldt at Chicago and others which might be located, are found.)"

We had made a trial run for Professor Coleman of the Silent Reading part of the A.C.E. *French Test—F10*, Form A, in December; in March, 1926, we ran it again in its printed form, together with the B form equivalent. No record was kept of the autumn administration in 1A. The results of the March administration in 1B were filed; they are the first objective evidence of reading achievement by the Reading Method derived from a standard test.

Thirty-six 1B students achieved a median score of 21.0 points (the maximum was 28), with a range of 13–28 and a time limit of 35 minutes. Their average was equivalent to the fourth-semester college norm (20.5) and the seventh-semester high-school norm (20.0). Another group of 36 1B students, tested on the same day with the B form, attained a median score of 19.1, the norm for third-semester college or sixth-semester high school. Similar results were obtained in German[44] and Spanish.

Our regular use of standard tests, however, did not begin until the autumn of 1927. From then until the present, their administration, either quarterly or annually, has been almost continuous.

In the summer quarter, 1926, the methodic features of French 1 were applied to the training of graduate students for the reading examinations in French required for higher degrees. There were six unlike sets of requirements in force in the university, but the usual recommendations for preparation in the case of a graduate student without previous experience in a language ranged from three to five quarters.[45] Those *with* experience apparently did not trust it, and haunted elementary language classes as visitors. For many of the graduate students the language reading examination was a hurdle before the conferring of the degree, their theses having been completed and accepted without the need for a foreign language proficiency.[46]

The regular French 1 course was uneconomical for the graduate student with only the reading examination in mind. Its oral-aural and speech-and-writing aspects were for him unwanted excess bag-gage. If these trainings could be eliminated, or at least considerably reduced, and if the preparation for reading could be shortened even more than in 1A, it might be possible for him to acquire a reasonable proficiency in reading in a single quarter-course. The course would be a condensation of 1ABC "for reading ability only." It would not be a so-called "scientific French" course. The university deans considered the proposal, at best, "audacious."

It was finally approved, but with composition retained, so firm was the common belief in the transfer values of speech and writing.[47] Accordingly, the following announcement appeared in the summer *Bulletin:*

301. *French for Reading Requirements.*—An intensive elementary course designed to enable the student to qualify for the reading requirements in French for advanced degrees. Its primary object is to establish the ability to read French. The foundation of a correct pronunciation is laid through phonetic study and drill. Oral and written expression are limited to the essentials. Reading accompanies the analysis of the language and is extended into the field of interest of the individual student. Laboratory practice, conferences, and reading reports. Bond, *Introduction to the Study of French, Sounds of French, Review Essentials of French Grammar;* Roth, *Contes des provinces;* Rambaud, *Civilisation française.* No graduate credit. Mj.

In the course as taught that summer, practice in speech and writing and use of the phonetic laboratory were omitted; the review of grammar was reduced to little more than the rules and their examples; and extensive reading was limited to about 200 pages in the student's special field.

Fifty-one graduate students registered for the two sections. Twenty-three of them had had no previous contact with French; twelve had had one year or less, ranging in recency from 4 to 14 years. Eight students were in the forty to forty-nine age range, 22 in the thirty to thirty-nine range, and 14 in the twenty to twenty-nine range. Thirty-three were doctoral candidates; the others were candidates for the Master's degree.

At the end of the 52 hours in the course, 23 students took reading examinations administered by the Department of Romance Languages in the Division, and passed. The others either deferred their examination until later or applied for it at other institutions. In the local examinations, the candidates were asked to translate orally passages from such authors as Renan, Novicov, Lebon, Sabatier, Legouis and Cazamian, Dolt, Poirier and Charpy, and Morat and Doyen. The passages averaged about 600 words.

Between 1926 and 1940, more than 1,000 students completed French 301 (also numbered 101G), and approximately the same number have taken the course in the last decade. Up to 1940, about 75 per cent of the students are known to have passed their language examination; for the later period no statistics are available. What is more important is proof that graduate students can be prepared for specialized reading in French in less than 60 hours of classwork.[48]

The phonetic laboratory, recommended first in 1923, materialized in 1926. The arguments for it had been approved: a saving in class time, improvement in pronunciation, larger class sections possible, remedial opportunity for the linguistically slow learner, a means for studying some of the problems of oral-aural instruction. But the cost had been prohibitive. The installation called for a "logophone," manufactured by the Student Educational Records, Inc., of Lakewood, New Jersey, and already in trial use by Professor R. E. Rockwood at Ohio State University. The price was exorbitant, but the budget-makers finally yielded, and a logophone was installed in our combination of office, library, and laboratory.

The instrument was an ancestor of the electric phonograph. It had three tone arms: one to convey the sound impulse to a control panel with a rheostat and switches to headphones plugged into a distributor box in the center of a table; a second arm with a diaphragm-type head; and a third equipped with ball point for hill-and-dale reproduction on wax records cut on the instrument by means of a special recording attachment. A telemegaphone could be attached for the purpose of amplification, and a hand transmitter resembling a microphone enabled the instructor to cut into the line leading to the headphones whenever he wished to give instructions. The turntable was operated by a small electric motor, but the sound-transmission system was operated from dry batteries stored in a compartment below the turntable. The wax blanks could be played only five or six times before it was necessary to shave them and re-record the selection.

It was a fascinating gadget, and in its first year amused and instructed 50 or more students in each of the three languages. More could have been serviced if it had been possible to accommodate more than 10 students at a time at its headphones. In 1928–29, in a single quarter, we gave a maximum of 8 hours of laboratory practice to approximately 200 students in French and Spanish 1A, on a basis of 10 students per hour.

Our first records were the quite unsuitable *Sperling Bibliothek* recordings[49] imported from Stuttgart. No other speech records were easily available, except some that had been made by the Student Educational Records of exercise material in the Fraser and Squair *French Grammar* (Heath). The high diction, rapid utterance, and dramatic rendition of the *Sperling* records made them of little value for beginners. We were finally obliged to make our own graded approach to the speech sounds[50] for the first stage of phonetic instruction in 1A.

From 1926 to 1951 the phonetic laboratory supplemented the classroom instruction in French 1, not only in training pronunciation, but in the programs in the history of French music and in masterpieces of French literature that served as part of the cultural background training in 1B and 1C. Its greatest contribution, of course, has been the saving of classroom time for other matters and the extended and repetitive experience that is so necessary in the early stages of oral French.[51]

Two important studies in second-language learning exerted considerable influence upon our investigation from 1927 on, namely, G. T. Buswell's experiment in eye-movements[52] and Michael West's report on bilingualism.[53]

Professor Buswell summarized his laboratory study of eye-movements and eye-fixations in reading a foreign language as follows (in part):

... (1) No notable difference between students who begin the study of French in high school and students who begin at the college level. ... (2) The maturity of reading which results from two years of study is decidedly greater with students taught by a direct method than with students taught by an indirect translation method. ... (3) During equal periods of time, approximately equal degrees of maturity are reached in the study of French, German, and Spanish when these languages are taught by similar methods and under similar conditions [p. 92].

Elaborating upon the second conclusion, he had this to say concerning the nature of true reading:

The psychological distinction between deciphering and reading can scarcely be overemphasized. The difference is clearcut. When students *read* they are rapidly fusing the word symbols into consecutive thought units with no consideration of the words as such. It is only this process of comprehending meaning that can properly be designated as reading. Students taught by a direct method[54] attain in two years' study of a foreign language those fundamental habits which are characteristic of the person who reads [p. 93].

This experimental study gave strong support to the reasoning underlying our courses and confirmed, through its scientific procedures, the conclusions at which we had arrived through personal experience. On one point there was still some question: were we getting for the average student in *one* year the reading proficiency which Buswell had in mind for two years?

Few books on learning a second language have had so widespread and penetrating an influence as West's closely documented report on the bilingual problems of teaching English to Bengali youth. Besides its specific bearing, it contributes to the broader field of foreign language teaching everywhere. Its effect is seen in the publications of the Modern Language Study and in the professional literature of two continents over the last twenty-five years. Most of the debated issues in foreign language methodology in the United States had, and still have, focal points in the West and Coleman reports.

It is obvious that we should be impressed by such statements in *Bilingualism* as the following:

... Our problem ... is to discover a means of producing silent reading ability in a foreign language and of doing this with the minimum expenditure of time and effort on anything else. ... This investigation involves two processes, —experimental teaching, and measurement of the result. ... Reading in a foreign language shows that it consists of three main elements: (1) Vocabulary, (2) Word by word reading, and (3) Skimming [p. vi].

In any system of practice the first essential is that the actual function to be developed should itself be practised, that the teacher should not rely, if it can be avoided, on the "transference" of effect from some indirect practice; for in all indirect practice here is a certain waste [p. vii].

Now speaking, writing, learning lists of words, saying the meaning of lists of words are not the same thing as Reading. ... Reading is best practised by reading. We must therefore devise a system so planned that from the very first unfamiliar words come to the student at regular intervals in the course of reading. ... He must be able to read easily and quickly so that his mind may spring at once from the foreign words to the ideas without the intervention of

the mother-tongue. Further, the matter of the reading-book must be of interest [p. vii].

By the use of these lists, i.e., word-frequency lists, it is possible to construct a
vocabulary of maximum usefulness at any given stage of progress . . . [p. viii].
It is therefore necessary to design courses of study which may possess a liberal
"surrender" value, and may as far as possible lead to subsequent independent
study. Hence . . . we must first of all enable the boy to read. This reading bond
is, moreover, the easiest of the four language bonds. The others, speech, hearing,
and writing, may be taught later to those who wait for them, are more able to
master them, and more likely to need them [p. 134].

The ability to read; to read directly, "fusing the word symbols
into consecutive thought units with no consideration of the words as
such"; to read material suited to one's maturity; to develop one's
skill systematically with surrender values at fixed stages; to postpone
speech, hearing, and writing for "those who wait for them, are more
able to master them, and more likely to need them"—all that was in
accord with our 1921 slogan: "the economical use of means aimed at
an end firmly fixed." The Calcutta experiment and the Chicago
experiment were both concerned, in the words of Michael Sadler,
with "making easier for the multitude of men and women the travel
and traffic of the mind." Both began in 1920–21 and, proceeding
independently and unknown to each other, had reached by 1926
similar conclusions from similar experiences.

The idea of deferring speech and writing until after the ability
to read has been attained, which seems to be difficult for some teachers to accept, West had found to be salutary and practical:

If it were possible to teach the child to read (of course with correct pronunciation) sufficiently fluently to make him enjoy reading and read a reasonably
large amount before permitting him to attempt any speech at all, the child
would, when he came to the speech lessons, have a Sense of the Language and a
feeling of what is idiomatic which would very greatly diminish his liability to
error and very greatly accelerate his progress.[55]

This was the "direct" reading method that Buswell had in mind.
It was also the pattern to which the foreign language courses in the
Junior College were being fashioned.

Four steps were yet to be taken: (1) a release from the restrictions
of a required fourth course, (2) freedom from preoccupations with
matters of local policy, (3) the preparation of graded reading materials utilizing the frequency word and idiom counts already avail-

able, and (4) a comprehensive, long-term investigation into the nature, amount, function, and products of reading, its implementation and motivation, means for its control and measurement, and its place in the chronological organization of an elementary language course. Five years were set as a term for the accomplishment of these four objectives.

## CHAPTER IV

# NON NOVA, SED NOVE

## 1. *From Old Plan to New Plan, 1927–32*

THE course of a classroom-conducted experiment never runs smoothly.[1] A course and its students cannot be kept at a constant pressure and temperature under a bell jar. Faculty rulings, changes in requirements, the time schedule, housing and the budget, executive comings and goings, general policies, national and international crises, and the like often wield the balance of power that determines the peaks and valleys in the curve of progress. That happened to our foreign language courses during the five years between 1927 and 1932.[2]

The "Commission on the Future of the Colleges,"[3] appointed by President Burton in 1923, during the following year recommended a plan "which was radical for the twenties but not unlike William Rainey Harper's unrealized 'blueprints.'" In an autonomous and physically segregated junior college, consecrated to general education, the curriculum would center upon the achievement of three types of independence, namely, in the processes of thinking, in aesthetic appreciation, and in moral living. One of the six subject matters enumerated as contributing to independence in thinking was "a reading knowledge of two foreign languages, including the necessary grammatical structure."

Admission to the College did not mean just "fifteen units chosen at random." In the case of a foreign language, "not less than a reading knowledge of that language" would be accepted. Graduation would depend not merely upon formal examinations or grades but also upon the evidence of an individual case history regularly assembled from the student's instructors. Entering and leaving the College, therefore, would depend upon demonstrated ability.[4]

The report stirred up violent opposition in the faculties, and the issue was not decided until January, 1927, when they adopted a *Report on a Theory of Education*. It was a compromise measure that changed conditions but little and referred all important matters to further committee study.

During the ensuing controversy between the "generalists" and the "specialists" and the debate over who should control the new College, the School of Education administration terminated its relations with the Junior College organization. The courses and staffs were reincorporated into the Colleges, but they were not reintegrated into their respective departments. For some time, the elementary foreign language courses wandered uncertainly, like Kipling's Tomlinson.

Before their official separation from the Laboratory Schools in March, 1927, the following memorandum was submitted by Superintendent Morrison to Dean Boucher of the College of Arts, Literature, and Science as a basis for the reorganization of the language courses:

I. It is understood that the first six majors of the program in French and Spanish constitute the elementary sequence, the essential learning products of which are:

1. Ability to read discourse which is without technical content and without specialized literary structure. Such ability implies interpretation of the printed page without intermediate transverbalization into the mother-tongue and with the true type of reaction which is characteristic of true reading in the student's vernacular. The ability is identifiable through characteristic symptoms.

2. Ability to use the language as a medium of written and oral expression with reasonable standards of accuracy in the same sense as that in which the student uses his vernacular for the same purpose.

3. Knowledge of grammar usage and idioms of the language as specified in a list of specific objectives to be worked out by, or under the direction of, the Department of Romance Languages.

II. Students will be *certified* in terms of the learning products as above defined and not in terms of the number of quarters registered in the elementary courses. If a student is found to have attained the specified learnings in two, three, or any other number of quarters, he will be so certified and will be held qualified for Senior College courses. Such a student will be *credited* with College majors in accordance with the number of quarters he has been registered in elementary courses, not to exceed six majors.

The memorandum was accepted. French and Spanish 1ABC and 2ABC constituted a "Junior College Division" of the Department of Romance Languages, under the personal supervision of Dean Boucher. The staff was installed in a suite of library, office, and audition rooms, adjacent to its classrooms on the fourth floor of Cobb Hall in the Arts quadrangle.

The reorganization plans for the courses were approved by the faculties in January, 1928. The more important changes were as follows:

1. Cancellation of French 2A, and the retention of 2B and 2C as continuation courses for 1ABC, designed for students desiring French courses in the Senior College.[5]

2. Retention of 1ABC as constituted, designed for noncontinuant, undergraduate students wishing to satisfy the language requirement of the Junior College.

3. Retention of French 301 (101G), as a special one-quarter course for graduate students preparing for the reading examinations for advanced degrees.

4. Accrediting according to the principles in the Morrison memorandum, with certification possible at any point in the two sequences, according to proved ability, the credits to correspond to the number of majors actually taken.

5. Deferment of credit for 1A and 1B until 1C (or equivalent) completed with grade of C or better.

6. Credit by advance standing for 1C to be contingent upon completion of 2A with the grade of C or better, or certification by the departmental examiner that "the student in question has a reading knowledge of the language."

7. Sectionizing of 1C for 1AB continuants and for new one and one-half- or two-unit entrants, to prevent retardation of continuants and to facilitate placement of new entrants.

8. Credit granted for course skipped, "provided, and when, the student makes a grade of B or better in the major in advance of the one he is recommended to omit."

The ten problems listed in the final report for 1921[6] were solved at last. French 1 was freed from higher controls. Admission, although still on a unit basis, was more closely adjusted to course achievement, thereby lessening predictable wastage. Certification was on an evidential basis, with accreditation raised to a C level. Sectionizing and promotional credit favored accelerated progress. French 2ABC, reduced to two quarters, rid of overlapping trainings, was free to develop specialized proficiencies as prerequisites for Senior College courses. And from the administrative standpoint a favorable continuance of our experiment was assured.

There were other changes to come, however. President Mason had questioned the validity of units and credits for entrance to the

Senior College or for the awarding of degrees.[7] In May, 1928, a committee report recommended the abolition of the current system of accounting in favor of five comprehensive examinations, one of which was to be in a foreign language.[8] It also established a board of examiners to administer the comprehensives. But before the report was acted upon, President Mason resigned, and approval of the recommendations had to wait upon the appointment of a new president.

The appointment came in April, 1929, in the person of Robert M. Hutchins. In his inaugural address in November he expressed clearly and forcibly his sympathy with proposed reforms within the College, speaking of them as "nothing revolutionary, [but] simply what was done here in 1891." The old debate between the generalists and the specialists in the faculties flared up anew. The next two years passed in endless, often fruitless, discussions. Finally, in March, 1931, the College faculty adopted its new curriculum, often referred to as the "New Plan."[9] By its provisions, certification in seven areas was to be made dependent upon educational achievement as measured by comprehensive examinations intrusted to a special board of examiners; class attendance was to be optional; student counseling was to be administered by a newly created dean of students and a body of advisers; and the student would be free to present himself for examination when he felt that he was sufficiently prepared.

Our system of tri-quarter reports on course personnel and instruction had disappeared with our transfer to the Arts quadrangles. Now student-teacher relations would be further weakened by the establishment of official advisers and the practice of the "freedom principle" of the New Plan.

According to the latter, liberally interpreted, the student was free (1) to absent himself from classroom practice and disciplines when he pleased; (2) to accept or to reject assignments; (3) to take or not to take tests and examinations, including the comprehensive at a specified time; (4) to follow a course program wholly or in part, regularly or irregularly, under one instructor or various instructors; and (5) to follow or to disregard counsel. In short, he was free to make his own decisions—and to abide by them and by their consequences.[10]

One more step remained to be taken. The College was not yet a four-year college, formed of the last two years of the standard high school and the first two years characteristic of the standard junior college. In December, 1932, the faculties took that step, and appointed a College Curriculum Committee to make a four-year program in general education to parallel the two-year program. Final ratification of the committee's recommendations was not obtained until March, 1937. Classes in the "New Four-Year College" began the following autumn.

The four-year program had little effect upon the foreign language courses. Of the 100 eleventh-grade pupils who entered the College annually from 1937 to 1943, only a few registered in French or Spanish during their first or second years. Our time schedule was reduced to four hours per week, with six hours for preparation. Progress reports replaced final grades based on quarterly examinations, and used a three-letter system, i.e., S (satisfactory), U (unsatisfactory), and R (insufficient evidence for an opinion).[11] Syllabi were made obligatory for all courses.

From the standpoint of modern language teaching, the experiences and changing conditions in the College from 1927 to 1932 highlighted at least one fundamental necessity for a successful method, namely, adaptability to external change. Without its flexibility, French 1 would have perished in the tumult of those five years.

## 2. *Basic Outline. II (1928)*

Until June, 1927, we had followed Basic Outline I,[12] with few modifications. From June, 1927, to September, 1932, we followed, with slight variations in procedure and materials, a general plan which is presented here as Basic Outline II. Its main argument and details had been discussed with and approved by Dean Boucher before the transfer of the language courses to the jurisdiction of the New College. Since this outline in form and in philosophy embodies much of what proved to be indispensable for the highest attainment in the language proficiencies envisaged by the course, and has formed the pattern for two decades of elementary language teaching in the College, it will be discussed in detail, together with some of its more important products and extensions.[13]

At the risk of being repetitive, certain generalizations follow in order to re-establish the setting and *raison d'être* for this experiment.

In the first place, the experiment was not the result of chance or of haphazard direction. It was not the result of a pedagogical theory imported from abroad as a language learning cure-all. It was a serious and patient attempt shared in by several persons to study the general problem of second-language learning in the laboratory of the classroom and to utilize the findings in improving modern language teaching in the University of Chicago and at junior college level. It was directed specifically at the production of a high and durable proficiency in the one aspect of language universally acknowledged to possess the highest surrender value obtainable in one year of formal study, namely, reading. Furthermore, it sought economy and assurance in the production of this skill. The development of the Reading Method was a local project to satisfy local needs. It was not conceived in the spirit of propaganda.

That it did not remain localized is due largely to the tidal wave of ink and vocal opinion that swept over the language teaching profession in the wake of the Modern Language Study upheaval from 1926 through the early forties. Off-campus the method was treated like certain pharmaceuticals which a tormented public purchases and consumes without first having its particular symptoms properly diagnosed and prescribed for. It was not a simple remedy or a panacea. It could, of course, be applied elsewhere and at secondary-school level, provided that the needs, conditions, and limitations of the proposed constituency were first surveyed and necessary adjustments made in the instructional and administrative details of the course.[14] But that did not often happen.

French 1 had a triple function: (1) to serve as a validating course for one-unit and two-unit entrants in French in the College; (2) to satisfy, as a terminal course, the modern language degree requirements of the university;[15] and (3) to provide a satisfactory foundation for continuation study in the language for an interested minority of its registrants. To these functions should be added the desirability of providing for the diversity of maturity, background, attitude, interest in language study, previous language training, and racial traits that is encountered in the student personnel of a large university.

As a validating course, it must progress in orderly and com-

mensurable stages and yet be flexible enough to give fair and ex-
peditious placement to incoming students who bring to the college
course divergent experiences with texts, methods, and teachers.
Registration must be subject to "readjustment in accordance with
the demonstrated ability of the student," operating for promotion as
well as for demotion, and conditioned upon performance, case history, conferences, and rigorous testing. Arbitrary placement may
work more harm than good.

As a terminal course, it must have a definite, realizable objective[16]
within its annual limits of 150 classroom periods and 200–250 hours
of preparatory study. The objective must be within the reach of all
purposeful students willing to make reasonable application to the
task. If reading skill, as that objective, is to be attained, it will be
possible only with the student's active and sustained interest and
co-operation. It will take an exercise of the will on the part of the
student, and not just on the part of the teacher.

It is at this point that a certain amount of re-education becomes
essential, such as removing the conception of time as a measure of
skill, discouraging lesson-getting as an objective, overcoming language inhibitions, explaining the working of a language-arts technique, actively promoting extensive reading, and guiding the student
in personal, interest-provoking projects. In the Reading Method as
presented here, re-education of the student plays a most important
role. So also does the re-education of the teacher. In this respect,
especially, it is a partnership enterprise.[17]

As a foundation course, it must make possible for those few who
may desire specialized training in French to continue into a second-
year course which has different aims and techniques. That French 1
was so qualified has been shown by the record of its continuants in
subsequent study situations, by the achievement of its promotional
cases, by its having brought about the reduction of the number of
majors required for entrance to Senior College courses in French, and
by its having made possible a change in the general nature of the
second-year sequence from translation and composition routines to
the exploration and appreciation of literature. These effects of a
first-year course upon a second-year course are interesting and
laudable, but they are of secondary importance in a consideration of
the true functions of the beginning course.

The main principles upon which the structure of French 1 rested included the trial-and-error principle of the language-arts,[18] the principle of "specific practice" as interpreted by West,[19] and the "single-phase" approach, which requires the deferment of speech and writing until after the recognition abilities are well under way. These three principles, with a firm commitment to the practice of individualized instruction, constituted the nucleus around which the course shaped itself during its first seven years.

The framework of the course as it was organized in 1928 is indicated graphically in Figure 1. The 150 fifty-minute periods of the year are divided into three equal quarter-sections, identified as 1A, 1B, and 1C. A quarterly examination is given at the close of each quarter, but credit for the full sequence is withheld until the completion of the third quarter with the grade of C or better. After the student has accumulated 18 majors, the sequence yields only half-credit; after 27 majors, it yields no credit.

Periods 1–5, inclusive, are devoted to a phonetic explanation of the sounds of French, working from spelling to sound and using choral response instead of individual recitation.

During periods 6–25, inclusive, the student concentrates on an analytical study of the variable forms of French grammar, without set vocabularies, rules for written usage, or composition exercises of any sort—a strictly passive, recognition-type approach to reading and to aural comprehension.[20] The initial phonetic instruction is reviewed twice in reversed order, spelling to sound and sound to spelling. A small amount of reading in a simplified text is done daily, in order to provide supplementary material for structural analysis. Assigned reading begins at the twentieth period. Since this is a time of information-giving, crowded with new language facts, the language of instruction is English. The use of French would be a barrier to understanding.

A rapid analysis of fifty-four irregular verbs[21] in periods 26–30, inclusive, concludes the formalized grammatical instruction in the sequence until the opening periods of 1C. From period 30 on, quantitative reading and aural experience replace formal, theoretical grammar with living construction patterns used in a meaningful context. This wide and deep exposure to oral and written French, with its "hit-and-miss" technique, as Morrison terms it, produces results not al-

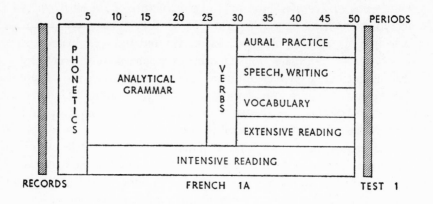

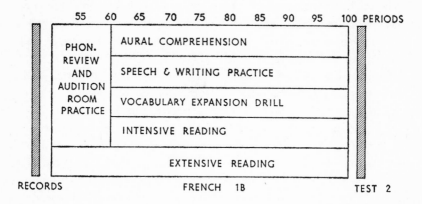

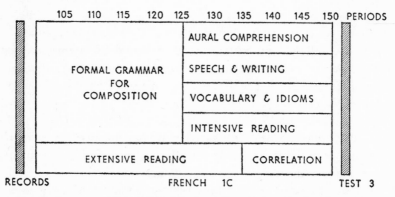

Fig. 1.—Structure of French 1ABC in the College, University of Chicago, 1928

ways to be had by the use of a standard XYZ grammar, as will be shown later.

In defense of the apparently absurd five-period scrimmage with the formidable French verb, it must be said that we still wore the shackles inherited from generations of Coquempots and could not yet think of reading ability apart from paradigms. We were capable only of a compromise, namely, a concentrated, recognition-type study of the commonest of the irregular verbs. By grouping analogous forms, the encounter was not so lethal as it might seem.

We were aware of more direct ways of approaching reading than by grammatical analysis.[22] The writer had dabbled privately in "grammarless" reading material in which the grammatical variables were treated as vocabulary, but the procedure seemed too cumbersome, too time-consuming, and even too juvenile for use in a college-level course, where factors of age, time, and money recommend the shortest route to the desired ends. Campus evidence to the contrary, college is no time for dallying.

Periods 31–50, inclusive, are occupied with practice in aural comprehension, the reading of intensive material subjected to vocabulary-building exercises, pronunciation drill, and the beginnings of direct oral and written expression based upon the reading text.[23] The active phase proceeds by substitution and repetition rather than by retranslation. In fact, translation from French to English is seldom resorted to; from English to French, not at all. With trial-and-error technique and with restraint on the part of the teacher, no small capacity for speaking and writing simply and understandably (though not necessarily correctly), in familiar situations, is possible for the upper fourth of the class by the close of the fiftieth period.

The reading experience, begun concurrently with the use of the analytical grammar, takes over the classroom program at the thirty-first period and continues unbroken in either intensive or extensive form until the last period of the year sequence. If he wishes, the student may begin his voluntary outside reading program at the mid-point of 1A. From then on, growth in reading power depends largely upon him. The class dissolves into persons.

The first quarter ends with a standardized test, usually a form of the *American Council Alpha French Test*. The period has been one of analytical approach to, and direct immersion in, the written and spoken language, with concentration upon reading.

We did not look upon the nature, materials, or chronological order of this 1928 version of 1A as final. Four years later, with the balance sheet for French 1 in our hands and improved implementation for the reading aim, we were still uncertain. Of one thing, however, we were sure, namely, the validity of two of the basic conceptions on which French 1 rested—the true nature of the reading process and the "law of initial diffuse movements."

Pillsbury and Meader define true reading as follows:

One must distinguish at least two sorts of reading, reading for words and reading for thought. . . . Reading for understanding is not word by word but sentence by sentence or even by larger units, for frequently later sentences serve to render clear what was not understood on the first reading. The meaning of a word is determined by this total setting rather than by the word itself and its immediate setting. But not only the immediate context determines the way in which the word shall be understood. The wider context is also important. . . . When one is reading for words, those and those only come to consciousness. . . . Reading, then, is a process of reconstructing the meaning of the author on the basis of a few unseen symbols in the light of the knowledge of the reader and in terms of the purpose that may be guiding him at the moment.[24]

This definition characterizes the procedure in 1A with its contextual setting for new words and its frequency and recency of associations, furnishing the running discourse that is the essence of the language-arts type of learning. By means of the techniques in 1A we hoped to prevent the characteristic mental set or inhibition traceable to the grammatical, daily-lesson type of language study.[25]

It is not easy to apply the "trial-and-error" technique. Self-discipline and alertness are needed in order for one to ignore in the first stage of the learning process the many errors committed in form and in sound and to accept relative attainment in lieu of mastery. The well-schooled instructor, fresh from graduate disciplines, finds it difficult to have faith in a theory that advocates "hit-and-miss" learning or to practice it. The student, however, has no such difficulty.

But the question is not so simple as that. The crux of the problem is when and where to bear down and when and where not to bear down. For instance, under the law of initial diffuse movements as defined by Morrison, when should the teacher correct errors in the interpretation or the use of the partitive article? Where should he begin: with the printed word or with the spoken word? Should he correct such errors on every occurrence (the "science" technique), in certain connections only, or at random? Should correction be restricted to errors in a particular pattern, e.g., in negative statements, until the particular pattern is mastered? Or should he omit all correction during the initial phase in the course? These questions are not easily answered. If they were answered in theory, there would still be the problem of applying the answer to the individual student in the classroom. For correction is a personal problem, a highly personal matter.

In French 1A, by the procedure outlined, oral and written work are treated merely as contributions to progress in reading through their motivation values. They abound in science-type and practice-type errors that go uncorrected for the most part. As the reading progresses and improves, they tend to improve, but not to the same degree. They gain potential, even in disuse.

During periods 51–60 in 1B there is an intensive review of pronunciation and aural problems, as a remedial treatment for persistent errors and as a check upon incoming one-unit students. The whole attention is fixed for a final brief time upon the sounds of the language, their identification in spelling, and their phonetic representation.[26] It is a period of corrective work in the laboratory with phonograph and recordings, a time for clearing up mistaken notions.[27] Extensive reading is the only other activity going on during this period of phonetic review.

Previously of a voluntary nature, extensive reading in 1B becomes a loose requirement of about 800 pages, subject to brief weekly reports on prepared forms, ungraded and nonreturnable. The choice of the material is left to the student, except in a few cases requiring special guidance. One of the five weekly periods is set aside in part or in whole for reading conferences or for comments on the reports. Much of the success of the year depends upon this quantitative reading. It must be carefully and sympathetically handled by teacher and student, with clear understanding of its function.[28]

Periods 61–100, inclusive, are occupied with a continuation of the classroom activities begun in 1A, namely, the intensive study of a reading text and practice in oral and written expression and aural comprehension. Speech and writing are viewed as contributory to the attainment of reading skill through their associative value in vocabulary-building and their contribution to the interest and pride of the student.

The student is not made too aware of his technical mistakes. His composition, like his reading, is so treated as to develop "a sense of ease in the use of the language, even to the neglect of accuracy in phonic and grammatical minutiae." There is seldom mention of grammatical rules and no translation of English to French. Asked for a reason for his correct use of a variable, he may answer that "it sounds right" or that it "looks right," or he may be in doubt.

French is the language of the classroom during these periods except on the days when reading conferences are held. The quarter closes with an alternate form of the *American Council Alpha French Test* or an equivalent standard test.

Periods 101–25, inclusive, composing the first half of 1C, center upon the study of formal, reproductive grammar and the rules of usage.[29] This is the first and only appearance of formal, standard grammar in the sequence. The student, able to criticize his own discourse, may now convert into a skill the reading adaptation which he has already made. Grammar functions here in its true place as a means of correction and co-ordination. It applies the *science* of language to the *practice* of language.

The remaining 25 periods are spent in oral-aural and written reworking of an intensive cultural text,[30] to which is again added an emphasis upon vocabulary-building and the recognition and use of common idioms. The course closes with a standard test, as in 1A and 1B.

The extensive reading in 1C has a minimum limit of about 1,000 pages, of which at least one-fourth concerns another subject matter or a personal interest of the student. Coming near the end of a year's reading experience, this integrated reading acts as a proof to the student that he now possesses the ability to read French for his own profit and pleasure. One cannot deny the educational and psychological values of such an object lesson.[31]

Figure 2 shows the relationship between the first-year sequence and the two quarter-courses of the second year. Note the limited amount of grammar in the five quarter-courses, the two concentrations on phonetics, the relative order of free and formal composition, the special attention to vocabulary study in 1ABC, the parallel development of intensive and extensive reading in continuous practice throughout the five courses, with aural comprehension supplementing the progress in reading, and the correlated reading in 1C. The

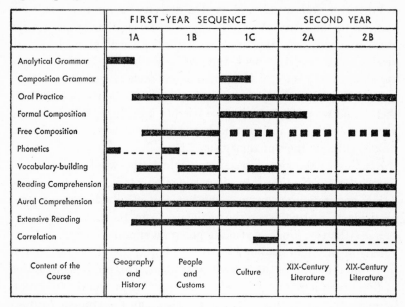

| | FIRST-YEAR SEQUENCE | | | SECOND YEAR | |
|---|---|---|---|---|---|
| | 1A | 1B | 1C | 2A | 2B |
| Analytical Grammar | | | | | |
| Composition Grammar | | | | | |
| Oral Practice | | | | | |
| Formal Composition | | | | | |
| Free Composition | | | | | |
| Phonetics | | | | | |
| Vocabulary-building | | | | | |
| Reading Comprehension | | | | | |
| Aural Comprehension | | | | | |
| Extensive Reading | | | | | |
| Correlation | | | | | |
| Content of the Course | Geography and History | People and Customs | Culture | XIX-Century Literature | XIX-Century Literature |

Fig. 2.—Distribution of instructional details in the first- and second-year French sequences in the College, University of Chicago, 1928.

continuation of first year into second year is little more than a prolongation of 1C.

Clearly, French 1 is not just a "reading course" in the common use of the term. Still less is it a "grammar-translation" course. And it is not a course in which reading is superimposed upon an "oral" or a "grammatical" method. Rather, reading is the foundation source of other activities in the language, the warp of the whole fabric. Few of the critics, teachers, and methodologists of 1927–32, in thinking or speaking of the "Chicago method," were acquainted with the real structure of French 1 as outlined above. That may explain in part the confusion in the literature of the time, although some of the misconceptions arose from the deeply rooted notion that a reading course must perforce be a translation course, which, in turn, must rest upon a grammatical basis, an immersion in linguistic science. It was difficult to think of grammarless reading except as a crackpot's dream.[32] Our articles, outlines, and conferences excited oralists and grammarians alike and consumed much needed time, so we withdrew from public debate.

Whatever oral, aural, and written activity occurs in French 1 is solely with the intent of developing or bettering the comprehension of the printed word. Whether these activities are all necessary or advisable, or only certain ones, and precisely what the contribution of any one of them is to the learning of a second language are questions for which there are only theoretical answers. We felt that they were useful, and we used them, but we tried to keep them subordinate to our reading aim. It is doubtful if we could have accomplished what we did without their auxiliary support.

Reading is the broad base upon which the whole structure of French 1 rests. No time is lost in getting down to it, and, once begun, it does not stop in one form or another. But it is its dual nature that particularly distinguishes the sequence from the usual beginner's course—the two kinds of reading going on simultaneously.

Part of this dual reading is "free," voluntary, and personal and is therefore the affair of the individual student. This point is disturbing to those who have not tried extensive reading or who have tried it by incorrect procedures. They ask: "How can the student read accurately at this stage? What can he possibly get out of his reading? Is he not making mistakes that he will be unable to correct, or to correct only with great difficulty?"

True, he does not read with absolute thoroughness. Few people do, even in their vernacular. Often his understanding of a paragraph read extensively is confused, sketchy, inaccurate. But is it essential in the early stage of language learning that the student comprehend fully and accurately what he reads? Thoroughness applies to mastery, and not to the practice stage. If the student is reading voluntarily what he finds pleasure in reading, and therefore continues to read, that is sufficient for the day. Intensive classroom reading, plus quantitative outside reading, will guarantee thoroughness in the end.[33] The proof of that statement will be found in the next chapter.

As has been said, in the practice stage the student uses properly

and effectively the hit-and-miss technique, which is much more productive of skill than the hunt-and-pick method of the transverbal-
izer. Would one think of acquiring the art of swimming by first
mastering Spaulding's manual on that activity, or would one use
trial-and-error methods? How does one obtain mastery in playing a
musical instrument?

The reading done by the students in French 1 resembled in manner their reading in the vernacular. When they met an unfamiliar
word, they read over it to the meaning of the sentence; if the word
did not fall into place, they read on, hoping to find it in a different
context, or a clarification of it through the meaning of the passage
as a whole.[34] Or they used means of inference, such as resemblance in
stem, derivation, cognate quality, or spoken value. As a last gesture,
they looked up the word in the glossary or passed on without it. In
sum, their reading was partly accurate and satisfactory and partly
inaccurate and unsatisfactory.

The ratio between accurate and inaccurate comprehension
changes rapidly according to the amount and nature of the outside
reading, for it is quantitative extensive reading, and not intensive
reading, that provides so much practice with content which has a
meaning and an appeal that the learning principle of initial diffuse
movements can be applied to its fullest extent and with strongest
motivation. It is the constant, repetitious procession of thousands of
speech units before the eyes and inner ear of the lone reviewer that
eventually brings the reading adaptation. Once the adaptation has
been made, the reader progresses quickly to the skill point, where
learning becomes a "matter of the final elimination of the misses."

### 3. "Outillage" for Reading

At the beginning of the third trial year (1922), it was recognized
that one of the twelve labors[35] for the staff would be the development
of suitable materials for the first stages of instruction. During the
next six years the staff prepared, tried out, and published basic
"grammars for reading" in French, German, and Spanish[36] but
made little headway with its program of readers.

By 1928, for use in the first quarter of the three language sequences, there were available in printed form *Terre de France,
Lecturas introductorias,*[37] and *Inductive Readings in German, Book*

*I*.[38] For the second stage (1B), a German reader was in trial form. The French reader for the third quarter had just appeared. By 1930, however, the missing texts for the full sequences in Spanish and German had been published. The second French reader, *Gens de France*, was abandoned half-done, and *Terre de France* shared with *La Semeuse* the intensive reading program of French 1 until the advent of the West-type readers in 1932.

These early French readers of the "Junior College Series"[39] had five characteristics that distinguished them somewhat from current foreign language texts; and, because these characteristics were of importance in our undertaking, they deserve some consideration here.

In the first place, they were for very early reading, beginning at the second or the fourth week of the first quarter-course. Their expository nature, as in Wilkins' *Italia*,[40] resulted in a high percentage of cognates and increased possibility of the exercise of inference, with a low percentage of idiomatic expressions. They were prepared before the publication of word and idiom frequency lists and so lacked the vocabulary gradation that marked later publications.

Second, they offered a reading fare suited to the maturity of junior college students. At a time when college students were reading in their language courses at the elementary level material prepared for and read by sophomores in high school without regard for differences in maturity, the preferences of the sexes, or the demands and aims of the two learning levels, the specificity of our texts was an innovation that did not carry very much weight with the teaching public at that time.

A third characteristic was their cultural content. We were thoroughly persuaded that a foreign language course should not divorce the study of the language from the country, people, and institutions which were so intimately linked with the development and expression of that language. There seemed to be no logical reason or need for postponing attention to the one until the other should be completed. Nor did it seem reasonable to expect a satisfactory picture of French civilization from the scraps of reading done in the classroom.

It should be possible to draw upon geography, history, folklore, philosophy, criticism, biography, and the sciences for material that would be readable, understandable, interesting, and informational for mature students. We have not withdrawn from that position. There has never been a valid reason for doing so.

Fourth, these first readers had no apparatus for speech and writing practice that involved retranslation. A large proportion of their drills dealt with vocabulary expansion and construction patterns, a trait that has characterized our materials since 1932.

The fifth and not least contribution of the "Junior College Series" was the physical attractiveness of the texts, which twice won national awards for the publisher. It was a time of drab, unrelieved bindings and undistinguished makeup for class texts. Any attractiveness of content was not matched by a similar appeal to the eye. The era of attractive packaging of groceries and cosmetics provided no uplift for the lowly language textbook. A change was in order. The "Series" made it with *Terre de France*.

The "Series" satisfied the need for mature, interesting, and cultural reading, but it did not have the smooth, even acceleration in vocabulary and syntax that we believed essential to a rapid and sound acquisition of reading skill.

Louis Marchand had explained his "Méthode scientifique"[41] at the Sorbonne in 1914. Harold Palmer announced his "scientific" method[42] of teaching English in London, three years later. In 1921, Palmer went to Japan as linguistic adviser to the Japanese Ministry of Education and head of the Institute for Research in English Teaching at Tokyo. Two years later, Marchand followed him to Osaka, to apply his method at the School of Modern Languages. In 1927, he was a member of the staff of Peabody College for Teachers, in Nashville, Tennessee. Meantime, Ernst Otto[43] had introduced some of the features of the Marchand method into Germany.

It was Marchand, more than Palmer, who appealed to us at first, in spite of his philosophy of "hear, speak, read, and write" and his exaggerated use of gesture, action, and *crescendo* in his teaching. He advocated word-building, contextual setting for vocabulary learning, controlled introduction of new words, the utilization of association, phonetics, choral repetition, the use of inference, phonic grouping, a continuous theme (*la Famille Dupont*), and a "reading staircase." To quote Marchand on the latter:

On aura donc à chaque étage un escalier (livre de cours) suivi d'un palier (livre de lecture) et autant d'escaliers suivis de paliers qu'il est nécessaire pour arriver à l'élaboration des 6,000 mots les plus importants de la langue. A chaque palier correspond une petite bibliothèque d'ouvrages qu'il faut choisir en tenant compte, aussi, de leur vocabulaire. Quand l'élève connaît 6,000 mots, il peut aborder les grandes œuvres classiques.

If we had a series of readers, *escaliers* and *paliers*, and allowed the grammar to generalize itself naturally, as it came to be needed, we might get better and more lasting results. The idea was attractive.

There were three questions to be answered first: (1) the exact nature of the total word list, (2) the choice of the first thousand words and of the succeeding thousands, and (3) a satisfactory procedure in introducing and teaching smaller vocabulary units in the basic books of the series.

The answers to the first two questions were not long in coming. In 1929, the Modern Foreign Language Study issued the Vander Beke *French Word Book*,[44] a range-frequency list of 6,067 words based on a count of over 1,000,000 running words from 88 sources, and the Cheydleur *French Idiom List*,[45] a range-frequency list of 1,724 idiomatic expressions based on a count of 1,183,000 running words taken from 87 units of French prose.

Michael West provided the answer to the third question, in 1926, in *Bilingualism*, and later in summarizing statements in the English press.[46] There was also the Palmer *Report*[47] in 1929. Two years earlier, in Canada, the Committee on Foreign Language Study, speaking of reading ability, had said: "The kind of reading which the Committee has in mind presupposes a new type of grammar and elementary reading texts. Their nature is set forth by West, and his new readers can serve as models."[48]

West's *New Method Readers*,[49] designed primarily for experimental use in teaching English to Bengali youth in 1924–26, were later expanded to include ten booklets (IA, IB, II–IX), each with a *Supplementary* written entirely within the vocabulary taught to that point, and a *Companion* booklet for vocabulary revision and drills. There were also *Composition* booklets at each stage for speech-and-writing practice. The series was a scientifically planned, tested, and closely integrated program for second-language learning of a calculated duration of five years for Bengali pupils. By 1928, the readers were in use in India, China, Ceylon, Palestine, Persia, Nigeria, Mombasa, and Uganda.

The popularity and effectiveness of these readers depended upon a number of features capable of application to the learning level of any second language, such as the selection of words according to their frequency and usefulness, the meticulous indication of new words on their first occurrence in the text, the proportion of new words to running words of text ("density"), the repetition of new words, care as to the suitability of the material to the age of the learner, and the division of the material into conveniently small units in order to provide for differing rates of progress and the individual reader.

For his *Readers* West selected approximately 3,500 words from Thorndike's *Teacher's Word Book*[50] and introduced them at the following rate for each of the ten booklets: IA (222), IB (236), II (300), III (300), IV (350), V (350), VI (400), VII (400), VIII (450), and IX (450). One new word was introduced every 60 running words, occurred at least three times and as often as possible in the rest of the story, and was printed in black type in the body of the text on its first appearance and repeated in the margin of the page. The text was broken into small units, the size of which increased as the reader progressed in the series. The *Supplementaries*[51] furnished plateau reading at six levels, i.e., 458 words, 758 words, 1,072 words, 1,415 words, 1,779 words, and 2,280 words. A *Supplementary* introduced no new words. All new words in the readers were illustrated, when possible, in thumbnail line drawings.

West's conception of text simplification and grading was revolutionary. It was apparent that our new series of readers were already obsolete and that another and different type of materials should be prepared.[52] The incentive to begin a second series came sooner than anticipated.

In May, 1927, en route from a meeting of the Modern Language Study Committee in New York, Miss Helen M. Eddy, then head of the Department of Foreign Languages in the High School of the University of Iowa and a member of the university staff, paid us a visit, inspected the materials and programs for French 1, and expressed a desire to adapt them to high-school instruction. Encouraged to undertake the project of preparing West-type readers for use at that level and assured of editorial assistance and a publishing outlet through the University of Chicago Press, she at once began work on the first-year materials, assisted by other members of the Iowa staffs. Between June, 1927, and December, 1929, the group prepared, tried out in the classroom, tested, and published a basic grammar, two first-year intensive readers, a workbook, a battery of progress and achievement tests, and a teacher's manual[53]—a remarkable performance by any standard.

In the preparation of their material, the authors were able to consult the manuscript of Coleman's *Report*, advance copies of Cheydleur's and Vander Beke's word lists, and manuscript copy of West's summaries of *Bilingualism* before their publication dates. Proofs of the Eddy texts were read by members of the French staffs at Wisconsin, Iowa, and Chicago and by West in Calcutta. Even before the volumes were on sale, advance copies were being used in experimental classes in Iowa, at Milwaukee, Minneapolis, Los Angeles, and the universities of Wisconsin and Illinois.[54] Reviewers and critics held a Roman holiday. What might have amounted to a sweeping reform in elementary French instruction at the secondary-school level was deprived, however, of much of its momentum by the appearance of Coleman's report on the *Teaching of Modern Foreign Languages in the United States*, in July, 1929, and the ensuing "Coleman controversy,"[55] the din of which has abated but not ceased at the present writing.[56]

Confident in the effectiveness of their approach to the textbook problem, the Eddy group moved forward into a program for the second year and for a series of "supplementaries." Between February, 1931, and October, 1932, they authored into print two first-year supplementary readers, a second-year basic reader, and a second-year supplementary.[57] Others were planned, but never executed.

Between 1932 and 1939, the Press published five "affiliated" supplementary readers,[58] more or less closely integrated with the "Eddy series," prepared by nonmembers of the Iowa group. Several of the books used experimental techniques, either in editorial mechanics or in the drills and exercises. In 1936–40, D. C. Heath and Company issued in two omnibus volumes[59] the basic materials for the two-year course, with a special version of the grammar for college use[60] and a new speech-and-writing text[61] based on the second year's work. With these two volumes the publication of the first series of West-type readers to be prepared in French in the United States, or elsewhere, came to an end. But a trail had been blazed where a highway would one day be built.

As a pedagogical venture, the series was reasonably successful. An integrated two-year high-school program, with the reading objective, a sound preparation for delayed speech and writing, and a respectable amount of cultural content, had been made available. It offered a reading fare of about 1,500 pages, or half a million running words, in a staircase arrangement under a ceiling of approximately the first 2,500 words in the Vander Beke frequency-range list and a corresponding range in the Cheydleur idiom list. The average new word density was 71, or about 14 new words per thousand running words. According to Haygood, the first 2,000 Vander Beke items, plus the 69 Henmon items in Part I of that list, yield about 90 per cent of running discourse. The series, therefore, provided a heavy concentration on Haygood's estimate of a "minimum vocabulary" for reading purposes.

The four semester levels facilitated testing schedules and readjustments to individual student progress.

In subject matter there was little new compared with traditional fare, either in the amount of grammar taught or in the nature of the stories read, if one considers the whole program with its reproductive finale. But there were two important differences between the Eddy-group program and current standard practice, i.e., the chronological order given to the various language activities and the greatly increased amount of reading that the order and the graded readers made possible.

It was not a perfect layout, nor was it suited to all teaching situations or to all teachers. No such complete series can be perfect in that way. Some of its defects were due to the untried nature of its basic materials—the frequency lists—and to difficulties encountered in applying West's procedures to a different linguistic medium and in a different educational milieu. For example, the restrictions imposed upon text reduction and simplification by the acceptance of what is essentially a range list for vocabulary control, the treatment of semantic divergences in counting words, the relative values of words in the early stage of learning, the use of associative relationships in word and idiom control, the practical worth of many of the so-called "common" idioms, the counting of variables, the treatment of cognates, the minimum density for safety, the use and editorial treatment of "outside" words—these are some of the new problems in textbook-making that the authors of the series encountered and had to solve.

There had to be an adjustment, in using the West principles, between a situation involving Bengali children learning to read English and a situation in which an American high-school boy or girl is learning to read French. Differences in background, maturity, studial environment, and the languages studied led the authors to impose larger vocabulary increments than did West, to make use of the cognate content of French and English (*Si nous lisions* is 34 per cent cognate, *Pierrille*, 37 per cent), to care less about "unit mastery" of vocabulary, and to be less precise about the counting of "new" words.

Finally, the whole project was affected by the traditional, grammatical set of language teaching, dominant then and now in the profession, and the failure to differentiate between the needs of the continuant and those of the noncontinuant.

During the preparation and publication of the Eddy-group texts, West maintained a lively correspondence with authors and editor, recounting the problems he had encountered in his own books and suggesting improvements for the French series. As an instance, he wrote concerning *Beginning French:* "It seems that you [Eddy] are rather hampered by syllabus, or perhaps by the conventionality of teachers (or is it of publishers?). I judge this from the very large amount of grammar which you present in proportion to use actually made of that grammar." And wrote, on the same subject: "Even Sanskrit needs much less grammatical preparation than . . . used in *Beginning French* for French." At the time (1929) he was himself preparing the foundation for a "grammarless reading course" in French.

He thought that the Vander Beke first-1,500-word range was "a rather large vocabulary for a book of this size. . . . I believe that the future will see English and American children saying all that they want to say in French in a basic vocabulary of 800 words, to which they may later add specific words according to their tastes and interests." The free use of cognates in the "Series" readers disturbed him, because of the liability of their becoming "dangerous" later on and because of their lack of usefulness in a minimum-use vocabulary.

He was also troubled by the high vocabulary limits of the first books in the "Series": "Eddy's texts are quite good, but they don't build up the first thousand words which are the most difficult of all, where the prepared text is most needed. I wish she would go back to the beginning and make a reading text (or texts), building up her first thousand words in continuous stories, relegating all the grammar to footnotes and appendices. . . . They [the Gurney books in the Oxford University Press series] all start *after* the first 1,000 (or after 2,000, or even 3,000). After 3,000 words the battle is almost over; I stop my *New Method* books at 3,000." A few months later, he wrote that he was making a study of "the initial stage, the first 1,000 words of a French reading and speech course" and that he was going to Paris to collect story-books for material for the twelve-year-old level. It is probable that he had the Canadian bilingual situation in mind, although later (1932) he made the error of failing to recognize the differences in study levels and reading tastes of French and American youth.

Again, in September, 1932, while Coleman was with him in Abingdon, he wrote: "We discussed Modern Language teaching and teachers in all its and their aspects. . . . He told me something about the French Vocabulary[62] and it sounds very interesting; the way he sets about his list is very similar to the lines I have been working on of late, though not perhaps quite so elaborate. . . . I only want to attack those first thousand words, so that a child may read right off from the word 'Go!' instead of having the rather discouraging preparatory process which is usual now."

Two months later, West accepted an invitation to collaborate with the author in the preparation of a new series of graded French readers for the first-thousand-word range, to interlock with the Eddy-group series at that limit. In June, 1933, the new "Direct Reading" series was under way, as an experimental venture.

West considered his New Method English readers as "explicitly experimental." To quote: "The experimental work for which they were designed has confirmed the principles upon which the books were constructed; it was not expected that they should confirm them in detail; rather that, if the principle proved sound, it should enable us to criticise them and suggest the details of something much better which might be constructed in the future. . . . A textbook is never finished, because the teaching of every new class reveals new respects in which the book might be improved. School textbooks should be kept, as H. G. Wells suggested . . . always standing in type, and no edition should exceed a year's demand. For every obscurity of the book is rebuked thousands of times by thousands of little victims of the author's carelessness or stupidity."[63]

The authors of the two language series which have been discussed shared in his opinion, but it was an opinion without weight with American publishers. Later, one experimental edition of an "inferential reader" was published by the University of Chicago Press, but it was also the final edition. Nevertheless, the truth of West's observation is something for authors and publishers to consider and for teachers to welcome. There is a very real need for "experimental textbooks" in a format and at a cost that will allow for repeated trial and revision.

## CHAPTER V

# READING FOR LANGUAGE POWER

## 1. *The Reading Collection*

ONE of the recommendations in the autumn, 1921, final report[1] referred to "provision for a departmental reading collection and selected reading lists, with prescribed readings for all students." The collection was established the following spring[2] and has functioned continuously for thirty years, having resisted successfully all efforts to reincorporate it into the General College Library.

The latter was formed in 1932, together with a library for the new residence halls and a special collection supporting President Hutchins' course in the "History of Western Thought." According to Director M. L. Raney, the modern language reading collection, transferred to the Cobb Hall quarters in 1927, "was the pioneer of the three, antedating the New Plan by a decade. It provided the model, too, for the apartment arrangement—library, class, and consultation rooms in juxtaposition. It had its beginning in 1923 [*sic*] in a shelf of books loaned from one of the School of Education libraries to the Junior College Modern Languages group."[3]

From 300 volumes in 1927 it grew in five years to 2,289 volumes, of which 1,060 were in French, 481 in Spanish, and 748 in German. All but 96 were in open circulation; the latter were general reference works on reserve. Nonfictional items included 317 French and 150 Spanish titles, the nucleus for the correlated reading in French and Spanish 1C.

For the first seven years, the staff took personal charge of the library; afterward, the management became one of the duties of the part-time secretary. It required about two hours a day to file charge cards, discharge books, reshelve them, index new additions, and attend to overdue notices.[4] The daily service cost did not exceed

$1.30. Annual purchases for 1927–32 averaged $95.60 for the three languages. In 1932, through the generosity of the Carnegie Corporation, 170 new books were added, at a cost of about $300.00. Since 1934, only a few volumes have been added to the French and Spanish sections, which now number about 1,700 titles.

Most of the collection originally was in foreign editions. Later, additions of textbook editions were made from private gifts, student donations, publishers' samples, and occasional duplicate purchases of laboratory material. Whenever practicable, foreign editions were preferred, in order to bring the student into direct contact with cultural material from France. The obvious drawbacks for inexperienced readers were offset by the motivating values of these firsthand contacts with foreign editions.

The mechanics of circulation were of the simplest. The books were shelved in alphabetical order by author in separate sections labeled according to general field, e.g., poetry, novel, social sciences, geography, and travel. A standard library charge card in a manila pocket on the inside of the back cover carried the necessary catalogue information, duplicated in a file on the secretary's desk. A vertical charging-out tray, a dating stamp and pad, and a box of signal clips to indicate overdue charges completed the equipment.

The procedure for withdrawing and returning books was equally simple, as the following rules indicate:

1. Only one book in a given language may be charged to a student at one time.

2. No book is to be retained more than two weeks without being renewed.

3. To withdraw a book, write legibly on the charge card your full name, university address, and the date. Place the card in the "charge" box, not in the filing tray.

4. To renew a book, write the request on a slip of paper, giving author, title, your name and address, and drop the slip in the "charge" box, as you would a card.

5. When returning books, put them in the wire basket marked "return" on the secretary's desk. *Do not shelve them.*

In six years, 1927–32, the collection serviced 18,845 calls, of which 13,911 were for French and 4,934 for Spanish; 2,676 were for works in nonfiction. Since the collection was open on an average of six hours a day with no one officially on duty during half that time and since a book could be obtained without being checked by a librarian, some loss, like laboratory breakage, could be expected. Yet in this period there were only 32 books charged out and not recovered, and 16 that were missing on the annual inventories, or a total of 48 missing volumes. The loss of one book for every 390 calls, over a period of six years, from an open-shelf collection without a regular, full-time attendant on duty is evidence enough of the co-operative spirit of its student users and the economy possible in a small departmental library in "apartment" arrangement with the staff office. It should be added, also, that no fines or penalties for overdue books were assessed or money handled.

Except for a brief period in the last twenty years, the collection has been housed in a large room together with the staff, the secretary, a Ditto machine, a row of filing cabinets, bulletin boards, library reading tables, and other office equipment. It has never had the ideal atmosphere of a library reading-room but rather that of a corner drugstore or a hotel foyer. The fact that the books were part and parcel of the office equipment, visible and accessible to all comers at all times, and not hidden away in some special nook, may account largely for the unusual use made of them.

There were, of course, other sources upon which the students drew for reading material, such as the College Library, which had a number of foreign language editions of works read in English translations in the Humanities survey courses, the Rental Library of duplicates, including 975 titles in French, Spanish, German, and Italian, that could be rented at the rate of one dollar per language per quarter, for as many books as the student wished; the main University Libraries; the Chicago Public Library and its branches; and private collections, usually composed of textbooks used by the student's parents in their own schooldays. But by far the greater amount of reading was done in books obtained from our small departmental collection.

## 2. *Selection and Reportage*

In selecting his reading material, the student exercised a free choice. That does not mean that no influences were brought to bear upon him. It means that the final decision was his. If he regretted it later, he could bring back the book and get another; he was under no compulsion to finish a book because he had begun it.

Besides the supplementary reading lists in the texts of the "Junior College Series" and in the Eddy-group readers, at certain points in the program of French 1 special, topical lists like the following were distributed as aids to the selection of material for individual reading programs:

1. Background material: geography, history, civilization.
2. The short story: from *fabliaux* to the twentieth century.
3. Graded readings: arranged by quarters (1A, 1B, 1C).
4. Reading in social sciences: anthropology, economics, education, political science, psychology, sociology, etc.
5. Reading in biological sciences (with call numbers to facilitate service through the special library).
6. French literary works set to music: by author, title, composer, and composition.[5]
7. The drama: from *Pathelin* to *Knock*, by centuries.
8. The novel: chronological listing, eighteenth to twentieth centuries.
9. Readings to correlate with humanities general courses.

There were also reading suggestions in foreign languages in the syllabi of other courses, as in the social sciences second-year *Syllabus for 1932*.[6] As an example of interdepartmental co-operation in promoting foreign language integration, the opening and closing paragraphs of the section on "Foreign Language Readings" are cited:

The staff of Social Science II desires to emphasize that thought in the social sciences cuts across linguistic boundaries, that no serious student of the social sciences can afford to be impeded in his advanced work by language difficulties, and that the best way to acquire facility in the use of foreign languages as a practical tool for the acquiring of knowledge is to begin early.

Students who plan to continue their work in the Division of the Social Sciences are urged to consult their instructors about the language requirements, as much time can be saved by an early and systematic approach.

It is suggested that students of this course who are also studying a foreign language may usefully correlate their language work with their social science work. The following titles are suggested, and your section instructor will be glad to suggest other foreign language titles on special subjects which may have caught your interest.

There follows a list of readings by author and title, grouped according to quarter levels. The section concludes as follows:

The above selections have been made with a view to providing material for students only moderately advanced in foreign language and social science. Many of the books are of a popular or journalistic type. Others are somewhat more technical, but none are considered too technical for students in this course. All are likely to prove fascinating as well as useful reading, and all will help to build the student's vocabulary in directions that will aid him considerably in advanced social science study or research.

The modern language departments of the University have willingly pledged their co-operation with the staff of Social Science II, and in language courses which do not necessitate the reading of specialized type of literature, selections from the above list may be made as part of the student's regular collateral reading in the course, after consultation with the instructor.

That is the sort of co-operation that can and must be made if foreign language study is to enjoy its full role in a program of liberal education.

The technique of reporting has been described for 1923. The printed slip used at that time was replaced in 1926 by a booklet[7] containing instructions for reporting, 22 detachable report forms, reading summary sheets for the instructor's files, and reading record sheets for the student's own use. Two sizes were available, one $8\frac{1}{2} \times$ 5 inches and the other $8\frac{1}{2} \times 11$.

The blanks greatly simplified the mechanical problem of controlling outside reading. Controls are needed over quality as well as quantity of the reading done by each student. Poorly controlled reading may result in half-learning and disaster. On the other hand, close controls mean a burden for student and instructor, unless some means are found to standardize the form of reportage and still leave the reader freedom in expression and interpretation. By means of the printed forms it was possible to check the weekly outside reading of a class of 30 students in a minimum of 30–45 minutes.

Furthermore, the forms called the student's attention to the essential aspects of his reading, required him to formulate his impressions, provided specific matter for discussion in conference, facilitated the keeping of records, and established standards for comparison. But what is more important, they enabled the staff to evaluate the reading achievement in other than quantitative terms, e.g., the degree of appreciation, personal reactions, perceptivity, critical ability, depth of sensitivity, analytical ability, and power of expression. They made possible information on not only what and how much was read but *how* it was read and what satisfaction was gained from the reading.

The Foreword in the booklet attempted to bring the activity of

extensive reading into a rational and personal relationship with the
student and his language study, thus:

Whatever may be your final objective in studying a foreign language, reading
is a necessity, and the ability to read should be the principal aim of your study.
If you feel the need of the fullest economy, you should gain this ability at the
earliest possible moment. To do this, you should practice two kinds of reading,
intensive and extensive.

The former serves as material for grammatical analysis, illustration of rules
of syntax, vocabulary building, and the development of literary appreciation,
and is the basis for oral and written exercises. It is confined normally to the
classroom textbook. It has a formal and pedagogical value.

Extensive reading has a different purpose and effect. It is the more rapid
reading of material of personal interest or value to the student, mainly for his
pleasure or profit, and not for conscious linguistic illustration. It offers the
reader a panorama of the language, its words, idioms, sentences, sounds,
rhythms, together with the concepts expressed, in an unbroken succession,
line after line, page after page. His conscious attitude toward the foreign
language breaks down and the growth of an unconscious feeling for the new
language begins, the firm establishment of which marks the acquisition of a
reading ability that may weaken but that will outlast the years. It is a substitute for the processes by which the child learns his mother-tongue. It bears
the same relation to intensive reading as the tennis court does to a manual on
*How To Play Tennis;* the expert must be familiar with both. They are comple-
mentary.

Read then, *judiciously,* for some reading is more worth while than other;
*copiously,* because it will take a great many repetitions of the foreign peculiari-
ties to enable you to grasp the spirit of the language; *understandingly,* or otherwise there will result loss of interest, discouragement, and misinformation;
*regularly,* that the day's gain in ability and confidence may not lapse. Reading
done thus, aside from bringing its own rewards, will react surprisingly upon
your more formal efforts and upon the abilities to write and to speak the foreign
language.

In the "Instructions to the Student" which followed, eight suggestions were made on *how to read*.[8] They have a value in estimating
how well the extensive reading was done, since it is not likely that
much reading would be done without some heed to the directions.
They are given below, verbatim:

*First,* read the introduction or preface to the book in order to get the general
idea of its contents, purpose, and place in its field.

*Second,* read more slowly and carefully the first pages. They contain the
exposition, the setting, the purpose of the whole, and they establish more or
less the vocabulary, style, and tone of the work.

*Third,* read by sentences rather than by words. Words assume their right meaning only when taken in conjunction with one another. The unknown word gathers meaning from its surroundings, its context. As your vocabulary increases, you will progress from phrase to sentence, and then pass from sentence to paragraph in your comprehension of the text. This should be your standard of achievement.

*Fourth*, use inference rather than the dictionary or the vocabulary in determining the meaning of unfamiliar words. Consider each word in the immediate setting or in the light of the previous or the following statement, or both. If you cannot get its meaning from the context, try to arrive at it by analogy or by derivation, bringing to bear upon it your knowledge of English, Latin, or other familiar language. It is often advisable to await its second appearance, when its meaning may be more obvious. If it occurs several times, "look it up." You should not "look up" more than you need in order to grasp the main facts or the gist of the material.

*Fifth*, take notes on your reading, either by underlining, abstract, or quotation. Your notes will coordinate your impressions, keep your ideas in sequence, and be useful in writing the report later.

*Sixth*, if a paragraph remains unclear, reread it before resorting to translation, and then never to literal, word for word translation, the "no man's land" of language. Reconstruct the thought of the original in your own tongue.

*Seventh*, progress in your reading from easy material (familiar content, if possible) to material of intermediate difficulty, and thence by easy stages to difficult reading. Determine your fitness to advance along the scale by the sense of ease acquired at a given point, measured roughly by the number of pages read per hour, plus the degree of understanding and the absence of undue vocabulary trouble. Do not hesitate to try the more difficult book, and do not hesitate to desert it if you find it too difficult. If it seems uninteresting, do not read it; find something that is interesting.

*Eighth*, take some active means of increasing your vocabulary, either by underlining all or a limited number of words in the day's reading, with periodic reviewing of the underlined words, or by compiling word-lists or copying the words on slips, and then alphabetizing or classifying them by topic or category, or by memorizing a set number of words daily, or by repetition through retelling orally or in writing. A vocabulary does not grow of itself.

To these recommendations the instructor added others in conference with students having special difficulties in their reading. It was general policy to explain to the learner the *why* and the *how* of what he was asked to do. He rarely failed to approve of the policy.

The writing of the report, if properly done, demanded effort and thought. Thirteen items of information were called for, namely, general nature of the material, subject, form, style, value, a summary (250 typed words), dominant idea, striking scene (or episode, fact, trait, statement), characters, a quotation, reasons for choice of quotation, personal impressions, and a comparison. The student was asked to show a regard for good form, neatness, correct spelling and punctuation, and accuracy in quoting from the original text. It was a discipline, to be sure, and sometimes met with rebellion, but it was a salutary discipline, usually accepted with good grace and appreciation of its function.

The reading record sheets indicated date, author, title, publisher, place of publication, year, and amount read for each reading report and provided the necessary data for the preparation of the reading summary form which was required at the close of each quarter for the office files. This summary showed the same information in totals for each book read during the quarter (in 1C, for the whole year). The reading summary and the personal record blank were filed together, forming a sort of *dossier* for every student.

Full instructions were given for reporting on each of the thirteen items, similar in type to the following on *style:*

Comment briefly on the style of the material, stating, for example, whether it is rhythmic prose, simple, complicated, didactic, expository, powerful, eloquent, persuasive, lavish in examples, rich in imagery, humourous, egotistic, exaggerated, coldly restrained, easy, elevated, pompous, analytical, artificial, impressionistic, etc. Consider your answer carefully and be prepared to defend your judgement, if necessary.

In estimating the value of the material read, its worth in its own field or to the reader, his studies or his plans could be considered. If there was more than one "dominant idea" in the material read, the student was to select the one that seemed to him to be the most important or the most interesting. The choice of the "most striking scene" and the "quotation" must be accompanied by a personal reason for the choice. Under "personal impressions," the student was asked to indicate impressions or judgments formed of the author's point of view, impartiality, mentality, erudition, discernment, literary or artistic skill, scientific vision, etc. On that point, the instructions called for an "honest personal conviction" and not a borrowed "label."

With a well-prepared report in hand, the instructor could tell with some degree of certainty whether the material had been read with understanding and profit. He could mark the progress in reading skill in a particular student, and he had the means of guiding him into full enjoyment of a reading proficiency in the language. He also had the means of knowing the real person back of a matriculation number—which is not a common privilege.

The question is sometimes asked about the risk of cheating through the copying of reports, the use of English abstracts or English translations in making out the reports, or other school misdemeanors in connection with outside reading and its reporting. The risk, of course, is no greater than that encountered in English theme writing, in mathematics problems, and in laboratory notebooks. Cases of dishonesty occurred, but they were so few and so easily detected that the staff gave them little weight beyond the case in point. The extensive reading activity was put on a strictly personal, noncredit basis; as in solitaire, the student found no incentive to cheat himself. The reports were not graded and had no part in setting course grades. The student knew that. The forms were not returnable; if the student wished, he could make a copy for his own use. The original reports were retained by the instructor until the end of the year and were then destroyed. Furthermore, a falsified report could prove embarrassing in a classroom discussion or in a private reading conference. The only serious problem which the staff had in connection with the extensive reading feature was the failure of many New Plan students to exercise good judgment about doing the reading.

Four separate studies were made between 1927 and 1933 of the extensive reading done in French 1.[9] Three of the studies were based on the reading reports and summaries. The fourth was an analysis of the circulation of books from the reading collection, based on charge cards and the shelf list.

The four studies revealed the nature, extent, rate, and distribution of reading done by courses, years, and special groupings of students over a period of five or six years when programs and procedures were comparatively stable. Some of the data derived from the studies are presented in the following pages. They constitute an impressive body of factual evidence that the Reading Method created in beginning language students both the will and the power to read to an unusual degree.

### 3. A Survey of Reading-Collection Calls

Director Raney of the University Libraries called for a statistical report on our reading collection in the autumn of 1933. The collection

TABLE 9*

| Range | A | B | CR | D | G | H | M | N | PE | PH | PSY | SC | SOC | SS | P | Total |
|---|---|---|---|---|---|---|---|---|---|---|---|---|---|---|---|---|
| 10–19.. | 4 | 14 | 6 | 21 | 12 | 12 | 2 | 50 | 2 | 2 | 2 | 2 | 1 | 18 | 2 | 151 |
| 20–29.. | ... | 2 | 2 | 9 | 1 | 6 | ... | 10 | ... | ... | ... | ... | ... | 11 | 1 | 42 |
| 30–39.. | ... | 3 | ... | 7 | 2 | 2 | ... | 16 | ... | ... | ... | ... | 1 | 6 | 1 | 38 |
| 40–49.. | ... | 6 | ... | 6 | ... | ... | 1 | 10 | ... | 1 | ... | ... | ... | 2 | ... | 20 |
| 50–59.. | ... | ... | ... | 5 | 1 | ... | ... | 7 | ... | ... | ... | ... | ... | 4 | ... | 17 |
| 60–69.. | ... | ... | ... | 4 | ... | ... | ... | 3 | ... | ... | ... | ... | ... | ... | ... | 7 |
| 70–79.. | ... | ... | ... | ... | ... | ... | ... | 2 | ... | ... | 1 | ... | ... | 2 | ... | 5 |
| 80–89.. | ... | ... | ... | ... | ... | ... | ... | 4 | ... | ... | ... | ... | ... | ... | ... | 4 |
| 90–99.. | ... | ... | ... | ... | ... | ... | ... | ... | ... | ... | ... | ... | ... | ... | ... | 0 |

* Key to abbreviations: A (art), B (biography), CR (criticism), D (drama), G (geography), H (history), M (music), N (novel), P (poetry), PE (political economy), PH (philosophy), PSY (psychology), SC (general science), SOC (social sciences), SS (short story).

TABLE 10

| Rank | Author | Title | Calls |
|---|---|---|---|
| 1........ | Malot | Sans famille | 470 |
| 2........ | Sand | La Mare au Diable | 343 |
| 3........ | Labiche | La Poudre aux yeux | 319 |
| 4........ | Mérimée | Colomba | 290 |
| 5........ | Maupassant | Huit contes choisis | 268 |
| 6........ | Molière | Le Bourgeois gentilhomme | 194 |
| 7........ | Dumas | Les trois mousquetaires | 174 |
| 8........ | Malot | Par terre et par mer | 168 |
| 9........ | Daudet | Tartarin de Tarascon | 160 |
| 10........ | Maeterlinck | Théâtre | 150 |
| 11........ | Daudet | La belle Nivernaise | 148 |
| 12........ | Maeterlinck | L'Oiseau bleu | 147 |
| 13........ | Rostand | Cyrano de Bergerac | 146 |
| 14........ | Labiche | Le Voyage de M. Perrichon | 146 |
| 15........ | Beaumarchais | Le Barbier de Séville | 142 |
| 16........ | Augier | Le Gendre de M. Poirier | 137 |
| 17........ | Clarétie | Pierrille | 135 |
| 18........ | Hugo | Notre-Dame de Paris | 135 |
| 19........ | Hémon | Maria Chapdelaine | 129 |
| 20........ | France | Le Livre de mon ami | 128 |

was closed for a week, and the accession cards in the author list were compared with the charge cards in the pocket of the books on the shelves, and the number of calls was transferred to the catalogue card. For books on the shelves that did not originate in the libraries a separate card index was made, showing author, title, and number of calls, forming an alphabetical list apart from the regular accession list. The reserve or general reference books were checked separately on the cards in the reserve-book tray. To the calls checked on the first two lists were added the calls taken from the full and discarded

TABLE 11

| Rank | Author | Title | Calls |
|------|--------|-------|-------|
| 1...... | (Larousse)* | *Encyclopédie par l'image* | 146 |
| 2...... | Daniels | *French Scientific Reader* | 71 |
| 3...... | Schoell | *Le Paris d'aujourd'hui* | 52 |
| 4...... | Voltaire | *Selections* (Havens ed.) | 46 |
| 5...... | Margueritte | *Fontenoy* | 39 |
| 6...... | Lesage | *Les Aventures du flibustier Beauchêne* | 36 |
| 7...... | Hugo | *Sur les bords du Rhin* | 36 |
| 8...... | Renan | *Ma sœur Henriette* | 33 |
| 9...... | Benjamin | *La Vie prodigieuse d'Honoré de Balzac* | 30 |
| 10...... | Foncin | *Le Pays de France* | 28 |
| 11...... | Rambaud | *Histoire de la civilisation française contemporaine* | 27 |
| 12...... | Valléry-Radot | *Pasteur: 1822–1895* | 26 |
| 13...... | Hourticq | *France* | 24 |
| 14...... | France | *La Vie en fleur* | 23 |
| 15...... | Guerber | *Marie-Louise et le duc de Reichstadt* | 23 |
| 16...... | Margueritte | *Strasbourg* | 22 |
| 17...... | Reymond | *Les Paysans* | 21 |
| 18...... | Ducoudray | *Histoire de France* (Super ed.) | 21 |
| 19...... | Badaire | *Précis de la littérature française* | 21 |
| 20...... | Valléry-Radot | *Vie de Pasteur* | 20 |

* Parentheses in this and succeeding tables denote editors.

charge cards preserved in the office files, thus giving the total number of calls for each item in the collection during the five-year period. This information was then transferred to check sheets, which showed the item index number, the author, the title, the library classification of the book, and the number of calls received for the item.

When completed, the check list contained 904 items, including reserve books, new accessions, and lost or missing items for which we had a charge card. There were 16 categories. In the five years, 13,911 calls were handled, ranging from 0 to 470 calls per volume. Of the 13,911 calls made by French 1 and French 2AB students, 34.7 per cent were for titles withdrawn ten times or more, and 65.3 per cent were for titles receiving less than ten calls per title. The indication was one of wide and varied reading.

As might be expected, the drama, the novel, and the short story received the larger number of calls, i.e., approximately two-thirds of the higher-bracketed titles. One title, the *Encyclopédie par l'image* (Larousse) in 24 volumes, a prime favorite for correlated reading, circulated 146 times.

Range played a much larger part than frequency in the circulation of the books, as Table 9 indicates. Very few titles circulated 100 times or more. Table 10 lists the 20 fiction titles receiving the highest number of calls. These 20 titles received 28.2 per cent of the total number of calls. It is fruitless to speculate on the reasons for their popularity; there are too many facets to a reader's choice.

That the reading in the higher ranges was not all in fiction is attested by the list of the 20 nonfictional titles in range 20–150, representing 42 per cent of the 1,762 calls. (Table 11). For purposes of correlation, readings were accepted in popular or fictionized form, as well as in purely expository form, the choice depending usually upon factors not in our control. This explains the presence of certain fictional titles in the list in Table 11.

## 4. *Extensive Reading: Quantity, Rate, and Kind*

In 1934 Professor Durbin Rowland and the writer completed a tabulation and study of the individual reading and reportage of 541 students enrolled in French 1ABC from 1927 to 1932.[10] The group read extensively and reported upon 769,093 pages, embracing 1,054 titles and 571 different authors.

The majority of the students were Freshmen, newly graduated from high school, carrying a normal study-load of three courses. Many of them were working at outside jobs and commuting. They were typical in their attitudes toward study and play. In general intelligence they were a representative cross-section of their entering groups.[11] They were not hand-picked.

Our investigation was based on two sets of data: (1) a check list showing the amount of reading done by each student in each of the three quarters in each of the five years under study and (2) a check list of the authors and titles reported upon by the 541 students, showing for each title its classification, the amount read by quarters, and the total amount read in the full period.

The source of the data was the reading summary sheet submitted to the instructor at the end of each quarter by all the members of his classes. Before filing, these summary sheets were verified by comparing them with the actual reading reports. The data, therefore, were factual, accurate, and complete.

The distribution by year and by quarter-course of the total number of pages read by the total group is indicated in Table 12.

The grand total for the five years is 769,093 pages, or better than three-quarters of a million pages. The difference between the annual totals for a given course, as 1A or 1C, has little significance, since the

TABLE 12

| Year | 1A | 1B | 1C | Total |
|---|---|---|---|---|
| 1927–28..... | 20,029 | 84,578 | 80,479 | 185,086 |
| 1928–29..... | 10,306 | 44,294 | 68,911 | 123,511 |
| 1929–30..... | 24,041 | 53,496 | 91,352 | 168,889 |
| 1930–31..... | 24,700 | 51,526 | 65,160 | 141,386 |
| 1931–32..... | 21,784 | 58,240 | 70,197 | 150,221 |
| Total.... | 100,860 | 292,134 | 376,099 | 769,093 |

number of enrollees varies from year to year. In five years, however, the differences between the grand totals for the three courses have more meaning. The fact that 13 per cent of the total amount read during the entire period was done in the first course (1A); 38 per cent in the second course (1B); and 49 per cent in the third course (1C) establishes for the three quarters a progressive ratio of 1–3–4. In other words, third-quarter reading equals in quantity the reading of the first and second quarters combined, and second-quarter reading trebles the first. When one considers the relative content and textual difficulty of the material read in the three quarters, this ratio becomes very significant.

Apparently, we have here an illustration of the old saying that "en forgeant on devient forgeron." The reading adaptation must come for the majority of readers at about the middle of the second course, and the skill level at or near the beginning of the third course, or how else can one explain the fact that almost 50 per cent of the total reading takes place in the last quarter? Furthermore, it must have been fluent, pleasurable, and reasonably accurate, or the

ratio would not have been so high in 1C, where the greater part of
the reading is in original scientific or expository material.

The exact reading average, quarter by quarter, for the total group
of 541 students is not obtainable from the foregoing data, because
they did not all take the three courses of the sequence. Since it was
desirable to learn the actual average increment per quarter, a second
check list was drawn up by quarters according to the student summaries. From this list the information in Table 13 was obtained concerning the average quarterly achievement.

TABLE 13

| YEAR | FRENCH 1A | | | FRENCH 1B | | | FRENCH 1C | | |
|---|---|---|---|---|---|---|---|---|---|
| | Total | $N*$ | $M*$ | Total | $N$ | $M$ | Total | $N$ | $M$ |
| 1927–28..... | 20,029 | 81 | 247 | 84,578 | 88 | 961 | 80,479 | 75 | 1,073 |
| 1928–29..... | 10,306 | 53 | 194 | 44,294 | 62 | 714 | 68,911 | 65 | 1,060 |
| 1929–30..... | 24,041 | 88 | 273 | 53,496 | 71 | 753 | 91,352 | 87 | 1,050 |
| 1930–31..... | 24,700 | 62 | 398 | 51,526 | 61 | 844 | 65,160 | 66 | 987 |
| 1931–32..... | 21,784 | 64 | 340 | 58,240 | 84 | 693 | 70,197 | 63 | 1,114 |
| Total... | 100,860 | 348 | 287 | 292,134 | 366 | 798 | 376,099 | 356 | 1,056 |

* In this and succeeding tables, $N$ represents the number of cases; $M$, the average score.

For the five-year period, the average amount read per student was
287 pages in 1A, 798 pages in 1B, and 1,056 pages in 1C. As in Table
12, the sum of the quarter averages is not particularly meaningful;
it amounts to 2,141 pages. Taken separately by years, the average
total reading per student is as follows: 1927–28, 2,281 pages; 1928–
29, 1,968 pages; 1929–30, 2,076 pages; 1930–31, 2,229 pages; and
1931–32, 2,147 pages. The averages are remarkably uniform, conforming to the 1931–32 pattern, which represents perhaps an ideal
curve of progress, with growth in proportion to exposure, in a
quarterly ratio of 1–2–3 and an average total reading experience of
about 2,150 pages. Considering the type of instruction during this
period, 2,150 pages no doubt represented "standard expectancy" for
extensive reading in French 1.

The students involved in the study did not constitute a homogeneous group. With rare exceptions, registrants in 1A were without
previous experience in French, whereas those in 1B were a mixed

group of 1A continuants, one-unit entrants, college transfers, and occasional repeaters. The 1C group was like 1B. The question arose: What would be the averages and the reading rate for a truly homogeneous group, one whose only experience in French would be limited to 1ABC?

To answer the question, we isolated the cases of "straight" continuants who had not received instruction in French previous to 1ABC and tabulated the reading amounts on their summary sheets. Table 14 summarizes their quarterly achievement in comparison

TABLE 14

| Group | French 1A | | | French 1B | | | French 1C | | |
|---|---|---|---|---|---|---|---|---|---|
| | N | Total | M | N | Total | M | N | Total | M |
| Total....... | 348 | 100,860 | 287 | 366 | 292,134 | 798 | 356 | 376,099 | 1,056 |
| 1ABC...... | 193 | 56,763 | 294 | 193 | 159,304 | 825 | 193 | 209,791 | 1,087 |

with the achievement of the total group. The 193 "beginners" who completed French 1ABC in unbroken continuation read a total of 425,858 pages, or an average of 2,206 pages per student reader. Their rate of reading averaged 294 pages for 1A, 825 pages for 1B, and 1,087 pages for 1C, which establishes a ratio of 1–3–4. The medians for the total group and the special group of continuants show only slight deviations, and the deviations are in favor of the 1ABC continuants. Apparently, the injection into the sequence of one-unit and transfer students did not raise the average amounts read either for quarters or for the year. Instead their presence seemed to depress the averages.

This yearly average of better than 2,200 pages and the rate ratio of 1–3–4 seemed less practical and desirable than the 2,150-page average and the ratio of 1–2–3. In later years, when we were reading more closely integrated material in 1A and 1B, the "unnatural gap between the accomplishment of the first part of the year and that of the middle of the year," referred to by Rowland, closed up, and our quantitative reading rate approximated the ratio of 1–2–3, the pattern established in 1931–32.

Table 15 shows the median and quartile scores by quarters for the group of continuants. The lowest individual score for three quarters was in the 1,300–1,399-page range; the highest, in the 3,300–3,399-page range. Half the group read more than 2,182 pages; one-fourth, more than 2,424 pages; and 10 per cent, more than 2,600 pages. These amounts do not represent the total reading experience of the students; the assigned classroom reading is not included. If it were

TABLE 15

| Measure* | 1A | 1B | 1C | 1ABC Total |
|---|---|---|---|---|
| $Q^3$........ | 382.80 | 1,011.67 | 1,144.23 | 2,424.68 |
| Md........ | 281.37 | 805.70 | 1,045.11 | 2,182.17 |
| $Q^1$........ | 190.00 | 681.62 | 1,013.79 | 1,971.64 |

\* Based on 50-page intervals for the quarters; 100-page intervals for total sequence. Md. is the middle score, and not the average ($M$), as in the preceding tables.

TABLE 16*

| Range (In Thousands) | N | French 1A | | French 1B | | French 1C | | Total | Per Cent |
|---|---|---|---|---|---|---|---|---|---|
| | | Pages | Per Cent | Pages | Per Cent | Pages | Per Cent | | |
| 50–20...... | 1 | 17,733 | 42 | 19,206 | 46 | 5,201 | 12 | 42,140 | 6 |
| 20–10...... | 11 | 35,876 | 25 | 61,496 | 42 | 47,162 | 33 | 144,534 | 19 |
| 10– 5...... | 16 | 13,512 | 12 | 46,632 | 41 | 52,943 | 47 | 113,087 | 15 |
| 5– 2...... | 36 | 12,357 | 11 | 43,756 | 40 | 53,681 | 49 | 109,794 | 14 |
| 2– 1...... | 77 | 7,280 | 7 | 41,836 | 37 | 62,489 | 56 | 111,605 | 15 |
| Total.. | 141 | 86,758 | 17 | 212,926 | 41 | 221,476 | 42 | 521,160 | 69 |

\* Reading the first line, in the 20,000–50,000-page range there was one title, contributing 42,140 pages, or 6 per cent of the total number of pages read by the group. The rate of reading was 17,733 pages, or 42 per cent, for 1A; 19,206 pages, or 46 per cent, for 1B; and 5,201 pages, or 12 per cent, for 1C.

included, each norm for 1ABC would be greater by more than 350 pages (*Terre de France, La Semeuse*).

The distribution of reading amounts by quarters, expressed in number of pages and in percentages of the total reading in the sequence, is shown in Table 16. The distribution of amounts less than 1,000 pages per title is not given in the table. One hundred and forty-one titles were read in excess of 1,000 pages each, contributing 69 per cent of the total number of pages (769,093) read by the special group. Of the 1,054 titles reported, 86 per cent (913) were read in amounts of less than 1,000 pages. Two-thirds of the reading was done within a small radius of about one-seventh of the number of books. Nonfictional reading was the principal cause of this wide scatter of titles in the low range. Apparently, correlated reading accounted for a large percentage of the thousand and more titles.

In the first quarter (1A), the decrease in range limits below 20,000 pages is accompanied by a decrease in amounts read within the range, whereas in 1C, range limits and amounts are in inverse ratio. The spread begins at the approach of the reading adaptation, as the more or less evenly distributed percentages for 1B suggest. It is at this mid-point that individual tastes and needs begin to control the selection of reading matter. The student feels secure enough in vocabulary and syntax to take to the open road. Only freedom and enthusiasm can explain his adventuring in the 913 titles which were read in amounts of less than 1,000 pages each.[12]

The 35 highest-ranking titles in amounts read, with the distribution of pages read in the three quarters of French 1, illustrate the general nature of the list and of the quarterly reading (Table 17). In the full list, as in the sampling in Table 17, one is impressed by the few cases of "premature" reading, as in the case of *Eugénie Grandet* (No. 20) for which 246 pages were reported in 1A. It was probably a "trial" on the part of one or more students who were interested in reading something by Balzac in the original.

Another type of misplaced reading is represented by the 456 pages read in 1C from *Si nous lisions*, a West-type graded reader suitable only for beginners in 1A. It may have been read in a remedial program for deficient students or by two-unit entrants without reading experience, or it may have escaped the control system. Staff conference minutes refer occasionally to the acceptance of substandard material in 1C and to the reading of too difficult material in 1A. Both were discouraged, but the policy was to advise and then allow the student to decide, prohibiting only when his choice would be definitely harmful.

We wanted to get rid of the universal practice of prescribing certain readings at certain levels of study and of restraining students from reading books prescribed for later stages of the course than the one in which they were engaged. This permissive or prohibitory aspect of language study, as one chooses to look at it, conflicted with our accepted theories of individualized learning and the growth of skill in an arts-type subject matter. Our philosophy was: "If he can, let him do it; if he can't, let him try." *Maria Chapdelaine* would not have been read in 1A and 1B if we had not held to that belief. The distribution of authors in the five ranges in Table 18 shows

TABLE 17

| Rank | Author | Title | 1A | 1B | 1C | Total |
|---|---|---|---|---|---|---|
| 1.... | Malot | *Sans famille* | 17,733 | 19,206 | 5,201 | 42,140 |
| 2.... | Lavisse | *Histoire de France** | 11,658 | 3,548 | 1,175 | 16,381 |
| 3.... | Dumas | *Les trois mousquetaires* | 1,273 | 9,575 | 4,570 | 15,418 |
| 4.... | Mérimée | *Colomba* | 63 | 7,226 | 7,204 | 14,493 |
| 5.... | Rostand | *Cyrano de Bergerac* | 0 | 3,884 | 10,034 | 13,918 |
| 6.... | Hugo | *Les Misérables* | 704 | 4,470 | 8,651 | 13,825 |
| 7.... | Labiche | *La Poudre aux yeux* | 3,042 | 7,919 | 2,523 | 13,484 |
| 8.... | Clarétie | *Pierrille** | 3,761 | 6,793 | 1,876 | 12,430 |
| 9.... | Labiche | *Voyage de M. Perrichon* | 2,051 | 6,727 | 3,391 | 12,169 |
| 10.... | (Eddy) | *Si nous lisions** | 10,336 | 1,137 | 456 | 11,929 |
| 11.... | Halévy | *L'Abbé Constantin* | 1,792 | 4,918 | 3,583 | 10,293 |
| 12.... | Daudet | *Le Petit Chose* | 1,196 | 5,299 | 3,699 | 10,194 |
| 13.... | Daudet | *Tartarin de Tarascon* | 353 | 4,644 | 4,544 | 9,541 |
| 14.... | Maupassant | *Huit contes choisis* | 1,696 | 4,874 | 2,399 | 8,969 |
| 15.... | Dumas | *La Tulipe noire* | 858 | 2,088 | 4,991 | 7,937 |
| 16.... | Malot | *Par terre et par mer* | 1,780 | 4,720 | 1,409 | 7,909 |
| 17.... | Sand | *La Mare au Diable* | 342 | 3,959 | 3,566 | 7,867 |
| 18.... | France | *Le Livre de mon ami* | 174 | 2,275 | 5,364 | 7,813 |
| 19.... | Verne | *Tour du monde ...* | 853 | 3,887 | 2,447 | 7,187 |
| 20.... | Balzac | *Eugénie Grandet* | 246 | 2,270 | 4,653 | 7,169 |
| 21.... | Molière | *Le Bourgeois gentilhomme* | 202 | 1,797 | 4,968 | 6,967 |
| 22.... | Labiche | *Cagnotte* | 727 | 4,419 | 1,611 | 6,757 |
| 23.... | (Bond) | *Terre de France** | 4,401 | 2,194 | 0 | 6,595 |
| 24.... | Hugo | *Notre-Dame de Paris* | 303 | 1,429 | 4,504 | 6,236 |
| 25.... | France | *Le Crime de S-.Bonnard* | 131 | 1,070 | 4,436 | 5,637 |
| 26.... | Maeterlinck | *L'Oiseau bleu* | 0 | 1,082 | 4,541 | 5,623 |
| 27.... | Hémon | *Maria Chapdelaine* | 1,026 | 2,013 | 2,573 | 5,612 |
| 28.... | (Ford, Hicks) | *New French Reader* | 420 | 3,911 | 937 | 5,268 |
| 29.... | (Morris) | *Easy French Fiction* | 4,529 | 74 | 204 | 4,807 |
| 30.... | Dumas | *Comte de Monte-Cristo* | 559 | 2,339 | 1,631 | 4,529 |
| 31.... | Hugo | *Hernani* | 0 | 1,352 | 2,981 | 4,333 |
| 32.... | Augier | *Le Gendre de M. Poirier* | 86 | 3,162 | 1,078 | 4,326 |
| 33.... | Labiche | *La Grammaire* | 553 | 2,231 | 1,069 | 3,853 |
| 34.... | Dumas *fils* | *La Question d'argent* | 149 | 1,611 | 2,014 | 3,774 |
| 35.... | Hugo | *Quatre-vingt-treize* | 24 | 360 | 3,134 | 3,518 |

\* Exclusive of intensive classroom use.

the same characteristics as indicated above for the titles read. The percentages in the fourth column refer to the total amount read in all ranges, including below 1,000 pages. Eighty-two per cent (622,509 pages) were read in the works of 96 authors. The remaining 475 authors contributed only 18 per cent of the reading. None of the latter authors was read in amounts exceeding 1,000 pages.

Over half the reading done was in 19 authors, i.e., Malot, Labiche, Dumas *père*, Hugo, Daudet, France, Molière, Maupassant, Lavisse (and Rambaud), Rostand, Mérimée, Balzac, Maeterlinck, Clarétie, Cochran and Eddy, Halévy, Erckmann-Chatrian, Verne, and Augier. They were read in amounts ranging from 10,078 to 50,049 pages.

The next highest-ranking authors down to the 2,000-page range were, in order: Sand, Bazin, Loti, Lamartine, (Bond), Dumas *fils*, Hémon, About, Flaubert, (Ford and Hicks), Voltaire, Romain-Rolland, (Morris), Scribe, (François), Bordeaux, Ch. Gide, Zola,

TABLE 18

| Range | Authors | Total Pages | Per Cent of Total |
|---|---|---|---|
| 20,000–50,000........ | 6 | 223,490 | 29 |
| 10,000–20,000........ | 13 | 183,416 | 24 |
| 5,000–10,000........ | 12 | 76,593 | 10 |
| 2,000– 5,000........ | 26 | 84,522 | 11 |
| 1,000– 2,000........ | 39 | 54,488 | 8 |
| Total............ | 96 | 622,509 | 82 |

Brieux, Sardou, Rambaud, Ponet *or* Dannemarie, Feuillet, Picard, Maurois, Beaumarchais, (Buffum), Lesage, Schoell, Margueritte, (Michaut), Forbin, (Dondo), Curel, Rébald, Gréville, Sarment, and Renan. The Michaut entry is his modernized version of *Aucassin et Nicolette*. These 38 authors contributed 21 per cent of the material read by the group.

The choice in authors was especially the student's. He invariably asked for "something by" Hugo, Molière, Maurois, Zola, etc., in making his early selections. If he had a definite title in mind, it was usually a standard work, such as *Les Misérables*, *L'Avare*, *Candide*, *Le Père Goriot*, *Les trois mousquetaires*, etc. In selecting nonfiction, he usually had a definite title that he wanted to read, following the recommendation of an instructor in a topical course.

Nonfiction netted 148,632 pages, or 19.6 per cent of the total number of pages read. There is a slight duplication in the count because biography was checked as such and also under the special category of the biographee's work.

The ranking of nonfictional general categories shows the social sciences, including history, political science, political economy, sociology, psychology, and geography, well ahead, with 82,999 pages, or nearly 56 per cent of the total amount of nonfictional reading. The humanities, including art, biography, music, criticism, and philosophy, are in second place with 47,635 pages. General science is third with 17,998 pages.

The distribution of nonfictional readings by categories and by quarters is shown in Table 19. In the first quarter, the nonfictional

TABLE 19

| CATEGORY | No. of Authors | No. of Titles | PAGES READ | | | | |
|---|---|---|---|---|---|---|---|
| | | | 1A | 1B | 1C | Total | Per Cent |
| Art................. | 27 | 31 | 185 | 1,312 | 6,557 | 8,054 | 5 |
| Biography........... | 50 | 61 | 932 | 4,429 | 18,288 | 23,649 | 16 |
| Criticism............ | 35 | 41 | 377 | 630 | 7,070 | 8,077 | 6 |
| Music.............. | 10 | 12 | 0 | 621 | 2,793 | 3,414 | 2 |
| Philosophy.......... | 15 | 18 | 0 | 776 | 3,665 | 4,441 | 3 |
| Geography, travel..... | 28 | 30 | 2,622 | 7,691 | 5,086 | 15,399 | 10 |
| History............. | 52 | 63 | 17,137 | 12,964 | 15,269 | 45,370 | 31 |
| Political science....... | 21 | 21 | 25 | 365 | 2,880 | 3,270 | 2 |
| Political economy..... | 16 | 19 | 65 | 69 | 6,614 | 6,748 | 5 |
| Sociology, psychology.. | 55 | 61 | 225 | 2,789 | 9,198 | 12,212 | 8 |
| General science....... | 71 | 77 | 241 | 2,498 | 15,259 | 17,998 | 12 |
| Total........... | 380 | 434 | 21,809 | 34,144 | 92,679 | 148,632 | ...... |

reading is predominantly in history, with geography and biography in second and third places, respectively. Only exploratory and negligible reading in the other categories occurs in 1A. That is correct procedure as background reading at that stage of learning. In the second quarter, history is less in amount but is still first choice. Geography (including travel), second in rank, is at its peak. Biography, sociology, psychology, general science, and art trail in that order. Biography, in the third quarter, takes the lead, with history and general science in second place, and sociology, psychology, political economy, and art following in the order given.

The reasons for these shifts are not wholly clear. There is, of course, the whim or need of the student. There are also the time schedule and the student's study program, since correlation with another course usually determines his choice. Then there are such reasons as accessibility, readability, the growth of critical judgment or of factual knowledge during the year, the recommendations of other persons, and changes in personal plans. Especially, there are the promptings, emphases, and influence of the student's instructors. In general, these shifts form a fairly clear pattern, in which the generalized tends to dominate the particularized, with the gap gradually narrowing as the sequence progresses.

The 20 most widely read titles in nonfiction are shown in Table 20

TABLE 20

| Rank | Author | Title | Amount |
|------|--------|-------|--------|
| 1...... | Rambaud | *Histoire de la civilisation française* | 2,895 |
| 2...... | Ch. Gide | *Principes d'économie politique* | 2,799 |
| 3...... | Maurois | *Ariel* | 1,803 |
| 4...... | Schoell | *Paris d'aujourd'hui* | 1,702 |
| 5...... | Valléry-Radot | *Vie de Pasteur* | 1,567 |
| 6...... | (Daniels) | *Scientific French Reader* | 1,543 |
| 7...... | Joran | *Histoire contemporaine* | 1,514 |
| 8...... | (Moffet) | *Lectures historiques* | 1,496 |
| 9...... | Hugo | *Sur les bords du Rhin* | 1,323 |
| 10...... | Doumic | *Histoire de la littérature française* | 1,212 |
| 11...... | Schinz | *Vie et œuvre de J.-J. Rousseau* | 1,049 |
| 12...... | Michaud | *Tableau de la civilisation française* | 1,080 |
| 13...... | Lefèvre | *Vie de Cyrano de Bergerac* | 1,067 |
| 14...... | Taine | *Philosophie de l'art en Grèce* | 912 |
| 15...... | Lévy-Bruhl | *Fonctions mentales des sociétés inférieures* | 910 |
| 16...... | Gallouédec | *Géographie de la France* | 880 |
| 17...... | Portalès | *Chopin* | 874 |
| 18...... | Renan | *Vie de Jésus* | 845 |
| 19...... | Boissier | *Cicéron et ses amis* | 797 |
| 20...... | Boutmy | *Psychologie politique du peuple américain* | 785 |

(*Terre de France* and *Histoire de France* excepted, since they were "pressurized" readings). The influence of the intended field of specialization on this list of readings is clear. The English major, the premedical student, the social science major, the art student, the student of natural sciences, are more evident here than the prospective specialist in Romance languages. The impression is accentuated when one examines the complete list of 434 titles. The acquired language proficiency has become useful; it is now a key for the unlocking of doors.

The diversity of reading is more apparent in a specific area, such as art:

Benoit, *Alberte Holbein;* Duret, *Histoire des peintres impressionistes;* (*Encyclopédie par l'image*): "Les Cathédrales françaises," "Histoire de l'art," "Rembrandt," "Rubens," "Versailles"; Gaultier, *Le Sens de l'art;* Gillet, *Watteau, Peinture;* Guyau, *L'Art au point de vue sociologique;* Hourticq, *Ars-una, Histoire générale de l'art, La Peinture;* Letallier, *Des Classiques aux Impressionistes;* Mâle, *L'Art religieuse du XIII<sup>e</sup> siècle;* Mérimée, *Étude sur les arts au moyen âge;* Michel, *Histoire de l'art;* Ottin, *Le Vitrail;* Poète, *L'Art de Paris;* Ary Renan, *Le Costume en France;* Rocheblave, *L'Art et le Goût en France;* Rodin, *Les Cathédrales en France;* Romain-Rolland, *Vie de Michel-Ange;* Rosenthal, *Louis David;* Séailles, *Essai sur le génie dans l'art;* Sicherat, *Histoire du costume en France.*

Painting, sculpture, architecture, stained glass, costume; monographs, general histories of art; histories of French art, religious art, movements, trends, and schools; genius in art; taste and meaning in art; the sociological implications of art—27 authors, 31 books, over 8,000 pages reported. That is really to read! "If he can, let him do it; if he can't, let him try." Does one think seriously that these books were read by persons who did not want to read or did not know how to read? Or that they were read so superficially that the reader got nothing substantial for his pains? Or that he had to translate to get at the meaning of the page?

The reading maturity of these 1B and 1C students must not be underestimated. By the *American Council French Test* given at the close of 1C, the average student in this group attained a median score in silent reading which was within one-half a point of the national norm for *seven college semesters.* One would hardly question the ability of a student who had completed three and one-half years of "college French" to read expository material of this nature.

Continuing the comparison, the lower fourth of the group of French 1ABC continuants referred to above surpassed the upper fourth of the national group in reading, vocabulary, and grammar, as of the end of one college year. Viewed in the light of this achievement, the performance of the French 1 students in extensive reading seems less illogical, less fantastic. We are dealing here with "mature" readers, and not beginners.

They knew what they wanted; they could read what they wanted to read; they got out of their reading what they wanted to get out of it. Can one ask more than that? For, after all, they were reading by and for themselves.

## 5. *Extensive Reading: An Appraisal of Values*

Perhaps the greatest single value of the extensive reading feature is its highly personalized nature, motivating or activating the whole course of study. In this one linguistic activity the class dissolves into so many individuals, each going his own way. The way may be for his good or for his ill. It is, however, the way of his own choosing. That is important.

His choice, as has been said previously, is not without information. His instructors have made recommendations, in the classroom and in private conference. Reading lists have been circulated, printed in the course syllabus, offered in the syllabi of other college courses, and indicated in his textbooks. There are the shelf catalogues of the reading collection, the rental library, and the general College library. He has free access to open shelves and the bibliographical works on the reference reserve shelves. New reading acquisitions are placed on a special "new-book" shelf, taken into the classroom, and "advertised" by the instructor. The bulletin boards carry reviews, clippings, notices, and other matter pertaining to books and authors recommended. Special displays of printed and pictorial material have been made on the tables of the reading-room: Louis XIV, Paris, Gothic art, Anatole France, the Romantic movement in art, in literature, etc. Classroom suggestions have been based on chance, the textbook, current events, local happenings, current productions of opera or motion picture, French arrivals in the United States, translations in current publications, international events, recitals, lectures, expositions, the university *Calendar*—anything, in fact, that served to integrate the study of French into contemporary living. The stimuli of phonograph recordings of French masterpieces, literary or musical, and of projections of slides and of opaque material (postcards, prints, illustrations) on the screen in the classroom have contributed to his selection of reading matter.

There are other influences, such as the availability, the readability, or the attractiveness of the book. Personal and home libraries, the influence of parents and of classmates, trends or fashions in the arts and the sciences, studial needs, academic requirements in upper-college courses, "job" influence, travel plans, the learning level in other studies, and even the necessity of filling quickly a "reading quota" may play a part in making selections. Especially, there are the reading habits of the student in his mother-tongue and his acquaintance with other literatures.

How, then, may his choice be judged as bad? Mainly, when it interferes with the smooth progression of his ability to read. If the material is unsuited to his level of achievement, because it is either too easy or too difficult, it is not good for him. If too easy, it may convey a false sense of security and accomplishment; if too difficult, it may cause discouragement or retard his language growth or encourage harmful reading habits. Superficiality in extensive reading is often the result of a poor selection of material, either because of its linguistic difficulty or because its subject matter is beyond the control or appreciation of the reader.

Certain weaknesses in the extensive reading feature appealed more to the instructor than to the student, as, for example, the matter of poor taste on the part of the latter in making selections. If the instructor felt strongly about the literary value of a certain choice, there were tactful ways of getting the student to change his mind, such as referring him to a good history of French literature or other critical appraisal of his selection. In nonfictional cases, the two volumes of *La Science française*[13] spared the instructor some embarrassment. Or the suggestion could be made that objectionable author X and acceptable author Y be read in reverse order, with the secret thought that author X might thereby be squeezed out of the program. After all, the question of taste in reading is not one to be made into a burning issue in the second quarter of a beginning French course.

Unbalanced, lopsided programs were more serious. We felt that a student for whom French 1 was to be his one and only contact with that language and its culture should leave the course with as wide and as representative a contact with the literature as possible. A student who insisted upon limiting his reading to the two thousand pages of the unabridged *Comte de Monte-Cristo* seemed to the staff to have a somewhat benighted idea of his opportunities. On the other hand, the staff condoned reading in a single author, genre, or period. The case was usually decided on circumstances.

There are many values in extensive reading. On the personal side, it promotes the interest of the individual student in his language study,[14] offers him a cultural broadening beyond the range of the classroom and the common textbook, contributes to the development of his personal stock of factual knowledge and critical judgments, furthers his international understanding, constitutes a definite and tangible reward for his efforts, and provides him with a relatively permanent basis for later linguistic development in other skills.

From the course-organizational angle, extensive reading favors the improvement of other instructional procedures through its release of classroom time normally devoted to "reading" or to "translation"; offers a solution to the problem of the slow and the fast learner; minimizes the need for sectionizing; prevents, to a considerable degree, the common curse of overlapping levels of instruction; facilitates objective testing; and places reading in the foreign language course in its proper emphasis and in a natural setting. To read is a natural and logical corollary of learning to read. Furthermore, extensive reading contributes to the acquisition of a high degree of reading skill in a very short time and to the promise of postschool use of the language—two most desirable objectives. Economy and long life, in learning as in clothing, are desirable qualities.

It must be said that, besides values to the individual and to the course, there are values to the teacher. Through the reading reports and conferences, teacher and student meet and come to know each other. Nor is the exchange one-sided in the area of culture and information. Any instructor, product of the usual course and thesis requirements of a graduate school, may find the role of teacher and pupil reversed in the perusal of an extensive reading report. Not all wisdom is locked up under a thatch of gray hair or in a graduate seminar. How many French teachers would choose to discuss *extempore* with an intelligent student already well versed in the elements of his chosen subject the informative data in a reading report on, say, a chapter in Renan, *L'Avenir de la science* or Maeterlinck's *Macbeth* or De Tocqueville's *De la démocratie en Amérique?* Two thousand five hundred pages per year per student form a challenge, if not a threat, to the language teacher. No one and nothing escapes the impact of a well-ordered program of extensive reading.

The results of the 1927–32 survey were a revelation to us. We knew something of what was going on, but we did not sense its full extent. The performance seemed explainable only on the basis of human differentiation and the desire for self-expression. If the 541 students had all been forced to read an "omnibus" text, a year-in-one-book and a book-in-one-year concoction, or just three or four prescribed texts, would they have averaged seven semesters of reading achievement in three quarters of time? Would they have acquired a live interest in another people's language and culture and the power to follow up that interest?[15] One would do well to reflect upon the ways of these college Freshmen left free in a maze of foreign print.

We now had concrete evidence of who read, what was read, how much was read, the rate of the reading, and some degree of its comprehension, and we held various reasons for justifying our techniques. It was time to measure objectively the products of those techniques.

## CHAPTER VI

# MEASUREMENTS. I

## 1. *Vintages of 1927–32*

IN ADDITION to the customary quarterly final examinations to establish course grades, from 1927 to 1932 the American Council on Education *Alpha French Test* in vocabulary, grammar, and silent reading was administered during the final week in each quarter to all students in the first- and second-year sequences. The A and B forms were used alternately during the year; the exact date of the examination was not announced; and the results were not discussed with the students. There was therefore little risk of the students becoming so familiar with the test items as to invalidate the results.

The test summary sheets provided the staff with a valuable means of estimating the effectiveness of the procedures and materials used from quarter to quarter or from year to year for the whole group, and at the same time they gave the individual instructor an objective rating of the students in his own sections. Supplemented by course grades and achievement-test scores, they formed a reliable index of achievement. The norms also made possible a comparison with the national norms and with the results obtained by experimental groups elsewhere and expressed our results in terms that could be generally understood and accepted.

Using the data in the test summaries, the information on the personal record cards, the final grade sheets in the registrar's office, and the reading report summaries, four separate analyses were made of the quarterly attainment of the registrants in the two sequences.[1] The first study was an analysis of the annual achievement of two sections for the period 1926–28. The second was a statistical analysis of A.C.E. test data for 596 French 1 and 205 French 2 quarter-completions during 1927–30, in order to obtain information on the comparative achievement of unit entrants, beginners, continuants in the second sequence, and promotional cases. The third was a study of the A.C.E. results for 1,085 quarter-students registered in French 1 and 400 quarter-students registered in French 2, for the period 1928–31, for the purpose of intergroup comparisons, correlations, and special information. The fourth was a multiple-factor analysis of attainment in vocabulary, grammar, and reading and the amount of extensive reading done by 107 straight continuants in French 1ABC during 1927–32.

Besides these investigations into our French product, similar ones were made during the same period into A.C.E. test results in Spanish and German, the work of continuants in Senior College courses in Spanish, and intercorrelations in German. It was a period of rather intensive self-examination.

Elsewhere, between 1925 and 1932, in Iowa, Illinois, Wisconsin, Minnesota, New York, and California, there were sixteen directed experiments that involved several thousand students, which purposed to test achievement in reading, vocabulary, and grammar, at high-school and at college levels, in classes professedly using our "direct reading"method and admixtures of our materials. While we were engaged in judging ourselves, we were being judged by others who were only slightly cognizant of what we were doing.

## 2. Grades, Curves, and Continuations

The faculties, in 1926, adopted a "grade curve" for the College, as follows: A, 11 per cent; B, 29 per cent; C, 39 per cent; D, 13+ per cent; F, 4+ per cent; and "Incomplete," not over 2 per cent. It was suggested that the instructor "satisfy himself that a variation is justified by the particular character of the personnel of his section, or modify his results in the direction of conformity with the scale." To encourage observance of the curve, the distribution of grades by each instructor was made public.

Since we had tried for some time to avoid giving D and F grades by holding student conferences, making tri-quarterly reports on deficient students, and placing one-unit and two-unit entrants according to early performance in 1B or 1C, our grade curves were badly skewed in the C and F brackets. For example, in 1927, French 1B, with 82 students in four sections, had an A range of 8.3–25.9 per cent, a B range of 22.0–75.0 per cent, a C range of 8.3–40.7 per cent, no D or "Incomplete" grades, and from zero to 11.1 per cent F grades. In fact, the College as a whole was not too successful in conforming.

In 1929, sanction was given to a procedure by which D cases were split into two groups: (a) to repeat the course and (b) to proceed conditionally to the next course. To prevent failures, we set as a prerequisite for continuation "a grade of C or better in the preceding course, or recommendation of the preceding instructor," and re-

TABLE 21

| Year | N | Honors (A, B) (Per Cent) | Median (C, D)* (Per Cent) | Failure (F) (Per Cent) |
|---|---|---|---|---|
| 1920–21 | 334 | 33.3 | 51.2 | 15.5 |
| 1921–22 | 400 | 36.4 | 50.2 | 13.4 |
| 1922–23 | 333 | 35.5 | 54.2 | 10.3 |
| 1923–24 | 423 | 39.6 | 48.8 | 11.6 |
| 1924–25 | 326 | 47.6 | 42.6 | 9.8 |
| 1925–26 | 319 | 50.0 | 42.2 | 7.8 |
| 1926–27 | 320 | 45.0 | 49.4 | 5.6 |
| 1927–28 | 389 | 43.2 | 48.3 | 8.5 |
| 1928–29 | 391 | 42.6 | 52.3 | 5.1 |
| 1929–30 | 428 | 45.1 | 53.5 | 1.4 |
| 1930–31 | 451 | 42.4 | 56.5 | 1.1 |

* From 1920 to 1927 (spring) cases of "no grade," representing course withdrawals before mid-terms, were computed in the median range with C and D grades; thereafter, such cases were subtracted from the enrolment total (N) for the year. Interyear comparisons are not appreciably affected by the change in procedure. Provisional grades were treated as regular.

ported to the dean the "stop" (F) cases and the "go" (D) cases at the end of each quarter. The procedure developed a more critical attitude by students and instructors toward the "barely passing" (D) mark; but the New Plan in 1932, by making quarter grades merely advisory, robbed the procedure of its force, and the practice was discontinued. Furthermore, a change in the marking system which designated S for satisfactory work, U for unsatisfactory work, and abolished the traditional marks, blocked any further experimentation with grading.

Table 21 shows the percentage distribution of honor, median, and failure grades for all sections of French 1ABC from autumn 1920 to spring 1931, inclusive.[2] A striking fact is apparent in this table, namely, that the honor grades increased progressively as the percentage of failure decreased. Failures dropped from a high of 15 per cent in 1920–21, the first experimental year, to a low of *1 per cent* in 1930–31, the eleventh experimental year and the first of the New Plan.[3] During this period, A and B grades increased from 33.3 per cent in 1920–21 to 42.4 per cent in 1931, with the high point (50 per cent) in the year preceding our transfer to the College of Arts, the year of our concentrated efforts in behalf of the exceptional student and of our most effective personnel work.[4]

Throughout the period, economy of learning and high standards of achievement were inseparable. From the first extensive reading average of 473 pages reported in 1C in the spring of 1922, the average

TABLE 22

| Course | N | A | B | C | D | F | Total Points* | Av. Pts. |
|---|---|---|---|---|---|---|---|---|
| 1A...... | 493 | 12.9 | 27.4 | 35.7 | 17.4 | 6.6 | 1,208 | 2.45 |
| 1B...... | 456 | 16.7 | 30.0 | 38.0 | 11.8 | 3.5 | 1,318 | 2.89 |
| 1C...... | 690 | 13.4 | 30.0 | 43.1 | 11.5 | 2.0 | 1,946 | 2.82 |
| Total | 1,639 | 14.3 | 29.2 | 38.9 | 13.6 | 4.0 | 4,472 | 2.72 |

* The scale rated A (6), B (4), C (2), D (0), F (−2) points.

amount for the full sequence rose to 1,184 pages in 1925; 1,581 in 1926; 1,739 in 1927; 2,281 in 1928; 1,968 in 1929; 2,076 in 1930; and 2,229 in 1931. Meantime, failures dropped from 15 to 1 per cent; honors increased from 33.3 to 50 per cent; and until 1926 (the last year that data were obtainable), there was only seven-tenths of 1 per cent (0.007) of failure in continuation study in the advanced French courses in the Senior College. Reading paid off in marks, the only educational currency recognized by recorders.

The grade distribution per course, expressed in percentages of the total number of marks, is indicated in Table 22 for the four-year period, 1927–31, the only years for which such data are at hand. The comparison shows (1) the depressive effect upon the percentage of A grades in 1C caused by promotions from 1B and by registrants with advanced standing; (2) a relatively stable percentage of B grades; (3) an increasing percentage of C grades, due in part to the policy in regard to the D grade; and (4) a progressive diminution in the percentage of F's. The grade-point averages approximate a "high C," with an average for the 1,639 grades of 2.72 points, or nearly B−.

Continuation data for French 1 students from 1920 to 1925 have been presented;[5] no further study was made for later years. For Spanish 1ABC, however, Professor John C. Ransmeier made an analysis of 154 continuants in 17 Senior College courses from 1927 to 1931. Since French and Spanish were under the same administration, followed similar procedures, had the same objectives, and had a parallel development, his findings for Spanish are germane to the present discussion. They are summed in Table 23. Professor Rans-

TABLE 23*

| Year | Group | N | Per Cent A | Per Cent B | Per Cent C | Per Cent D | Per Cent F | P.A. |
|------|-------|---|------------|------------|------------|------------|------------|------|
| 1927–29..... | Junior College | 24 | 20.8 | 62.2 | 16.7 | ..... | ..... | 4.08 |
| | Non-Junior College | 171 | 15.2 | 40.1 | 38.6 | 5.2 | ..... | 3.29 |
| 1930–31..... | Junior College | 93 | 24.5 | 46.2 | 27.9 | 1.0 | ..... | 3.89 |
| | Non-Junior College | 90 | 14.5 | 37.7 | 40.0 | 6.6 | 0.1 | 3.18 |

* The Junior College group in 1927–29 received 100 per cent of their training in Spanish 1ABC. There were 37 students who received 81 per cent of their training in Spanish 1; they averaged 3.83 grade points in later continuation study. "P.A." = point average for the group.

meier made two separate studies, as shown in the table. No failures were on record for either Junior College group. The superiority of the Junior College group at all grade levels is quite apparent. In the second study (1930–31) the Spanish continuants, evenly matched with non–Junior College trainees, held a strong lead over their competitors, averaging 3.89 grade points per completion, or approximately a B grade. The reading emphasis in Spanish certainly was not detrimental to specialization in that language.

### 3. *Special Group Studies*

The first administration of the newly obtainable American Council French tests was made quarterly in 1927–28, which was the first year of our installation in the College of Arts. As a test of French 1 products under the new conditions, checks were made on two sections for extensive reading, correlation, continuation, and achievement in vocabulary, reading, and grammar.[6]

For 100 quarter-students in the two sections, the extensive reading averaged 2,215 pages, a gain of 23 per cent over the average for the preceding year. In 1C, spring 1927 and 1928, the average amount read in correlation was 403 pages, distributed in 19 categories. Twenty-four students used their reading for general background knowledge; 18 in term papers and themes; 16 in classroom activities; 14 in various reports; and 4 in preparing for examinations. Twenty-eight made no formal use of it, giving as reasons a lack of encouragement or of opportunity in the special field.

All but 9 students liked to do correlated reading. They gained a different point of view (27 cases), found in it a "tool" value (26), consulted original sources (15), gained new values of aesthetic appreciation (13), and renewed their interest in the language (5).

TABLE 24*

| Course | $N$ | Vocabulary | Grammar | Reading |
|--------|-----|------------|---------|---------|
| 1A...... | 111 | 30.1 (II) | 15.2 (I+) | 13.4 (I+) |
| 1B...... | 68 | 41.1 (III+) | 19.9 (II+) | 16.0 (II) |
| 1C...... | 128 | 42.5 (III+) | 32.1 (V+) | 20.1 (IV) |

* 50 cases in 1A and 43 in 1B were taught by a substitute instructor hostile to the method. Two sections of 1B omitted the test through an error. For 1C vocabulary, $N = 107$; grammar, 104.

Those who disliked it found it too technical or uninteresting or of no use to them.

Of the 389 grades earned in all sections of French 1 during the year, 43.2 per cent were honor grades, 48.3 per cent median grades, and 8.5 per cent failure. Achievement on the A.C.E. tests, except for 1A, was lowered by shifts in teaching personnel and section changes. The median scores in vocabulary, grammar, and reading for all sections are indicated in Table 24. The roman numerals in parentheses refer to semester equivalence according to the standard norms.[7]

In a comparison with college semester norms, 1A exceeded the one-semester norms in all three skills; 1B reached or surpassed the two-semester norms; and 1C equaled three semesters in vocabulary, five semesters in grammar, and four semesters in reading. The marked increase in grammar in 1C no doubt came from the intensive review of grammar and the influx of two-unit registrants in that quarter. On the Cheydleur *Grammar Test,*[8] a section of 24 students in 1C scored a median of 53, which is better than the third-semester norm (51) for that test.

The 53 "straight" continuants in the total group scored a median of 41.5 in vocabulary, 29.9 in grammar, and 20.0 in reading, in the third quarter of the sequence. Except in grammar, the deviation was slight. On a time equivalence of one college year, the 1C continuants had a percentile rank of 93 in vocabulary, 78 in grammar, and 90 in reading. By national standards, our M student was a "$Q^3$," with honors in vocabulary and reading.

## 4. *The Baird Survey, 1927–30*

Three years after this preliminary check on French 1, a statistician, H. D. Baird, was commissioned to make an analysis of the A.C.E. test results in French, Spanish, and German 1ABC and 2AB, in order to obtain the following data: (1) norms to be used in grading, counseling, and placing our students and for comparative purposes; (2) objective evidence of the effect upon achievement in advanced courses caused by the practice of "skipping"; and (3) evidence of the influence upon attainment in the first-year sequences of students entering with language credits. The survey covered all foreign language completions between autumn, 1927, and winter, 1930, inclusive. Unfortunately, the spring, 1930, results were not available at the time of Baird's report.

The data for the total French group, including 2AB, are presented in Table 25, showing the median scores in vocabulary, grammar, and reading on the A.C.E. *Alpha French Test*, college semester norms, and plus or minus deviates from these norms. Except for 1A, these results are for mixed groups, containing "straight" continuants, delayed continuants, cases of demotion and promotion, repeaters, transfer students, students with advanced credit, students-at-large, and a few graduate students. The constituency no doubt was fairly representative of the average college beginning language class.

The comparative data in Table 25 bring out clearly the economy in time effected through French 1. In one year of 150 fifty-minute class hours (French 1ABC), the *average* student acquired a proficiency in vocabulary equal to the four-semester norm (45.4), a proficiency in grammar approximating the seven-semester norm (35.9), and a reading proficiency equal to the seven-semester norm

(22.9), or three and one-half college years. Two of the major objectives of the standard elementary French course—reading and grammar—were attained to a degree reported by the Modern Language Study for more than three times the exposure of French 1.

That the trainings in 1ABC were effective for advanced and specialized study, including the active use of the language, is apparent from the medians for 2A and 2B, the two courses in the second-year sequence which were prerequisite for Senior College work. Their equivalence is more than the fifth and seventh semester norms, respectively.[9]

The A.C.E. tests, of course, furnish no direct evidence of oral-aural proficiencies. Indirectly, however, the accomplishment of

TABLE 25*

| COURSE OF STUDY | VOCABULARY (75) | | | | GRAMMAR (50) | | | | READING (28) | | | |
|---|---|---|---|---|---|---|---|---|---|---|---|---|
| | N | M | Norm | Dev. | N | M | Norm | Dev. | N | M | Norm | Dev. |
| 1A..... | 200 | 25.8 | 23.8 | 2.0 | 201 | 12.3 | 12.4 | − 0.1 | 202 | 13.1 | 12.5 | 0.6 |
| 1B..... | 187 | 37.8 | 28.7 | 9.1 | 187 | 18.5 | 21.5 | − 3.4 | 186 | 19.1 | 14.9 | 4.2 |
| 1C..... | 208 | 45.1 | 40.4 | 4.7 | 208 | 33.7 | 22.8 | +10.9 | 207 | 22.2 | 19.1 | 3.1 |
| 2A..... | 79 | 49.5 | 45.4 | 4.1 | 79 | 32.5 | 27.3 | + 5.2 | 78 | 22.7 | 20.5 | 2.2 |
| 2B..... | 126 | 59.2 | 52.8 | 6.4 | 126 | 39.5 | 28.9 | +10.6 | 127 | 24.8 | 21.4 | 3.4 |

* The national norms given are for college semesters, the comparison being between Junior College quarters and regular college semesters. The deviates are between quarter and semester scores. All deviates are *plus*, except in grammar for 1A and 1B.

French 1 continuants in 2A and 2B, as indicated here, supports the contention that students trained by the Reading Method can and do effectively carry on in courses that require the use of the spoken language.[10] It may be argued that only exceptional students were involved in further course work. That was no doubt true of upper Senior College courses, but it was not true of 2A, which at this time was a required fourth major for the validation of 1ABC.

When one considers the great number of students in our colleges who study a foreign language for one year and who, for one reason or another, do not pursue the study further,[11] the question invariably arises as to the degree of skill which the average student takes away with him, in that case. How would the French 1 student compare

with college students in general with the same exposure to the language?.

In order to arrive at a fair answer, Baird separated from the total group the cases of training limited to 1ABC only. Since the A.C.E. norms were for students without previous contact with the language, comparison between them and the average scores $(M)$ for the group of 1ABC beginners should yield accurate information. His data, summarized in Table 26, include the mean scores for the French 1

TABLE 26*

| COURSE OF STUDY | VOCABULARY (75) | | | | GRAMMAR (50) | | | | READING (28) | | | |
|---|---|---|---|---|---|---|---|---|---|---|---|---|
| | $M$ | P.R. | Sem. | Norm | $M$ | P.R. | Sem. | Norm | $M$ | P.R. | Sem. | Norm |
| 1A.... | 26.6 | 65 | I | 24 | 13.3 | 59 | I | 12 | 13.5 | 62 | I | 12 |
| 1B.... | 39.2 | 86 | II | 31 | 19.9 | 46 | II | 19 | 19.1 | 86 | II | 16 |
| 1C.... | 46.0 | 99 | II | 39 | 31.3 | 79 | II | 24 | 22.7 | 98 | II | 19 |

* The 1ABC scores are *means*, not medians. The percentile rank for the mean is shown according to the *semester* scale; no quarter scales are published. The norms, also, are for semesters.

subgroup, the percentile ranking, and semester norms, the comparison being between quarter and semester since quarter norms are not available. The number of cases involved were 200 for 1A, 124 for 1B, and 59 for 1C. The number was small for 1C because the study was made before the close of the spring quarter, 1930. Although all cases were strictly the product of 1ABC, not all were straight continuants, taking the three courses in unbroken succession.

In general, the subgroup was slightly superior to the total group discussed above, except in 1C grammar. Instead of raising the general level in reading and vocabulary, the presence of students with previous experience had the opposite effect.

The data reveal that students who drop out of a language course after one quarter or one semester take little of value with them. At the end of 1A, the average student would have a percentile rating of 65 in vocabulary, 59 in grammar, and 62 in reading in a semester comparison, while the one-semester student represented by the norm would, of course, have only a 50 percentile rating in each of the three skills.

Few students withdraw at the end of 1B, whereas many drop out

of language study at the end of the second semester. In the case of
1B withdrawals, the average student would have a percentile rank
of 86 in vocabulary, 50 in grammar, and 86 in reading in a two-
semester comparison. The average student who drops the language
study at the end of two semesters has a percentile rank of 67 in
vocabulary, 46 in grammar, and 67 in reading. It is clear that the
1B student takes more with him at the end of two quarters in all
three proficiencies than his fellow-student elsewhere at the end of
one year.

The French 1 student has still one quarter to go before quitting
the study of the language temporarily or permanently. At the end of
his third and last quarter he has a P.R. of 99 in vocabulary, 79 in
grammar, and 97 in reading, *on the average.* He ranges in proficiency
from four semesters in vocabulary to seven semesters in reading,
compared with his fellow-student. And he has saved two and one-
half years, approximately, in time.

If this seems preposterous, recall that we are in 1927–30. Reread
Coleman's summary of conditions at that time[12] or Hagboldt's report on achievement in German 1 in 1927–28.[13] And as evidence that
times may change without our changing with them, one may consult
the placement data for 1946–48 and the Cooperative test data for
1934–48 presented in a later chapter.

Up to this point, we have discussed the average student. What of
the superior students in the upper quartile who were promoted or
"skipped" over a course in French 1 or French 2? Baird made a
separate tabulation of such cases and compared their mean scores
with the mean scores for the total group. There were 39 cases, 2 of
which were "double skips," i.e., from 1A to 1C to 2B, five quarters
in one year. In Table 27 the mean scores in vocabulary, grammar,
and reading are given for each of the five types of "skips," including
all courses taken by the students, and for the total group.

In not a single instance did a student who was promoted to a
higher course fail to score in the upper quartile or to better his
previous score in the course from which he was promoted or to show
a plus deviation from the mean of the total group. Furthermore, if
one compares the mean scores for the subgroups in reading with the
maximum possible score (28 points), it becomes obvious that for
some of the "skips" the A.C.E. test in silent reading no longer

measured the full degree of their proficiency. For our local purposes, the analysis showed that the 1A/1C and 1C/2B types of promotion were the most promising. We had found a solution to the common problem of overlapping in the upper quartile.

TABLE 27*

| COURSES TAKEN IN 1ABC AND 2AB | N | VOCABULARY (75) | | GRAMMAR (50) | | READING (28) | |
|---|---|---|---|---|---|---|---|
| | | Special Group Mean | Total Group Mean | Special Group Mean | Total Group Mean | Special Group Mean | Total Group Mean |
| 1A/1C..... | 12 | 40.0 | 26.6 | 23.0 | 13.3 | 21.3 | 13.5 |
| | | 49.2 | 45.3 | 38.8 | 33.0 | 23.8 | 21.7 |
| 1ABC/2B.. | 7 | 31.5 | 26.6 | 25.1 | 13.3 | 16.6 | 13.5 |
| | | 44.4 | 38.3 | 28.0 | 19.4 | 20.9 | 19.0 |
| | | 48.7 | 45.3 | 39.4 | 33.0 | 23.7 | 21.7 |
| | | 60.1 | 58.8 | 39.4 | 37.7 | 26.6 | 24.8 |
| 1A/1C/2B. | 2 | 55.5 | 26.6 | 38.0 | 13.3 | 28.0 | 13.5 |
| | | 63.0 | 45.3 | 38.0 | 33.0 | 25.5 | 21.7 |
| | | 70.5 | 58.8 | 43.0 | 37.7 | 28.0 | 24.8 |
| 1C/2B..... | 16 | 52.7 | 45.3 | 42.7 | 33.0 | 23.0 | 21.7 |
| | | 62.3 | 58.8 | 41.0 | 37.7 | 25.5 | 24.8 |
| 1B/2A..... | 2 | 45.5 | 38.3 | 28.0 | 19.4 | 23.0 | 19.0 |
| | | 53.0 | 49.8 | 33.0 | 31.9 | 23.0 | 22.3 |

* Five types of "skips" are indicated: 1A/1C, 1ABC/2B, 1A/1C/2B, 1C/2B, and 1B/2A. The oblique line indicates the location of the course skipped, e.g., 1A/1C means that the student took 1A, skipped 1B, and took 1C.

### 5. *The Mosier Survey, 1928–31*

Thorough as the Baird survey was, it did not cover the full academic year 1929–30, nor did it analyze the "straight" continuants in whom we were particularly interested. We lacked information also on the work of repeaters, as well as certain correlational data. Consequently, in 1932, an educational psychologist, Mr. E. Mosier, was asked to make a thorough and final study of the A.C.E. test results for the three full academic years 1928–31. He rendered a painstakingly accurate and comprehensive report with 50 tables and graphs and a detailed account of his procedures, of which only a fraction can be presented here.

For the total group, the situation is summed in Table 28, which covers 1,482 administrations of the A.C.E. *Alpha French Test* in the three-year period. Medians, means, and standard deviations are given for both 1ABC and 2AB.

The results are slightly higher for all levels and skills than in the Baird survey. At the end of the first-year sequence the average attainment is equivalent to four semesters in vocabulary, approximately seven semesters in grammar, and seven semesters in reading, with the upper fourth of the group squeezed into narrow limits below the maximum score. The peak of growth in vocabulary and reading is in 1B; in grammar, in 1C. Inasmuch as the type of grammar (functional) tested received special attention in 1C for the first time

TABLE 28

| COURSE | VOCABULARY (75) | | | | GRAMMAR (50) | | | | READING (28) | | | |
|---|---|---|---|---|---|---|---|---|---|---|---|---|
| | N | Md. | M | S.D. | N | Md. | M | S.D. | N | Md. | M | S.D. |
| 1A..... | 298 | 27.1 | ...... | ..... | 295 | 12.5 | 13.8 | 8.1 | 293 | 13.6 | 13.8 | 5.7 |
| 1B..... | 317 | 38.3 | 38.5 | 9.1 | 317 | 20.1 | 20.7 | 8.6 | 316 | 20.0 | 19.8 | 2.2 |
| 1C..... | 470 | 46.0 | 46.0 | 9.4 | 469 | 34.3 | 33.9 | 8.4 | 468 | 22.4 | 22.0 | 3.8 |
| 2A..... | 183 | 52.6 | 52.5 | 8.5 | 183 | 37.3 | 35.4 | ..... | 182 | 24.1 | 23.5 | 3.6 |
| 2B..... | 214 | 60.7 | 59.5 | 8.5 | 214 | 40.6 | 39.2 | 7.4 | 214 | 25.5 | 25.1 | 2.6 |

in the sequence, the gain in grammar proficiency in that quarter is quite understandable. But for the staff the growth of vocabulary and reading in the second quarter was more important.

Overlapping between the courses was not excessive,[14] as can be seen from Figures 3, 4, and 5, percentile graphs from the frequency tables with the right-hand $y$-axis numbered down, rather than up, to show the proportion of the group exceeding a given score.

In 1A, 8 per cent of the students do as well as, or better than, the average 1B student in vocabulary; 18 per cent in grammar; and 15 per cent in reading. In French 1B, 20 per cent of the students equal or exceed the average for 1C in vocabulary; 7 per cent in grammar; and 29 per cent in reading. In 1C, 23 per cent equal or exceed the average for 2A in vocabulary; 38 per cent in grammar; and 34 per cent in reading.

The upper quartile comparisons are equally significant. In French 1A, the upper 25 per cent of the students do as well as, or better than, 30 per cent of 1B in vocabulary; 42 per cent in grammar; and

34 per cent in reading. The upper quartile of 1B equals or betters 47 per cent of 1C in vocabulary; 21 per cent in grammar; and 57 per cent in reading. The upper quartile of 1C equals or exceeds 46 per cent of 2A in vocabulary; 68 per cent in grammar; and 62 per cent in reading. There is ample justification in these comparisons for the 61 promotions that were made during this period.

Again, as in the Baird survey, the 1ABC students without previous training in French were separated from the total group, but

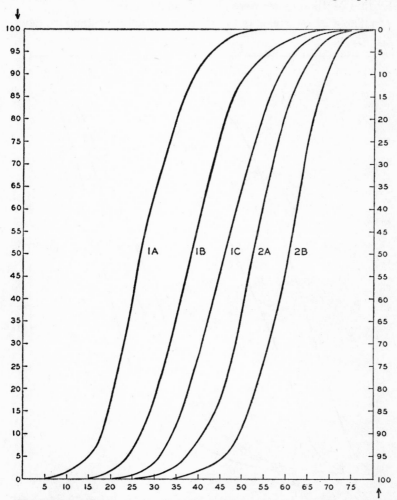

FIG. 3.—Percentile curves of scores in Vocabulary, A.C.E. French Test, for French 1A, 1B, 1C, 2A, and 2B.

Mosier considered only those whose study was continuous through the three courses of the sequence. There were 119 such cases. Since the students took the A.C.E. test at the end of each quarter, the norms represent achievement as measured at definite, known intervals of time, i.e., approximately three, six, and nine months within one and the same academic year. No delayed continuants, repeaters, "skips," or students with advanced standing were included in Mosier's data. The special group was as "pure" a product of the Reading Method as we were able to get.

In Table 29 the mean and median scores and the standard devia-

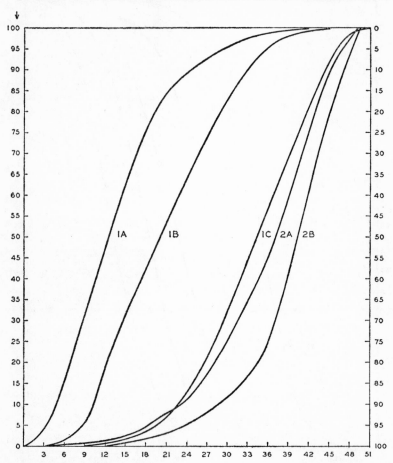

FIG. 4.—Percentile curves of scores in Grammar, A.C.E. French Test, for French 1A, 1B, 1C, 2A, and 2B.

tions on the A.C.E. *French Test* are given for each of the three quarters of French 1, for 119 "straight" continuants. In comparing the medians for this group with the medians for the total group (p. 162), one notes slight losses for the former in 1B and 1C vocabulary. In grammar the special group is superior to the total group at the 1A level, evens off at 1B, and drops below the latter at 1C. In reading, there is an equivalence throughout the sequence. When one

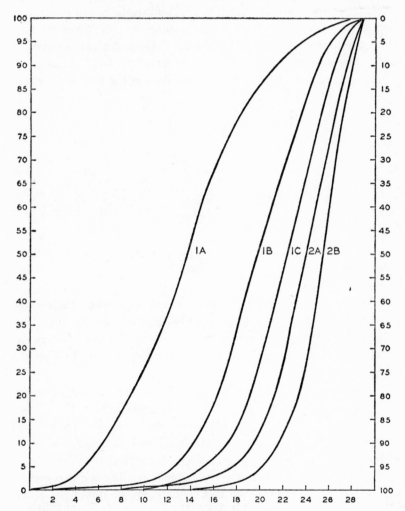

Fig. 5.—Percentile curves of scores in Reading, A.C.E. French Test, for French 1A, 1B, 1C, 2A, and 2B.

considers the constituency of the total group and the fact that 23 superior students skipped 1B, the performance of these 119 continuants demonstrates conclusively the validity of the procedures by which they were taught.

In order to analyze the effect of French 1 training as compared with high-school training, special tables were prepared, representing separately the distribution and medians for each course alone or in combination for vocabulary, grammar, and reading. The cases were then grouped by their first college course, any previous training being presumably taken in high school. Here are two sources of possible error: first, some cases no doubt were transfers from other institutions, and, second, the tests were given at the end of the quar-

TABLE 29

| Course | Vocabulary (75) | | | | Grammar (50) | | | | Reading (28) | | | |
|---|---|---|---|---|---|---|---|---|---|---|---|---|
| | $N$ | Md. | $M$ | S.D. | $N$ | Md. | $M$ | S.D. | $N$ | Md. | $M$ | S.D. |
| 1A..... | 119 | 28.1 | 28.4 | 7.4 | 119 | 13.1 | 13.8 | 6.0 | 118 | 13.6 | 14.0 | 4.8 |
| 1B..... | 119 | 37.5 | 37.1 | 8.9 | 119 | 20.0 | 20.4 | 7.9 | 119 | 20.3 | 20.4 | 3.7 |
| 1C..... | 118 | 43.8 | 45.0 | 9.0 | 118 | 31.4 | 28.0 | 7.6 | 118 | 22.1 | 21.7 | 3.7 |

ter, thereby adding one quarter of college work to any previous experience. However, such error would tend to obscure, rather than to exaggerate, the effect.

Table 30 sums the median scores in the three skills for each of the five courses (1ABC, 2AB). It is cross-indexed, the first vertical column showing the course first taken in the College (and hence the amount of previous training) and the horizontal lines showing the levels, or courses, in which the median score was made.

If we select, as an example, French 1B as a point of entry into the College sequences and if we compare the medians on the second horizontal line with the scores that lie above or below in the vertical columns, we note that the 1B "starters" had an average score of 38.5 in vocabulary, compared with 38.0 for the students that entered at the 1A point, and that in grammar and reading the two groups were equally proficient. Since the 1B entrants no doubt presented one unit of French from high school, representing nine months of exposure, their total exposure at the end of 1B (when the test was

given) amounted to twelve months. Yet they were no more proficient than the 1A beginners, who had had only half that exposure
at the time of the 1B test. Furthermore, at the 2A and 2B levels, the
1A group definitely surpassed the 1B group in all three skills.

In fact, the 1A beginners, who did all their work in the College
sequences, were clearly superior in performance to all other groups,
except for the 1C group in vocabulary. Since the 1C entrants had at
least 21 months of training at the 1C test level, and the 2A and 2B
entrants had, respectively, 25.5 and 30 months of training in the
language, there would seem to be no doubt about the tremendous
saving in time possible through beginning the language study in 1A.

TABLE 30

| FIRST COURSE TAKEN | LEVEL | | | | | | | | | | | | | | |
|---|---|---|---|---|---|---|---|---|---|---|---|---|---|---|---|
| | Vocabulary | | | | | Grammar | | | | | Reading | | | | |
| | 1A | 1B | 1C | 2A | 2B | 1A | 1B | 1C | 2A | 2B | 1A | 1B | 1C | 2A | 2B |
| 1A.... | 27.1 | 38.0 | 44.8 | 53.3 | 63.5 | 12.5 | 20.1 | 32.5 | 36.4 | 40.3 | 13.6 | 20.0 | 22.3 | 26.4 | 26.9 |
| 1B.... | | 38.5 | 44.5 | 51.3 | 59.4 | | 20.0 | 33.5 | 35.7 | 39.8 | | 20.0 | 22.5 | 24.1 | 26.5 |
| 1C.... | | | 46.8 | 53.5 | 59.2 | | | 36.7 | 40.9 | 42.0 | | | 22.4 | 24.0 | 25.7 |
| 2A.... | | | | 50.9 | 63.1 | | | | 31.3 | 41.6 | | | | 23.4 | 26.3 |
| 2B.... | | | | | 60.7 | | | | | 40.0 | | | | | 25.0 |

The average 2B entrant spent 30 months in doing what he could
have done as well or better in half that time, had he taken the five
courses offered in the College.

In another set of graphic studies representing the median and
lower quartile points of the Chicago group and the upper quartile
norms of the national group, plotted against time by quarter and
semester, respectively, the statistical significance of the Chicago
group was very apparent. In all cases except grammar below the 1C
level, the performance of the lower quartile exceeded that of 75 per
cent of the national group.

The validity of these comparisons may be judged from the data
in Table 31, which presents the means, standard deviations, and
standard error for French 1C and for two semesters, with the differ-

ence between the means, the standard error of the difference, and the critical ratio.

An attempt was made within the limitations of the data to learn whether or not the superiority was due to superiority in method of training or to superiority in initial ability. The result of the investigation is shown in Figure 6, a graphic representation of the superiority in intelligence compared with the superiority in achievement in French 1C.

At the left is the distribution of scores for 36,667 students (American Council norms) on Thurstone's *A.C. Psychological Examination*, followed by the distribution for 679 entering Chicago Freshmen of the same year (1932).[15] Then appears the same type of distribution

TABLE 31

| | VOCABULARY (75) | | | | GRAMMAR (50) | | | | READING (28) | | | |
|---|---|---|---|---|---|---|---|---|---|---|---|---|
| | $N$ | $M$ | $\sigma$ | $\Sigma$ | $N$ | $M$ | $\sigma$ | $\Sigma$ | $N$ | $M$ | $\sigma$ | $\Sigma$ |
| 1C............ | 470 | 46.0 | 9.4 | .41 | 470 | 33.9 | 8.4 | .37 | 470 | 22.0 | 3.8 | .17 |
| 2 semesters..... | 297 | 29.1 | 7.9 | .46 | 297 | 22.7 | 10.1 | .59 | 297 | 14.2 | 4.2 | .24 |
| Difference...... | .... | 16.9 | ..... | .61 | .... | 11.2 | ..... | .70 | .... | 7.8 | ..... | .29 |
| Ratio.......... | .... | ..... | 27.7 | .... | .... | ..... | 16.0 | .... | .... | ..... | 26.9 | .... |

for total group vocabulary, grammar, and reading at the 1C level, the only level at which the Chicago and American Council groups are comparable. The shaded areas in every case represent the *interquartile ranges*.

In this analysis there are three assumptions necessary, which do not, however, appear unreasonable: (1) The distribution of intelligence of students taking French, both here and elsewhere, is comparable to the distribution of the total group. This assumption was tested for 88 students who took 1ABC in the College and was found to be true of them.[16] (2) The distribution of intelligence of the A.C.E. French test group is comparable to the distribution for the A.C.E. intelligence test norms. For this assumption there was no empirical check, but it does not appear to be an unreasonable one. (3) Intelligence is a fair criterion of initial ability to learn French.[17]

If these assumptions are granted, the interpretation of the diagram may be made in the following manner. On the American

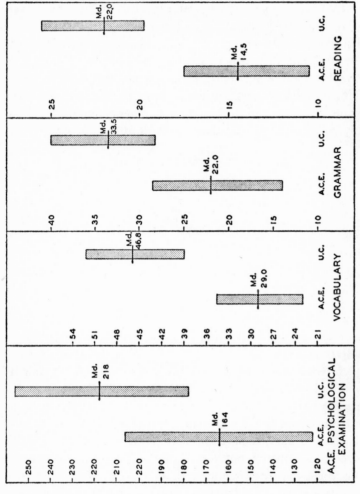

Fig. 6.—Superiority in intelligence compared with superiority in language achievement. Interquartile ranges for the national one-year college group and the University of Chicago French 1C group on the A.C.E. tests.

Council psychological test there is a sizable proportion of the inter-quartile range lying below the median of the Chicago group and above the median of the American Council group and having the same mean intelligence. Given this overlapping of intelligence by the two hypothetical groups, one can expect to find a similar over-lapping in the interquartile range of the language tests. The fact that there is none between the two groups in any of the tests leads to the inference that some other variable than general intelligence is operative here. From this and other evidence the variable would appear to be the difference in instructional procedure, the known major difference between the two groups under comparison. This is the only solution which the data at hand afford. In view of the

TABLE 32*

|  | Vocabulary | Reading | Grammar | Art. Lang. | Analogies | Total Score |
|---|---|---|---|---|---|---|
| Vocabulary....... | ......... | .5514 | .5743 | .0310 | .0853 | .3767 |
| Reading.......... | .5514 | ......... | .4076 | .1139 | .1514 | .4535 |
| Grammar......... | .5743 | .4076 | ......... | .1783 | .0900 | .3065 |
| Art. lang......... | .0310 | .1139 | .1783 | ......... | ......... | ......... |
| Analogies......... | .0853 | .1514 | .0900 | ......... | ......... | ......... |
| Total score... | .3767 | .4535 | .3065 | ......... | ......... | ......... |

* Partial correlations, holding intelligence constant, with total score, Thurstone A.C.E. psychological test: vocabulary/grammar, .520; vocabulary/reading, .460; grammar/reading, .318.

reasonableness of the assumptions on which it is based, it is very probably the correct one.

Other intercorrelations were computed for a group of 88 "straight" continuants in French 1 who had taken the A.C.E. psychological test, namely: 1C vocabulary, 1C grammar, 1C reading, and total score, artificial language, and analogies from the Thurstone test. The data are tabulated in Table 32. The intercorrelations of the language skills, although not very high, are significant, particularly between vocabulary and reading. In 1948, the College examiners found a correlation of .53 between vocabulary and reading in a French 1 comprehensive examination taken by 236 students; and again, in 1949, a coefficient of .55 in an examination taken by 222 students. The coefficient of .5514 for this special group would there-fore seem to correspond with later findings.[18]

In fact, the dominant single factor in both whole and partial correlations appears to be vocabulary, and *not* grammar! The fact that the highest single correlation is between vocabulary and grammar and that the lowest is between grammar and reading is perhaps explainable by the emphasis placed upon learning grammar as vocabulary throughout the sequence.[19]

The prognostic value of the two parts of the A.C.E. psychological test (artificial language, analogies) in respect to the language abilities tested is quite negligible; of more importance is the relation of total score to reading.

Mosier completed his survey with three studies: (1) the effect of promotion on exceptional students, (2) the effect of repeating a

TABLE 33

| TYPE OF PROMOTION | N | VOCABULARY | | | GRAMMAR | | | READING | | |
|---|---|---|---|---|---|---|---|---|---|---|
| | | Md. | M | S.D. | Md. | M | S.D. | Md. | M | S.D. |
| 1A/1C.... | 23 | 37.2 | ...... | ...... | 24.1 | 24.6 | 7.5 | 20.4 | 20.4 | 5.2 |
| | | 48.9 | 49.0 | 10.4 | 38.6 | 38.0 | 7.4 | 23.7 | 23.4 | 3.5 |
| 1B/2A.... | 4 | 45.0 | 44.0 | 3.8 | 24.0 | 24.0 | 4.5 | 24.7 | 24.4 | 0.3 |
| | | 50.0 | 57.5 | 3.2 | 36.0 | 34.5 | ...... | 25.0 | 25.0 | 1.4 |
| 1C/2B.... | 34 | 55.0 | 54.5 | 7.5 | 42.0 | 41.7 | 4.6 | 24.9 | 25.0 | 1.8 |
| | | 62.3 | 62.5 | 5.5 | 41.9 | 41.5 | 5.7 | 26.7 | 26.4 | 1.9 |

course failed, and (3) a comparison between Old Plan and New Plan students.

Between 1928 and 1931 there were more than 61 promotions: 23 cases of 1A/1C, 4 cases of 1B/2A, and 34 cases of 1C/2B. The first type was preferred practice with beginners; the third, with 1ABC continuants and two-unit entrants. Medians, means, and standard deviations for each of the three types are shown in Table 33. In each bracket the first horizontal row indicates the median, mean, and deviation in the course *from* which the student was promoted; the second row, similar data for the course *to* which he was promoted. The data in this analysis differ very little from the data given by Baird for the 1927–30 promotions, some of whom were included in the Mosier tabulation. As in the previous study, promotion led in every case to higher achievement in the three skills, despite the already high initial attainment.

For the 25 "repeaters" whose subsequent work was analyzed, the dividends were indeed small. Only in 1A and 1B vocabulary, on their repeating the course, did they attain a median score equal to, or better than, the median for the total group. In all cases the gains over the first scores were slight, particularly in grammar at the 1A and 1B levels. Only the upper fourth achieved a passable language proficiency. Those who repeated 1B and 1C derived more profit than those who repeated 1A. In general, the evidence indicated only a small chance of satisfactory accomplishment on a course retaken.

The special study of Old Plan and New Plan continuants in French 1 was not very fruitful because of the small number of cases (47) for the New Plan period. The latter group showed a slight advantage in reading but lost heavily (5.9 points) in third-quarter grammar. The formal disciplines of grammar and composition seemed to have suffered somewhat by the new freedom.[20]

## 6. *The Cheshire Factor Analysis*

Statistical proof was lacking in respect to the relation between the *amount* of extensive reading done at a specific level of learning and achievement in vocabulary, grammar, and reading at that level. Had quantity of reading anything to do with skill in reading, and, if so, in what degree or ratio?

Miss Leone Cheshire, a statistician in the employ of the University examiners, undertook to find an answer to the question by means of a factor analysis of the twelve variables: French vocabulary, grammar, and reading scores and amount read in 1A, 1B, and 1C, based on a sample of 107 University of Chicago College students who completed French 1 in straight continuation between 1927 and 1932.

The sample included most of the 119 continuants analyzed by Mosier. Their reading amounts were obtained from the check list of extensive reading, which served as part of the basic data on quantity, rate, and kind of extensive reading discussed in the preceding chapter.

The sampling of cases shown in Table 34 is illustrative of the nature of the data sheet on which the Cheshire study was based. The data sheet lists for each case the scores on the A.C.E. French test and the extensive reading total for each quarter-course. The reading amounts are cumulative for 1B and 1C, because any effect that the reading might have on the growth of the language abilities would be an effect of the total amount of reading done, up to the time of the test on those abilities.

From the data sheet, tables were made showing the distribution of scores, percentile ranks, and norms in preparation for the calculations. Table 35 is a summary of the norms on the A.C.E. test

TABLE 34

| Case No. | French 1A | | | | French 1B | | | | French 1C | | | |
|---|---|---|---|---|---|---|---|---|---|---|---|---|
| | Voc. | Gram. | Read. | Amt. | Voc. | Gram. | Read. | Amt. | Voc. | Gram. | Read. | Amt. |
| 1...... | 27 | 13 | 11 | 348 | 26 | 27 | 25 | 1,164 | 46 | 37 | 23 | 2,175 |
| 15...... | 29 | 17 | 11 | 110 | 30 | 14 | 18 | 747 | 26 | 24 | 11 | 1,644 |
| 79...... | 30 | 18 | 21 | 393 | 43 | 31 | 22 | 1,896 | 41 | 34 | 25 | 3,054 |
| 237...... | 23 | 8 | 8 | 130 | 42 | 11 | 15 | 680 | 47 | 21 | 19 | 1,475 |
| 346...... | 35 | 21 | 21 | 378 | 51 | 25 | 27 | 1,288 | 46 | 36 | 27 | 2,382 |
| 496...... | 25 | 9 | 12 | 246 | 33 | 12 | 23 | 1,828 | 42 | 22 | 18 | 2,975 |

TABLE 35*

| | Vocabulary | | | Grammar | | | Reading | | | Amount Read | | |
|---|---|---|---|---|---|---|---|---|---|---|---|---|
| | $Q^3$ | Md. | $Q^1$ | $Q^3$ | Md. | $Q^1$ | $Q^3$ | Md. | $Q^1$ | $Q^3$ | Md. | $Q^1$ |
| 1A | 33.8 | 28.3 | 23.8 | 19.8 | 15.0 | 11.0 | 18.3 | 13.6 | 11.2 | 383.6 | 250.0 | 168.9 |
| 1B | 42.5 | 36.9 | 31.8 | 28.1 | 22.7 | 15.1 | 22.2 | 19.5 | 16.8 | 1,276.8 | 1,046.4 | 792.5 |
| 1C | 51.2 | 44.0 | 37.8 | 37.4 | 32.4 | 27.6 | 23.4 | 20.9 | 18.1 | 2,327.7 | 2,108.4 | 1,858.3 |

* Decimals have been reduced to one point. The norms for amount read are for cumulative reading amounts. Md. is the median, or middle score.

and for the amount of extensive reading at each of the three levels of French 1, for the 107 straight continuants. There are only a few minor deviations between the median scores for this group and those for the Mosier group discussed above.[21]

Using the Pearson product-moment formula, Miss Cheshire calculated the 66 experimentally independent intercorrelations of these twelve variables. She then used the Thurstone multiple-factor technique to isolate the general factors or primary abilities accounting for the major part of the correlations, first locating the twelve variables with reference to an arbitrary set of orthogonal axes by

Thurstone's centroid method and later rotating the centroid axes into a new set of axes giving all positive or zero loadings, using Thurstone's analytic method.

The five centroid co-ordinates for each test are recorded in the respective rows of Table 36. The first entry in each row is the projection of that test on the first centroid axis; the second entry in each

TABLE 36

| Test | I | II | III | IV | V | $h_s^2$ |
|---|---|---|---|---|---|---|
| 1A—Voc...... | .712 | .095 | .029 | −.277 | .062 | .6402 |
| 1A—Gram.... | .618 | .278 | −.164 | −.480 | −.115 | .7297 |
| 1A—Read.... | .669 | .310 | −.173 | −.119 | .605 | .9538 |
| 1A—Amt..... | .480 | −.674 | −.096 | −.054 | −.137 | .7156 |
| 1B—Voc...... | .605 | .371 | .400 | .077 | −.040 | .6712 |
| 1B—Gram.... | .734 | .260 | −.289 | −.083 | −.342 | .8137 |
| 1B—Read..... | .743 | .191 | −.177 | .255 | .161 | .7108 |
| 1B—Amt..... | .513 | −.789 | −.030 | .043 | .155 | .9125 |
| 1C—Voc...... | .660 | .346 | .406 | .211 | −.081 | .7712 |
| 1C—Gram.... | .746 | .193 | −.128 | .075 | −.354 | .7411 |
| 1C—Read..... | .614 | .224 | −.100 | .405 | .182 | .6343 |
| 1C—Amt..... | .524 | −.736 | .060 | .081 | .042 | .8282 |
| $\Sigma a^2$.......... | 4.9305 | 2.2498 | .5803 | .6246 | .7371 | ......... |
| $\Sigma a$.......... | 7.618 | .069 | −.082 | .134 | .138 | 9.1223 |
| Maximum contribution... | .557 | .623 | .165 | .230 | .366 | ......... |

row is the projection of that test on the second centroid axis, and similarly for the remaining three factors.

The total variance for each test is unity. That part of the variance accounted for by these factors, i.e., the common factor variance ($h_s^2$), is indicated in the last column of the table. From this column, we see that the five factors (numbered in Roman numerals) contribute from 63 to 95 per cent of the total variance for each test.

Projections on a sixth and seventh centroid axis were also calculated, but their maximum contributions were too nearly the size of expected errors to be significant, and they were discarded.

In order to determine the meaning of the five factors, it was necessary to rotate the axes into a new set of axes which would give all positive or zero loadings and which would maximize the number of zero loadings. The results are shown in Table 37. Each horizontal row gives the five co-ordinates of the test referred to the new axes, which are now no longer orthogonal, but oblique. Negative loadings as high as −0.12 are allowed; some negative loadings near zero would be expected, because of experimental error. Inspection of the variables having highest loadings in each column should enable us to identify each of the five factors. This process of "naming" is, of course, arbitrary and entirely independent of the mathematical analysis. However, in this analysis, the names seem to be self-evident except for Factor I, which might be interpreted in a number of ways.

Factor I is present to a fairly high degree in vocabulary, grammar, and reading for all three units (1A, 1B, 1C), with the predominant

TABLE 37

| Test | I | II | III | IV | V | Check |
|------|------|------|------|------|------|-------|
| 1A—Voc. | .52 | .26 | .36 | .42 | .15 | 1.71 |
| 1A—Gram. | .55 | .00 | .02 | .45 | .40 | 1.42 |
| 1A—Read. | .92 | .00 | .01 | .59 | .00 | 1.52 |
| 1A—Amt. | − .07 | .77 | − .12 | − .04 | .19 | .73 |
| 1B—Voc. | .44 | − .03 | .55 | .11 | .25 | 1.32 |
| 1B—Gram. | .44 | − .01 | − .11 | .02 | .76 | 1.10 |
| 1B—Read. | .61 | .08 | − .03 | .04 | .42 | 1.12 |
| 1B—Amt. | .02 | .91 | − .08 | .06 | − .05 | .86 |
| 1C—Voc. | .42 | .00 | .54 | − .01 | .33 | 1.28 |
| 1C—Gram. | .35 | .06 | .02 | − .10 | .73 | 1.06 |
| 1C—Read. | .52 | .00 | .01 | − .08 | .36 | .81 |
| 1C—Amt. | − .03 | .87 | .02 | − .02 | .03 | .87 |
| Check Σ. | 4.68 | 2.92 | 1.18 | 1.45 | 3.57 | ........ |
| Actual Σ. | 4.69 | 2.91 | 1.19 | 1.44 | 3.57 | 13.80 |

loadings in reading, and with a tendency for 1A to exceed 1B and 1C. This factor is conspicuously absent in amount of extensive reading. It may possibly be a factor of general intelligence; but if this is true, why should 1A exceed 1B and 1C, since the same group was tested at all three units? It may possibly be a knowledge of subject matter as derived through reading ability, where the largest amount of this ability is present in 1A. This factor could also be a general verbal factor, but this could not be determined without the addition of some verbal variables distinctly different from language tests. Or it could be a general language factor uncorrelated with amount read.[22] Whatever it is, it is related particularly to reading ability and to the work of 1A as compared to the later units.

Factor II is conspicuously *amount of extensive reading*. All other loadings are near zero except 1A vocabulary. This latter loading may be interpreted as vocabulary learned in 1A through extensive reading. Here is clear evidence of the constant value of the quantitative reading experience in French 1.

Factor III is *vocabulary*, since the only loadings of any significance are in vocabulary at each of the three learning levels. The loadings for 1B and 1C are of the same order of magnitude and are greater than for 1A. This would seem to indicate greater attention to vocabulary-building in the last two units.

Factor IV is quite definitely the *training in 1A*, since all other loadings vanish for all practical considerations. The 1A training in reading seems to be more significant than that in vocabulary and grammar. As in the case of Factor I, here also 1A tends to exceed the other two units. If Factor IV is indeed the training of the first unit, then (as a colleague said) "we have something with which to frighten our children of 1A." There seems to be statistical support here for our long-standing belief that the materials and methods of the first unit in the sequence set the mold for all subsequent work. Factor IV may well be the "reading approach."

Factor V has its highest loadings in *grammar*. In this case, 1B and 1C loadings exceed the loading for 1A. The oral and written composition in 1B and 1C and the review of grammar in 1C would account for the predominance of Factor V in the last two units. The fairly high loadings for vocabulary and reading in 1BC may indicate the degree to which the study of formal grammar and language use contribute to those commands. Conversely, the zero loading in 1A reading may indicate the lack of formal reproductive grammar at that level and consequently the lack of grammatical contribution to reading ability.[23]

The Cheshire analyses closed the long series of measurements begun in 1927 and ending in 1932. Her findings were indexes of relationships and not necessarily of causes within French 1. The causes could be extremely indirect. But, taken with the Baird and Mosier findings and our own data and opinions, the Cheshire study rounded out the body of proof that we needed to establish the validity of our procedures. We rested the inquiry there.

## 7. *Tryouts*

From 1927 to 1932 there was a fairly consistent attempt, nation-wide, to modify modern foreign language instruction so as to conform more or less to the recommendations of the Modern Language Study. Despite the protests of the "oralists," the ranks of the "direct reading methodists" were swelling, especially in the Middle West and West, and the interest in objectively scorable tests grew rapidly.[24]

Acting as a sort of laboratory and service center for anyone interested in the Reading Method, the College language staff tried out and criticized a score of attainment tests for a number of teachers and schools.

Among the tests were Coleman's true-false form to replace his "Silent Reading" section in the A.C.E. *Alpha French Test* (1929), a French version of the Burgess *Silent Reading Test* (1926), an adaptation of the Thorndike-McCall *Reading Test* (1926), the A.C.E. trial form FT-10 of the *French Test* (1926), the A.C.E. *French Grammar Test* (selection type, by F. D. Cheydleur) (1927), the Lundeberg-Tharp *Audition Test in French* (1928), the Iowa *First Semester French Examination* (1930), the Iowa *Reading Comprehension Test* (1930), the Iowa *Second Semester French Examination* (1930), the Iowa *First* and *Second Year French Comprehension Tests* (based on the "Chicago French Series") (1929——), the Eddy *French Progress Tests* (1928–29), and French scholarship and placement examinations for the University of Chicago (1930–32).

The tryout of the Iowa *First Semester French Test* (1930 form) illustrates the type of service we tried to render. The test, based on vocabulary, grammar, and pronunciation material in *Beginning French, Si nous lisions*, and *Pierrille*, was administered to 253 students in 12 sections at the University of Iowa. The maximum score was 168; their median was 98.8; lower quartile 72.3; and upper quartile 129.7. On the A.C.E. *Alpha French Test*, Part II (silent reading), their median score was 9.75, with a lower quartile of 6.7 and upper quartile of 12.3. We were asked to check the group against our French 1A and to criticize the test.

The two tests were administered to a winter section of 1A composed of repeaters, unclassified students, validation and limited-credit cases, several belated beginners, and a faculty wife. A more homogeneous group was not available at that time of the year. The 1A group attained the following norms: (1) on the A.C.E. reading test, a median of 14, lower quartile 9, upper quartile 16; (2) on the Iowa *First Semester Test*, a total score median of 116, with a lower quartile of 91 and an upper quartile of 153, and a range of 73–156. A comparison of the two groups gave the advantage to 1A.

The Iowa French test had four parts: Part I tested reading comprehension, using two techniques, i.e., translation of selected items in a continuous French passage, and English response to French questions; Part II tested vocabulary, using three techniques, i.e., matching, English equivalents, and selection of opposites; Part III tested pronunciation, using matching and correspondences; and Part IV tested grammar comprehension, using multiple-choice, four-response technique, in English. The time set was 90 minutes. The maximum score was 168, without weighting of the items, to which Part I (reading) contributed less than half (78 points).

Four recommendations were made: (1) to reduce the time to 75 minutes, since one-third of the test group completed the test in less time; (2) to lower the credits for Parts II, III, and IV, since it was possible for a student to pass the test without proof of reading ability gained through Part I; (3) to omit the section on recognition grammar because of its doubtful validity in a test of reading attainment at the end of a semester's training; and (4) to omit the section in Part I which involved proverbs because of their impractical and puzzle-solving values. These recommendations were put into effect at Iowa the following year.

After 1932, general interest in experimental studies in foreign language teaching waned. Mainly a few colleges in the Middle West and isolated investigators continued experimenting along the lines suggested by the Modern Language Study.[25] The early attempts to transplant a reading method to unprepared or unsuitable terrain or to engraft it upon a alien or traditional procedure or to force it upon a teaching staff unsympathetic toward its principles[26] did not meet with conspicuous success. Today, if one sifts through the hundreds of articles, addresses, reports, and abstracts for 1925–33, one recovers only a small residue of substantial, proved facts that apply to the

Reading Method. And even less is to be found during the depression years, World War II, and the A.S.T.P. mirage.

Nevertheless, during these eight years there were sixteen definite, directed experiments outside the University of Chicago, which purposed to evaluate achievement in vocabulary, grammar, and reading in high-school and college classes, employing a "direct reading method" in the Chicago or the Iowa pattern and evaluating their achievement by means of standard, "new-type" tests. Since the

TABLE 38

| CASE | TERM | LOCATION | DIRECTOR | INDEX No. |
|------|------|----------|----------|-----------|
| | | I. Colleges | | |
| 1...... | 1925–27 | Univ. of Iowa | C. E. Young and J. Daus | I, 199 |
| 2...... | 1926–27 | Univ. of Illinois | J. B. Tharp and E. Murray | I, 197 |
| 3...... | 1927–28 | Univ. of Wisconsin | F. Cheydleur | I, 192 |
| 4...... | 1930–32 | Univ. of Iowa | G. Cochran | .......... |
| 5...... | 1930–32 | Univ. of Wisconsin | F. Cheydleur | II, 387 |
| 6...... | 1930–33 | (Group B) | F. Cheydleur | II, 387 |
| | | II. Schools | | |
| 7...... | 1926–27 | Univ. H.S. (Iowa) | G. Steep | I, 195 |
| 8...... | 1926–29 | Minneapolis | G. Steep and A. Gay | I, 195 |
| 9...... | 1927–29 | Univ. H.S. (Iowa) | H. Eddy | I, 171 |
| 10...... | 1929–30 | Milwaukee | C. E. Young | I, 200 |
| 11...... | 1930–32 | Milwaukee | Coleman, Young, *et al.* | II, 388 |
| 12...... | 1931–32 | Reading, Pa. | C. L. Cassel | II, 386 |
| 13...... | 1932–33 | New York City | S. Wolfson | II, 392–93 |
| 14...... | 1930–32 | Los Angeles | W. H. Shield | II, 387 |
| 15...... | 1930–31 | (Group B) | F. Cheydleur | II, 387 |
| 16...... | 1930–33 | (Group A) | F. Cheydleur | II, 387 |

experiments have some bearing upon the University of Chicago experiment, they are tabulated here (Table 38) in their chronological order, and commented upon briefly. With the exception of case 4, the results were published and are abstracted in the first two volumes of Coleman's *Analytical Bibliography*, the index numbers to which are given in the last column.

In case 1, Young and Daus, profiting by the mistakes of the first year, in the second year applied fairly closely our 1925–26 procedures and materials to two matched groups of six sections each.

At the end of the first semester, their total score median for reading, vocabulary, idioms, and pronunciation was 148.38 for the experimental group, and 132.16 for the control group taught by a grammar-translation method. At the end of the second semester, the median for the experimental group was 169.2 compared to 133.0 for the control group. The investigators expressed no conclusion.

In the Preface to his *Introduction to the Study of French* the author stated that twenty recitation hours were a "workable minimum of time for grammatical preparation for reading" and that supervised reading could be undertaken safely after twelve lessons. The statement drew the fire of the reviewers (Sparkman, Krappe, *et al.*) and prompted the Modern Language Study committee to commission Professor Tharp to set up a trial group at the University of Illinois (case 2) to test the ability of beginning college students to "learn to read things really worth while in a year."

The experimenters did not follow our reading method, did not complete the *Introduction to the Study of French*, ignored oral-aural practice, used translation as the sole check on reading, and omitted from their published report such essential data as second-semester procedures, amounts read, editions used, reading averages, time exposure, and number of cases involved. The only "outside" reading was 100 pages (unspecified) the first semester and *La Tulipe noire* the second semester. Class or assigned readings during the second semester included *Le Pêcheur d'Islande*, *Le Livre de mon ami*, and *Colomba*.

On the Iowa *Placement FT-1 French Test* and the A.C.E. *Alpha French Test*, Part III (silent reading), given at the end of each semester, the "reading" sections surpassed the "grammar" sections by 20–25 per cent in vocabulary and by 26–40 per cent in reading, and achieved from 16 to 41 per cent of the grammar learned in the regular sections. The experimenters concluded that "early and much practice in reading is an excellent way to read French and like it."

The third college experiment (case 3) involved control and experimental sections of comparable size and general intelligence. The director was given an outline of the method used in French 1, but, in practice, the experimental "method" consisted principally of the basic materials of French 1 and an increased amount of reading.[27] The final report, more favorable to the control than to the experimental sections, expressed belief that the data were inconclusive because of the presence of elements unlike those in the Iowa and Chicago experiments. In his correspondence with the author, Professor Cheydleur left no doubt as to the nature of the administrative barriers that impeded his research.[28]

Using the Eddy series and following rather closely the procedures recommended in her teacher's manual, *Training for Reading*,[29] Miss Grace Cochran directed two successive groups of beginners at the University of Iowa (case 4) in a reading method, with the results shown in Table 39 and obtained at the end of the first semes-

TABLE 39

| Group | Vocabulary (75) | | | | Grammar (50) | | | | Reading (28) | | | |
|---|---|---|---|---|---|---|---|---|---|---|---|---|
| | N | Q¹ | M | Q³ | N | Q¹ | M | Q³ | N | Q¹ | M | Q³ |
| 1931..... | 238 | 27.1 | 32.4 | 38.8 | 231 | 18.3 | 23.5 | 29.4 | 239 | 13.1 | 16.1 | 18.6 |
| 1932..... | 171 | 28.0 | 33.1 | 39.3 | 170 | 21.1 | 26.4 | 33.4 | 170 | 13.5 | 16.9 | 19.7 |
| National*. | 389 | 18.7 | 23.8 | 28.6 | 1,568 | 30.3 | 36.4 | 42.9 | 299 | 8.8 | 12.5 | 16.0 |

\* The national norms are for one semester, college level.

ter on the A.C.E. *Alpha French Test*, with the Cheydleur selection-type *Grammar Test* substituted for Part II, the grammar section prepared by Coleman.

In a comparison of the Iowa and the national norms, the Iowa group gained in vocabulary 36 per cent for the 1931 contingent and 39 per cent for the 1932 group; reading gains were 29 per cent in 1931 and 35 in 1932. The loss in grammar decreased from 35 per cent in 1931 to 28 in 1932. Sixteen per cent of the students reached or exceeded the fourth-semester norm in reading; 21 per cent exceeded the norm in vocabulary. Nineteen per cent attained the first-semester norm in grammar, "a carry-over from functional to synthetic grammar, [states Miss Cochran] which should form a strong foundation upon which to build the speech and writing units." The fourth college experiment met more fully the essential conditions of the Reading Method than any other experimental tryout in the eight-year period.[30] It ran continuously until its merger into the Iowa Individualized Study Plan in 1934.

Undaunted by his 1927–28 experience, Professor Cheydleur

launched a second and a third trial of the reading method at the University of Wisconsin (cases 5 and 6) between 1930 and 1933. The results were combined with others obtained in the wider investigation (cases 14, 15, 16) reported in detail in Volume XVII of the *Publications* of the Modern Language Study.[31] Undertaken at the instigation of the Committee on Modern Language Teaching and financed in part by the Study, it was the most ambitious and extensive attempt to evaluate attainment by the reading method that was made. Any shortcomings in Cheydleur's data are the inescapable result of the premises he was obliged to accept and the conditions in the fifty or more institutions which he could not control. In many instances he was forced to assume or to interpret conditions, procedures, and attitudes on which he lacked specific information and which no doubt affected his final conclusions.

The experiment involved approximately 2,400 students and 200 teachers, distributed geographically as follows: *High Schools:* California (10), Connecticut (1), Illinois (3), Iowa (4), Maryland (1), Michigan (1), Minnesota (3), Mississippi (1) Montana (1), New Hampshire (1), New York (2), Ohio (5), Pennsylvania (1), Tennessee (1), Utah (1), Vermont (1), Wisconsin (7). *Colleges:* Georgia State College for Women, Burlington Junior College, St. Ambrose (Davenport, Iowa), Fort Dodge Junior College, State University of Iowa, Washington (Iowa) Junior College, Macalester College, William Woods College (Fulton, Missouri), Hiram College, Otterbein College, Knoxville College, University of Tennessee, University of Wisconsin.

These were among the 200 schools named by the University of Chicago Press as using the "Chicago French Series," i.e., *Beginning French, French Workbook, Progress Tests, Si nous lisions,* and *Pierrille.* They agreed to administer the A.C.E. tests periodically and to report the results to the director.

The investigation proceeded mainly by correspondence over a period of three years and included one-semester and two-semester results, lack of funds and materials preventing any observation of repeated experience in teaching or in second-year continuation study with the reading method. It was a herculean task performed under difficult conditions.

Some of the limitations of the inquiry[32] should be of interest to anyone contemplating the investigation of language instruction on a large scale. The financial limitations excluded the extension of the experimental study into the critical second year and did not permit comparisons with other procedures, except in three city systems, namely, Rochester, Cleveland, and Milwaukee. The educational limitations resulted from the number, size, nature, and location of the co-operating schools; the lack of uniformity in time exposure, class size and composition, maturity levels, studial requirements, and test conditions; the lack of positive knowledge by the director concerning the adherence to the principles and texts of the method on the part of some of the teachers,[33] and the unwarranted spread of the first-year materials over two years by some of the high schools and over two semesters by most of the colleges, tending to lower the medians in comparison with the national norms. The premise was faulty that institutions purchasing the "Chicago French Series" texts were *ipso facto* following a reading method or that a uniform method could be deduced from the materials and followed by 200 teachers in 50 schools, in spite of the instructions issued in manuals, prefaces, and correspondence.

Information was lacking on admission requirements, standards, intelligence quotients, the presence of repeaters or other types of nonbeginners; on the attitude, experience, and co-operation of the teachers involved; and on the reliability of cross-sections of previous scores obtained by eclectic methods and furnished by the teachers.[34] There were also such matters as the disparity in section size (seventeen numbered between 10 and 20 students), failures to complete the program, the unsuitability of series materials for college classes, and the lack of greater representation among the co-operating schools in respect to the average standard of instruction responsible for the national norms.

The survey attempted to do what, in all probability, was impossible. Had the director been able to set up and supervise in person each experimental unit, the results would have been quite different and more reliable. Nevertheless, it is not without value as a demonstration of what can be accomplished by a mass application of new and unfamiliar methods to language teaching.

The results were measured by means of the A.C.E. *Alpha French Test*, Part I (vocabulary), Part III (silent reading), and the Cheydleur selection-type *Grammar Test* in place of Part II (Coleman's grammar section).

In vocabulary, 19 of the 47 schools surpassed the national median by from one to three semesters. For the total group of 1,200 high-school students at the second-semester level, the median was 26.2 (norm, 21.7) and the mean, 27.2. In reading, the experimental group was superior to the national group at both quartile and median points. Fifteen per cent of the lower quartile performed as well as the upper quartile of the national group. In the upper quartile, 6 schools matched or surpassed the national fifth-semester norm; 12 others equaled or surpassed the fourth-semester norm; and 23 others attained the third-semester norm.

Grammar achievement showed a loss of 6.8 points at the median and 3.8 points at the mean. From his Wisconsin experiences in 1927–28 and these outcomes, Professor Cheydleur was prompted to say in his final report that "the vocabulary . . . and the reading scores . . . offer positive evidence of compensatory attainment [for the loss in grammar] in the case of the students whose scores supplied the data for the present study."

Comparing the percentile ranks for the composite scores, he noted that "fair and poor students are more likely to do 'passing' work with the reading method than with any other method," a conclusion at which he had arrived previously in the Wisconsin experiments. In an analysis of 903 cases at the one-semester level in college, the coefficient of correlation between vocabulary and reading was $.54 \pm .02$; between vocabulary and grammar, $.265 \pm .02$; and between grammar and reading, $.287 \pm .02$. In the higher correlation between vocabulary and reading lies, perhaps, the reason for the greater insurance for lower quartile students.

Professor Cheydleur's report concludes with a résumé of his findings in respect to the "reading" procedure, summarized as follows:

1. It is superior for vocabulary-building.
2. It is superior for attaining the reading objective.
3. It is inferior for attaining mastery in grammar.
4. It is superior for the three language functions combined.
5. It can yield "at least an equal attainment" in pronunciation at the first-year level.

6. It seems preferable at the first-year high-school level, as judged by matched group performance.

7. It would seem less preferable at the second-year high-school level, judged by matched groups of superior cases.

8. It is preferable from the point of view of "the mortality of students and the consequent enrolment in language courses."

9. It offers students, through the sense of accomplishment, "greater pedagogical and psychological motivation for continued language study and for the attainment of both immediate and more remote objectives, such as an improved reading technique and a widened cultural background."

10. "Finally, while we believe that our investigation reasonably demonstrates that the 'reading' method is probably the preferable plan to follow in the average two-year high-school or college course, where most students do not take foreign languages longer than that time, it does not demonstrate that a 'modified direct' or 'eclectic' method may not be more desirable in courses in which students actually continue the subject for a longer period."[35]

In the last conclusion, Professor Cheydleur voices the general concern of the language teaching profession for the sacred remnant of beginners who "go on," a concern that has made of the elementary language course a sort of Procrustean bed for decades in American education.[36] The assurance of continued high achievement in advanced courses by students trained by a "reading" method, which Professor Cheydleur did not find in the outcomes of his study, was factual in the case of French 1 continuants in the University of Chicago, as has been shown above. That assurance could be duplicated elsewhere, given the necessary adjustments and favorable conditions.[37]

High-school experiments Nos. 7, 8, and 9 were the first and in some ways the most influential experiments in a reading method at that level. All three were directed by Miss Eddy, were controlled with great care, and adhered strictly to a preconceived plan and a coordinated set of materials. They accomplished much in publicizing the "reading approach," in calling attention to the findings and suggestions of the Modern Language Study, and in applying the theories and principles advocated by West, Palmer, and others to the teaching of French and the preparation of materials.

They were especially valuable for the example they set for the use of objectively scorable tests in a planned program of course evaluation. In her 1927–29 trial sections in the University of Iowa High School (case 9), Miss Eddy administered 10 standard French tests per year, including the A.C.E., Harvard, Columbia Research Bureau, and Iowa Placement tests, and recorded the gains and losses for her pupils, semester by semester. Her astonishing results, although vitiated by the small number of cases, showed language teachers what could be accomplished by a "reading" method;[38] it was a "demonstration lesson" unlike the rehearsed performances staged at modern language conferences.

In his report on an experimental reading class (case 12) in a senior high school, Mr. Cassel[39] states that in the third-year classes, where traditionally trained groups and the experimental class were combined, "the latter showed far better reading ability and only slightly less skill in speaking and writing." This statement should be compared with Cheydleur's tenth conclusion, above.

There were other "reading" method experiments during this period and after, but the net results of them all sum up to these: increased reading power, greater vocabulary control, lessened grammatical efficiency but higher composite percentile ranking, increased interest, and lowered academic mortality. For these results there was sometimes statistical evidence gathered by means of objective-type tests of proved reliability. But for oral, aural, and composition abilities there was little or no evidence that was not subjective, largely because accurate measuring devices were lacking. At present, the aural gap is partially bridged, but the oral gap still separates the investigator from an answer to one of the most contentious issues in modern language teaching.[40]

## 8. *Query and Answer*

As the earliest experimenters with a "reading" method, the modern language staff of the College received an annual barrage of inquiries from teachers in all types of schools, public and private, and from administrators, supervisors, educators, and investigators in the United States, Canada, and abroad. Between 1924 and 1932 the inquiries for French alone averaged from 60 to 70 a year. In many instances the answers led to a chain of correspondence, which resulted in experimental courses elsewhere and in new lines of thought for us. It was not a one-way traffic.

Among the earliest inquiries were those of Professor J. Van Horne (1923), of the University of Illinois, who asked for titles and amounts read in elementary French and to whom we sent the annual lists for 1920–23 and an outline of French 1; of Professor C. E. Ficken (1924), of Macalester College, with a like request; of President R. E. Vinson, of Western Reserve University (1925), and Dean W. G. Leutner, of Adelbert College, asking for outlines and data.

In 1926, the twenty-page *Questionnaire to Selected Teachers* of the Modern Foreign Language Study was returned with complete data on French 1, sets of tests, and staff publications. In the same year, outlines were sent to Professor C. E. Young, of the University of Iowa, for his trial of the "reading" method; and Professor Helen M. Eddy conferred with the staff, examined files and materials, and questioned us about procedures and results, in order to set up her own experiment in the University of Iowa High School. In 1927, Professor R. Keith Hicks, of the University of Toronto, special investigator for the Canadian Modern Language Study committee, interviewed us and received data, outlines, and publications, from which he later wrote his account of the "Bond Reading Method" in Volume I of the committee's *Publications*.[41]

In June, 1927, Professor F. D. Cheydleur, of the University of Wisconsin, planning to use our analytical grammar in experimental sections in a "reading" method in the autumn, asked for our current outline and comments. The outline was sent with the following comment:

The inclosure is a copy of the content outline for 1A, which is the keystone and foundation (if there be such a combination) of the first year. Problem cases there that resist correction remain problem cases throughout 1ABC, in general. Occasionally a student does not develop to his best until 1B is over, but the case is uncommon. Hence we work hard in 1A and loaf, if at all, in 1C. . . . We have tried earnestly to make the first year what it is for most students, the beginning and end of their language instruction, and as such to make it as permanent and as valuable to the student as possible. We are not building graduate courses or senior college courses *per se;* if the proportion of continuants has increased and the quality of their preparation has become better, it has been as a by-product and not as an aim. Our interest in the outline, therefore, is like that of one who sharpens a tool to make shorter and better work of a job—and less work for the workman.

Not all correspondents wanted general information. In September, 1927, Professor E. C. Hills, of the University of California, asked specifically about class size, week-hours, teacher-load, and the composition of our staff, e.g.: "Is the modern language faculty of the Junior College a distinct organization from that of the university proper? What type of men do you have as instructors to help you? Are your instructors graduate students working for advanced degrees, or are they men who have already taken the advanced degree and who have settled down to teaching for life?"[42] (a question touching the business of educational slave labor). There was no dodging the issue in the reply:

> The staff of the Junior College group is distinct from the staff of the Senior Colleges and Graduate Schools. The members of one group do not teach courses in the other group, except in extension courses in Downtown College. To be specific, the 69 sections in French, German, and Spanish 1ABC and 2AB in the Junior College are all taught by the nine members of the Junior College staff ... of whom four have the Ph.D. degree, three have the M.A. degree, and two hold the B.A. degree with Master's requirements fulfilled. All are primarily interested in teaching rather than in productive literary scholarship. .... Every member of the staff has had at least ten years of college teaching, except one, who has had a mixed experience. Five of the nine members have been departmental executives; eight are productively interested in linguistic pedagogy applied at the college level; by autumn, five will have published in that field. ... The youngest is between thirty and thirty-five years old; six are married, with families; all have had foreign residence; and all are American citizens, and with one exception, of American birth.

It is the writer's opinion that the foundation courses in modern languages in college should be manned by similarly constituted staffs. Less than that is to cut the garment short at both ends.[43] It is a shortsighted policy that skimps at the expense of the college Freshman. The role of the teacher in the learning process cannot be overestimated.

From David A. Robertson, assistant director of the American Council on Education, came the following request (1928):

> At the Boston meeting of the Department of Superintendence I am scheduled to report on the work of our American Council on Education Committee on Personnel Methods. To illustrate one of the plans of my own Committee on Personality Measurement, I wish to refer to the very valuable reports which you and your colleagues used to make on students in the junior college Romance courses. You will remember the reports to Professor Morrison which found their way to my desk concerning both high grade and probation cases.[44] Will you be good enough to send me five or ten illustrations of these reports?

As a former dean in the University of Chicago, Mr. Robertson got the ten sample reports.

By 1928, the inquiries centered about the problems of extensive reading, like the request of Professor Neil C. Arvin, of the University of Rochester, for our "method of getting the students to do it." The answer, in part, follows:

Reading is encouraged from the first day; the staff never lets up on classroom advertisement of every opportunity for increasing the reading experience of the student. With our personal record data before us, we shape each student's reading to a definite end, fitting it into his tastes or needs on an orderly plan, but allowing him to take the lead and select the actual material. The next step is to make the material accessible, which we do through an open-shelf, departmental reading collection in nineteen classifications, mainly of French editions, with a few American texts. . . . One day a week is set aside for reading reports on prepared forms and for conferences. When we do not have any business on hand, we use the days for testing.

Professor Robert J. Kellogg, of Ottawa (Canada) University, found a reference to our "Thousand-Pages-a-Quarter Club" and wanted to know what it was all about. It was an embarrassing question, since the plan ended after our transfer to the College of Arts. It had functioned one year in the following manner, as reported to our Ottawa correspondent:

Every student reading 1,000 pages as extensive reading and reporting upon the material in units of 50 pages or less in a single quarter, was listed on a departmental bulletin board, and offered a chance for promotion to a higher course the following quarter, his other work being of high grade. It was intended that credit should be given for the course skipped (an intention realized a few weeks ago). It was further intended to form a social club of these students, to meet fortnightly for travelogues, theater or movie parties, discussions of plays and books, and informal talks by French visitors. There would be no formal organization, dues, minutes, and the like, a "factotum" serving as the one officer, and the meeting place to be the departmental headquarters. . . . It was even planned to have the members get out a mimeographed French news-sheet, as the spirit moved. . . .

In 1929, Professor Harry Kurz, at Knox College, asked for "methods, procedures, and devices in connection with language teaching *in order to reach the individual student.*" The italics are his. Of necessity, the reply was long, covering such subjects as conference hours, personal and study records and their use, reading reports and conferences, the reading collection, use of the audition room, bulletin board service, activities suggested by film showings and operatic programs, and attendance at French lectures, musicales, exposi-

tions, and club programs. But the Reading Method itself was probably the most effective means of reaching the individual student.[45]

From 1929 to 1933 the inquiries redoubled. Not content with
correspondence, Professors Stephen H. Bush and R. E. House, of the
University of Iowa, spent two days with us, examining files, visiting
classes, and interviewing students and instructors. Professor Philip
H. Churchman, of Clark University (1929), sent manuscripts of
articles for criticism and of his replies to our critics.[46] For three
years Professor Robert D. Cole, of the University of Pennsylvania,
maintained an exchange of data and opinions with Professors
Hagboldt and Ransmeier and the writer. George W. H. Shield,
supervisor of Modern Languages, Board of Education of Los
Angeles, through correspondence and conferences laid the ground-
work for the Los Angeles experiment with the reading method and
kept us informed of its progress until its cancellation in June, 1932.

Finally, there were the many personal contacts and exchanges of
ideas and materials between the members of our staff and Professor
Cheydleur, of the University of Wisconsin, particularly in reference
to testing and techniques at both institutions, not only during the
1930–33 survey described above but also during the war years.

Such contacts as these formed a web of inquiry and research in
which no experimentally minded person or group could long remain
isolated. Much more could have been accomplished in time, had the
web not been destroyed by the events of 1940.

## CHAPTER VII

# TWENTY YEARS AFTER

## 1. *The Day of the Systems*

BEGINNING with the two-year "New Plan" College in 1931, there followed in the next twenty years a rapid and somewhat bewildering succession of structural changes[1] in the collegiate section of the University of Chicago. Touching all phases of college life and work, these changes influenced in many ways the content and conduct of our language courses. Their influence, however, did not affect the basic pattern or its philosophy. Instead, they served only to fix them more firmly.

There is a value in scanning briefly some of these changing conditions, inasmuch as one proof of an effective method of teaching is its ability to withstand external changes and vicissitudes without impairment of its efficiency and to adapt itself to the new and the unforeseen. Survival depends upon flexibility. As will be seen, the Reading Method survived many systems.

The Two-Year College Plan was in operation from 1931 to 1937, when the Four-Year College came into active existence,[2] adding to the earlier plan the last two years of high school and setting up a curriculum of liberal education leading to the Bachelor's degree.[3]

In January, 1931, at the request of the Curriculum Committee, we drew up a two-year program to conform to the projected College Plan. It retained 1A and 1B as constituted[4] but sectionized 1C into "Humanities" and "Tool" sections. The latter concentrated on the "intensive reading of special material in fields of other Divisions." French 2, reserved for students planning to enter the Division of the Humanities, added a third-quarter survey of literary masterpieces.

Nothing came of the proposed changes. The question of merging the College language staff with the divisional staffs made changes inadvisable for the moment. In January, 1932, the question of merger was resolved by an official decree of "separate maintenance," resulting in an autonomous foreign language department within the jurisdiction of the College, a unique status retained until lately. In April, the German staff chose to merge with the divisional group. Two years later, experimentation in the teaching of German, for ten years under the skilful guidance and inspiration of Peter Hagboldt, ceased. The old routines took over.

Departmental policies shifted with New Plan developments. In January, 1932, the practice of demotion and promotion of students had to be abandoned, because the College suddenly discontinued the practice of "staggering" courses. Henceforth, the comprehensive examinations would be given only at the end of the year, in June, and not on application of the student when he considered himself to be prepared.[5] The Divisions also discontinued staggered schedules, so that promotion from French 2 was no longer possible except at the end of the year.

Furthermore, since the faculty had ruled that two units (the face value of French 1) satisfied the foreign language requirements in the College, only 15 of the 386 students in 1ABC in the autumn of 1932 would have to take the June comprehensive in order to satisfy degree requirements. With the necessity of validating 1ABC by means of a fourth major removed and with College language requirements satisfied at entrance by all but a handful of students, what would be the future for our experiment? Already, regardless of U and S grades, students were free to come and go in the sequence, without let or hindrance.[6] The reading conferences were abandoned in March, 1932, because of the shortening of the time schedule from five hours to four hours per week and the refusal of the students to attend a voluntary fifth hour for that purpose. We lost thereby our most effective check upon the reading progress and personal reactions of our course personnel. Another means would have to be found to insure the old standards.

Absenteeism became a plague. During the last three weeks of the winter quarter, 1932, a check on the attendance in the French, German, and Spanish classes showed an average loss of instruction time of 10 hours (two and one-half weeks) per student. Absences in German amounted to 11.7 per cent of the time available in the three-week period; in French, 17.6 per cent; and in Spanish, 21 per cent. "Floater" trouble developed: students who, though registered in a certain section, attended other sections spasmodically or regularly, without authorization. The language staffs proposed the status of "visitor" in cases of excessive absenteeism. The proposal was accepted, resulting in more ambiguity for the R grade and no diminution in absenteeism.[7] Seventeen years later, in *one day*, of 7,278 course registrants, only 63 per cent attended class, and 9 per cent (650) were "floating." Twenty-eight per cent were somewhere else. In French 1, 63 per cent (including 13 floaters) were in their classrooms. And again, at the close of the winter quarter in 1951, the R grade was recorded for 34 per cent of all students in the College, the payoff for the abuse of freedom.

Absenteeism in a foreign language class pays low dividends. Of 44 students who received R in the spring, 1951, French 1C final report, 11 incurred the grade of F in the comprehensive, 2 received the grade of D, and 15 failed to report for the examination, although they had registered for it.[8] In German, 35 of the 44 failures on the comprehensive were earned by students whose absence from class routines had not enabled the instructors to evaluate their achievement by means of a standard letter-grade. Somewhat belatedly, the faculty took action to restrict the student to taking "informed choices" in the matter of class attendance, namely, choices based upon previously demonstrated records of attitude and achievement.[9] Some learning can be had, apparently, only through experience.

Agitation for the creation of the Four-Year College began in the autumn of 1932,[10] plans having been discussed with Carnegie Fund representatives early in May. President Hutchins' proposal to extend the College to the last two years of high-school work was approved by the University Senate in November and by the Trustees in January, 1933. But curriculum and other troubles developed which led to a stalemate that was not broken until autumn, 1937, when the first classes of the New College began.

At the beginning of this period of uncertainty the French staff was concerned mainly with the place of foreign language study in the curriculum being formulated for the New College. It did not appreciate the committee's recommendation to the faculty[11] that two years of foreign language study be made *elective,* and its qualification of the instructional procedure to be applied, as "the multiple approach to immediate reading [*sic!*]," having as its aim "the reading adaptation within the radius of the pupil's ideational background." The educational jargon concealed more than it revealed.

In October, 1934, the foreign language question was placed in the hands of a curriculum subcommittee composed of a representative from each of the interested university bodies, i.e., the High School, the New College, and the Division of the Humanities,[12] who were to develop a four-year program in language as part of the new curriculum.

The new program was reported in March, 1937, and was adopted by the faculty. All students were to follow the same basic college program, with time made "available" for special interests. The fifteen basic courses of study included the "mastery of one foreign language *equivalent to two high school units.*" With fifteen comprehensive examinations to pass in four years, it was obvious that "available" time for special interests would not exist for the rank and file of College students. The old inadequacies of the place and function of foreign languages in the two-year program had not been corrected in the four-year program. We merely had more of the same.

In respect to methods, aims, and achievement, French 1 was obliged to change but little until the 1937 action of the faculty marked it as a "terminal" course,[13] severing its continuity with French 2, which became a detached elective, a nebulous "special-interest" course. The principal change other than this accentuation of its already terminal nature was the experimental trial of the Individualized Study Plan developed at the University of Iowa and applied to the 1934–35 program for French 1.[14] However, conditions in the College became more and more unfavorable for the successful operation of the Iowa plan, and it was dropped four years later, to be replaced by the programs and procedures described in the 1938 and later syllabi, of which the 1941 *Syllabus* is the best example. After 1941, having received special permission to depart from the College policy of publishing its syllabi annually, the French staff issued, instead, quarterly outlines and schedules. That is our present practice.

In these twenty years the problems of course evaluation assumed

an increasing importance, drawing upon the time, energy, and ingenuity of the staff until, at times, they threatened the proper
balance between the teaching and testing functions. In a later chapter dealing with measurements it will be easily seen to what extent
the making and giving of tests and examinations shared in our work.

Dean Boucher warned us in January, 1928, when the New Plan
was in the making: "I am inclined to believe that by an examination
which involved written, oral and aural work on the part of the
student, we would be safe in permitting a student to gain exemption
from the language requirement. . . . I think we could safeguard our
standards if we even granted course credit for informal language
work on the basis of examination. . . ." By 1932, the second statement was a fact. And by 1945, the first was an established practice.

After 1932 the quarter-sections of French 1 had no separate
unity; credit of any sort required the successful completion of a
comprehensive examination based on the work of the three quarters
as a whole, and offered normally at the end of the academic year.
Quarterly examinations had only advisory or counseling value.

In 1935, the French staff began the systematic measurement of
each quarter's achievement in vocabulary, reading, and grammar
by means of the Cooperative Test Service (American Council on
Education) French tests,[15] using the data for advisory and planning
purposes. The program is still in force. In 1946, when all foreign
languages, ancient and modern, were placed on a basis of "choice by
examination," a choice made mandatory for all applicants for admission to the College, our accumulated Cooperative test data made
placement in French easy and reliable.

Army training programs began in 1941. Already, war conditions
were affecting adversely an experiment in administering "split comprehensives," i.e., a type of cumulative examination in three parts,
administered at the completion of 1A, 1B, and 1C. The plan was discarded, and we returned to the former single, three-hour examination on the completion of 1C.

The shortage of war-workers led (1942) to two three-day shifts
per week, which condensed the four-day program of French 1 into
three days, in alternation. The A.S.T.P. program the following year
did not interfere with the regular language courses, which continued
on their three-day-a-week schedule. In fact, some of the instruc-

tional and testing materials used in the A.S.T.P. training courses, notably tests of oral and aural proficiencies and topical materials for conversational practice, were tried out in French 1 sections at various stages of revision. Both programs benefited considerably. Later the French 1 sequence served as a proving ground for the United States Armed Forces Institute (U.S.A.F.I.) materials.

No instructional changes were made in French 1 when the influx of World War II veterans began in 1946. An administrative change was made that permitted veterans who registered in January to complete the course in June, condensing the work of three quarters into two. It was accomplished by lengthening the week to five days and by extending the quarters into the usual examination periods. The trial arrangement lasted two years and was highly successful, owing largely to the caliber of the "GI" registrants.

In 1946 the special course (101G)[16] for graduate students preparing for the reading examinations was discontinued in the College and was turned over to the Department of Romance Languages in the Division to administer. In twenty years, 1,009 graduate students had completed the one-quarter summer course, 40 hours in length. In its place appeared a "capsule" French 1 course, offering three quarter's work in one quarter, utilizing from 10 to 12 hours per week for 10 weeks, and ending with a comprehensive examination that was identical with the June examination for the year sequence. The "intensive" nature of the summer course required that no other course be carried by the registrant at the same time. It has been fairly successful. The chief defect is the shortened reading period and consequent lessening of reading proficiency. But it is still the routine performance of 1ABC.

## 2. *The First Syllabus, 1932*

Under the date of February 7, 1931, the Curriculum Committee sent its plan for the New College to the faculty; it was adopted and was approved by the University Senate in March. Its legislation required a printed syllabus for each course offered in the College, to assist students in preparation for the required examinations.

There were, of course, other purposes to be served by the issuance of course syllabi, as Dean Boucher pointed out:

In the first place, since the examinations are based on the syllabi, the student who is qualified and desires to do so, may work independently in one or more fields and thus save both time and money. Secondly, courses are more likely than not to be better designed, organized, and presented when faculty members in charge are required to follow programs of work that they have had to make available in print for inspection by their colleagues and their students. Thirdly, the requirement of a printed syllabus for each course means that the proponents of a course must be able to show not only that it will vindicate its existence in general terms but that it will serve a specific purpose in the entire program of studies if the course is to pass muster before the Curriculum Committee. . . . Fourthly, it means an end of the type of course . . . that begins any place, drifts along at any pace determined by the caprice of the instructor, and ends any place attained by the end of the course.[17]

The first syllabi, considered experimental, were ready by September, 1932. A nineteen-page mimeographed booklet carried the requisite details for French and Spanish 1ABC and 2ABC.[18] Only the "General Remarks" and the section dealing with French 1ABC are reproduced here, as the earliest published syllabus of our Reading Method and as an indication of the nature of the course until its modification in 1934, referred to above.

### SYLLABUS FOR FRENCH AND SPANISH 101 TO 106
#### GENERAL REMARKS

I. Each year sequence consists of three parts, one quarter in length. The first year sequence is indicated by the numbered series 101–102–103 [1ABC] and the second year sequence by 104–105–106 [2ABC]. In both sequences the quarter parts are merely portions of a whole, have no individual entity, and receive officially no separate recognition; they are but stages in a continuous line of development.

II. The *First Year Sequence* in French or Spanish is designed for the following classes of students:

1. Those without adequate previous instruction in modern foreign languages and who desire to begin the study of French or Spanish to satisfy the language requirement of the College.
2. Those who intend to enter the Humanities Division and who wish to offer either French or Spanish as a second (foreign) language. . . .
3. Students of the Social Sciences Division, and of other Divisions, who desire to acquire the ability to use French or Spanish as a tool for research purposes, or for personal enjoyment in the field of their major interest.
4. Students other than those indicated above who may desire to learn to read with considerable facility modern French or Spanish of moderate difficulty, and to receive elementary training in other phases of the language.

III. The *Second Year Sequence* in French or Spanish is intended primarily for those students who wish to enter the Humanities Division, and is a prerequisite for more advanced work in either language in the College.[19] It will also meet the needs of other students who may desire to continue the study of French or Spanish beyond the first year sequence, thus integrating the recognition and reproductive trainings in so far as may be possible in two years of language study.

IV. In both sequences students are given individual guidance and encouragement to go as far beyond the achievement norms of the class as they may desire and be able to do, resulting often in promotional opportunities.

V. Regular class attendance, although on the same voluntary basis as in other courses in the College, is particularly imperative in these sequences, due to the inherent nature of language learning with its oral and aural trainings largely limited to the classroom experience. Attendance at individual conferences and periodic tests is required; students who do not attend these tests and the appointed individual conferences are liable to transfer to the inactive class list.[20]

VI. Extensive, or outside, reading in all sequences permit a wide range of choice in accord with the needs and interests of the student. Every effort is made to make the extensive reading as useful and as interesting as possible to the individual student, conforming whenever advisable to his reading habits in English. To this end, correlated reading, reinforcing other courses, is actively encouraged. The cooperation of instructors in other departments in this respect is welcomed.

Class and individual reference to general histories of French or Spanish literature, access to the open shelves of a departmental reading collection, the privileges of a well-stocked rental library,[21] the use of mimeographed reading lists and guide sheets, classroom talks and personal conferences on reading materials and programs: these are some of the means by which the student is aided in making up a reading program and in gaining access to the books. Reporting on such reading is made, in general, through the use of *Reading Report Blanks*, supplemented by oral conferences as desired.

VII. Compositions, particularly in the second year sequence, which are deemed unsatisfactory will be required to be rewritten as often as the instructor may judge necessary. The importance of writing a composition as well as possible before it is given to the instructor is stressed to the end that errors may not tend to become fixed by repeated writing.

VIII. Special oral and aural practice is required in certain portions of the first year sequences in French or Spanish, and in all three parts of the second year sequences whenever, in the latter case, it is considered necessary for the correction of speech habits in the foreign tongue. This special practice includes the memorization of poetry, auditory practice with the phonograph, dictation from recordings, corrective phonetic drills, and aural and pronunciation tests. Student initiative is urged in cultivating the oral and aural aspects of the language studied through such means as may be had beyond the limits of the classroom, such as attendance at the *Circulo Español* or the *Cercle Français*, listening

to French or Spanish plays, radio programs, or lectures, or forming pairs or groups for informal oral-aural practice. Counsel by the instructor is always available in such matters.

IX. At the beginning of the second year sequence in French or Spanish, a *Placement Test* is administered by the Board of Examiners to serve as an index for the proper placing of the student in the second year sequence according to his various language abilities.

X. Both sequences are subject to *Comprehensive Examinations* covering the work of the three quarters, administered by the Board of Examiners at the close of the sequences in June.

### OUTLINE OF THE FIRST YEAR SEQUENCE IN FRENCH (101–102–103)

#### FRENCH 101 [1A]

No. of
Periods                              Type of Activity

0– 2. . . . . . Explanation of the nature of the course, its single objective (direct comprehension of simple French, written and spoken), its materials and organization. Discussion of certain attitudes and methods of study in language learning. The taking of personal records.[a]

3– 6. . . . . . Phonetic introduction to the sounds of French developed from spelling to sound, with drill on isolated words practiced in chorus. Choral reading of connected discourse.[b]

7–21. . . . . . (1) Analysis of the variable grammar forms, with drill in their recognition, aural and visual. Considerable emphasis on the language facts common to both French and English in an attempt to lower the student's resistance to the foreign language and to bring the differences between English and French into relief. All active composition is deferred.[b]

(2) Double review of pronunciation: first, from spelling to sound; second, from sound to spelling, using IPA symbols. Limited practice in reading from phonetic transcription.[b]

(3) Unassigned classroom reading of connected discourse to supplement the analysis of the grammatical structure and to further develop linguistic aptitude or fluency.

(4) Oral practice in concert reading of special groupings of isolated words and of connected discourse. Practice in the comprehension of the spoken language by means of oral-aural recitation on the grammar exercises, and the comprehension of simple narrative, anecdotes, and comment kept within the vocabulary range. The conduct of the class otherwise remains in English.[b, c]

22–25. . . . . . Rapid analysis of the irregular forms of 54 common irregular verbs, with practice in their recognition.[b]

26–40. . . . . . (1) Assigned daily reading in a reading text, on which are based drill in pronunciation and oral reading, aural comprehension,

vocabulary expansion, reading comprehension, recall in vocabulary and irregular verb forms, and a limited amount of free
composition.[c, d]

(2) Voluntary extensive reading with simple reports, confined to
items on a graded reading list. The recommended minimum is
350–400 pages, if kept within the limits of the first 2,000 words
of the Vander Beke word list; less, if the material selected is less
carefully graded.

*Materials:* (*a*) *Personal & Study Record Blanks* (supplied). (*b*) O. F. Bond,
*Introduction to the Study of French*, University of Chicago Press, 1925. (*c*) Wil-
liams-Cochran-Eddy, *Madame Thérèse* (Erckmann-Chatrian), University of
Chicago Press, 1932. (*d*) For verb recall: Bond, *French Verb Blanks*, University
of Chicago Bookstore. For study guidance, the student is referred to Peter
Hagboldt, *How To Study Modern Languages in College*, University of Chicago
Press, 1925.

## FRENCH 102 [1B]

| No. of Periods | Type of Activity |
|---|---|

0– 2. . . . . . .Explanation of the nature of the course and its single major objective (direct comprehension of moderately difficult written French
and simple spoken French), its materials and organization. Discussion of certain attitudes and study methods. Bringing of personal records up to date.[a]

3–10. . . . . .(1) Intensive phonetic review, using a specially prepared manual[b]
and phonograph recordings of the graded exercises.[c] A period of
intensive study of the sounds of French intended to correct faulty
individual pronunciation. A satisfactory pronunciation is one of
the ultimate aims of the sequence. Special attention to individual problems.

(2) Extensive reading with a minimum recommendation of 600–
700 pages for the quarter, subject to reading reports,[d] conferences, and general guidance. The reading is selected in part
from an approved list.

11–40. . . . . .(1) Special drill in speech and writing, converting passive knowledge to active ability, not as an end in itself, but as a fixative
for reading ability.[e] No formal grammar.

(2) Daily vocabulary expansion drill suggested by the intensive
classroom text: synonyms, antonyms, homonyms, cognates,
word-groups, definitions, word choice, idioms, etc.[f]

(3) Intensive reading, with assignments and testing for reading
comprehension. Oral and aural practice.[f]

(4) Continued extensive reading, of which a part must be *cultural*,
including French history and geography. The reading should be
regular, continuous, and not subjected to linguistic or literary
analysis. Formal reports.[d]

(5) Use of the French language is stressed in the classroom.

(6) Various means of motivation are used throughout the quarter: maps, phonograph recordings, charts, postcards, photographs, magazines, prints, bulletin board service, announcements (plays, new books, concerts, opera, radio programs, international happenings), talks on French manners, customs, institutions, etc.

*Materials:* (*a*) As for 101. (*b*) O. F. Bond, *Sounds of French,* University of Chicago Press, 1925. (*c*) Recordings of the exercises in *Sounds of French,* University of Chicago Press. (*d*) O. F. Bond, *Reading Report Blanks,* University of Chicago Press. (*e*) Special unpublished material. (*f*) Struble-Cochran-Eddy, *Les Trois Mousquetaires* (Dumas), University of Chicago Press, 1932.

## FRENCH 103 [1C]

| No. of Periods | Type of Activity |
|---|---|
| 0– 2. . . . . . | Explanation of the nature of the course, its major emphasis (formal grammar and its application to speech and writing), its primary aim (accuracy in the comprehension of written and spoken French), and the study methods and attitudes involved. Completion of the personal records for the year sequence.[a] |
| 3–40. . . . . . | (1) Completion of the study of a formal, synthetic grammar of a brief, review type, with written, oral, and aural drills based on a literary text. A review of all of the common irregular verbs and 100 common idioms. Practice in free composition.[b] |

(2) Intensive, classroom reading of a small amount of material of moderate difficulty, preferably a short play or a collection of short stories or essays, subjected to exacting standards in respect to accuracy of comprehension.[c]

(3) Extensive reading of a recommended minimum of 800–900 pages of standard works, preferably in several literary genres and to the extent of one-third, at least, in some special field of interest to the individual student. In certain cases, the entire reading may be done in correlation with other courses or with special interests. The reading is subject to conferences and formal reports, as in previous quarters. The third quarter reading should bring the total reading experience for the sequence to at least two thousand pages.

(4) Auditory training through dictation, classroom talks in French on a variety of matters (books, authors, literary movements, manners, customs, institutions, provinces, travel, etc.), telling of stories and anecdotes, audition tests, phonograph recordings.

(5) Motivation as for 102. Recommended reading of French periodicals and newspapers in the departmental reading room, or through private subscription. Travel literature and advice.

*Materials:* (*a*) As for 101, 102. (*b*) O. F. Bond, *Review Essentials of French Grammar and Composition,* Macmillan, 1926. (*c*) Selected reading from the following: D. Rowland, *Contes de Maupassant;* T. Stanley, *Croquis d'un flâneur;* and B. W. Woodbridge, *La Semeuse* (in the Junior College French Series).

The 1932 *Syllabus* was only a memorandum and a chalk-line. It did not differ essentially from the 1928 *Outline*.[22] It was directed to the teacher rather than to the student, who could find in it little assistance for independent study. The unsettled nature of our organization and the College policies and our inability to foresee the effect that the New Plan would have upon classroom routines explain the omission of detailed assignments and time schedules. Nevertheless, the *Syllabus* was a needed step in the right direction.

## 3. *The Fifth Syllabus, 1936*

In 1934 Daniel Feder submitted a doctoral dissertation at the University of Iowa, entitled "A Study of Individualized Instruction at the College Level."[23] It was a lengthy technical report of a closely controlled experiment in teaching elementary French, using a traditionally taught group as a control. The two groups were considered about equal in linguistic ability.

The main characteristics of the experimental course were (1) recognition of the individual, (2) a predetermined outline, (3) each student working at his best rate, (4) minimum standards of achievement determined in terms of objective measures of satisfactory performance, (5) extension of time over subsequent semesters for completion of partial work done, (6) responsibility of attainment vested in the student, (7) the classroom as a "socializing" agency, (8) sectioning on the basis of ability, and (9) examinations as a means of instruction and self-evaluation.

The eleven standardized examinations of proved reliability administered during the year demonstrated the superiority of the experimental group, a greater homogeneity of learning through the reduction of chance to do poor work, and the salvaging of more than 18 per cent of the students from D and F grades. There resulted also greater motivation and a general betterment of study habits. During the course a great many self-administering and self-scoring progress tests with alternate "retake" forms were used, based on small units of instruction confined to the "Iowa Group" texts.

The experiment interested us because of our experience with the Reading Method, our knowledge of the materials used, and the writer's personal acquaintance with the working details of the Iowa course.[24] We decided to try the plan in French 1 and organized the 1934–35 *Syllabus* on an individualized study basis.

The best example of the syllabi for 1934–38, while the plan was in force, is the *Syllabus* for 1936. It was a bound, planographed booklet of 82 pages, 6 progress test charts, and 5 base maps.[25] The contents consisted of general remarks on the nature of the course (6 pp.), an introduction to the course of study (10 pp.), outlines, schedules, and lists (35 pp.), and nine appendixes.

The general remarks discussed such topics as the types of students for whom French 1 was designed, class attendance, extensive reading, means of procuring and reporting upon reading material, supplementary oral-aural practice, conferences with the instructor, special tutorial periods, the reading collection, the bulletin boards, Honors work, and comprehensive examinations. With the exception of the statements about tutorial sections and Honors work, the topics will be discussed later in connection with the 1941 *Syllabus*.

Voluntary tutorial periods were introduced in the winter quarter, 1933, "for additional or remedial practice in pronunciation, oral and written language, and aural comprehension." They were scheduled in the late afternoon to avoid conflicts, and instructor's permits were required for registration.

The service was discontinued four years later because of indifference on the part of the students, difficulties in scheduling, and consensus of the staff that little was accomplished that could not be done through the regular conference hour.[26] Furthermore, the student problems were so diverse and so often personal that group treatment was impractical and ineffective. And for the registrants who did not need remedial aid, but who wanted additional practice in language use, there were other and more effective and satisfying means.

The statement in regard to Honors read as follows:

In June of each year the Department awards Honors to all students in the first year sequence who (1) read for Honors in each of the three quarters, and (2) achieve a total score in the quarterly departmental and final tests falling within the upper quartile of the total distribution for the course.

Reading for Honors amounted to about 700 pages in satisfaction of six "supplementary projects," which were spaced in the outline to correspond roughly with the end of the quarters. Supplementaries 1–2 required the reading of West's *Le petit roi d'Ys*, an inferential reader in the VB-1,000 word range; supplementaries 3–4, the reading of the Williams, Cochran, and Eddy edition of *Madame Thérèse;* and supplementaries 5–6, the reading of approximately 300 pages of unedited material of the student's own choice. The supplementary reading, added to the minimum requirement, brought the total experience to 2,500 pages for Honors candidates.

The second condition to be met by the candidates was an upper quartile ranking in the distribution of the composite scores on 22 "departmental" or achievement tests and on each of the quarterly administrations of the Cooperative French test.

The winners were announced during the comprehensive examination period, presented with de luxe bound volumes of French classics, congratulated by the dean of the College, and given publicity in Chicago and home-town papers. A member of the Board of Trustees financed the annual cost (less than $30.00). After three years the feature was discontinued for lack of new sponsors. It had stimulated a fourth of our enrolment to greater effort, had resulted in 19 awards, and had been acclaimed by students, staff, and administration.

Two cases taken from the files illustrate the efficiency of the recipients and their attainment:

*MM.*—Nineteen years old, graduate of Englewood (Chicago) H.S. No previous experience in French. Winter total score: 415 points, ranking third in 81 contestants. Spring total score: 412 points, ranking twelfth in 71 contestants. Winter Cooperative test total score: 169 points, equal to a P.R. of 80 per cent on a 2-year college rating. Spring Cooperative score: 201 points, equal to a P.R. of 83 per cent on a 3-year college scale. Read extensively 2,268 pages, 568 pages above the required minimum, plus 700 pages which were read for Honors. Awarded leather-bound editions of Maurois, *Lyautey*, and Stendhal, *La Chartreuse de Parme.*

`DH.*—Seventeen years old, graduate of Opelika (Alabama) H.S. No previous experience in French. Winter total score: 434 points, ranking first in 81 contestants. Spring total score: 495 points, ranking first in 71 contestants. Winter Cooperative score: 191 points, equal to P.R. of 90 on a 2-year college rating. Spring Cooperative score: 252 points, equivalent to 99 per cent on a 3-year college scale. Read 2,429 pages, 759 pages in excess of requirements, plus 700 pages for Honors. Reading included Loti, *Le Pêcheur d'Islande;* Pourtalès, *Chopin;* France, *Jocaste, Le Chat maigre;* and Hugo, *Hernani.* Awarded de luxe editions of France, *Les Dieux ont soif,* and Maurois, *Byron* (2 vols.). Recommended to French 107 (third year), omitting the second-year sequence.

A simple award for exceptional work done by a college Freshman in a routine course sometimes leads to something besides statistics. It is no mere coincidence that, of the nineteen Honors students in French 1, six skipped French 2 and entered divisional courses while they were still in the College, four became teachers of Romance languages, and four received their doctoral degree from the University of Chicago. Of the latter, one became a well-known college president, two are members of the present foreign languages staff in the College, and the fourth is a nationally known professor of French and literary critic in a midwestern university.

The last three sections of the "Introduction to the Course" in the *Syllabus* explained the nature of the Individualized Study Plan. They are presented in slightly condensed form:

I. *The Plan.* (1) Division of the year's work into 65 "projects," subject to study and checking by the individual student. (2) Substitution of lesson assignments, supervised study and drill, self-testing of progress, conferences on language problems and typical errors, advice on the materials and conduct of the course, and short talks on France and French culture, for the usual classroom recitations. (3) Oral-aural practice daily, as supplementary activities to learning to read. (4) Standardized examinations quarterly as a means of measuring relative achievement.

II. *Advantages of the Plan.* (1) The organization into "projects" enables the student to progress at a rate of study determined by his own will, circumstances, and ability. (2) The supervised study feature of the classroom period enables the student to profit by the instructor's suggestions and corrections while the work is going on. (3) The self-scoring progress tests taken at the completion of a given project enable the student to check his own progress, step by step. (4) The project organization releases part of the class period for student-teacher conferences on learning problems, removing the difficulty often met in making appointments. (5) The Plan frees the class period for general directions and comment on objectives, methods, and choice of reading, etc. (6) The Plan also allows for more classroom drill in the spoken language. (7) The Plan provides for an enlarged program of cultural talks, in French and in English.

III. *General Instructions for Work on Projects.* (1) Do not leave a project until you have mastered it; as a rule, it will require from three to five hours to insure control. (2) As soon as a project is completed to your satisfaction, take the progress test, score it, and enter the percentage score on the Progress Test Chart in the *Syllabus.* (3) If the test results in 80 per cent correct responses, go to the next project. (4) When you have completed the tests in the folder, return the folder to the instructor; it will be returned to you later. (5) It is important to keep up all records: the Progress Chart, the Personal Reading Record sheet, and the Student Personal Record card. (6) In some instances, it is possible to be working on more than one project at a time; you should consult your instructor. (7) Questions on difficulties encountered in working the projects must be written on slips and presented to the instructor at the beginning of the period when the answer is desired. Only problems presented in this way will receive attention in the five minute period set aside daily for their discussion. (8) Departmental final tests are not based on specific assignments; they are achievement tests for the measurement of reactions to new material. They are announced in advance and given only on the date announced; they are not open to review. The results are posted on the office bulletin board. (9) By comparing your score with the table of norms (p. 73), you may find your ranking relative to past performance in the course.

That was our version of the Iowa plan. The basic materials were those of French 1, i.e., *Introduction to the Study of French, Sounds of French, Terre de France,* with the addition of Landry's *French Word and Idiom Book*[27] and a trial edition of his *Outline of Minimum Essentials of Grammar,* and Book I of the *Graded French Readers.* Eight graded readers from the "Chicago French Series" constituted the extensive reading material for the first two quarters.

It was the first use of "staircase" and "plateau" readers in the first two quarters of French 1 and the parallel use of objectively scorable progress tests on the extensive reading. The staff had often discussed the advisability of a prereading stage that would develop the VB-2,500 word range by means of a graded approach such as seemed possible through the interlocking West-type and allied readers of the "Chicago French Series." The staff also wanted to study the effect of a testing program in conjunction with reading reports and paced according to a fixed plan of study.

The four years during which the Individualized Study Plan was in operation revealed fully the strength and weakness of such a procedure. In the autumn quarter, the medians in reading and vocabulary, as measured by the Cooperative test, were the highest for any year recorded previous to 1946. In the winter and spring quarters, 1934, the medians showed no marked improvement over previous records. The prereading stage had apparently eased, but not materially bettered, the approach to "free reading."

The results of applying test controls and forcing the pace of the extensive reading were quite negative. Many students were content to do the required readings and no more, coming up to the comprehensive examination with a vocabulary limitation of VB-2,500, gained largely through a cramming process abetted by the Landry text, and resenting strongly the inclusion in the test of any word outside that range. Other students who completed the graded readings late in the year or delayed too long the reading of unsimplified material read too little and too superficially to be much benefited by the experience. In nearly all cases the progress tests on the extensive reading were either ignored or perfunctorily done. To be sure, the tests were arbitrary in content, sometimes absurd and trivial, of little instructional value and, in the student's mind, wholly negligible.

The staircase approach was fruitful, but in this instance it was too long-drawn-out, too rigidly controlled, tending in some cases to produce a false sense of security, and on the whole became a routine that destroyed some of the psychological advantages of free reading. Local conditions may have had something to do with the mediocre results of the plan, although the staff felt that they were due to over-regimentation and to the expressed distaste of the students for the reading bill of fare.[28] In extensive reading the diet must be palatable, or the appetite is soon lost.

The testing program, which was a very vital part of the plan, was viewed as another form of compulsion. After the innovation wore off, it reacted upon students and instructors like a pair of handcuffs, keeping them together and preventing either party from running away or doing the other violence, but ruinous to initiative, freedom of movement, and the joy of learning. The burden of preparing 54 progress tests, 22 departmental tests, and 76 alternative forms; the constant need for revisions and new stencils; the preparation of test folders for the students; the replacement of folders lost or mislaid; the maintenance of stock files; the collection of test charts; the costs of materials; and the statistical work entailed in scoring, making distributions, and computing norms—all this created for the staff a time-load and a chore that lost luster within a brief space of time.

The 76 tests were viewed with still less enthusiasm by the students, for whose good, presumably, they were made. Once the novelty of scoring one's own test wore off, the test program fell into disuse. Since the departmental tests were given according to a posted schedule, there was no need of the "grapevine" to keep the student from unwelcome encounters that might be of an incriminatory nature. However, the tests were there for whomever chose to use them, and they provided an unusual opportunity for self-evaluation and progressive measurement in specific language abilities.

The departmental tests formed a rather complete coverage of the course activities, as the following list of titles shows:

    I. Phonetics (ISF, 1–12; matching technique)
   II. Grammar recognition (ISF, 1–12; items in context, 5-choice)
  III. Vocabulary, VB-1,500 (sentence context, 5-choice)
  IV. Pronunciation (diagnostic form, 50 items, 6-choice)
   V. Silent reading (paragraph, best-answer type)
  VI. Grammar recognition (ISF, complete; context, 4-choice)
 VII. Idioms-1 (CH-100, in *Si nous lisions*)
VIII. Irregular verbs (ISF, complete; context, 4-choice)
  IX. Oral reading (prose passage, sight; reading scale)
   X. Idioms-2 (CH-200, in *Pierrille*)
  XI. Pronunciation (SF, complete; sentence context)
 XII. Vocabulary VB-1,800 (sentence context, multiple choice)
XIII. Idioms-3 (CH-300, in *Les trois mousquetaires*)
XIV. Audition (Lundeberg-Tharp, complete form)
 XV. Vocabulary VB-2,500 (based on *Les trois mousquetaires*)
XVI. Cultural background-1 (geography of France)
XVII. Dictation (100-word sight passage)
XVIII. Reading comprehension (Iowa 1933 form)
XIX. Oral reading (Voltaire, *Lettre à Rousseau*)
XX. Grammar (A.C.E. *Alpha French Test*, Part II, Coleman)
XXI. Cultural background-2 (history of France)
XXII. Vocabulary VB-3,000 (sentence context, 4-choice)

The following are representative of the 65 "projects" into which the assignments in French 1 were divided:

*Project 2.*—Study Lessons I, II in the *Introduction to the Study of French* (abbreviated, ISF) and do the exercises. Those that deal with pronunciation should be done orally, with two repetitions. Those capable of being written should be written in a notebook, checked with the text, corrected, and kept for further reference. This is practice work; its value is mainly in the doing. If you are satisfied with your results, take Progress Test ISF-1, score it yourself (the key is in the right hand margin which should be turned under before you begin), and enter the percentage correct in the Progress Chart. If the score is

80 per cent or better, go to the next project. This is the regular procedure for subsequent projects.

*Projects 28/29.*—Procure a copy of Haygood's edition of Bazin's *Les Oberlé* or Limper's edition of Daudet's *Le Petit Chose*, both of which are edited within the range of vocabulary of *Si nous lisions* and *Pierrille*, which you have just completed. The Bazin and Daudet books are therefore "plateau" readers, intended to consolidate and strengthen your stock of idioms and words within this basic range. You should read the book chosen *rapidly*, in as few sittings as possible, with your attention directed on content. Progress Test PC-Com-1 for *Le Petit Chose*, or OB-Com-1 for *Les Oberlé*, should then be taken. Since the tests are arranged by chapters, they may be taken while the reading is in progress. Don't fail to turn under the marginal Key before you start.

*Project 46.*—Read TFR, Chs. 15, 16; prepare exercises 15 (A, B, C, D) and 16 (A, B, C). Take Progress Test TFR-8. As part of the test, make an oral reading of *Le Cor* to your instructor. You will find the rest of the poem in Vreeland's *Anthology of French Prose and Poetry*, pp. 288–291, and in many other anthologies. If you want to read more of the great epic poem *La Chanson de Roland*, ask your instructor to locate for you a modern French version in the reading collection. The tailpiece in TFR, p. 96, reads as follows: *signum KaRoLuS caroli gloriorissimi regis*. It is a copy of an authentic signature of Charlemagne. What does it mean?

Supplementing the assignments in the projects was a varied program of activities in the classroom, devoted to "language use, the discussion of problems and procedures, talks on France and French civilization, testing, and supervised study." The following titles in the outline indicate the nature of these talks and discussions: French grammar versus English grammar, *être* as auxiliary verb, inference in reading, homonyms and dictation, Provence and Alsace, Normandy and *Perrine* country, the great epic poems, reading in correlation, Rousseau and Voltaire, building a French bookshelf, the French Revolution in art and literature, Paris, Hugo and the Romantic movement, Realism and Balzac, "Going to France?" What this list does not show, of course, is the integration of these talks with the assignments, the outside reading, and the audio-visual program.

Syllabi, like itineraries planned six months in advance of setting out, do not always happen according to scheduled arrangements. Our copy had to be in by March 1 for the following autumn. But they were indispensable guides, and the eventual happenings usually represented 85 per cent of the original plan.

In applying Feder's procedures, we omitted two, i.e., sectioning for ability and the extension of time for completing projects. The former was not possible under our local conditions, and the latter was made unnecessary by the latitude allowed by the College relative to taking comprehensive examinations at specified times.

To summarize, the positive values of the experiment were mainly evidential, such as the desirability of an early stage of integrated intensive and extensive reading in material suited to the maturity level of college students; a closely knit program of assignments, classroom practice, and informative talks; a wide distribution of progress and achievement tests; and a syllabus written for the student *and* the teacher.

On the negative side, there were the evils of lock-step organization, a burdensome and sometimes needless use of tests, an excessive work-load for the teaching staff, a high cost of maintenance, a constant source of confusion, and an incentive to lax study habits and low standards. Indeed, this trial of the Iowa plan fitted too well into the students' misconceptions of the new curriculum and policies of the College. Readers of the *Maroon*, the student newspaper, in reading an editorial on our syllabus, may well have stopped with these words: "Placing the course more completely under the spirit of the new plan, class assignments and recitations have been abolished, and the work has been divided into 65 'projects' which can be completed in a length of time which depends on the individual's ability and *inclination*." The italics are the author's.

We may have wrought too well!

## 4. *The Last Syllabus, 1941*

The ninth and last published edition of our French *Syllabus* appeared in 1941. Since then we have issued only the daily time schedule for the quarters of the sequence. What began as an economy measure in the war years, like others of the kind, has persisted to the present.

Because the 1941 *Syllabus* describes the Reading Method succinctly and completely in a practicable, orderly form and is a comparatively recent application, as much of its contents as is germane to the present discussion is reprinted in the following pages. Dates, references, and comment have been kept as in the original booklet.

It is hoped that the description of the two preceding syllabi and the reproduction of the essential parts of the 1941 *Syllabus* will provide sufficient information about what really went on in French 1 to enable one to interpret the products of the course and to understand the processes by which they were obtained. The recounting of products without an explanation of the ways and means by which the products were secured is to tell only the end of the story. The ways and means were not exactly the same, of course, year in and year out or from instructor to instructor. We never composed or followed a "teacher's manual," abhorring the stereotyped. Each instructor interpreted the schedule in much his own way, and thereby injected a sizable $X$-factor into the end-products of his course. But the syllabus held us together, kept our eyes fixed on the objectives, and charted our way.

FRENCH 101, 102, 103—SYLLABUS[29]

(Ninth Edition, 1941)

PART I. GENERAL REMARKS

1. The sequence covers the three quarters of the scholastic year; it is indicated in the *Announcements* by the numbered series 101–102–103. For students in the College, the quarter parts are merely portions of a whole and have no value as separate units. Divisional students taking a sequence as an elective receive official credit at the successful completion of the work of the separate quarters.

2. Daily class attendance is required.[30] Students who, because of absences, lose their grasp of the steady progress of the daily classwork, and students who are not present at the departmental examinations at the specified time will not be given quarter credit for the course.

3. At the time of the *first* Departmental Test, any student wishing to be considered inactive, i.e., an R student, must declare his intentions. No change in status, from inactive to active or *vice versa*, may be made subsequently in the course quarter.

4. Extensive (outside) reading is the underlying experience of the sequence. As practiced, it allows a wide choice in accordance with the needs and interests of the individual student, and conforms more or less to his reading tastes in English. A part of the extensive reading is correlated in nature, reinforcing other courses, with the cooperation of instructors in other departments.

Students in French 103 (Spring Quarter), particularly, are encouraged to ask for reading suggestions in French from instructors in other courses that especially appeal to them.

For students registered in the *Humanities General Course,* a list of suggested readings in French is given on pages 31–34 of this syllabus. A selected list of French readings is given in the current syllabus of the Humanities course, also.

For students registered in the *Social Sciences II General Course*, a number of suggestions for correlated reading will be found in the syllabus for that course; additional titles may be had on application to the instructors.

Class and individual assistance, references to literary histories and other bibliographical aids, access to the open shelves of the Departmental Reading Collection (Cobb 412), the privileges of the Rental Library (University Bookstore), classroom talks and personal conferences on reading materials, programs and procedure in reading and reporting, are some of the means by which the student is aided in his extensive reading. Reports are made, in general, on Bond's *Reading Report Blanks*, supplemented on occasion by oral conferences with the instructor.

5. Oral and aural practice *supplementary* to the regular classroom work of the sequence is required whenever it is thought necessary for the correction of wrong speech habits or of inadequate understanding of spoken French. This supplementary practice includes the memorization of literary selections, auditory practice with phonographic recordings, individual dictation drill, corrective phonetic exercises, and the taking of aural and pronunciation tests.

The student who wishes to secure a considerable facility in the oral-aural use of the language must *early* realize that the brief classroom experience cannot adequately supply it, and that he must extend the experience beyond the limits of the classroom through such available means as attendance at the meetings of French clubs or at French "tables" during the lunch hour, listening to French plays, radio programs, informal illustrated talks, and talking motion pictures, or through forming pairs or groups for practice or discussion.

6. Each instructor has a schedule of conference hours to which his students are expected to come for the explanation of difficulties which have not been solved in the classroom, and which they cannot solve for themselves. Grammatical difficulties, reading problems and programs, language study techniques, personal inhibitions and handicaps, as well as plans, projects and ambitions, are all proper subjects for discussion with the instructor. This applies alike to all students.

7. Attention is called to the various French publications received by the Reading Room, Cobb Hall 412. The reading of such publications as *L'Illustration, Marie-Claire, Réalités Françaises, Plaisir de France, Revue de Paris, Monde et Voyages, Larousse mensuel, Le Petit Journal*, etc., however occasional or fragmentary the reading may be, not only enlarges materially one's knowledge on matters of contemporary life and current world happenings, but increases one's French vocabulary and contributes markedly to other language abilities.

8. A Reading Collection of both fictional and non-fictional works in French (Cobb 412) is accessible to all students registered in the First Year sequence. Notices of the hours and regulations governing the withdrawal and return of books belonging to this collection are posted on the glass-encased bulletin board in the hallway near the entrance door. A complete shelf-list, alphabetized by *author*, is located in the Reading Room. Since the collection is administered

on the self-serve plan, each user is asked to adhere strictly to the few simple rules governing its proper use, particularly the renewal regulations. A copy of these *Rules for Procedure* is included in this syllabus, page 24.

9. Special bulletin boards for French clippings, posters, notices, announcements, pictures, cartoons, etc., have been placed in the classrooms and in the departmental office. Attention paid in passing to the material posted on these boards will help enrich one's language experience. Class members are invited to make contributions to the boards that may be of general interest.

10. The sequence is subject to a Comprehensive Examination administered by the Board of Examinations. These examinations test *achievement only*.

### PART II. INTRODUCTION TO THE COURSE OF STUDY

#### 1. OBJECTIVES

The primary object of the First Year sequence is to learn to read French of a normal degree of difficulty, *not* through translation, but by direct and immediate comprehension, easily and accurately.

Training in the understanding of spoken French and in the writing and speaking of the language is developed only to an extent consonant with the rapid development and attainment of reading power.

The emphasis on reading power is the result of many years of experimentation in this department. It is an emphasis that has come to be accepted for the American school and college by many of those educational workers who are interested in the improvement of modern foreign language teaching.

The reasons for this emphasis are too numerous to detail here, but one may note in brief the following: (*a*) of the four aspects of language learning—reading, writing, speaking, and understanding the spoken language—reading alone is open to mastery in a one-year course of limited classroom exposure (approximately 125 hours); (*b*) the majority of students either do not wish or cannot afford to give more than one year to the study of a foreign language in college; (*c*) of the four language aspects, reading is basic for the acquisition of the others and makes possible further study of the language; (*d*) reading is a "tool" skill, an instrument for the enlarging and deepening of the student's intellectual and emotional life; (*e*) reading holds the most interest for the majority of students.

Practice in speaking and hearing French is a valuable aid in learning to read, as well as a useful accessory to reading ability. It provides for the inner speech that accompanies silent reading. It contributes forcefully to memory and recall. It assists in explaining forms and structure of the language as written. It affords pleasure through its use. For these and other reasons, the oral-aural side of French receives constant attention throughout the course.

#### 2. FOUR PHASES OF LEARNING TO READ A FOREIGN LANGUAGE

The development of a reading ability in a foreign language resembles closely the process of acquiring skill in artistic, musical, dramatic and literary appreciation and creation, or re-creation. It has, or should have, similar techniques of study and the same imperative need for constant and copious practice. Practice in *reading* is the fundamental prescription in a course with the reading objective; this should not be lost to mind. It is only through practice that one gains the mastery to do something.

In this process there are, roughly speaking, four important and interlocking steps, as follows:

1. The ability to pronounce correctly the foreign language.
2. The building of a large and rich vocabulary of words, grammatical forms, idioms, and speech "patterns" (or ways of speech), particularly from the recognition standpoint.
3. A considerable amount of practice in reading material built almost wholly within a known and limited vocabulary, simplified in its grammatical structure, and gradually rising in the scale of language difficulty to an approximation of what may be termed "standard."
4. A breaking-away from the reading of simplified, prepared texts and the beginning of independent reading of original material, fictional or nonfictional, general or technical, in much the same manner and with much the same degree of appreciation or profit that may be had from similar reading in English.

It is idle to comment here on the relative value of these four steps, or on which one, if any, may be slighted or omitted; too little is known objectively of their exact relationships to reading mastery. There is but one course for the student to follow, namely, to give to all four phases equally serious attention.

### 3. SOME DO'S AND DON'T'S

It would be neither practicable nor sensible, at the beginning of the course, to give all the useful instructions and cautions; their nature and number might easily create a perplexity like that of Carolyn Wells' famous centipede. One would not know what to do first, or next. A certain amount of trial-and-error procedure must be followed, as in music or art lessons, golf or swimming. But the following ten points of the "game," if read carefully and thoughtfully at the start of the course and re-read at intervals, may prevent a deal of stumbling, costly delays and discouragements:

1. PLAN your college study and make a definite, regular allowance in it for this course. To help you plan your work, we have provided this syllabus with an outline of the year's projects, a tentative schedule for their completion, a time-schedule of the classroom activities, and lists of reading suggestions. Draw up a work program with definite week hours for yourself, and try to keep to it.

2. COMPLETE one project before you pass to another; there are no "royal roads" to a language. Grammars are but rule books, and not the game, any more than Spaulding's *Manual of Tennis* is tennis. Time and labor in learning to read French have no value unless their expenditure brings results. You cannot slight or omit parts of the course here and there, postpone practice to the night before an examination, or ignore an important phase of the work, and get mastery of the skill that you seek. The bill, however, will always be yours to pay.

3. Do not get discouraged at your RATE OF PROGRESS, unless you have done little or nothing to further it. If you are working regularly, honestly and according to instructions, and you do not seem to be progressing as rapidly or as well as you expected, consult your instructor and get his opinion. Language is an elusive thing; there where you think to lay hands upon it, it evades you at times. But you may feel sure that there is no real reason why *you* cannot learn to read French in a satisfactory manner.

4. The principle of REVIEW underlies all learning; language study is not exempt. Fortunately, much of the material for this course provides for the necessary review; then, too, the oral-aural practice deals with the same forms, words, structures as the printed page, thus providing further repetition or review. But the student must go further; he should review systematically vocabulary, idioms, and irregular verb and changeable grammar forms.

5. Take every opportunity you can to enlarge and enrich your contact with the SPOKEN WORD and to practice French speech. It is of the highest importance that you do so, if you seek the highest degree of reading power. This is easy to say and to resolve to do, but the doing is involved and beset with difficulties. You have first your own, particular set of speech production problems to solve, as well as those that are general to English speech *vs.* French speech; second, you have to overcome the various difficulties encountered in comprehending foreign speech; and then come your own troubles with the phrasing of the spoken response. It is all a very complicated bit of human activity. One must realize that fact, be patient and observant, and work hard and steadily. Good results bring an immense satisfaction.

6. You cannot, of course, read without a VOCABULARY. One should not need to debate that statement, yet many language failures and near-failures owe their being to just that cause! It is obvious that one cannot read without an initial stock of words, and that this stock should have a very high frequency and should be capable of expansion. Such a stock is provided in the early graded reading material of the course. Do not fail to master it. Secondly, do not fail to use it as a means of sensing through the context the meaning of new and unknown words. This latter procedure, called "inference," is vastly superior to dictionary and word-list thumbing, which should never be resorted to until inference has failed.

7. Do not mistake the use of GRAMMAR in this course. It is, in the beginning, a means of getting quickly to reading through its analysis of the variable forms of the language, pointing out, as it does, the means of recognizing the relationships of person, time, quantity and quality, gender, etc. It is not an end in itself; in fact, here, it is little more than structural vocabulary, ordered and presented with reading power in mind. Later in the course, when the reading adjustment has been made, it appears again in even briefer form, as a summary of the usages already become familiar through reading and partly assimilated, subconsciously. Keep yourself free from the grammatical consciousness that tends to make one decipher or translate word for word; deciphering is fatal to true reading power.

8. TRANSLATION into English, whether word for word or "free," whether

silent or audible, is something to be studiously avoided in learning to read a foreign language. Old study habits from Latin, for example, must be dropped. Read silently, thinking only of the content of the story; read as rapidly as you can, trying, of course, to make it as meaningful as you can; reread known material for the general flow of ideas; try to anticipate what is to come next in the story; and, above all, master your basic vocabulary and the grammatical variations that make inference and rapid reading possible. Once the habit of direct reading has been established, pay close attention to the idioms encountered, also, for at that stage it is the idiom that will slow you up and tempt you to translate into English.

9. IDIOMS are perhaps best unquestioned; they seldom yield gracefully to word for word analysis. Most of the picturesqueness, flavor, and distinction of the language lies in them. That is true of all language, English as well as French. Your final stage of reading in original, normal material will possess ease and accuracy to the degree to which you have mastered these idiomatic expressions. They are legion in number and often complicated and "blind" from an English viewpoint. But the soul of the French people and of French civilization is caught within them. They are worth struggling with.

10. Last, but not least in importance, do not forget that there are more avenues to MEMORY and learning than through the eye. If the eye alone is not sufficient, add the sound image of your voice, or the impression of the sound and rhythm received by your ear, or the curiously complicated but immensely valuable assistance to learning given by the movements and act of writing. These four avenues to memory combined can make permanent the possession of a language fact or usage that one avenue alone may not suffice to fix even temporarily. Do not neglect any of these avenues of learning, if they are available to you.

#### 4. ARRANGEMENT OF THE COURSE

The main features of the plan followed in the First Year sequence in French are as follows:

1. Division of the year's work, in so far as study of the printed word is concerned, into 120 projects, subject to study and checking by the student.
2. Daily classroom practice in the comprehension of spoken French, and in the speaking of French, as supplementary activities to the study of the printed word. Classroom activities also include instructions and advice on the methods, materials, and objectives of the course, and short talks in French or in English on France and French civilization.
3. Measurement of progress and achievement through objective type tests, dealing with such specific language abilities as reading, vocabulary, grammar, aural comprehension, pronunciation, and knowledge of cultural background material.

#### 5. TESTS AND RECORDS

Self-scoring progress tests (abbreviated PT in the *Program*) are taken at the completion of certain projects, more or less regularly spaced in the schedule.

They enable the student to check upon his mastery of specific material, such as certain assigned readings, grammatical topics, irregular verbs, phonetics, etc. They are primarily instructional tests and are not used in estimating the student's general achievement in the language.

As soon as a progress test has been taken, the date of its completion and the percentage score (*not* the raw score) should be entered on the *Test Chart* to be found at the end of the *Syllabus*.

The departmental achievement tests (abbreviated AT) provide a basis for the comparison of the achievement of the individual student with that of the whole body of students following the sequence. This relative measure helps the student to determine what changes he should make, if any, in the rate and emphasis of his future study. It is upon these tests, and the Quarterly Test (final), that the quarterly grade report is made to the Bureau of Records.

All achievement tests are announced in advance. They are not given on dates other than as announced. The papers are not open to review. As soon as an achievement test score has been reported, enter it in the appropriate space on the *Test Chart;* you will find the cumulative record interesting and valuable.

There are two other records necessary to keep up from quarter to quarter and required for the permanent files of the department: the *Personal Record* card (Project 1) and the *Personal Reading Record* slip in the pad of reading report forms.

## PART III. APPENDICES

### A. CORRELATED READING

One asks sometimes: Why try to read material in correlation? Among the defensible answers are: (*a*) it is highly personal and individual in its appeal; (*b*) it challenges more fully the ability of the student to read and understand the foreign language, thereby coinciding with the major goal of the course; (*c*) it presents all the problems of reading French as they affect the particular learner, as well as all the satisfactions and rewards; (*d*) it demonstrates clearly and forcibly to the individual learner the progress that he has made toward the ultimate skill desired. There are no really valid reasons for deferring this test of skill. There are no valid reasons for deferring correlated reading. It is a worthwhile and useful experience.

How may one know what to read? An answer is possible in one or more of the following sources: (*a*) the bibliographical data given in the next appendix; (*b*) the lists of supplementary readings in the textbooks used in the course; (*c*) the items suggested in the special lists in *Appendices* F and G; (*d*) special lists available through your instructor; (*e*) the advice of instructors in other courses with which correlation is desired; (*f*) the special subject shelves of the Reading Collection, Cobb 412; (*g*) the subject catalogue items in the General Catalogue of the University Libraries (Harper W-31); and (*h*) the advice of the members of the French staff in the College.

How can one meet the obstacle of the special vocabulary needed for reading such material? Certainly not by reading only graded material, and not by the memorizing of word-frequency lists. In fact, there is at present no way of acquiring a special vocabulary except by reading material with a special vocabulary, and using a dictionary whenever inference, a knowledge of word formation in French, or common cognates fail to suggest the right equivalent or the correct meaning. Special glossaries are rare. But one must be reasonable: if one has the basic reading vocabulary that is sufficient for ninety percent of running discourse, one must be patient in acquiring the two or three percent that is special vocabulary. Get a good dictionary and use it properly. Your instructor will make recommendations, if you ask him to do so. Seek advice before purchasing a pocket dictionary; it may be shortsighted economy.

A few cautions may save you wastage and disappointment: (1) Do not choose a book which is too specialized in content or too statistical. (2) Do not choose a book which is beyond your control or preparation in the subject matter. (3) Do not leave the correlated reading to the last minute or try to crowd it; it requires thought as well as the ability to read French. (4) Read intelligently, not carelessly. (5) Make the reading reports show *how* you have read rather than merely *what* you have read. They may be irksome to prepare, but they are all your instructor has on which to judge the quality of your reading.

### B. BIBLIOGRAPHICAL NOTES

A selected bibliography of French science, covering a score of fields, with an historical introduction to each field, is contained in the two volumes of *La Science Française*, published by the French Ministry of Education (cf. reserve shelf, Cobb 412).

There are several specialized collections of works that one may consult for material in a particular field. The *Série Armand Colin* numbers more than 180 titles in all fields of knowledge, each volume of uniform size and written for general consumption (cf. special shelves, Cobb 412). The *Rieder Collections* number a hundred monographs, with illustrations, on subjects in art, music, sculpture, architecture, applied arts, and literature, and include biographical monographs as well as general works (cf. special shelves, Cobb 412). The Nelson *Collection Gallia* is a French "Everyman's Library" of fiction, numbering several hundred volumes of uniform size, good quality, and low price; they are specially recommended for private purchase. Another excellent collection of fiction is the *Mainz Collection*, published in Vienna, attractively bound and low priced, and the cheap but excellent editions of the *Classiques Larousse* (standard fiction, mainly).

For authors, titles and movements in literature and allied fields, consult the new Thieme, *Bibliographie de la littérature française de 1800 à 1930*, a three-volume work of exhaustive nature. Lanson's *Manuel bibliographique* is the standard bibliography for the older period 1500–1800. Both works are on the reserve shelf in Cobb 412. Excellent bibliographical assistance in French literature, including history, criticism and philosophy, may be had in many of the standard histories of French literature, such as: Lanson, Bédier and Hazard,

Petit de Julleville, and the briefer manuals of Lanson, Abry-Audic-Crouzet, Des Granges, Mornet, Nitze and Dargan (in English), and others.

Henri Berr's monumental series of treatises on *L'Evolution de l'Humanité*, each volume prepared by a specialist in the particular field or period of world and cultural history, has reached the end of the Ancient World (in forty volumes), and continues towards its amazing goal of writing the complete history of the world's civilization.

Under the editorship of Gabriel Hanotaux, a staff of collaborators has prepared an exhaustive *Histoire de la Nation française*, superbly printed and illustrated. See also, the twelve-volume *Histoire générale du IVe siècle à nos jours*, by Lavisse and Rambaud.

Under the direction of Vidal de la Blache and L. Gallois, a *Géographie universelle* has now reached fifteen volumes, magnificently illustrated and printed. André Michel directs the publication of an equally detailed *Histoire de l'Art*, and J. Combarieu has prepared a three-volume *Histoire de la Musique*.

The remaining five appendixes are omitted here. Appendix C explained the rules for the use of the reading collection. Appendix D listed the reading material for classroom use, the prescribed outside reading, and the plateau readers. Appendix E indicated, in order of popularity, 90 of the 100 most widely read titles in French literature reported in the Rowland-Bond survey of extensive reading for 1927–32.

Appendix F cited in chronological order 40 authors and their works, with modernized or standard French editions, which could be read in correlation with the Humanities general course and copies of which were accessible either in the College library or in our reading collection. Outside reading in nonliterary fields was suggested in Appendix G, which listed 168 titles in art, biography, criticism, geography, travel, history, music, philosophy, political science, political economy, sociology, psychology, physical sciences, and biological sciences. The choice was based on the list of books read by students in French 1 and reported in the Rowland-Bond survey.

These appendixes, with the two preceding parts, composed the permanent section of the *Syllabus*, which was followed by the 1941–42 program or schedule, printed as a separate section on colored paper stock. It was intended that this section (Part IV) would be replaced annually, or when necessary, to conform to administrative, calendar, textbook, and instructional changes. The 1941 program follows:

## PART IV

### A. PROGRAM FOR FRENCH 101–102–103

#### 1. MATERIALS FOR THE SEQUENCE

The following materials are purchasable by the student; they are the basic material for the three quarters. Extensive reading material is not included.

1. Staff, *Syllabus for French 101–102–103* (University Bookstore).
2. Bond, *En Route!* (grammar), D. C. Heath & Co.
3. Bond, *Graded French Readers*, Books I to X (D. C. Heath & Co.). The readers are available as separate booklets, or in two volumes: *Première Etape* (I–V), *Deuxième Etape* (VI–X)
4. *French Verb Blanks* (University Bookstore)
5. Bond, *Sounds of French* (phonetic manual), D. C. Heath & Co.
6. Chinard, *Scènes de la vie française*, Ginn & Co.
7. Bond, *Reading Report Blanks*, D. C. Heath & Co.

#### 2. SCHEDULE FOR THE AUTUMN QUARTER

There are 43 classroom hours in the Autumn Quarter. For convenience in administration, the activity of one classroom hour, plus the equivalent of two hours of preparation, are considered as *one project*. There are, therefore, 43 "projects" in the autumn schedule, numbered from 1 to 43, inclusive. Included in the outline are assignments for homework, classroom practice, classroom talks or discussions, requirements for extensive reading, progress and achievement tests, and special recommendations. Abbreviations: ER (*En Route!*), SC (*Sept-d'un-coup*), AN (*Aucassin et Nicolette*), CE (*Chandeliers de l'évêque*), PG (*Les pauvres gens*), PT (Progress test), AT (Achievement test).

Project                                        Description
1 . . . . . . . Preliminaries: texts, filling of Record Card, assignments, office hours. Discuss ER, ch. I, pars. 1–6 (phonetics). Assign reading of Syllabus, Parts I, II; ER, I, 1–6.
2 . . . . . . . ER, I, 1–6; exercises I, 1–7. Choral practice. Oral reading: SC, ch. I. Talk: Phonetics *vs.* reading.
3 . . . . . . . ER, I, 7; exs. I, 9–11 (vowel sounds). Talk: Phonetic triangle.
4 . . . . . . . ER, I, 7; exs. I, 12–15 (vowels, semi-consonants). Oral practice: SC, II. Talk: Elision and liaison.
5 . . . . . . . ER, I, 8–9; exs. I, 16–19 (elision, liaison, review). Oral practice: SC, III. PT-1 (checking ER, I, pars. 1–6).
6 . . . . . . . ER, II complete, with exs. 1–6. Reread *Syllabus*, II, sect. 3, par. 7 (use of grammar). Talk: Grammar *vs.* reading. PT-2 (ER, I, 7–9).
7 . . . . . . . ER, III, 7–16; exs. III, 1–4 (present action). Review drill, ER, I. Talk: Verb mastery and irregular verb reduction.
8 . . . . . . . ER, III, 17–20; exs. III, 5–6 (present action, irreg. vbs.). Board identification quiz. Talk: Stress *vs.* irregular verb forms in present tenses. PT-3 (ER, III, 7–19).

Project                     Description

9......ER, III, 20–22; exs. III, 7–9 (present action, irreg. vbs.). Board identification quiz, pronuncaition irreg. vb. forms.

10......SC, III (review), IV–VI (advance). Rapid translation and choral reading. Identification by infinitive of irregular verb forms.

11......ER, IV, 23–27; exs. IV, 1–4 (agreement). SC, VII: oral reading and analysis of agreements. Talk: Hints on oral practice. AT-1 (Phonetics-1). Review ER, chapter I.

12......ER, IV, 28–30; exs. IV, 5–7 (agreement). Talk: Agreements in dictation and aural comprehension. PT-4 (ER, III, 20–22).

13......ER, V, 31–36; exs. V, 1–3 (limitation). SC, VIII–IX; oral reading and translation. "Structural" dictation (SC). PT-5 (ER, IV, 23–30).

14......ER, V, 37–39; exs. V, 4–5 (limitation). SC, X–XI: oral reading and analysis of limiting words. Structural dictation.

15......ER, V, 40–42; exs. V, 6–7 (limitation). Memorize par. 42 (common adverbs, prepositions, conjunctions). PT-6 (ER, V, 31–42). AT-2 (Verb identification-1, present action).

16......ER, VI, 43–48; exs. VI, 1–3 (reference). SC, XII–XIII: oral reading, analysis of unstressed pronouns. Talk: Stressed pronouns.

17......ER, VI, 49–51; exs. VI, 4–6 (reference). SC, XIV–XV: oral reading, analysis of personal pronouns. Talk: Structural value of pronouns.

18......ER, VI, 52–56; exs. VI, 7–10 (reference). Talk: Analysis of forms and use of relative and interrogative pronouns.

19......SC, XVI–XX: oral reading and translation. Review ER, II (word order); III, 19–21 (irreg. vb. forms). Talk: Question and answer in French. PT-7 (ER, VI, 43–56).

20......SC, XXI–XXV: oral practice and translation. Review ER, III, 19–21. Talk: Inference in reading.

21......SC, XXVI–end: oral practice and translation. Review ER, 19–21. Talk: Importance of the "initial" word list.

22......SC, vocabulary drills: oral and board practice. PT-11 (SC, vocabulary and idioms), as classroom practice.

23......ER, VII, 57–65; exs. VII, 1–3 (past action). AN, assignment 1. Board quiz on identification of past tense forms.

24......ER, VII, 66–69; ex. VII, 4. Tense drill on present perfect. AT-3 (Recognition grammar-1).

25......ER, VII, 68–70; exs. VII, 5–7 (irreg. past tense forms). AN, assignment 2: analysis of past tense forms. Oral quiz on recognition of type-forms, past tenses.

26......ER, VIII, 71–76; exs. VIII, 1–4 (future action), AN, assignment 3: translation. PT-8 (ER, VII, 57–70).

27......ER, IX, 77–83; exs. IX, 1–3 (measurement). Learn ER, IX, 79–80 (numbers). PT-9 (ER, VIII, 71–76).

28......ER, IX, 84–end; exs. IX, 4–5 (measurement, review). AN, assignment 4. PT-10 (ER, IX, 77–86). Note: Further work with ER will

Project                                    Description

be with the verb outlines, pp. 88–98, completing the grammatical introduction to the course.

29.......ER, Verb Outlines, I–III (-er, -re, -ir types): verb blank drill. AN, assignment 5: oral and translation. Talk: Hints on verb conjugation and use of blanks.

30.......ER, Verb Outlines IV, V (avoir, être): verb blank drill. Aural identification of forms of avoir, être. AT-4 (Verb identification-2).

31.......ER, aller. Verb blanks and board drill in recall. AN, assignment 6: oral-aural practice.

32.......ER, dire. Verb blank drill. AN, vocabulary drills: board work and oral recitation. Analysis of affixes.

33.......ER, faire. PT-13 (AN, vocabulary and idioms), as classroom practice. AT-5 (Grammar recognition-2).

34.......ER, pouvoir. CE, assignment 1. Discussion: Pouvoir as an auxiliary verb. Talk (in French, with slides): Toulon, Marseille, Digne (as background for CE).

35.......ER, prendre. Verb blank drill (review). CE, assignment 2. AT-6 (Vocabulary-1; initial vocabulary). Cf. initial vocabulary list in PE (Première Etape), or mimeographed copy.

36.......ER, savoir. CE, assignment 3: oral-aural, translation, and questionnaire.

37.......ER, venir, tenir. Discussion of compound forms. CE, assignment 4: oral-aural, questionnaire, translation.

38.......ER, voir. CE, vocabulary drills; oral and written practice. Talk: Word families and derivatives.

39.......PG, assignment 1: oral and translation. PT-14 (CE, vocabulary and idioms), as classroom practice.

40.......ER, vouloir. Verb blank drill (review). PG, assignment 2: oral-aural and translation. PT-15 (Regular verb forms).

41.......ER, conduire group. Verb blank drill, or boardwork. PG, assignment 3. Talk: Importance of idioms.

42.......ER, craindre group. PG, assignment 4 (translated orally by the instructor to demonstrate problems in interpretation). PT-16 (PG, vocabulary and idiom). AT-8 (Irregular verbs-1).

43.......QUARTER FINAL EXAMINATION.

### 3. SCHEDULE FOR THE WINTER QUARTER

There are 43 classroom hours in the Winter Quarter; there are, therefore, 43 projects, numbered consecutively from 44 to 86, inclusive. Included in the outline are assignments for homework, extensive reading, classroom practice and talks, discussions, lectures, conference hours, audition room schedule, recordings, and progress and achievement tests. Abbreviations: AM (L'Attaque du moulin), EDB (Evasion du duc de Beaufort), ANG (L'Anglais tel qu'on le parle), SF (Sounds of French), CO (Contes), LG (La Grammaire), RV (La Ronde de la vie), TM (Les trois mousquetaires), PT (progress test), AT (achievement test), RR (Reading report).

| Project | Description |

44.......Quarter preliminaries. Personal Record card brought up to date. Demonstration of use of Audition Room. Schedule AT-7 (Pronunciation diagnosis test administered in individual conference). AT-9 (Vocabulary-2; Books I–IV).

45.......AM, assignment 1: oral-aural, questionnaire. Talk in French: *L'Alsace et la Lorraine* (postcards, slides). Beginning of audition room practice: program changes *twice weekly* (see posted schedule).

46.......AM, assignment 2: translation, and content summarizing. Dictation on assignment, simplified text.

47.......SF, II, pp. 23–27; exs. 5–8 (front vowels). Group listening to recorded exercises, repetition chorally and rotative. Practice in imitation without the manual.

48.......AM, assignment 3: oral-aural practice. AT-S1 (Reading comprehension-1).

49.......AM, assignment 4: selected translation, questionnaire. Talk: *La Guerre de 1870–71.*

50.......AM, vocabulary drills: oral and written. Extension practice in use of affixes, synonyms, antonyms, semantic values.

51.......SF, II, pp. 32–35; exs. 13–16 (back vowels). PT-17 (AM, vocabulary and idioms).

52.......EDB, assignment 1: questionnaire. Talk in French: *Richelieu, Mazarin et Vincennes* (slide sequence).

53.......EDB, assignment 2: questionnaire. AT-S2 (Vocabulary-3, Books I–V, PE). Review basic vocabulary words in heavy type.

54.......EDB, assignment 3: practice in translation. Practice in verb identification, based on EDB.

55.......SF, II, pp. 39–42; exs. 20–23 (rounded front vowels). Sentence drill based on SF, in review.

56.......EDB, assignment 4: questionnaire, selected translation. Board dictation based on EDB, word order emphasized.

57.......EDB, assignment 5 (final). EDB, vocabulary drills. AT-10 (Audition-1; T–L technique).

58.......ANG, assignment 1: dramatic reading, assigned parts. PT-18 (EDB, vocabulary and idioms).

59.......SF, II, pp. 45–47; exs. 26–29 (nasal vowels). Sentence drill. Recording: *La Cigale et la Fourmi,* choral repetition.

60.......Outside reading of TM begins (cf. *Syllabus,* II, sect. A, 7–14). Explanation of procedure in reading TM. AT-11 (Vocabulary-3; Books I–VI). Talk: *Dumas et "Les trois mousquetaires"* (slide sequence).

61.......ANG, assignment 2: oral reading, by parts. Outside reading of TM continued.

62.......ANG, assignment 3: as before. Outside reading, TM continued.

63.......SF, II, pp. 48–50; exs. 30–32 (nasal vowels). Outside reading, TM. AT-13 (Idioms-1; Books I–V).

Project                                     Description

64.......ANG, assignment 4: as before. Outside reading, TM. Some translation of idioms in ANG, as review.

65.......ANG, assignment 5 (vocabulary drills). Outside reading, TM. Individual oral reading of *La Feuille* (SF, II, p. 51 and recording).

66.......CO, assignment 1: translation and questionnaire. Outside reading, TM. Audition room practice with SF ends, except for remedial work. PT-19 (ANG, vocabulary and idioms).

67.......CO, assignment 2: vocabulary quiz. AT-16 (Pronunciation-2).

68.......CO, assignment 3: questionnaire, idioms. Outside reading, TM.

69.......CO, assignment 4: selected translation. Outside reading, TM. AT-12 (Vocabulary-4; Books I–VII).

70.......CO, assignment 5: questionnaire. Outside reading, TM.

71.......CO, assignment 6 (vocabulary drills): board work. RR-1 due on TM (cf. instructions in Foreword in pad of forms). Talk: *La Géographie de la France* (illustrated).

72.......LG, assignment 1: dramatic reading, questionnaire. Outside reading of plateau-B or ungraded reading begins; personal conferences. PT-20 (CO, vocabulary and idiom).

73.......LG, assignment 2: oral-aural practice. Outside reading continued. AT-17 (Vocabulary-5; Books I–VIII).

74.......LG, assignment 3: oral-aural practice. Structural dictation, unknown material. AT-15 (Reading comprehension-2).

75.......LG, assignment 4: translation of assigned roles. Board dictation from LG. Outside reading continued.

76.......RV, assignment 1. Outside reading continued. PT-21 (LG, vocabulary and idioms).

77.......RV, assignment 2. RR-2 due; continue with outside reading. All-French conduct of classroom begins.

78.......RV, assignment 3. Outside reading continues. Talk: *Villages de province* (with slides, maps).

79.......RV, assignment 4. Board dictation, based on RV. Outside reading continues.

80.......RV, assignment 5. Outside reading continues.

81.......RV, assignment 6. AT-21 (Reading comprehension-3; range, VB-2500).

82.......RV, assignment 7. Outside reading continues.

83.......RV, assignment 8. AT-20 (Vocabulary-6; Books I–IX). RR-3 due, with *Reading Report Summary* sheet for autumn and winter quarters, showing accurately all reading done to date, intensively and extensively. Return books loaned from Reading Collection.

84.......RV, assignment 9; vocabulary review, questionnaire.

85⎫
    ⎬......QUARTER FINAL EXAMINATION
86⎭

There are 40 classroom hours in the Spring Quarter; the projects are numbered from 87 to 126, inclusive. The extensive reading program calls for a minimum of 600 pages, of which at least 400 *must be in correlation*. Reading programs should be arranged with the instructor the first week of the quarter. Abbreviations: SVF (*Scènes de la vie française*), PT (progress test), AT (achievement test), RR (reading report).

Project                     Description

87.......Quarter preliminaries. Records. Discussion of correlated reading (cf. lists in *Syllabus*, III). AT-Special 3 (Cultural background-1).

88.......RV, assignment 10, with questionnaire. Dictation on RV. Outside reading begins.

89.......Talk: *Les Ecoles littéraires du XIX siècle en France.* Trial note-taking on the lecture.

90.......RV, assignment 11: questionnaire. Material and discussion of dangerous cognates. AT-19 (Dictation-1).

91.......RV, vocabulary drills. Board work on cognates. PT-23 (Cognates-1).

92.......RV, assignment 12: questionnaire. Dictation from RV.

93.......RV, assignment 13: questionnaire, translation of idioms.

94.......AT-32 (Vocabulary-7; Book X). PT-22 (RV, vocabulary and idioms).

95.......SVF, assignment 1. RR-4 due. AT-27 (Idioms-3).

96.......SVF, assignment 2. Oral-aural practice, questionnaire SVF. Material and discussion of reflexives.

97.......Board work on reflexive usage. PT-24 (Semantic change-1). Recording, and individual recitation: *Le Corbeau et le Renard.* Discussion of J.-H. Fabre's commentary on the fable of *La Cigale et la Fourmi.*

98.......Talk: *La France romaine et féodale* (slides, cards, books). PT-25 (Audition-1).

99.......SVF, assignment 3, with questionnaire. RR-5 due on extensive reading.

100.......SVF, assignment 4. Dictation, oral-aural practice.

101.......SVF, assignment 5, with questionnaire. Paragraph composition based on SVF assignment.

102.......Talk: *Les Paysans français* (with slides, cards). AT-23 (Audition-2).

103.......SVF, assignment 6, with questionnaire. RR-6 due on extensive reading. AT-25 (Dictation-2).

104.......SVF, assignment 7. Dictation.

105.......SVF, assignment 8, with questionnaire. Dictation on SVF. Material and discussion of prefixes.

106.......Discussion of prefixes. PT-26 (Semantic change-2). AT-22 (Vocabulary-8; VB-3000).

107.......SVF, assignment 9, with questionnaire. RR-7 due on extensive reading.

108.......Talk: *Les Cathédrales* (slides, cards, books). Dictation based on the talk.

Project | Description
109.......SVF, assignment 10, with questionnaire. Board dictation.

110.......Audition room practice: recording of *Le Soir* (Hugo). Memorization drill.

111.......SVF, assignment 11, with questionnaire. RR-8 due on extensive reading.

112.......Talk: *La France au travail* (slides). Audition room practice: *Lettre à Rousseau*, for individual oral reading.

113.......SVF, assignment 12, with questionnaire. Composition, based on SVF.

114.......SVF, assignment 13. AT-28 (Idioms-4).

115.......SVF, assignment 14, with questionnaire. RR-9 due on extensive reading. AT-24 (Vocabulary-9; VB-3500).

116.......Talk: *Les Villes universitaires* (slides, maps). AT-26 (Cultural background-2; SVF, II, III).

117.......SVF, assignment 15, with questionnaire. Dictation. Material on suffixes.

118.......Discussion of suffixes, with board work. PT-27 (Semantic change-3).

119.......RR-10 due on extensive reading. SVF, assignment 16, with questionnaire.

120.......Talk: *Paris à travers les siècles* (slides, cards, books).

121.......SVF, assignment 17, with questionnaire. AT-29 (Audition-3).

122.......Talk: *La France artistique* (cards, prints, books). Dictation based on talk.

123.......SVF, assignment 18, with questionnaire. Turn in *RR Summary* sheet, showing all reading, intensive and extensive, done during the entire year. Fill out the special report sheet for reading done in correlation. Return all books loaned from the Reading Collection.

124.......AT-31 (Vocabulary 10: VB-3000/4500). Final conferences.

125.......AT-30 (Cultural background-3: SVF, Part IV).

126.......FINALS: Standard Achievement Test (required of everyone).

Comparing the 1932, 1936, and 1941 editions, one sees in all three syllabi the same fundamental framework of the Reading Method, differing only slightly from the *Basic Outline* of 1924. In fact, the general pattern is easily recognizable in all the course programs of the last twenty-seven years. Only small details—texts, the testing programs, and chronological shifts of such matters as the phonetic review or the introduction of cultural material—mark the changes from year to year. The third quarter saw most of the changes, because it was more directly affected by the fortunes of the second-year course. When French 1 was freed from the weight of 2A, it was possible for 1C to assume its proper role in the sequence. In these changes there was a slow process of improvement, of instructional refinement, not yet completed. It is doubtful whether the potential of a course of study can ever be fully realized.

To some teachers the idea of a syllabus is distasteful. It suggests a rigid, static, lock-step type of course. As an illustration of how flexible French 1 could be, consider the 1949–50 program. The phonetic review and remedial practice in the audition room shifted to the thirtieth period in the autumn and extended into the first part of the winter quarter. The *Graded French Readers* of the alternate series were introduced as plateau reading concurrently with the intensive use of the first series, establishing for a second time a closely knit relationship between the two types of reading from the start of the course. Progress tests were issued for home use instead of in the classroom. Quarterly achievement examinations, two hours long, replaced the batteries of tests previously used in the autumn and winter quarters. Approval of extensive reading programs was required. The cultural reader, Parker and Grigaut's *Initiation à la culture française*, replaced the Chinard text and was completed in the winter quarter, freeing the spring quarter for the reading of *Pierre et Jean* (Maupassant), *Petite anthologie* (Palfrey and Will), and *Lectures françaises*, a special anthology of selections from Michelet, Mérimée, Voltaire, and Bergson prepared by the staff. The audio-visual program was enlarged to include two one-hour programs of phonograph recordings illustrating the history of French music from the twelfth to the nineteenth century. Here was variety without the sacrifice of essentials.

Changes such as these in the mechanical implementation of a course affect teaching and learning. That is why we maintained such a system of checks and counterchecks on each quarter's work. If a royal road to language learning is ever found, it will probably be a superhighway equipped with electronic devices, recorders, public address systems, automatic signals, metering instruments, and under- and overpasses. The language teacher will need a training course in language engineering, laboratory techniques, and educational statistics. This is no longer the age of Ollendorff.

## CHAPTER VIII

# MECHANICS

## 1. *In Search of One Thousand Words*

IN A preceding chapter,[1] consideration was given to two attempts to solve the old problem of the initial stage in learning to read a foreign language, in particular that part of the problem centered about the material to be read, its nature, vocabulary, and arrangement. In both attempts, various economies were sought, i.e., in time spent, in the memory burden, and in the learning effort. At the same time, higher yields in pleasure and profit were demanded, with longer retention and greater promise of postschool use. The "Junior College French Series" and the "Chicago French Series" were the results of the two experiments, the former at the college level, the latter at the secondary-school level.

Both attempts failed fully to satisfy the editors, the teachers, or the student users of the readers. The ventures offered only a partial solution to the stubborn problem, item No. 9 on the 1922 agenda,[2] which had so long and so persistently plagued the French staff. The college series had provided maturity of content, cultural richness, attractive formats, a greatly shortened prereading stage, material for vocabulary expansion, and motivation for extensive reading. But it lacked the smooth, even acceleration obtainable by careful vocabulary selection and gradation, and it presented too many difficulties for a highly profitable initial stage.

The high-school series, particularly the "Iowa Group" texts,[3] were pioneering in their application of word counts and West techniques to reading material in French. Their "staircase" layout, their observance of the principles of new word density and repetition, their limitation of vocabulary according to range and frequency, their vocabulary-building exercises, and a new emphasis upon the foreign word in English marked them as a new and important step in textbook-making and in foreign language methodology.

228

They were short of the ideal, as has been pointed out. Their overload of grammar in theory and in practice, their oversized vocabulary radii, too high vocabulary limits in the early stage, a not too
skilful handling of forced-in words and idioms, a debatable choice of
reading material,[4] and too close adherence to the original texts were
some of their weaknesses. They were weaknesses which were more or
less inherent in the use of new and untried materials and of new
procedures in the making of French textbooks.

Could we in a third attempt avoid these weaknesses, while retaining the advantages of the earlier ventures? It was worth trying.

The project began in 1930 in the mind of the author, following the
receipt of a letter from Michael West in Dacca, India, addressed to
Miss Eddy. Only a part of the project has been realized to date, but
that part has taken on at times international aspects, influencing
second-language learning in Canada, England, France, Holland, the
Belgian Congo, Mexico, Ecuador, and New South Wales.

West wrote as follows:

You are correct in supposing that I make no distinction between Grammatical
Vocabulary and Reading Vocabulary; it is not necessary in English. . . . In regard to size of vocabulary, I find it more and more necessary to emphasize the
distinction between Minimum Reading Vocabulary and Minimum Speech
Vocabulary. Minimum Reading Vocabulary is such a vocabulary that one does
not have to look up an excessive number of unknown words in the dictionary in
attempting to enjoy an ordinary novel in its original form (or similar nontech-
nical material).

The Minimum Speech Vocabulary is the least vocabulary which will enable
one to express all ordinary ideas with reasonable elegance, e.g., to retell the
above novel at full length but in one's own choice of words.[5] (In preparing Supplementary Reading Material such as that in the *New Method Series*, one is, of
course, using the Minimum *Speech* vocabulary. This slightly subtle point has
caused some confusion of thought amongst my critics.[6]

In *Bilingualism*, the Minimum Reading Vocabulary was estimated at about
5,000 words: the estimate is necessarily rather vague, since it depends upon the
definition of the term "enjoy," and this depends on the incentive of the student.
A student who has left school will not read a French novel for his enjoyment if
he has to look up an appalling number of words in the dictionary. But, even if
he has to look up a pretty fair number, but has previously acquired a taste for
French fiction (thanks to your supplementary readers), he might still do so.
Hence it is possible that, in such a case, a slightly smaller Minimum Reading
Vocabulary would suffice.

My estimate of Minimum Speech Vocabulary has changed very considerably.
The reason will be apparent if you compare the original *New Method Supplemen-*

*tary Readers* with the Second Series (*Famous Fairy Tales, Gulliver's Travels, Monte Cristo, Cloister and the Hearth, Treasure Island*). I found in writing these books that I was able to say far more with these limited vocabularies than I had anticipated. . . . I have classified words under four heads—Essential (e.g., "say"), General (e.g., "enquire"), Common Environmental (e.g., "sleep"), and Specific (e.g., "dollar").[7]

It is not possible for the schoolmaster to foretell what will be the adult specific vocabulary of any child. He may need French in order to correspond with French business houses, or to study art in Paris, or to frequent the Folies-Bergère. Even if the teacher could make the prediction, he could not deal with the thirty different sets of requirements in his class. The vast bulk of the spoken and written word-populations consist of Class I (Essential), the earlier part of Class II (General), and Class III (Common Environmental). Their bulk in a word-frequency count is overwhelming; the Specific words (Class IV), though they are very frequent each in its own context, are in the language as a whole, extremely rare. Moreover, owing to their extreme frequency in the individual context, they are very easily and automatically acquired in real life, when that "context" comes.

Our function as schoolmasters is therefore, as I believe, to teach the essential and general words of the language (with as few specific words as possible) so that the child may be able, when he leaves school, to talk fluently and correctly about—*nothing in particular*. The vocabulary of the *something* in particular will be acquired after he leaves school. In other words, place him in any situation and give him its specific words . . . and he will talk as well as any native. The problem is: What is the size of the Minimum Speech Vocabulary? This means what is the number of Essential words, of General words necessary for elegance, and of useful Common Environmental words? Or in other words (from the practical, experimental viewpoint), how many words are needed to retell an ordinary novel at full length, if the Specific words involved in its plot are supplied extra? . . . I have come to the conclusion that this Generalized Speech vocabulary is between 1,000 and 1,500 words, probably near the smaller figure.

Although West was concerned primarily with speech-and-writing vocabulary in this letter, it seemed reasonable to suppose that the theoretical difference between a minimum speech vocabulary and a minimum reading vocabulary might lessen in practice, or even disappear in a minimum adequate reading and definition vocabulary. The latter would be a sort of compromise list compiled from a word-frequency count (like Vander Beke's) known to be complete and adequate, by taking the first four or five thousand items, reducing them by eliminating synonyms, duplicates, and less useful words, completing all the essential categories (such as colors, shapes, numbers, directions, etc.), and, finally, testing the list through the writing of stories, the making of a dictionary, and the development of speech-and-writing material.

The idea of such a "minimum adequate vocabulary" was shelved for a time; the author was in France, and efforts to effect a meeting with West failed. The latter left the Continent for India, but in June, 1932, from Calcutta, in acknowledging the receipt of the author's *Yearbook* article on adapting modern language instruction to individual needs,[8] West restated his belief that prepared texts which would build up the first 1,000 words would be an enormous asset to the initial stage in French 1; that "unpeptonized" material (even as outside reading)[9] should not be read until a 2,000-word vocabulary had been acquired; and that our reliance on French-English cognates to "pull our students through" might lead to dangerous half-understandings at a later stage.[10]

In August, when he was back in Abingdon, England, still worrying about the problem of recognizable and deceptive cognates and much concerned about the first thousand words, he wrote that he was "amusing himself by designing a little study of the initial stage, the first thousand words of a French reading and speech course" and that he was going over to France to make a collection of the study-books which French children aged twelve *actually read* ("Have they no Edgar Wallace, Sexton Blake, Conan Doyle?")[11] Also he had received a tentative offer from the University of Toronto to undertake experimental work of a bilingual nature, and he would be pleased "to co-operate with anyone on French reading," if he came.

In November the University of Chicago Press, which had just initiated the new series of *Graded German Readers* under the editorship of Peter Hagboldt, joined with the author in inviting West to participate in a like venture in French, as a co-operative undertaking to "develop a series of short, inexpensive readers, graded four ways and within the VB-1,000 word range, or *a minimal vocabulary*, if preferred, leading directly to reading at the high-school or college level, or both if distinctions of level are not thought worth while. The series would be developed independently of the Iowa-group materials, although interlocking with them near the 1,000-word level (probably *Pierrille*). . . ."

West accepted the invitation. But work on the new series would have to be delayed until spring, 1933; meantime, he would have a try at writing a modern French thriller in Vander Beke's first 1,069 words, in particular to test that radius for story-telling and to determine the degree to which one could depend upon cognates for inferential reading. He would not be in Toronto until late summer; we could have a long conference on the results of his "try" at Vander Beke, on the merits of frequency and range in establishing minimum vocabularies, on the selection of reading material, the treatment of cognates, the introduction of grammatical variables as vocabulary items, the manner of dealing with "outside" words, etc.; and then we could settle down to the long, hard task of drawing up a minimum adequate vocabulary (a provisional one, be it understood!) and of writing a grammarless French course, a series of readers and supplementaries, that would meet the specifications which he had indicated in the *New Era*, as follows:

No language course (except perhaps in pure reading) has yet been successfully constructed on the basis of a selected minimum adequate vocabulary, rather than on a grammatical basis. . . . But when that is done . . . we shall have French and German courses setting out to teach a certain adequate vocabulary, courses in which the grammar is introduced as needed in order to enable the child to use his vocabulary, courses with a fixed and definite vocabulary goal, courses which, when they reach that goal, say: "Stop here! You don't need any more words. Practise those you have got until you have mastered them. And, when you have done that, you will find that you can speak the language!" When that comes it will reduce the time-cost and increase the efficiency of modern language teaching—very considerably.[12]

The conference was held at Windyedge in the Michigan dunes during the month of July, 1933. At its close, West went on to Toronto, and from then until our contract with the Press was dissolved in 1940, except for a May meeting of the Federation of Modern Language Teachers in Chicago, we conducted our co-operative undertaking by correspondence. Sustained active participation by West ended in 1935, following the second London conference on vocabulary selection (the "Carnegie Report"),[13] for reasons of ill health, private affairs, and publishing demands in respect to his English publications. The author gathered up some of the loose ends of the project and tied them off, but for the most part the "Learn To Read Series" went into the limbo of lost causes.

Something of value was achieved, however, besides experience.

By March, 1933, we had a French "inferential reader" written within the VB-1,000 word radius, the first of its kind: *Le petit roi d'Ys*.[14] By October, we had the first draft of a grouped-frequency modification of the Vander Beke *French Word Book*, showing 4,759 words grouped under 2,049 heads ordered by total frequency. The cognates in the first 2,000 grouped frequencies in this list were being checked against Dale's correction of Thorndike's first 8,000 words for familiarity to fourth-, sixth-, and eighth-grade pupils.[15]

By March, 1934, a provisional draft of a grammarless reader for the first-semester course at high-school level was ready for revision: Jules Verne's *L'Île mystérieuse*, told in approximately 20,000 running words by means of 969 different words, representing 582 West-Swenson "units of learning." This was the only application to a French text of their since discarded system of new-word rating.[16]

In June, 1934, a provisional draft of a *Minimum Reading and Definition Vocabulary* for French went to press.[17] It consisted of 1,701 items listed under 1,157 "head-words." A supplementary list grouped each item under one or more of 61 logical classifications.

We were now ready to test the reliability of the vocabulary by story-telling, dictionary-making, newspaper writing, "stretching," comparison with other word counts in English and in foreign languages, checking against so-called "subjective" small-radius lists that had been used in retelling stories, and by the application of various techniques of word selection, such as the use of the double-column comparison, the analysis of forced-in items, etc. There was also the question of how satisfactory the "MAV" (as we called the list) would prove to be as a minimum speech vocabulary, a question that could really be answered only by trying to write a speech-and-writing course within it.

In short, we had a list of one thousand words "more or less" as Palmer said of his own thousand-word English list.[18] How good was it? What could it do? How could it be improved?

During the next four years, directly or indirectly, a dozen persons in Canada, England, and the United States gave some of their time and thought to seeking the answers to these questions, but world affairs, geographical distances, and personal fortunes played a stronger hand. None of the questions, by 1950, had more than a partial answer.

A great many attempts have been made to find a "Northwest Passage" to reading. Bibliographies on vocabulary control, such as Dale's, Fries's, Coleman's, and Bongers',[19] indicate a formidable succession of "word-counters" since the historic count by Kaeding in 1891–98.[20] Already, by 1932, there were the English word counts of Eldridge, Ayres, Jones, Packer, Thorndike, and Horn; the German counts of Kaeding and Morgan (a layering of the Kaeding count); the Spanish counts of Keniston,[21] Cartwright, and Buchanan; and the French counts of Henmon and Vander Beke. There were also the idiom counts of Keniston in Spanish, Hauch in German, and Cheydleur in French, which had been made available by the Modern Language Study.

From 1932 onward, with the exception of the Thorndike and Lorge[22] extensions of earlier counts and the Dutch word count by De la Court,[23] activity in the field of vocabulary control was mainly on the part of lexicologists (like Palmer); "critics-amenders" like Faucett and Maki, Palmer and Hornby, Eaton, West, Bond, Tharp, and Bongers; analyzers of texts (like Haygood, Emery, Miller, and many others); and committees on selection, such as the Federation of Modern Language Teachers' committee on Basic French[24] and the Carnegie Conference on English vocabulary selection. The efforts of most of these workers extended both *downward* and *sideways* (to borrow West's terms),[25] seeking to define or to evaluate a "word"[26] or to find the smallest number of "words" with the largest number of "meanings" or usages and the widest range of usefulness. The miraculous thousand-word list was, and no doubt still is, a goal that is "without imminent realization."

Our own search began with the first 1,000 words of the Vander Beke list, plus the 69 high-frequency Henmon items which constitute Part I of the *French Word Book*.[27] It was commonly supposed that these 1,069 words, because of their high rank among the 6,136 words that occurred in more than 5 of the 88 units that furnished the 1,147,748 running words checked by the compilers, constituted a minimum and adequate vocabulary for the first stage in learning to read French.

Miss Eddy and her associates, however, in preparing the materials for their first-year high-school course, found it more expedient in writing *Beginning French* to select 677 words and 105 idioms, "as far as possible from those of high range" in the Vander Beke and Cheydleur counts, and to introduce as *new words* in the two readers (*Si nous lisions, Pierrille*) used concurrently with *Beginning French* approximately 993 words and an unstated number of idioms, "bringing the reading matter of this first unit within the highest *quartile* of the Vander Beke and Cheydleur counts." The figure of 1,595 words shown as the total vocabulary at the end of *Pierrille* seems to indicate that some of the vocabulary of *Beginning French* was not repeated. If one adds to this total the large number of variants of idioms and the special "story-telling" words of low frequency used in both readers, one obtains a vocabulary that is neither minimum nor adequate.[28]

Their experience led West to try out the first 1,069 Vander Beke words, supplemented by a small number of "outside" words (about 30) needed for the story, and by approximately 950 cognates, easily recognizable or inferrible, the English equivalents of which were in the first 8,000 words in Thorndike's *Teacher's Word Book*.[29] The cognates were included for the purpose of testing their inferribility.

For material, he chose Toudouze, *Le petit roi d'Ys*, a "thriller" for boys and girls between the ages of twelve and sixteen. The "outside" words were explained at the head of the chapter where they first occurred. All words used in the book outside of VB-1,069 were indexed by page and line where they were first introduced and listed without English equivalents. Teachers were urged to mark all cognates whose meaning the majority of the class failed to infer and to send a marked copy of the book to the author or the publisher, to be replaced by a new one without charge. He was overoptimistic; not one marked copy was returned.

A trial check was made in two sections of French 1A in the twelfth week of the course. Only 11 out of 50 students reported any difficulties with the cognates. Their list contained 51 words, such as *cartouche, grade, loisir, graisse, canot, pétrole, supprimer, cave,* etc. They read the book in one or two sittings, without using a dictionary. It is doubtful whether some of the words would have been correctly inferred had West not rewritten the whole surrounding passage so as to make the reader guess the right meaning, a technique that he had used in his *New Method* English readers.

There were two questions unanswered: What would have been

the results with less mature or less intelligent readers, aged twelve to sixteen? And what difference would it make if the 950 cognates were screened according to Dale's study of Thorndike's *10,000 Word Book?*[30] In a preliminary test, Dale had found a correlation of about .55 between rank in the Thorndike list and familiarity of the word to tenth-grade pupils. Later, Tharp required that all cognates, to be included in his *Basic French Vocabulary*, should be in Thorndike's list and known to at least 75 per cent of eighth-grade pupils according to Dale's check list.

West did not get from *Le petit roi d'Ys* the information on the inferribility of cognates that he expected. But he did learn some of the difficulties in the way of retelling a story within the first 1,000-word radius of the Vander Beke list. Some of his reactions he related in his correspondence, thus:

In selecting these 1,000 plus 69 words, I assumed that they would be, as in the case of Thorndike's first eleven hundred words, enough to constitute a minimum adequate vocabulary. As a result of this experiment, I observed certain marked differences between the words of this list and those of other (English) lists with which I have been accustomed to work. In one respect, the Vander Beke first thousand words are too rich; in another respect, they are remarkably weak. In fact, the list of words chosen proved to be neither minimum nor adequate. There proved also to be an unexpected technical difficulty inherent in the use of range, as contrasted with a frequency list.

In vocabulary-building West insisted always upon the principle of teaching together words which are very closely connected, i.e., different parts of speech formed from the same root. A new suffix (for him) had the difficulty and value of a new word and should be treated as such in the vocabulary; but, once the suffix had been taught, new regular compounds of that suffix made with previously learned word roots did not count as new words, unless the compounds deviated abnormally in meaning. Now the Vander Beke list, being ordered by range, tends to separate widely the related members of a word group. It lists separately adjectives and adverbs and verbs or adjectives and abstract nouns.

For example, *acheter*, range 44 and frequency 113, is separated by over 3,000 words from its derivative *acheteur*, range 9 and frequency 21. In the *admirer* group, *admirable* (r. 43, f. 80) and *admirer* (r. 36, f. 70) are in the first 1,000 words, but *admiration* (r. 32, f. 50) is in the second 1,000, and the adverb *admirablement* (r. 11, f. 11) is in the fourth 1,000. If these four words were grouped together under the index of their total frequency, they could be taught in the first 500 words.

In criticizing the original *Basic French Vocabulary*[31] at the 1934 Iowa conference, Professor Morgan pointed out the inconsistencies of the Vander Beke list. It groups all verb forms presumably on the assumption that the verbs are learned as wholes, whereas actually the case is clearer for words like the *admirer* group than for verb forms, which often differ greatly from their infinitive root. And, in practice, certain verb forms are often deferred, while adjective and adverb tend to go together.

As a solution to the difficulty, West proposed a regrouping of the first 2,000 words that would eliminate the "splitting":

> The effect of this splitting is to lower the credit of the words split. In this way the validity of the list is affected; common words are thrust downward and less useful words are thereby promoted. The Vander Beke list carries the policy of splitting further than any other list, and its value consequently is gravely impaired, in my opinion. . . . In a frequency list this defect is not serious because it is easily rectified . . . by adding up the total occurrences of the various forms, and so get the true credit. In the case of a range list such addition is not legitimate, for ranges are number of sources; if you add them, you assume that all the sources are different. . . . The only solution is to decide which credits should be grouped, and to group them by going over the original material again.

There were three other possibilities. We could use a "merit formula," as Buchanan had done for his Spanish count, but Vander Beke had discarded the formula for very good reasons. Or we could rectify the Vander Beke range placements by converting total frequencies into range by a formula derived from his coefficient of correlation between range and frequency for the first 1,000 words,[32] but his correlation index of .77 did not hold much promise for successive thousands. It would be possible also to compare with the Vander Beke range list another list ordered by frequency and, by drawing off the words in common within a fixed radius, to construct a third list after the method used by Ford and Hicks in constructing their "Toronto List."[33] But Ford and Hicks found only 430 words common to both range and frequency ordering of Vander Beke's first 500 words.

It was decided, therefore, to proceed with West's suggestion and to make a grouped-frequency redistribution of the Vander Beke list down to a point that would yield 2,000 "units."

There was another difficulty in the way of obtaining a minimum adequate vocabulary:

> We find among the first 1,000 Range words in Vander Beke the following words, and many others of similar type: *répéter, distinguer, émotion, retraite, proposer, titre, immense, énorme, imposer, profiter, entièrement, rôle, réclamer, disposition,* etc. . . . . They are refined General words of narrow connotation whose main idea is expressible by an Essential word, or can be done without. A little undue richness of vocabulary is no disadvantage; it merely indicates that the first 1,000 words of the Vander Beke list are by no means a *minimum* adequate vocabulary. It is obvious that the first 1,000 words are capable of considerable reduction; this reduction could be done to a certain extent by the reordering consequent on grouping. But there is need also of elimination of narrow words and of synonyms. By so doing, it should be possible to obtain a vocabulary of about 500 words capable of retelling any ordinary text suitable for this stage.

A third difficulty in using Vander Beke's first 1,000 words was the poverty of that radius in respect to objective words, the "words we talk about." That is a result, of course, of ordering a list according to word *range.* A "pure" range vocabulary based equally on all sorts of material will contain almost no objective words. In the Vander Beke list, 56.4 per cent of the materials are set in the ordinary French environment of novels and plays; hence there is considerable environmental influence on the list, as shown by the presence of such words as *glace, joue, lampe, plume, tableau, chat, poche, église,* etc., within the first 1,000 words. But, compared to Thorndike or any other frequency list, the Vander Beke list is extremely poor in objective words, and the objective words tend to be placed lower, which, in turn, means that their placement tends to be less reliable.

Compare, for example, the following words in the first 500-word radius of Thorndike that are *not* found in the first 1,000 words of Vander Beke: "east," *est* (3,940); "mountain," *montagne* (1,342); "summer," *été* (1,117); "bird," *oiseau* (1,067). Or the following words in Thorndike's second 500 words and not in Vander Beke's first 1,000: "dog," *chien* (1,220); "farm," *ferme* (1,416); "island," *île* (1,608); "fruit," *fruit* (1,157). These are only a few of such instances.

Obviously, we do not know what all the students want to read about, and it is equally obvious that general words are of value in *all* cases. Yet the student in the initial stages must read some simple material of an objective nature, and in so doing he will encounter necessarily some objective words. Objective words are less certain and more wasteful predictions than are general words; and yet we must have some.

The problem of their selection was discussed in a letter from West, as follows:

One solution is to make them as few as possible, to do what the Range list does—keep them out. One can do quite a lot of "keeping out" by throwing the objective words into inferable cognates or by treating them as "inevitable outside" words (not listed in the end-vocabulary), but they may become numerous and burdensome. . . . One must assume that, whatever be the ultimate intention of the students, they will all in the initial stage read an objective type of literary material—probably stories. And we must therefore *allow* or *provide* such objective vocabulary as will enable the textbook writer to construct suitable material for their needs.

If we *allow*, the objective words outside the range are left unfixed; each author will introduce those words necessary for his story. . . . Some criterion is desirable in order to keep the number small, [besides] an objective vocabulary must be, so far as it goes, complete; and it must be capable of expressing the meanings of words not contained in it, i.e., it must have power of definition. . . .

The remaining alternative is to *select* a set of objective words; and (in my opinion) the best way of doing this is by the technique of Reduction which was used in selecting the Universal English vocabulary on which we were engaged last year at Dacca. The technique is elaborate, and it requires a thorough knowledge of the language. Its result is not objective in the sense that a Range or Frequency list is objective. On the other hand, it works successfully—which is the great thing. It does produce a *complete* set of words, with no waste, a vocabulary which is self-sufficient and equal to all ordinary needs. If it is not objective, it is at least more reasonable than an objective list; for if a word is omitted or included, one can give a reason, whereas there is no practically satisfactory reason for deferring the number "eleven" and the month "October" until the second thousand words (as in Vander Beke's list).

All who have used a frequency or range list "reserve the right to depart from it in a small number of instances"; in fact, they follow the list "with common sense." The function of a Reduced Objective vocabulary is to minimize this element of individually exercised common sense and to standardize it, so that supplementary readers can be written by anyone and examination papers can be set within a definite assumed vocabulary which will not demand an undue number of Outside words and Exceptions.

Supposing we add such a set of objective (Content) words: to what extent will this dilute the really more valuable general vocabulary of Form-words? Very considerably at the beginning, but less and less in the later stages. For, once having got a complete and adequate set of Content words, the textbook writer is compelled to add but very few others in retelling later material. He will be compelled to add only the indispensable technical terms inextricably connected with the plot of each book. . . . Thus, in a minimum adequate vocabulary of 1,000–1,200 words, objective words will be about 40 per cent; in a 3,000-word vocabulary, they will be about 13 per cent.

Three steps were agreed upon as necessary in our project of constructing a minimum adequate vocabulary in French, i.e., (1) a regrouping of the Vander Beke list in the descending order of the total frequency credit of a word or a group of related words; (2) a reduction of the first 1,000 "units," so as to provide a minimum vocabulary of form words; and (3) the preparation and addition of a minimum adequate list of content words, which, together with the form words obtained by the reduction process, would provide the MAV that we desired.

The first step was taken in July, 1933; Professor Louis Limper, of Kansas State College, was engaged to make an alphabetical card index of the Vander Beke frequencies. In August, West (in Toronto) received the original alphabetized frequency list from Professor Vander Beke. By October, we were able to compare the original list with Limper's card index for verification, make up the regrouped list, classify the first 2,000 "units" by hundreds, and take out the first 700 "units" for the completion of categories. It was expected that this filling-up would raise the 700 "units" to 1,000 or 1,300 words, an experimental first year's vocabulary. On the principle that "what is taught together must be counted together," it was decided that irregular verb forms should be added to the infinitive, especially since this was to be a reading vocabulary.

At this point, West started on the second and third stages, using the first draft of the regrouped frequency list as a basis, although it was clear that the draft was not entirely accurate. He also began "writing down" Jules Verne's *L'Île mystérieuse* in order to test the provisional MAV list and to discover needed content words. Meantime, the author, assisted by members of the College staff and West's group in Toronto,[34] undertook to verify and revise the frequency list and its alphabetical index; to provide two appendixes, namely, one on fifty Latin roots and their common French derivatives and a second on common French prefixes and suffixes, with derivation, values, and examples; and to put the material into shape for publication. The last draft was finished in June, 1937, four years after the beginning of the project, but the *Word List* was not published until 1939.[35]

Compared with the first draft, the published form shows a reduction of a few group credits, an increase of about 10 per cent in the number of entries, the addition of a score of groups, and the correction of some of the credit indexes. It was doubtful, however, whether these changes would materially affect the order of the first draft used in 1933 by West in establishing the provisional minimum vocabulary.

In the process of assembling the word groups from the items in Vander Beke's *Word Book* several perplexing questions arose, caused mainly by the ambiguities and inconsistencies in the listing or counting, such as the failure at times to indicate usages in the case of homonyms (e.g., *reporter, prêt, voisin, lâche, désert*) or the lack of information as to the meanings responsible for the indicated frequency of the word, e.g., *adresse, coupe, faux, gauche, importer*, etc. What meaning or usage should be tagged to the symbol?

A particularly troublesome matter was the question of allowing etymological relationship to control the constitution of a group when the logical relationship found in present-day usage was no longer close or obvious and so might lead to misuse or misunderstanding of the questionable items. An example of this type of question is presented in the *tour* group: *tour* (m.), *tour* (f.), *touriste, tourelle, tourner, tournant, tournée, tournure, tournoi, entourer, entourage, retourner, retour, détourner, détour, autour, autour de.* In such groups it seemed best to make the final grouping logical at the expense of etymological relationships. In the case of items with multiple meanings, it was decided against the practice of "splitting" the credits, since the relative frequencies of the meanings could not be known. Inasmuch as each item in the published list was given with its Vander Beke frequency index under the group index, the teacher or the textbook-maker was free to reassign any questioned item according to his own wishes and so to readjust the ranking order of the groups.

From the grouped-frequency list West drew off the first 1,100 groups (i.e., above credit f. 76) and began the writing of *L'Île*

*mystérieuse* within the first 500-word radius. When the first draft of
the story was completed, he had used up approximately 590 items
of the first 1,000 in the West-Bond list, plus 271 items in the second
1,000 and about 60 "outside" words, all cognate except 6 (*canot,
cochon, crayon, gâteau, huile, soif*) which were needed for the story.
It was obvious that the *grouped*-frequency list was not in itself the
MAV that we were looking for.

A different approach to the problem was decided upon. West had
compiled an English vocabulary of 1,158 words (2,032 words by
"open" count), which he had reduced from a list of 1,415 words
"known, by the experience of writing two novels within it,[36] to contain a minimum adequate vocabulary." The reduced list had been
revised further after comparing it with Thorndike's first 1,000
words, Horn's first 1,000, the first 1,000 in the Adult Education
Society and the American College (Sofia) lists, Palmer's 600-word
and 1,000-word lists, and Ogden's *Basic English* vocabulary.

The West list was transposed into French. The French list was
then checked for residuals in the first 1,000 frequency groups in the
West-Bond list and compared with the original *Basic French Vocabulary* as published in the *Modern Language Journal* (January,
1934). Items forced in or out after such comparisons were analyzed,
discussed, and subjected to the "double-column treatment" before
being admitted or excluded.

Two more checks were made: (1) against the vocabulary of *L'Île
mystérieuse* for the nucleus of essential form words (roughly the first
500 of the West-Bond list) and for a collection of content words competent to serve as a nucleus for a speech-and-writing vocabulary;
and (2) for residuals, against the English definition vocabulary being
used by West and his associates in preparing the *New Method English
Dictionary*.[37] This was the original list of 1,779 words used in defining
approximately 24,000 items.

The cognate study by Miss Frazer to which we have referred did
not get out of the card-index stage, and the "item stretch" that was
to furnish the usages and meanings for a "service list" to accompany
the minimum adequate vocabulary as a guide for users of the list,
was postponed until after the Carnegie conference. It was never
completed. *L'Île mystérieuse*, which got down to reading after five
introductory chapters in which a minimal amount of grammatical

material needed for reading was presented as vocabulary, affrighted textbook publishers in Canada, England, and the United States with its unconventional techniques, and so the dog-eared manuscript was retired from circulation.[38]

The MAV list, however, furnished the vocabulary base for the writer's series of *Graded French Readers*,[39] in the preparation of which it has been highly useful, flexible, and adequate, regardless of the type of literary material being retold or simplified. Only 56 words have not been used in preparing the 20 books of the original and alternate series, the material of which includes short stories, folk literature, condensed novels, plays, radio skits, history, and anthologies of prose and poetry. Of these 56 unused words, 33 are derivatives of known head-words, e.g., *aiguiser, certitude, facilité, gazeux, imprimeur, meubler*, and 23 are head-words included in MAV mainly for definition purposes, as *acide, caoutchouc, cire, craie, élastique, enfler, graisse, gramme, huile, mâle*, etc.

On the positive side, *Sept-d'un-coup* (Book I), written in approximately 8,500 running words, has a total vocabulary of 370 words, including the 69 Henmon items in Vander Beke's list (Part I), plus 28 variables to complete the categories.[40] Ninety-three per cent of the total vocabulary is within MAV. Ten of the "outside" items are special, story-telling words needed for *Sept-d'un-coup*, i.e., *caverne, ceinture, corne, fromage, géant, licorne, mouche, sanglier, sou, tronc*, and allowable for that purpose. The others, e.g., *brave, camarade, accepter, formidable, héros, orange, mariage*, could have been avoided, but their cognate quality made the effort of removing them rather pointless, and they were retained.[41]

In *Aucassin et Nicolette* (Book II), a much more difficult subject to work with, since it was desirable to keep some of the medieval flavor, 93 per cent of the total vocabulary of 500 words (exclusive of irregular verb forms) falls within MAV. Of the 28 "outside" items, *berger, casque, chevalier, comte, écu, enfer, épine, fée, jongleur, paradis, lance, rose, sire, tournoi, vicomte, viole*, and *lion* are recognizable as story-telling content words needed for that particular tale. Of the remaining items, several, like *autant, lèvre, misère, robe*, and *souffrir*, were put on a "provisional" list for observation.

The process of reduction and simplification of Zola's *L'Attaque du moulin* was accomplished, however successfully, at the cost of only

42 "outside" words, of which 28 are cognates and 14 are noninferrible story-telling words, i.e., *fiancer, haie, peuplier, lierre, dot, aboyer, durer, sembler, volet, sourd, matelas, mentir, noce,* and *boulet.* Again, some of them could have been avoided; others, like *mentir* (we had *mensonge*), *sommeil, sourd,* and *durer,* deserved to be put on probation.

After the first five books (*Première étape*),[42] the proportion of inside to outside items among the new words was reversed. With 1,108 of the 1,701 head-words and derivatives in MAV already introduced, it was no longer necessary to exercise the close control used to build up gradually the first 1,000 words. The first stage in grading reading material, which is the slow, methodical building of the essential vocabulary, providing an increasingly greater command of the more frequent items and patterns of speech, and establishing a sense of confidence and achievement in the learner, had been completed. In the last five books of the series, the problem was to lead the student more precipitously through stages of less frequent items to material that would be wholly ungraded, as in *La Ronde de la vie.*[43]

There are four means of easing the difficulty of the "weaning" process in so far as vocabulary is concerned, i.e., a gradual lessening of new-word density, a stepped-up percentage of cognates, an increase in the percentage of derivatives, and the maintenance of a fairly large percentage of vocabulary overlap from one book to another. How this was done in the case of the first series of the *Graded French Readers* may be seen from Table 40.

The average new-word density for the ten books is 38, that is, one new word to every 38 running words of text. More meaningful, however, is the volume density of the new *noninferrible* words, since they form the real *new* learning burden. In the critical first five books, the density of new noninferrible words does not drop below 45. In Book V (*L'Attaque du moulin*), it rises to the equivalent of 8 words per thousand, which is much less than the 33 words per thousand considered by West to be safe in a highly cognate situation such as we have here.[44] In the remainder of the series, the density index does not drop below this rate.

It is very important to keep a low ratio of new words per thousand running words of text in the first stage of learning to read. As Palmer says: "The degree of fusion should be proportionate to the degree of frequency of occurrence of the symbol. . . . Therefore, the words must be fused as you go, particularly in the earliest texts, if one is to read with economy."[45] But repetition of a limited vocabulary does not alone make easy reading. Miller's analysis of the vocabulary of ten widely read French texts[46] shows that density ratings change very materially the order of readability established by the percentage of difficult vocabulary, i.e., words ranked by Vander Beke outside the 2,000-word limit. For example, *Ramuntcho* ranked fourth in percentage of difficult vocabulary (46.62 per cent), but eighth in density of difficult vocabulary per page (12.15 words), whereas *Les Misérables*, which was ninth in percentage of difficult

TABLE 40

| | BOOKS | | | | | | | | | | TOTAL |
|---|---|---|---|---|---|---|---|---|---|---|---|
| | 1 | 2 | 3 | 4 | 5 | 6 | 7 | 8 | 9 | 10 | |
| Total new-word density............ | 31 | 43 | 41 | 33 | 50 | 46 | .... | .... | .... | .... | ...... |
| New noninferrible density............ | 45 | 68 | 93 | 76 | 125 | 89 | .... | .... | .... | .... | ...... |
| Per cent of cognates...... | 13 | 11 | 18 | 17 | 18 | 24 | 24 | 29 | 25 | 24 | 31.7 |
| Per cent of derivatives.... | 7 | 11 | 12 | 13 | 12 | 15 | 13 | 11 | 19 | 35 | 31.0 |
| Per cent of noninferrible.. | 46 | 51 | 46 | 48 | 51 | 40 | 41 | 62 | 46 | 72 | 61.0 |
| Per cent of overlap........ | .... | 77 | 63 | 70 | 78 | 77 | 72 | 69 | 72 | 55 | ...... |
| Per cent inside MAV..... | 93 | 91 | 86 | 83 | 86 | 56 | 62 | 50 | 55 | 19 | 48.0 |

words (52.37 per cent), was second in rank according to density (7.36 words) per page. Controls are needed over both *rate and kind* of vocabulary increment.

Of the 3,423 words used in the *Graded French Readers,* Books I–X, almost a third (31.7 per cent) are dependable cognates in the given context. The volume percentages are lower for the first five books than for the second five, owing to the relative infrequency of cognates in the MAV being developed in Books I–V. The increased percentages of cognates in the later books, coupled with increasing percentages of derivatives of known items, substantially offset the effect of the rise in the ratio of noninferrible words, as in *La Ronde de la vie* (Book X), which is an unsimplified literary anthology nearly twice the size of any other book in the series.

In a "staircase" series of readers, the new-word quotas are the vertical risers, and the overlapping vocabulary forms the horizontal treads. Both are necessary, but overlap in vocabulary helps in the ascent only when it extends very appreciably beyond the limits of the new-word increment. Only then can there be a minimum of learning wastage. The repetition of 77 per cent of the words used in Book I makes Book II easier to read and helps greatly in the matter of fusion. The 63 per cent overlap in Book III helps to consolidate the vocabulary of Books I and II, and similarly from step to step in the reading staircase. At the top, in *La Ronde de la vie*, the learner still has 55 per cent of known words surrounding the 45 per cent of unknowns to help him meet the final test of ungraded and difficult reading.

Judged by the test of the *Graded Readers*, our minimum adequate reading and definition vocabulary was a satisfactory nuclear vocabulary for general reading purposes.[47] The evidence from its use in the alternate series further strengthened that statement.[48]

Theoretically, it could be improved by comparing it with Tharp's revision of *Basic French* and the corrected edition of the West-Bond *Grouped-Frequency French Word List;* by checking it against the "Interim Report on Vocabulary Selection," Palmer's *Thousand-Word English*, and Bonger's recent *K-L-M English Word List*,[49] and by examining the "forced-in" items of graded readers by Eddy, Ford and Hicks, Coleman, and others. But to what end? For it is likely that there can be no truly objective minimal list of words such as we were looking for.[50] In the final analysis, it would be a list of "one thousand words—*more or less*." And yet, as West has said, "the most important unsolved problem in modern language teaching is the Nature and Size of the Minimum Adequate Vocabulary. For a large proportion of the pupils never get any further; indeed, under present conditions, very few get so far; and, if they do not get so far, they get nothing worth while out of all the labour they have expended."

## 2. *Audio-visual Aids*

It has been repeatedly pointed out that oral-aural skills and cultural information had an integral share in French 1 from its beginnings. A reasonably correct pronunciation, the ability to understand normal spoken French, and an acquaintance with the history and cultural heritage of the people whose language was being studied were held to be axiomatic in the rationale of the Reading Method. Their implementation, therefore, especially the mechanical and non-textual materials used, deserves consideration.

In the early reports[51] to Superintendent Morrison, recommendations were frequently made for the transfer of some of the phonetic instruction from the classroom to a laboratory, or "audition room," and for the purchase of visual material to supplement the cultural matter in the course programs. The collection of the latter began in 1923, but the audition room did not materialize until 1926.[52] Since that time it has been in steady use and has become a valued part of our physical equipment. Some of the apparatus purchased twenty-five years ago is now outmoded, although still serviceable and sufficient for our needs. Part of the equipment is listed, as follows:

### PROJECTION

Victor Animatograph sound-film projector, model 40
Spencer-Lens Delineascope, model D (for glass slides)
S.V.E. 35-mm. projector (slides and strip-film), model DD
True-Vue film-viewers
Portable and wall Da-Lite screens
Multiplex lantern slide cabinet, No. 51 (960 slides)
Classroom projection stand

### SOUND

Webster-Chicago wire recorder, model 80
Presto Compac instantaneous recorder, model D (disk)
Ansley Dynaphone, model D-1 (record player, portable)
Garrard automatic record changer, model RC-30 (78 r.p.m.)
Webster-Chicago dual speed record changer, model 256-1
Trimm "professional" headsets (booth equipment)
Microphones (hand and floor), amplifiers, loudspeaker

Duplication in the equipment is due to an attempt to keep up with the changing models and improvements of late years. Our major needs would be well met today by a portable record player, a tape recorder, and a tri-speed record changer, as far as sound equipment is concerned. And in visual equipment, single projectors can now be had that handle glass, 35-mm. and micro-slides, and 16-mm. and 35-mm. stop-films, reducing the apparatus needed and the cost.

Mechanical aids can be liabilities. There are teachers who cannot or will not learn how to operate a motion-picture projector or who are helpless before a recorder. There are students who blow fuses, burn out tubes and lamps, crack lenses, and ruin records, in spite of simple instructions and cautions. There are teachers who do the same thing. There are temperamental instruments that do not choose to run until the repairman comes. And, unless soundproofing is used, there are one's colleagues to be reckoned with. The use of audio-visual aids is exacting, and, unless one is ready to respond fully and intelligently to their needs, it is better to forego them.

The present audition room is a very modest affair compared to the elaborate and expensive installations at Cornell, Purdue, the University of Louisiana, and elsewhere.[53] It has no closed booths, multiple hookups, soundproofed control cabinet for the operator, dual arrangements for listening and recording of individual speech, and the latest in sound systems. Nevertheless, as Figure 7 shows, it is a compact layout capable of serving up to 33 students at one time, with or without the assistance of an instructor. It is equipped for the playing of disk or wire recordings, class or individual listening, single or multiple record playing, recording on wire or disk, and is quickly convertible for visual projection of any type or for listening to a program over a loudspeaker.

The plan indicates the suite arrangement of the departmental office (room 412) and the audition room (413). The outer office contains a slide cabinet (near the fire exit, *left*), a row of steel filing cabinets, a service desk by the entrance door, a Ditto machine, open wall cases shelving the reading collection, a library table, and five desks for the staff.

In the audition room, around the four walls and in the center are 33 open stalls approximately 22 inches wide and 14 inches deep, with 18-inch-high partitions, and 29 inches of clearance from the floor. The material is 1-inch white pine, oil-rubbed and shellacked. Each cubicle is fitted with a Mallory jack connected in parallel with the steel control cabinet in the alcove to the left (*bottom*). Two single-pole, single-throw switches with a pilot light connect the trunk line to the cubicles and the line to the loudspeaker on the right wall with the amplifier and record changers in the cabinet and a hand microphone on the shelf to the left. The red pilot light glows when the current is on, as a reminder to the users of the room to throw the switch before leaving.

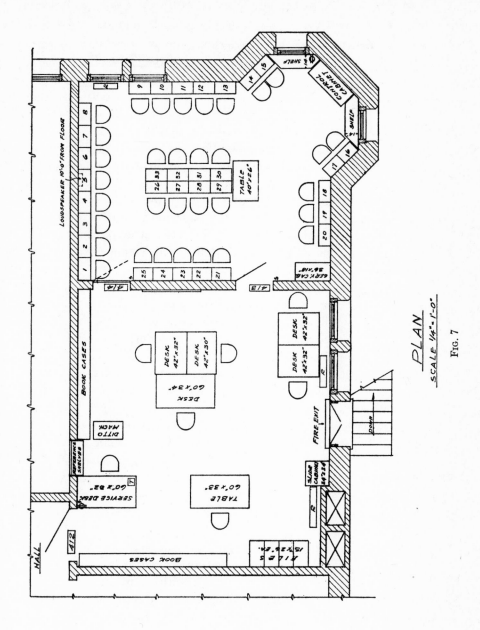

PLAN
SCALE ¼"=1'-0"

FIG. 7

A specially built amplifier is located on the top shelf of the cabinet; on the shelf below are the record files, and below them the two automatic record changers, connected independently to the amplifier, so that either one may be put on the line to the cubicles or to the loudspeaker. There are connections also for the microphone, a headphone, and the wire recorder. The space at the bottom of the cabinet serves as storage for the Presto recorder and the projectors. The cabinet can be securely locked.

When the equipment is in operation, the only manual attention needed is to throw the switch beside the pilot light. The repetition of single records is possible by means of the Garrard changer. For individual listening, the Ansley player with its own tone, volume, and speed controls, is placed on the small table and plugged into an outlet near the pilot light. In group practice the instructor can listen in on his headphone and cut into the line with comments over the microphone.

The record collection is inadequate on the speech side and will probably remain so until someone produces a *graded* set of disk recordings to follow the initial presentation of speech sounds. For the latter we have relied upon the graded recordings of the *Sounds of French*, prepared in 1925,[54] and now out of stock. It was intended to continue with a graded approach to the common patterns of speech and intonation, using a general rather than a narrowly specific vocabulary; but the continuation records were not made.[55] Consequently, we have had to use such material as *Spoken French* (Denoeu and Hall), *French by Sound* (Weeks and Allard), some of the old Stephan and Coustenoble recordings in *Sperlings Phonothek*, and transcriptions of current grammar texts. Intended for particular situations or for higher study levels, none of these materials offers the type of gradation desired.

We agree with Dunkel that "a set of 'graded listeners,' so to speak, is as badly needed as were the graded readers. Until equally well-organized materials are available for aural practice (which will lead the student from the ability to work with simple items of high frequency to that of understanding whatever is said to him), we cannot expect achievement in aural comprehension to equal that in reading."[56] Certainly, the high diction of literary and dramatic selections, e.g., Boyer's *Liberté, Égalité, Fraternité*, or the relaxed diction of the U.S.A.F.I. records[57] is not the logical sequence to an introduction to French speech sounds. Because of this no man's land in oral-aural speech material, after the middle of 1B[58] the audition room is used mainly for auditing literary and musical recordings in connection with the cultural programs of 1B and 1C.

Something of the nature of these cultural programs may be learned from the following entries taken from the 1950 *Outline:*

FRENCH 1B

La Renaissance: (Villon), Marot, Ronsard, Du Bellay.

La Musique française avant le XVIIe siècle: Blondel de Nesles, Perrin d'Agincourt, Richard Cœur-de-lion, Pérotin-le-Grand, Adam de la Halle, Ars Antiqua (minor forms), *Conduct de Saint-Louis,* "mélismas," "estampies," Guillaume de Machut, Guillaume Dufay, Josquin des Pres, Clément Jannequin, Guillaume Costeley, "pavanes," "branles," "danses."[59]

République et Empire: Rousseau, Danton, La Fayette, Hugo.

La Comédie bourgeoise: Molière, *Le Bourgeois gentilhomme.*

La Musique française aux XVIIe et XVIIIe siècles: Lulli, Rameau, Clérambault, Couperin, Destouches, Robert de Visée, Jean Mouret, Jean-Jacques Rousseau.

FRENCH 1C

Molière et La Fontaine: *L'Avare, La Cigale et la Fourmi, Le Corbeau et le Renard.*

Daudet: *La dernière classe* (complete), *Le Petit Chose.*

Maupassant: *Sur l'eau* ("L'Esprit du mot").

La Fontaine: *La Laitière et le pot au lait, Le Coche et la Mouche. Les Animaux de La Fontaine* (operatic).

Anatole France: *Le Crime de Sylvestre Bonnard.*

Popular and Folk Songs: *Le Roi d'Yvetôt, Noëls, Pont d'Avignon, Frère Jacques, Du bon tabac, Chevalier de la ronde, Au clair de la lune,* etc.

Voltaire: *Traité sur la tolérance, Lettre à Rousseau.*

Le Romantisme: Hugo, *Les pauvres gens, Tristesse d'Olympio;* Lamartine, *Le Lac;* Musset, *La Confession d'un enfant du siècle;* Vigny, *Le Cor, La Mort du loup.*

Rostand, *Cyrano de Bergerac* ("Ballade du duel," "Le Tirade des nez," "Non merci ... ," "La Lettre de Christian.")

Most of the literary recordings are old, of poor quality judged by modern standards, and are increasingly difficult to get or to replace. A series of modern recordings of literary masterpieces by well-qualified artists is badly needed. Meanwhile, much can be done on wire or tape by French members of the language staff. But little serious learning can come from the audition room until it is given a serious place in the program of instruction.[60] Used with discrimination and intelligently, it can free the student from the artificial stimulus of textbook exercises, with their anticipated situations, and offer endless and changeless repetition, the core of language learning.

The stock of projection materials consists of standard and 35-mm. slides, postcards, photographs, "pochettes," stop-films, color and black-and-white prints, and book illustrations. There are approximately eight hundred $3 \times 4$ glass slides, most of which are from the author's own collection, and one hundred 35-mm. color slides that form the nucleus of a collection planned to cover the high points in French art. Over a thousand postcards and "pochettes" are filed according to general subject matter. There is rarely a topic to illustrate for which suitable cards cannot be found. With the Balopticon (opaque projector), a portable screen, and window shades drawn, an ordinary classroom brings the visual image to the aid of the spoken word, easily and effectively, and at little cost. Cards, prints, stamps, maps, illustrations, and the printed page—the form and variety of materials are inexhaustible.[61]

With the reading collection and the university library as sources, we have drawn upon the book for visual aid to the work of the classroom. For displays in the classroom or in the staff office, we used such books as the illustrated reference works published by Larousse that deal with art, the provinces, literary history, political history, the natural sciences, etc.; a two-volume collection of color prints of paintings in the Louvre; the *pays de France* collection by Hachette; bound volumes of Christmas and special issues of *L'Illustration* and *Plaisir de France;* the Rieder illustrated monographs on art, literature, sculpture, music, architecture, and applied arts; Dayot's *L'Histoire par l'image;* and the indispensable *Encyclopédie par l'image* published by Larousse, a separate brochure for each subject. Organized around some person, event, or topic under discussion or study in the course program, such "exhibits" were valuable adjuncts to the daily lesson, stimulating and informative.

Fusion of the spoken and printed symbol with the thing itself, extension of the oral-aural training beyond the textbook and the recitation, and integration—"the relation of language learning activities at a given time to the other learning activities the student is engaged in during the same week, month, and year"[62]—these are the ways in which audio-visual aids and practices contributed to the learning process in French 1.

### 3. Tests and Test-making

In an experimental course the making and giving of tests are secondary only to the teaching. At times, they are fully as important, for besides their function as accrediting devices they have instructional values and are a means of "clarifying many of the linguistic issues involved in the experimental program."[63] It is a common mistake to view tests solely from the accrediting angle; they often reveal more about the course and the teacher than they do about the students.

In an experiment in learning, tests assume perhaps more than ordinary importance and themselves become an object of experimentation and analysis. There must be many of them, with variant forms, and they require continual revision and recasting into better forms, as determined by analyzing the results of their predecessors. The process is unending.

The task of test-making, giving, analyzing, and revising is the duty of the whole staff,[64] and not an assignment for a defenseless member; for if it is justly considered, it is a task to challenge the collective know-how and endurance of the whole group, the success or failure of which reflects upon not one, but all, of the teaching force.

Holding to this view, the members of the College French staff, during the last twenty years, have co-operated in the production, administration, and criticism of 20 comprehensive examinations, 12 quarterly examinations, more than 80 achievement tests, and 60 progress tests for the first-year sequence, besides a number of special examinations for scholarships, placement,[65] and remedial groups. In addition, there have been quarterly administrations of national standardized tests. "Know as you go" is part of what Morrison called "the essence of direct teaching."[66]

In the case of progress and achievement tests, as long as they applied to the course and were effective, they were used repeatedly and formed a dependable and ready supply of stock tests that could be drawn upon in any emergency.

Comprehensive examinations, which must be released for sale within a specified time after their first administration, had to be made anew each year. From 1938 onward, the staff had the technical advice and assistance of a representative on the Board of Examiners, who also cared for the administrative details. Since 1939 the papers have been scored mechanically.

Progress tests usually had marginal keys that could be folded under while the test was being taken. They were short, rarely more than fifteen minutes in time and a single sheet of paper in length. Achievement tests were longer, more difficult, and did not represent

TABLE 41

| Number | Nature | Technique |
|--------|--------|-----------|
| PT-1......... | Pronunciation, ER, I | m-c, T-F, and matching; no symbols |
| PT-2......... | Pronunciation, ER, I | Same |
| PT-3......... | Present tenses, ER, III | m-c, 3-response, and recall |
| AT-1......... | Phonetics | m-c, 3-response, T-F; no symbols |
| PT-4......... | Irregular pres. forms | m-c, 3-response, and recall |
| PT-5......... | Agreement, ER, IV | m-c, and recall |
| PT-6......... | Limitation, ER, V | Sentence context, recall |
| AT-2......... | Verb recognition | m-c, 3-response in English |
| PT-7......... | Reference, ER, VI | Paragraph context, recall |
| PT-11......... | GFR, Book I, vocabulary | s-c, m-c, 3-response in English |
| AT-3......... | Recognition grammar-1 | s-c, m-c, 4-response in English |
| PT-8......... | Past tenses, ER, VII | s-c, and sentence context, recall |
| PT-9......... | Future tenses, ER, VIII | Same |
| PT-10......... | Measurement, ER, IX | s-c, m-c, 3-response; translation |
| AT-4......... | Verb recognition, ER | m-c, 3-response in English, in context |
| AT-5......... | Recognition grammar-2 | As in AT-3 |
| AT-6......... | Initial vocabulary | m-c, 3-response in English, in context |
| PT-13......... | GFR, Book II, vocabulary | As in PT-11 |
| PT-14......... | GFR, Book III, vocabulary | Same |
| PT-17......... | Review of regular verbs | Sentence context, English recall |
| PT-15......... | GFR, Book IV, vocabulary | As in PT-11 |
| AT-8......... | Irregular verbs-1 | Sentence context, English recall |

any particular assignment. Until 1946, batteries of these tests served to determine the grades reported to the advisers and the recorder for temporary use in counseling, cases of probation, applications for scholarship extensions, withdrawals, transfers, etc. After that date, quarterly examinations, which were miniature two-hour comprehensives, replaced the achievement tests for grading purposes.

As an example of the coverage afforded by these tests, the schedule for the autumn quarter, 1941, is given in Table 41, with indications of the content and the techniques used in each test.[67]

The question may rise as to the total time required for the full testing program in the year. Actually, the 30 achievement tests scheduled in 1941 did not take more than 12 hours of class time. The progress tests were usually done on the student's time, outside class hours. Quarterlies required two hours each for the autumn and winter administrations; there were none in the spring. Except for the first two or three forms, the comprehensive examinations required three hours, in one sitting. Quarterlies and comprehensives were given on the student's own time, following the completion of classwork. At the most, testing on class time occupied 10 per cent of the total year's allowance for the course, which does not seem to be excessive, particularly in the light of the surprising uniformity of product in French 1, year by year, due in large measure to this means of observing the breadth and depth of progress *in situ*.

Some account of the French 1 comprehensives is necessary because their internal structure is, in a way, indicative of the nature of the end-products envisaged in the course and also because the grades assigned through their use replace the usual "teacher's marks" and transcend the latter as impersonal indexes of achievement. Each of the twenty forms is presented, therefore, in chronological order, with such information as may be useful in estimating the extent of the skills being measured and the validity of the techniques.[68]

*1932 form.*—Specifications: *I. Grammar:* 100 items adjusted to multiple-choice, substitution, and completion techniques; vocabulary within VB-3,000 radius. *II. Reading:* 75 items; narrative, descriptive, dramatic, and expository passages, with questions in French and write-in responses in English; vocabulary limits, VB-3,000 and CH-250. *III. Vocabulary:* 100 items within VB-3,000, sampled as follows: 25 items from the first thousand, 33 items from the second thousand, and 42 items from the third thousand; tested out of context, with multiple choice in English. *IV. Aural comprehension:* 70 items; sentence completion and definition techniques. *V. Pronunciation:* 30 items; oral reading of continuous passage of 100 words, of which 30 were on the check list. Total credits: 375. Time, 5 hours, in two sessions. Median score, 262 (70 per cent). $N = 26$.

This form became a model in its general layout for successive examinations for several years. The distribution of grammar items was made according to a composite of the item frequencies in five standard tests, i.e., Columbia Research Bureau, A.C.E. *Alpha* (Coleman), A.C.E. *Selection-Type Grammar* (Cheydleur), Ford and Hicks, Toronto, and Cooperative grammar (Wood).

In selecting the distractors for the vocabulary items, we submitted part lists of the French words to the students in 1B, and then collated the meanings which they supplied before making our final choice. It was the most devastating vocabulary test in the history of French 1. The students, in their ignorance, produced more likely distractors than the staff could devise in their collective wisdom. For instance, the students sometimes selected a meaning because of its resemblance to the French word in sound, spelling, root, or physical mass, e.g., *maintenant* is too long to mean "now." At other

TABLE 42*

| SUBJECT | FRENCH 1ABC | | | | FRENCH 2 PLACEMENT | | | |
|---|---|---|---|---|---|---|---|---|
| | $N$ | $Q^1$ | $M$ | $Q^3$ | $N$ | $Q^1$ | $M$ | $Q^3$ |
| Vocabulary..... | 68 | 58.5 | 66.0 | 72.0 | 50 | 49.2 | 59.2 | 70.5 |
| Grammar....... | 68 | 56.1 | 69.0 | 76.8 | 50 | 41.5 | 59.3 | 68.1 |
| Reading........ | 68 | 105.7 | 117.9 | 126.9 | 50 | 77.5 | 96.7 | 114.2 |
| Total...... | 68 | 225.0 | 252.0 | 267.5 | 50 | 165.0 | 217.0 | 246.2 |

* All scores are raw scores. Maximum scores: vocabulary (100), grammar (100), reading (75 × 2 = 150), total (350).

times, they confused the French word with another French word bearing a real or fancied resemblance in sound, spelling, mass, or association. A few derived a meaning for the French word indirectly through a resemblance to a word in Spanish or Latin. The selection of pure chance equivalents was uncommon. As a result of the test, care was taken in the comprehensives to select distractors based upon resemblances rather than upon chance.[69]

*1933 form.*—Specifications as for the 1932 form. Time: 4 hours. The reading section included passages in description, biography, criticism, science, narration, anecdote, and dramatic dialogue. Technical and low-frequency words were explained in the text when essential. Total credits: 450. $N = 68$.

This form was administered a second time as an autumn placement test for two-unit registrants in French 2, with the results in Table 42.

In each of the three subject matters and at each of the three range levels, the French 1 group was superior to the applicants for admission to French 2. In the total distribution, 23 per cent of the

French 1 group and 52 per cent of the two-unit group of incoming registrants were below the lower quartile norm (225.0) for French 1.

*1934 form.*—Specifications: *I. Vocabulary:* Paragraph context, vocabulary range VB-3,500. *II. Grammar:* Three techniques, i.e., underlined items in context, with English recall; double column (French, English), with blanks in the French version; and translation of French passage into English. *III. Reading:* As previously, except that weighted responses replaced the questionnaire technique. *IV. Pronunciation:* Connected passage and 10 phrases repeated from the passage. No aural test. Time: 4 hours. Total credits: 308 (written parts, 268). $N = 97$. Norms on Parts I, II, III: 135.8 ($Q^1$), 155 (Md.), 177.5 ($Q^3$). Maximum, 268. Median equaled 58 per cent of total credits for Parts I–III.

The 1934 examination was unsatisfactory. It was the first year of the application of the Iowa plan[70] and the graded readers in the "Chicago French Series" to the first-year course and of the use of the Iowa "penetration" technique in testing reading comprehension. That technique presented students with four or five choices graduated in accuracy from wholly correct to wholly false, and weighted accordingly. It too often resulted in hair-splitting and irrelevancies. In the grammar section, the double-column technique was time-consuming, confusing, and difficult to key and score.[71]

The shift from isolated-word technique to paragraph context in testing vocabulary was a result of a staff argument over the respective merits of the two procedures and of the opinions of Judd and Huse.[72] The final decision in favor of contextual testing followed Stalnaker's analysis of a trial test given to 1A sections.

The trial test consisted of four sections of 25 words each selected from VB-1,500 limits and tested objectively by four different procedures, namely, (1) multiple choice of English equivalents for the French word out of context, (2) double-column matching of opposites in French, (3) three-choice sentence completion in French, and (4) English translation of underlined words in French sentence context. The Pearson correlation coefficients for the four techniques are shown in Table 43.

Mr. Stalnaker concluded that underlined items in context calling for translation (D) was the best technique and that testing vocabulary in isolation (A) was the least desirable. Matching of opposites (B) and multiple-choice sentence completion (C) were second and third choices, respectively. He pointed out a possible error, in that the same items were not used in all four parts of the test. Working with Professor William Kurath of the College German staff in a later experiment with contextual and noncontextual testing of vocabulary,[73] his conclusions were that the context technique is slightly more reliable (.97, compared to .95 for best answer); is preferred by a small majority of students as fairer; and correlates slightly higher with teachers' marks (.63, compared to .60 for best answer) and with intelligence scores. Consequently, we adopted testing in context as standard practice.

The increase from VB-3,000 to VB-3,500 as the range in vocabulary for French 1 comprehensives was a result of an analysis by Professor Lawrence Andrus of the B Form of the *Cooperative French Test*. He found that 83 per cent of the vocabulary section and 89.8 per cent of the reading section were within the first 3,500 words of

TABLE 43*

| Part | A | B | C | D | Total |
|------|------|------|------|------|-------|
| A..... | ....... | .58 | .56 | .67 | .78 |
| B..... | .58 | ....... | .67 | .76 | .88 |
| C..... | .56 | .67 | ....... | .72 | .85 |
| D..... | .67 | .76 | .72 | ....... | .90 |

\* $N$ = 108; average time: 35 minutes.

the Vander Beke list. The French 1 medians obtained on the Cooperative test by 1C students justified the acceptance of these limits for the comprehensives. We have kept to them, except in a few cases when we wished to explore the 3,500–4,500 range.

*1935 form.*—Specifications: *I. Reading-vocabulary:* Combined, using double-column method. In the left column, the continuous French texts with items of vocabulary, idioms, variable grammar forms, and phrases underlined; in the right column, the items repeated, with blank spaces for write-in equivalents. Underscored pronouns required the identification of the reference. Vocabulary range for items, VB-3,500. Contextual values, rather than dictionary meaning, called for. Eight passages including narration, history, nature description, anecdote, and philosophic verse. *II. Pronunciation:* As previously. *III. Aural comprehension:* Lundeberg-Tharp test, Parts II (sentence completion) and III (definition). Hand-scored. Maximum credits: 257 plus 50 (aural); total, 307. $N$ = 100. Norms: (on written part) 158 ($Q^1$), 199 ($M$), 219 ($Q^3$); (on aural part) 32 (Md.).

*1936 form.*—Specifications as for 1935, except (1) vocabulary range exempted first 500 of the VB-3,500 radius; (2) Lundeberg-Tharp test given in full. Hand-

scored. Maximum credits: 290 plus 100 (aural); total, 390. $N = 91$. Norms: (aural test) 48.4 $(Q^1)$, 61.0 $(M)$, 74.5 $(Q^3)$. Standard median on the L-T test was 70.4.

*1937 form.*—Specifications nearly the same as for 1936. Vocabulary range, VB-500/3,500 and CH-300. Hand-scored. Maximum credits: 300. $N = 78$. Data lost.

*1938 form.*—Reading and vocabulary combined. Grammar and pronunciation sections omitted. Lundeberg-Tharp complete form used. Vocabulary limits, VB-3,500. Passages selected from Courier, Charbonnier, Voltaire, Thierry, Solari, and Renan. Double-column layout, numbered items from passages (left) and multiple choice, 4-response in English (right). The first of the machine-scored tests, using standard answer sheets. Maximum credits: 300 plus 100 (aural); total, 400. $N = 96$.

An item analysis of the 1938 form revealed that 20.66 per cent of the reading-vocabulary section was *unprofitable,* the items being correctly answered by 95–100 per cent of the candidates. Another 23.33 per cent was of *doubtful* value, inasmuch as they were answered correctly by 90–94 per cent of the candidates. In sum, 44 per cent of the test was dispensable. Pronoun references and grammatical variables from Vander Beke's list of 69 Henmon items were totally useless as test items. An inspection of the contextual settings and the item distractors showed that (*a*) extremely high-frequency items were excess baggage; (*b*) inference played a larger role than thought possible; (*c*) an item was as good as its weakest distractor; and (*d*) the best items were those with logical choices. The last point was made a special issue in the next comprehensive.

*1939 form.*—Specifications similar to the 1938 form. Lundeberg-Tharp form, complete, for aural comprehension section. No change in techniques except in the choice of distractors; all four English choices, including the correct response, were selected in logical sequences in so far as practicable, eliminating absurd and pure-chance choices. Maximum credits: 300 plus 100 (aural); total, 400. $N = 117$.

By making the choices as logical as possible, we hoped to reduce the percentage of unprofitable items and to increase the reliability of the test. How well we succeeded may be judged by the tabulated results of the test and an item analysis (Table 44). There were still 14.0 per cent of unprofitable items and 20.33 per cent of doubtful items in the written test, or a total of slightly more than one-third of the items that could be dispensed with and not greatly affect the spread of scores. But we had improved the 1938 situation by 10 per

cent. Evidently the test was a highly satisfactory instrument of measurement, if one may judge by its high coefficient of reliability (.97), a mean total score equivalent to 75 per cent of the maximum number of points possible, and a wide scatter. How much had the selection of distractors to do with the improvement in the number of discriminative items and with the high reliability of the examination? We could not be sure of the answer, for want of adequate controls, but we agreed that a close relationship seemed to exist between the two.

TABLE 44

|  | Reading-Vocabulary | Aural | Total |
|---|---|---|---|
| No. of items......... | 300 | 100 | 400 |
| No. of points........ | 300 | 100 | 400 |
| Mean score (points)... | 239.33 | 62.34 | 301.42 |
| Standard deviation... | 36.82 | 18.44 | 50.71 |
| Reliability index..... | .97 | .94 | .97 |
| Standard error....... | 6.38 | 4.52 | 8.78 |
| No. of cases......... | 117 | 117 | 117 |

The circumstances governing comprehensive examinations do not permit controlled experimentation. But inspection of many of the papers convinced us that we had successfully induced some of our students into error by the sequential nature of the wrong choices. The practice is somewhat questionable, in spite of the observation that in normal reading the erroneous understanding of a word may lead to further misconceptions along the line of the original error, the reader finding in the context a fictitious support for his continued misunderstanding. In short, one error may set up a sort of chain reaction of errors. It is regrettable that the staff did not explore this idea further.

*1940 form.*—Specifications: *I. Reading-vocabulary:* In context, multiple-choice technique, VB-1,000/4,500 range, CH-400. *II. Reading comprehension:* Paragraph, sentence completion, 3-choice in French. *III. Aural comprehension:* Lundeberg-Tharp aural test, Form B, all parts. Weighting: I, 200 items × 1; II, 25 items × 4; III, 100 items × 1. Total, 400. (Five reading passages: narration, drama, history, anecdote, description, verse.) Machine-scored. $N = 94$.

Because of the greatly increased vocabulary range from VB-1,000 to VB-4,500 and the separation of vocabulary from reading comprehension as a trial procedure, an analysis of the test was made by the examiner, Lawrence Andrus, with the results shown in Table 45.

The mean total score is 71 per cent of the maximum number of points, which may indicate that the examination was rather easy or that the group had achieved satisfactory results in the areas covered by the examination. The first interpretation seems untenable because Part III was a standardized test applicable to various levels of achievement, and the vocabulary difficulty in Part I was so controlled that words of highest frequency (VB-1,000) were not in-

TABLE 45

|  | Vocabulary I | Reading II | Aural III | Total |
|---|---|---|---|---|
| No. of items........ | 200 | 25 | 100 | 325 |
| No. of credits...... | 200 | 100 | 100 | 400 |
| Mean.............. | 145.10 | 77.15 | 62.30 | 284.12 |
| S.D............... | 28.86 | 21.59 | 16.38 | 59.02 |
| Variance........... | 835.12 | 465.93 | 268.25 | 3,483.46 |
| Reliability......... | .97 | .91 | .92 | .97 |
| Standard error...... | 5.00 | 6.48 | 4.63 | 10.22 |
| N................. | 94 | 94 | 94 | 94 |

cluded as items. The mean scores on Parts I and II together represent 69 per cent of the maximum number of points for the combined parts. The mean score on Part II seems rather high (77.15 per cent), but this is balanced by a large standard deviation, which would normally indicate that the test is excellent for purposes of classifying students in rank order. It seems fair, therefore, to interpret the mean score on the entire examination as indicating a satisfactory general level of attainment.

The reliability coefficient for Part II (reading comprehension) is as high as those reported for many standardized tests, and the coefficients for Part I and for the whole test are higher than usual for standardized tests. If Part II were extended to 100 points, by use of the Spearman-Brown prophecy formula, we could predict a reliability coefficient of .975.

The standard error of measurement of the whole examination is less than 4 per cent of the average score; that of Part I, little more than 3 per cent. These values are satisfactorily low. The higher standard errors for Parts II and III depend somewhat upon their shorter length. The low standard error of measurement for the whole examination means that the ranking of candidates in order of merit and the subsequent assignment of letter grades for certification are done with reasonably high precision. Ninety-four students took the examination; their grade distribution was as follows: 9 A's (9.6 per cent), 23 B's (24.5 per cent), 36 C's (38.2 per cent), 12 D's (12.7 per ent), and 14 F's (14.8 per cent). Correlations between the three parts of the examination are given in Table 46.

TABLE 46

| Part | I | II | III | Total |
|------|------|------|------|------|
| I......... | ........ | .77 | .54 | .94 |
| II........ | .77 | ........ | .55 | .82 |
| III....... | .54 | .55 | ........ | .79 |
| I, II..... | ........ | ........ | .56 | .95 |
| I, III..... | ........ | .78 | ........ | ........ |
| II, III.... | .65 | ........ | ........ | ........ |

The almost identical correlations of Parts I and II with Part III, although relatively low, are satisfactory, since presumably Part III (aural comprehension) measures an ability somewhat different from those measured by Parts I and II. Since the latter measure similar but not identical abilities, their correlation of .77 is reasonable, although not high enough to justify the omission of one of these two parts. The fact that the lowest correlation of a part with the entire examination (that of Part III) is greater than the highest inter-correlation (Part I with Part II) is significant. It means that the parts are so combined that each part contributes an important element to the entire examination, and the total score becomes a well-integrated single index of a student's competence in the abilities measured by the several parts.

An item analysis was carried out for Parts I and II. Theoretically, items passed by too large or too small a percentage of the group are either unprofitable or of doubtful value, in that their discriminative power is slight. In this connection, items passed by 95 per cent or more of the contestants were classified as unprofitable; items passed by 90–94 per cent, as of doubtful value. In Part I, 35 items (17.5 per cent) were answered correctly by more than 95 per cent of the contestants, and 30 items (15 per cent) by 90–94 per cent. The total percentage (32.5 per cent) of unprofitable and doubtful items in the vocabulary section, plus the 20 per cent of the items in Part II (reading) which were correctly answered by better than 90 per cent of the contestants, if reduced, would make the entire examination more discriminating.

*1941 form.*—Specifications: *I. Reading-vocabulary:* 150 items in paragraph context, multiple-choice response; range VB-1, 500–4,500, and CH-400, checked against the items passed by 90 per cent of the contestants in the 1940 examination. *II. Reading:* 50 items (100 credits) based on unedited passages; completion type, 3-choice in French response. *III. Aural comprehension:* Lundeberg-Tharp test, complete (100 items). *IV. Pronunciation:* 100-word passage, 25 items checked. Maximum credits: 375. Time, 4 hours. Machine-scored. $N = 59$.

An innovation in testing pronunciation in the 1941 examination became standard practice in succeeding tests. The oral test was scheduled previous to the comprehensive date. In a three-minute period, the contestant read a passage of 100 words before a panel of three judges, who checked the pronunciation of certain items only and certain qualities of connected speech, averaged their ratings, and reported the scores to the examiners. The contestants were allowed from 3 to 5 minutes to prepare silently, under supervision, for the oral reading. Later specifications stipulated weightings for such general qualities as elision, liaison, grouping, intonation, fluency, etc.

*1942 form.*—Specifications: *I. Vocabulary:* Double-column layout, with item in sentence context (left) and item repeated with write-in space (right); 120 items (100 in VB-3,500 range, and 20 items in VB-2,000–4,500). *II. Reading comprehension:* Five passages (novel, history, biography, sociology, criticism), questionnaire technique; 40 items (80 credits). *III. Aural comprehension:* Lundeberg-Tharp, Parts II, III (50 items). *IV. Pronunciation:* As for 1941. Maximum credits: 275. Time, 3 hours. Hand-scored. $N = 46$.

*1943 form.*—Specifications: *I. Vocabulary:* Sentence context; range VB-3,500, with few items in VB-4,500; 100 items. *II. Vocabulary-reading:* 125 items in paragraph context; four passages from Margueritte, Samains, Faguet, and Carrel. *III. Aural comprehension:* As for 1942 (50 items). *IV. Pronunciation:* As for 1941. Hand-scored. $N = 32$. (Old material.)

*1944 form.*—United States Armed Forces Institute lower-level French Test, Experimental Form LFV-1-B-4, in a trial run of the vocabulary and reading sections. Grammar omitted. Special *cultural background* section: Sentence completion, in French, 65 items. *Pronunciation:* As previously. Time, 4 hours. Partly machine-scored. $N = 30$. No data filed.

*1945 form.*—Specifications: U.S.A.F.I. reading, vocabulary, aural, and

grammar sections, lower-level B Form (upper-level form for vocabulary).
*Cultural background:* As previously, 50 items. *Pronunciation:* As previously.
Time, 4 hours. Partly machine-scored. $N = 52$.

The 1945 form was an experimental run, under the direction of the
examiner, Lawrence Andrus, of the complete battery of U.S.A.F.I.
French tests. The time allowance for the U.S.A.F.I. parts was 130
minutes for reading, vocabulary, and grammar sections, and 30
minutes for the aural test. The results are summarized in Table 47.

TABLE 47

| Part | Maxi-mum Points | Mean | Range |
|---|---|---|---|
| I. Vocabulary.... | 80 | 56.12 | 32–76 |
| II. Reading...... | 47 | 40.60 | 24–47 |
| III. Grammar..... | 60 | 32.65 | 18–52 |
| IV. Aural......... | 85 | 36.31 | 8–82 |

A descriptive leaflet of the U.S.A.F.I. tests and norms[74] indicates
that the college two-year norm in vocabulary, based on 734 cases
in 56 schools, was 39. The French 1 mean was at the ninety-first
percentile. The reading mean was at the ninety-sixth percentile in
the distribution for one college year, based on 810 cases in 40 schools.
In grammar, the average attainment equaled the norm for one
college year, based on 826 cases in 39 schools. There were no norms
for the aural comprehension test. The adaptation of the U.S.A.F.I.
aural test made later by Agard and Dunkel[75] differed from it in the
number and nature of the items and in the use of phonograph
records instead of a reader.

In the summer quarter, 1945, the U.S.A.F.I. tests (without the
grammar section) were administered as part of the comprehensive
examination in a special, "intensive" French 1 course, which provided the instruction of the regular sequence in the ten weeks of the
summer session. Twenty-one students took the test. They attained
a mean score of 57.67 in vocabulary (upper level), 37.86 in reading
(lower level), and 55.76 in aural comprehension. The results were
highly satisfactory and assured the intensive course of a permanent
place in the summer programs of the College.

*1946 form.*—Specifications: *I. Aural comprehension:* U.S.A.F.I. form, 85 items. *II. Vocabulary:* Sentence context, multiple-choice, 4-response, 100 items. *III. Reading comprehension:* Four passages (poetry, science, philosophy, narration), sentence completion, 4-choice, no vocabulary limitation; 20 items (100 credits). *IV. Civilization:* Sentence completion in French, 3-choice; 50 items. *V. Pronunciation:* As previously. Maximum credits: 360. $N = 47$ (summer quarter, 49). No data for the June administration filed. Summer quarter mean score on the U.S.A.F.I. aural test: 64.4, or 76 per cent of the maximum.

Testing cultural background knowledge as a course product is a thorny matter. If it is derived from a special textbook, the choice seems to lie between an account of contemporary French civilization subjectively related and an encyclopedic history of French civilization from Gallo-Roman times to the world war, replete with names, dates, and places which are confusing and uninteresting to the average undergraduate language student. A second choice is whether to teach the subject matter thoroughly, as in an "area" course, or superficially, in which case the instructor would have to select the points to bear emphasis and the form of the statements to be made about them. If the subject matter is to be a part of the comprehensive, he must further determine the time and manner of presenting the required facts in the course and must agree with his colleagues on their selection and presentation. There would then be the problem of how best to test this body of cultural knowledge, presumably held in common by the contestants, and what weight to give that subject matter relative to the other subject matters of the examination.

An alternative would be to do nothing in respect to the acquisition of cultural information other than to bring out of the intensive reading material such cultural content as it might contain or suggest, and to deal with the content in whatever way one wished, without consideration for a uniform and universal body of information for which all students in the course could be held responsible. The results of such an alternative are normally chaotic, one-sided, individually slanted, and quite subject to chance.

The first real attempt to attack the problem was made in the 1946 form by constructing a 50-item test that (*a*) had a proportionate distribution in time (periods and centuries) and in topics and (*b*) minimized the need for memorization of names, titles, and dates. The topical distribution of the 50 items was as follows: history (10), literature (10), geography (5), architecture (5), provinces (5), church and government (4), arts and sciences (5), Paris (5), and industry (1). The technique used was that of the incomplete statement with multiple-choice response, all in French. In the summer administration of the test, the norm was 34, or 68 per cent of the maximum number of points. It was an improvement over the preceding haphazard tests, but it was still too arbitrary and too exacting.

*1947 form.*—Specifications: *I. Aural comprehension:* U.S.A.F.I. test, Parts II, III (completion and definition), 50 items (25 credits). *II. Vocabulary:* 100 items (50 credits) in sentence context, 4-response, multiple-choice; range VB-3,500 and CH-300. *III. Reading:* Passages, with sentence-completion items, 4-choice, in French; 25 items (100 credits). *IV. Civilization:* Two techniques: selection, sentence completion; 50 items (50 credits). *V. Pronunciation:* As previously (25 credits). Maximum credits: 250. Machine-scored. $N = 127$.

Since this comprehensive was the first to be administered to a group composed mainly of war veterans, a special analysis was made of the results by the examiner, Hugh Walpole. His findings are summarized in Table 48.

TABLE 48*

| NAME OF PARTS | PART | INTERCORRELATION | | | | MAX. | MEAN | S.D. | r. |
|---|---|---|---|---|---|---|---|---|---|
| | | II | III | IV | V | | | | |
| Aural comprehension... | I | .40 | .26 | .27 | .54 | 50 | 38.75 | 7.06 | .84 |
| Vocabulary............ | II | ..... | .45 | .32 | .50 | 100 | 79.36 | 11.14 | .88 |
| Reading.............. | III | ..... | ..... | .45 | .27 | 25 | 15.65 | 3.31 | .49 |
| Civilization........... | IV | ..... | ..... | ..... | .25 | 50 | 30.51 | 7.61 | .81 |
| Pronunciation......... | V | ..... | ..... | ..... | ..... | 25 | 16.73 | 4.48 | .75 |

* $N = 96$. Reliability coefficients are based on the short form of the Kuder-Richardson formula, on a basis of one point per item.

The highest intercorrelation (.54) is between aural comprehension and pronunciation, as would be expected. "As one speaks, one hears" is not an empty phrase. In his own administrations of the Lundeberg-Tharp aural test, Professor Tharp[76] found a correlation of .82 to .93 between disk recordings of speech and the "phonetic accuracy" sections of his test, and a correlation of .82 between the disk ratings and scores on the Seibert-Wood[77] test.

The aural comprehension and vocabulary means suggest that those parts of the examination were relatively easy; the former is 77 per cent of the maximum, and the latter is 79 per cent. The omission of the phonetic accuracy section from the U.S.A.F.I. aural test would account for higher scores, as it may well account for a lower correlation between the aural and pronunciation sections than would have been found had the phonetic accuracy part been retained. The phonetic accuracy technique is usually highly discriminating. As for the vocabulary section, evidence points to too low a range (VB-3,500, without restriction) and too many non-discriminating choices.

The reading mean is relatively not high, being 65 per cent of the maximum. The low standard deviation (3.31) indicates a lack of spread in the scores and explains the relatively low index of reliability (.49). The 25 points were weighted heavily, counting 100 credits toward the total of 250, with a variance of 282.31, or 45.1 per cent of the total variance of the test. Its intrinsic contribution of 175.22, or 28 per cent, is slight. If reading ability is the principal aim of French 1 and if it is desirable to test that aim in the comprehensive examination, then the reading part of the test should contribute more to the total test, not just by excessive weighting of items, but by a larger number of items, and particularly of more discriminating items.

*1948 form.*—Specifications: *I. Aural comprehension:* Sentence-completion and definition type, 50 items. *II. Vocabulary:* Sentence context, 4-choice, VB-2,500–4,000, CH-300, 75 items. *III. Reading comprehension:* 5 passages (Voltaire, Maurois, Calmette, Hérédia), sentence completion, 4-choice, emphasis on interpretation, 39 items. *IV. Civilization:* 50 items, four sections: (*a*) references to reading sections; (*b*) relation of people, works, and events to five chronological divisions in French history; (*c*) relation of statements to four specified provinces; (*d*) identification of persons, movements, works of art or of literature), 4-choice in French. *V. Pronunciation:* 10 isolated words and 2 sentences (for elision, liaison, fluency, and general accuracy), with limited penalties, panel of judges, and composite rating; 20 credits. Total score: 292 points. $N = 207$ (College) and 29 (divisional): total, 236. Time, 3 hours.

There were several innovations in this test form: (1) a vocabulary section shortened in the number of items, time allowance (20 minutes), and range limits (VB-2,500–4,000); (2) longer reading passages and the inclusion of a complete short story (*Naissance d'un maître*) to be read "extensively" in a short time allowance; (3) four different techniques in the civilization section, one of them consisting of references to statements made in a historical passage in the reading section; and (4) an attempt to shorten the pronunciation test and to improve its objectivity, without too much loss of flexibility.

In scoring the test results, College and divisional students were graded separately, in order to learn to what extent, if any, the latter affected the grade distribution for the former. The influence of the 29 divisional students upon the total distribution was really slight. They earned between 15 and 16 per cent of the three highest rankings (A, B, C), 4 per cent of the barely satisfactory grades (D), and 5 per cent of the failures. The group constituted about 12 per cent of the enrolment. No separation of the two groups was made in subsequent test administrations.

In Tables 49 and 50 are given the intercorrelations of the five parts of the test, the mean scores for the parts, the standard deviations,

TABLE 49

| DESCRIPTION OF PARTS | PART | INTERCORRELATIONS | | | | | | MAX. SCORE | MEAN SCORE | S.D. | r. |
|---|---|---|---|---|---|---|---|---|---|---|---|
| | | 1 | 2 | 3 | 4 | 5 | Total | | | | |
| Aural comprehension | 1 | .... | .18 | .18 | .03 | .54 | .43 | 50 | 33.25 | 7.00 | .80 |
| Vocabulary | 2 | .18 | .... | .53 | .49 | .28 | .78 | 75 | 59.02 | 8.96 | .86 |
| Reading | 3 | .18 | .53 | .... | .41 | .23 | .77 | 39 | 30.98 | 4.02 | .63 |
| Civilization | 4 | .03 | .49 | .41 | .... | .15 | .64 | 50 | 31.38 | 7.24 | .80 |
| Pronunciation | 5 | .54 | .28 | .23 | .15 | .... | .49 | 20 | 13.22 | 3.54 | .68 |
| Total | | .... | .50 | .88 | 1.00 | .75 | .62 | .... | 292 | 216.48 | 26.39 | .92 |

TABLE 50

| Description | Part | 1 | 2 | 3 | 4 | 5 | Total |
|---|---|---|---|---|---|---|---|
| Aural comprehension | 1 | 17.64 | 6.77 | 9.12 | 0.91 | 8.03 | ....... |
| Vocabulary | 2 | 6.77 | 80.28 | 57.32 | 31.79 | 8.88 | ....... |
| Reading | 3 | 9.12 | 57.32 | 145.68 | 35.83 | 9.83 | ....... |
| Civilization | 4 | 0.91 | 31.79 | 35.83 | 52.42 | 3.84 | ....... |
| Pronunciation | 5 | 8.03 | 8.88 | 9.83 | 3.84 | 12.53 | ....... |
| Variance | | 17.64 | 80.28 | 145.68 | 52.42 | 12.53 | 308.55 |
| Per Cent | | 3 | 12 | 22 | 8 | 2 | 47 |
| Covariance | | 24.83 | 104.76 | 112.10 | 72.37 | 30.58 | 344.64 |
| Per cent | | 4 | 16 | 17 | 11 | 5 | 53 |
| Total variance | | 42.47 | 185.04 | 257.78 | 124.79 | 43.11 | 653.19 |
| Per cent | | 7 | 28 | 39 | 19 | 7 | 100 |
| Total possible score | | 30 | 75 | 117 | 50 | 20 | 292 |
| Per cent | | 10 | 26 | 40 | 17 | 7 | 100 |

and the separate coefficients of reliability, with the contributions of the parts to the total variance. In computing the reliabilities, the short form of the Kuder-Richardson formula was used. Weightings were used only in computing the data for total score. The intercorrelations between total score and part scores have been corrected for attenuation.

The 1948 form was a better test than its predecessor. But the improvement was not wholly the product of our efforts; chance, as usual, played a part in it.

The correlation coefficient of .54 for aural comprehension and pronunciation is the same as for the 1947 test, but the index of reliability for the pronunciation section (.68) is lower. Its contribution to the total test is small. The mean, however, when expressed in percentage of the maximum (66 per cent) is equivalent to that for the longer and more complicated form of the previous year. It seemed worth while to try the experimental procedure again.

The vocabulary mean of 59.02 is 78 per cent of the total possible, and the standard deviation of 8.96 indicates a good spread for the scores. Reliability is satisfactory (.86), giving assurance that that part of the test is measuring accurately what it does measure. The mean on the 1947 form was 79 per cent of the maximum, and the reliability index was .88. By reducing the testing time for that part to 20 minutes and the number of items from 100 to 75 and by compressing the range between VB-2,500 and VB-4,000, we had saved space and time, but we had not materially improved the test as we thought to do.

The results on the reading sections are not easy to interpret. The time allowance of 90 minutes was much too long. The examiner held the contestants to the full time, which affected the results upward, as the high mean (79 per cent of maximum) and small scatter (S.D., 4.02) show. Again the reliability is low (.63). The heavy weighting of the 39 items ($\times 3$) further complicates an analysis. There are two factors present in the situation, no doubt, i.e., a lack of discriminating items in sufficient number and a homogeneous group of examinees in knowing how to read. On the full test they incurred the lowest percentage of failure (8 per cent) in twenty years.

*1949 form.*—Specifications: *I. Pronunciation:* As for 1948; 40 items (20 credits). *II. Aural comprehension:* Completion and definition techniques; 25

items (25 credits). *III. Vocabulary:* Sentence context, 4-choice; range VB-1,000–3,500 and CH-300; 65 credits. *IV. Reading:* Five passages from Balzac, Gautier, Taine, Lanson, and complete short story by Scholl; sentence completion, 4-choice. *V. Civilization:* Three techniques: references to passages in Part IV, identification of items by provinces, and identification by movement, person, or title; 41 items (82 credits). Two credits added to Part V for two experimental items. Total points: 235. Time, 3 hours. $N = 222$.

The form differed from the 1948 test in four ways: (1) the aural test was halved, with the choices in French, on a theory that the flow of thought should be kept in the same language; (2) some items in the Balzac passage referred to statements or incidents in *Eugénie Grandet* that were not specifically covered by the selection but were presumably known from assigned study of the novel in the spring quarter; (3) the Taine and Lanson selections expressed separate views on the *Querelle des anciens et des modernes,* and three of the eleven items required comparison of the two points of view; (4) in Part V almost half the items were suggested by the reading passages in Part IV.

The inclusion of "known" material in the reading section may be censured in an examination purporting to measure independent skills. As a disciplinary action, it was neither defensible nor effective, although it was understandable, for during the year student attitude and co-operation had been at low ebb. Of 270 registrants, 222 took the comprehensive; and, had the usual standard of 65 per cent of the maximum number of points been maintained for a passing grade (D), 34 per cent of the contestants would have failed.

That the examination was, on the whole, a satisfactory instrument seems to be borne out by the data in Table 51. The percentage values of the part means, to be sure, were relatively low, but the coefficients of reliability were quite high, with the exception of the aural comprehension test. The standard deviations indicated a fair spread of scores for the several parts.

The reliability of the pronunciation section was the highest (.89) for the five parts. The percentage of its mean (67 per cent) was equal to the 1948 percentage (66 per cent), when the technique was first applied. The separate evaluation of specific items, the use of a checking chart and a panel of judges, the assessment of penalties for general deficiencies, and the allowance of four minutes for the preparation and oral reading of the material appeared to be a satisfactory solution to the problem of testing pronunciation objectively in a final examination.

The change in the technique of testing aural comprehension was unfortunate. As far as the examinees were concerned, the theory of "keeping the flow of thought in the same medium" ran counter to practice. Their aural competency depended too much upon the ability to convert the French stimulus rapidly into an English reaction. When the conversion was blocked by French instead of English choices, without the needed time to review mentally the

TABLE 51

| Part | Description | 1 | 2 | 3 | 4 | 5 | Total |
|------|-------------|---|---|---|---|---|-------|
| 1..... | Pronunciation | ....... | .42 | .35 | .32 | .33 | .50 |
| 2..... | Aural comprehension | ....... | ....... | .31 | .32 | .29 | .47 |
| 3..... | Vocabulary | ....... | ....... | ....... | .55 | .55 | .80 |
| 4..... | Reading | ....... | ....... | ....... | ....... | .66 | .85 |
| 5..... | Civilization | ....... | ....... | ....... | ....... | ....... | .76 |
| Mean score.................. | | 13.5 | 15.5 | 45.4 | 58.5 | 28.6 | 161.5 |
| S.D......................... | | 4.1 | 3.0 | 10.2 | 12.8 | 6.5 | 29.3 |
| Reliability.................... | | .89* | .36 | .88 | .81† | .79 | ....... |
| Maximum score............... | | 20 | 25 | 65 | 82 | 43 | 235 |
| Mean, in per cent.............. | | 67 | 62 | 70 | 71 | 67 | 69 |

\* Computed on the unweighted score (40).

† Computed on 41 as maximum score.

aural stimulus, they floundered in guesses. The aural section had the least reliability (.35), the lowest mean score (62 per cent), and the least scatter (S.D., 3.0).

A special attempt was made to increase the number of items in the reading section and to lessen the amount of the weighting. The mean score was equivalent to 71 per cent of the maximum number of points, with a satisfactory spread in individual achievement. The coefficient of reliability for that part of the examination (.81) seemed to indicate that the test measured satisfactorily what it really measured. But there was an open question: What did it really measure? Was it reading proficiency, or critical ability, or the knowledge of familiar content, or a blend of all three? For all three elements were present in the test.

*1950 form.*—Specifications: *I. Reading comprehension:* 6 passages (Prévost, Maupassant, Lanson, Saulnier, Du Bellay, Gautier), sentence completion, 4-choice. *II. Civilization:* General items, sentence completion, 4-choice. *III.*

*Aural comprehension:* Two techniques: (*a*) reaction to stimuli, (*b*) short oral passage with 3-choice English responses. *IV. Pronunciation:* As before. Total credits: 248. Weighting of parts not known. No analysis. $N = 215$.

This form was an experimental essay by the examiner, Roger Oake. He made four departures from previous practices: (1) the omission of a vocabulary section as a separate subject matter; (2) a compensatory increase in the length of the reading part and in the nature and number of its items; (3) the use of geometric designs as a medium of response to aural stimuli; and (4) the use of discourse in paragraph form for aural comprehension.

The vocabulary section was omitted in order to provide more time for the reading sections and to find the validity of the latter without reference to specific vocabulary or to grammatical variables (a part of the material in previous vocabulary tests). No limitation was placed upon vocabulary or idiom content in the examination, with the exception of the aural part. Theoretically, skill in reading with understanding such material as was presented in Part I implied a satisfactory command of forms, structure, and words. If our aim was reading skill, we should be able to test it by *direct* techniques applied to continuous discourse in prose or in verse and thereby eliminate testing vocabulary per se from an examination intended to measure only end-products. That was the theory.

The 1950 comprehensive, however, produced no clear evidence (if the results in letter grades were an index) of the success or failure of the theory in respect to "testing reading by reading only."

There were five possible reasons for its failure to produce convincing evidence: (1) the basic passage, a 2,000-word excerpt from Prévost's *Le Pas relevé*, required too much scanning and turning of pages in order to select from the 72 choices the 18 right answers, resulting in loss of time and effectiveness; (2) the inclusion of presumably known material (*Pierre et Jean*) from class and outside reading, and items that were unanswerable in the given passage; (3) the almost puzzle-solving technique needed for the identification of the correct responses to the 10 items of comparison based on the Lanson and Saulnier passages; (4) the presence of cultural background items (16 per cent) among the 56 items of the reading section; and (5) a purely arbitrary weighting of credits.

Part I was a test of reading skill, factual knowledge, reading content that was presumably known because of having been assigned, critical ability, and the comprehension of philosophical subtleties. Too many different things were being tested in too many different ways for any positive measurement of the validity of the whole as a test purely in the ability to read French.

In the aural comprehension part the comparative validity of either technique used could not be ascertained. In the use of geometric designs (circles, squares, triangles, quadrilaterals, intersecting lines, alone or in combination) as a means of reacting to spoken stimuli, the speech vocabulary is, of necessity, very limited and repetitive, and the general situation resembles a maze, exit from which too often depends upon the comprehension of one word of a structural nature, e.g., preposition, adverb, or connective. On the other hand, the paragraph-best-answer procedure has its shortcomings in the lengthened memory span necessitated by the selection of a number of responses from three or four times that number of choices.

The examination was not analyzed. It was obvious from the grade distribution that its validity as a whole was questionable; a passing grade of 60 per cent of the total number of credits would have failed 31 per cent of the contestants. But the test had demonstrated two things: (1) new approaches to testing reading and aural comprehension and (2) the difficulty in keeping achievement, accrediting, and discipline in their proper places.

*1951 form.*—Specifications: *I. Civilization:* Two parts: (*a*) 29 items, 4-choice completions or identifications; (*b*) 5 items, 4-choice identifications of historical events relative to time periods (34 credits). *II. Reading comprehension:* 6 passages (Montesquieu, Hugo, Maupassant, Corneille, Siegfried, Seignobos), sentence completion, 4-choice, 53 items ($\times 3$), 159 credits. *III. Aural comprehension:* Using line drawings to check reaction to oral stimuli, 12 items ($\times 2$), 24 credits. *IV. Pronunciation:* As before, 20 credits. Total credits: 237. $N = 141$. Mean: 159.9 points (67 per cent); S.D., 28.2 points (12 per cent).

In the 1951 examination, the examiner, Hugh Davidson, experimented further with testing reading comprehension without a vocabulary complement and in a heavy concentration of time and credits. It was a "power" situation. He included comparative and cultural items among the simple reading comprehension items, on the theory that both are (or may be) present under circumstances attendant upon reflective reading and therefore should be present under test conditions if depth as well as breadth of reading ability is to be measured.

The presence of cultural and comparative items, as stated previously, complicates the evaluation of a "reading" test. In this case, in order to determine whether Part II actually tested proficiency in vocabulary (and in grammar) independent of any contribution derived from a vocabulary test such as had been included in the comprehensive examinations previous to 1950, an analysis was made of the scores on the reading section of the comprehensive and on the R-form of the *Cooperative French Test* for a group of 88 students to whom the standard test was administered a few days before the comprehensive. The results are shown in Table 52.

TABLE 52

|                       | Mean    | S.D.  |
|-----------------------|---------|-------|
| A.C.E. vocabulary.... | 79.72   | 6.48  |
| A.C.E. grammar......  | 57.46   | 8.71  |
| Part II, reading*..... | 111.48 | 16.82 |

Correlations

A.C.E. vocabulary/Part II, reading.... .578
A.C.E. grammar/Part II, reading...... .340

\* Raw scores. A.C.E. scores are scaled.

The vocabulary mean exceeded the norm for two college years (77.4) by 2.3 points, with a percentile rank of 61. The standard deviation indicated a good spread. The grammar mean had a minus deviation of 5.3 points from the one-year college norm. Both means fell short of a twelve-year average; in fact, the total score on the Cooperative test (cf. p. 290) was the lowest for 1C since 1934.

Did the reading comprehension section of the comprehensive reveal this general weakness? Apparently not, since the coefficient of correlation between A.C.E. vocabulary and Part II was only .578, and between A.C.E. grammar and Part II, a low .340. One may conclude that the reading section in the 1951 comprehensive did not indicate a satisfactory ability to deal with vocabulary and grammar. It did not compensate for the omission of the vocabulary section of older test forms in the total situation.

The use of line drawings[78] instead of geometric figures to indicate reactions to oral stimuli avoided all the pitfalls of the latter technique tried out in the 1950 form and promised a very satisfactory solution to an old and perplexing testing problem.

In this discussion of past examinations three major purposes were in mind: first, to furnish informative data in lieu of the actual test forms for the fuller appreciation of the achievement in French 1, expressed in letter grades or in means on standard tests, to be presented in the following chapter; second, to indicate some of the problems that confront anyone who attempts to measure with accuracy attainment in a foreign language; and, third, to illustrate some of the devices and procedures employed to that end.

More could have been attempted and accomplished, had our efforts not been confined largely to final examinations primarily intended for grading students, or had it been permissible to repeat the whole or parts of a test, either in the original or in a revised form. Fundamentally, of course, an end-of-the-year examination is not the best time to try out experimental testing techniques, particularly when that examination affects the academic status and future of the examinees.

Good comprehensive examinations are not easily come by. Perfect ones, if once obtained, could in all likelihood not be duplicated in series. The task has to be performed anew each year. But the techniques can be sorted out by trial and retrial, by analysis, by concerted effort, and by perseverance.

## CHAPTER IX

# MEASUREMENTS. II

## 1. *Comprehensive Examination Grades*

SINCE 1932 the Office of the University Examiner has reported 2,419 grades for the first-year French sequence, of which 1,975 were incurred in the June administrations of the comprehensive examination, and 444 in the September administrations. With few exceptions, the former represent the product of the regular sequence, and the latter the product of the intensive ten-week "capsule" course in the summer quarter. The data for these two groups will be kept separate for purposes of comparison.

Since 1938, on nine occasions, the examiners have scheduled December examinations. Approximately 100 grades have been awarded on these examinations; they are not included in the following statistics because the majority of the cases were "retakes" because of previous failure or in order to improve a grade previously conferred.

To the description of the contents and techniques of the comprehensives discussed in the preceding chapter should be added certain information concerning the rules and procedures established for the administration of College comprehensive examinations. The following extracts from the *Résumé of Examination Rules and Procedures* (spring, 1950) furnish these facts:

Students must register not later than April 15 for all Spring quarter Comprehensive examinations at the Office of Test Administration. . . .

Your examination number should be printed in the spaces provided on each answer sheet and examination booklet. . . .

Each examination is based on the last syllabus which has been in use for three quarters.

After a student has been admitted to the University he may take any comprehensive examination. He need not register for nor attend any specific course before taking the examination. However, the fee for a comprehensive examination taken in fulfillment of the requirements of the College by a student who does not register for the courses offered to prepare him for that examination is . . . [the same as for the course].

A student who has completed a course is not required to take the comprehensive examination immediately upon the completion of that course. A student who has failed in an examination may take it again at any time the examination is scheduled in the future. He need not have attended any course nor have been in residence in the meantime.

A student may, if he wishes, repeat an examination in order to raise his grade. The higher grade is counted on the student's record. However, a student who has completed the requirements in the College may not repeat a College examination in order to raise the grade. [*Note:* A special fee is charged each time.]

If a student registers for an examination in a course and fails to report at the time and place designated, he is marked absent and no grade is recorded. . . . If a student does report for any part of an examination, a grade will be recorded for him. Thus, if he reports and answers none or a few questions, a failing grade will be recorded.

A comprehensive examination is based upon the entire year's work, even though the course has not been completed at the time of the examination.

The examinations are based on the syllabus and the indispensable readings listed in the syllabus. The policy of the Board is to require, insofar as it is feasible, that the student demonstrate that he can integrate, correlate, and apply the facts and principles of the course.

The papers are scored and the grades established without reference to the student's name. The grades are set by the instructional staff in cooperation with the Examiner, subject to the final approval of the appropriate Dean and the University Examiner. The student's grade is determined solely by the examination, with no reference to course records.

From the above statements it is evident that the number and identity of the students taking a certain comprehensive examination in a given year may not (and usually do not) coincide with the number and identity of the registrants for the course of study preparing for that examination; that there is no regular progress through the College by "years" and therefore no particular level of study represented by the registrants in a given course; that examinations, and *not* courses, explain progress through the College; and that not only may a student delay action in respect to a given examination, but he may take the examination without having either registered for or followed the course of study offered by the College in preparation for the examination.

Under these conditions, it is virtually impossible to track down the experiences of individuals or groups of individuals. One can perceive clearly, if at all, only mass progress in generalized terms. It is no longer possible to get back of the F grade, to explain an A grade, to promote or to demote, to analyze continuation study, to be sure in interpreting test performance, or to evaluate an instrument of measurement beyond a given moment. In this imprecise situation, stability and directions can be maintained only by such means as

TABLE 53

| Year | N | Per Cent A | Per Cent B | Per Cent C | Per Cent D | Per Cent F | Per Cent Passed |
|---|---|---|---|---|---|---|---|
| 1932 | 26 | 4 | 23 | 54 | 8 | 11 | 89 |
| 1933 | 68 | 7 | 22 | 46 | 18 | 7 | 93 |
| 1934 | 97 | 9 | 20 | 31 | 20 | 20 | 80 |
| 1935 | 100 | 10 | 18 | 46 | 13 | 13 | 87 |
| 1936 | 91 | 12 | 20 | 43 | 14 | 11 | 89 |
| 1937 | 78 | 13 | 14 | 45 | 17 | 12 | 88 |
| 1938 | 96 | 13 | 14 | 60 | 7 | 6 | 94 |
| 1939 | 117 | 11 | 19 | 41 | 16 | 13 | 87 |
| 1940 | 94 | 10 | 25 | 38 | 13 | 15 | 85 |
| 1941 | 59 | 5 | 21 | 44 | 20 | 10 | 90 |
| 1942 | 87 | 9 | 15 | 52 | 11 | 13 | 87 |
| 1943 | 32 | 3 | 22 | 53 | 3 | 19 | 81 |
| 1944 | 30 | 10 | 17 | 47 | 17 | 10 | 90 |
| 1945 | 52 | 12 | 19 | 42 | 15 | 12 | 88 |
| 1946 | 47 | 13 | 19 | 42 | 15 | 11 | 89 |
| 1947 | 127 | 6 | 22 | 44 | 18 | 10 | 90 |
| 1948 | 236* | 10 | 19 | 41 | 22 | 8 | 92 |
| 1949 | 223 | 11 | 19 | 35 | 21 | 14 | 86 |
| 1950 | 215 | 11 | 20 | 39 | 18 | 12 | 88 |
| 1951 | 141 | 9 | 21 | 38 | 14 | 18 | 82 |

* This number includes 29 divisional cases.

course outlines and standardized tests. They are the great stabilizers in teaching.

The results of twenty annual June administrations of the French 1 comprehensive, expressed in percentages of the total number of grades assigned each year, are given in Table 53. Of the 1,975 grades, 9.4 per cent were A's; 19.4 per cent B's; 44.0 per cent C's; 15.0 per cent D's; and 12.2 per cent F's. Of the total number of students, 87.8 per cent received passing grades. When one considers that between 1932 and 1952 there were depression, prewar, wartime and postwar years, the record is, to say the least, satisfactory.[1]

The percentage range for various grades shows considerable deviation from the standard "grade curve." For instance, the A grade ranges from 3 per cent in 1943 to 13 in 1937, 1938, and 1946; the F grade from a low of 6 per cent in 1938 to a high of 20 in 1934. The minutes of "post mortem" staff meetings contain conjectural explanations for such fluctuations; but sometimes there was factual evidence on hand to account for them, as in the case of the downward shift of percentages from C to D to F (20 per cent) in 1934, the first year of the application to French 1 of the "Iowa Plan," with the unsatisfactory results related in the preceding chapter, or the reverse swing upward from F to D to C (60 per cent) in 1938, when the vocabulary and reading sections of the comprehensive contained

TABLE 54

| Year | $N$ | Per Cent A | Per Cent B | Per Cent C | Per Cent D | Per Cent F | Per Cent Passing |
|------|-----|------------|------------|------------|------------|------------|------------------|
| 1945 | 21 | 14 | 19 | 38 | 15 | 14 | 86 |
| 1946 | 49 | 8 | 23 | 38 | 18 | 13 | 87 |
| 1947 | 123* | 10 | 15 | 42 | 15 | 18 | 82 |
| 1948 | 98 | 13 | 28 | 26 | 18 | 15 | 85 |
| 1949 | 78 | 6 | 18 | 24 | 28 | 24 | 76 |
| 1950 | 75 | 7 | 20 | 38 | 19 | 16 | 84 |

* A small group of veterans who began the regular sequence in the winter quarter and completed it in the summer is included in this figure.

unprofitable and doubtful items to the extent of 44 per cent of the total number of points.

Particularly noticeable in Table 53 are the high percentages of the passing grades for the four "GI" years, 1947 to 1950 inclusive. Here the human factor outweighed the mechanics of testing and the law of averages. This "language learning business," as Palmer and Redman called it,[2] is as complicated and fortuitous as business in the commercial sense.

The first "intensive" French 1 course was offered in 1945, in the ten weeks of the summer quarter; there have been six repetitions of the course to date. The comprehensive examinations were identical with the regular (June) forms. The grade percentages are shown in Table 54. Of the 444 grades, 9.7 per cent were A's; 20.5 per cent B's; 34.2 per cent C's; 18.7 per cent D's; and 16.7 per cent F's. The percentage of passing grades (83.3 per cent) was 4.5 per cent less than the passing percentage for the regular sequence. The trend was downward from C to D to F, which confirms the belief of the staff that the closely packed, intensive, summer course is too concentrated and does not afford the protracted spread of language practice needed to produce the best results. No small factor in the lessened quality and quantity of the products is the summertime in Chicago. The experiment proves, nevertheless, that the Reading Method can be used in an intensive course with profit.

## 2. Aural Proficiency

Since 1932, with the exception of 1933, an auditory test has been a part of the comprehensive examination for French 1. From 1935 to 1943 inclusive, the form used was the *Lundeberg-Tharp Audition Test in French*;[3] from 1946 to 1948, the U.S.A.F.I. aural test; and from 1949 to 1952, specially prepared forms of a tentative nature. The scores obtained on these tests were added to those on the other parts of the comprehensive to form the total score used in ranking, except in a few instances when part analyses were made. The scattered analyses are presented here as objective proof of the quality of aural attainment possible in a reading method course.

The Lundeberg-Tharp test was composed of three parts: (1) fifty groups of four near-homonyms, each one of which must be identified when spoken; (2) a series of twenty-five incomplete statements, the key word to which must be supplied in English or in French; and (3) a series of short definitions which must be identified in similar manner. The maximum number of points possible was 100, subject to the usual formula for the correction of guessing. Only the data for four administrations are obtainable (Table 55). The mean score for the 402 cases is 62.4 per cent of the maximum number of points, which seems to indicate a fairly high degree of achievement, considering the difficulties usually encountered in auditory tests. Since the tests were administered by someone not on the teaching staff of French 1, the results were free of that particular source of influence.

The only norms for the Lundeberg-Tharp test known to the writer are those published in 1929 in connection with the tentative form, which are wanting in precise information about the sources of the data. The norm for "two college semesters" is 56.6 points, or 56.6 per cent of the maximum number possible; for "three college quarters," 70.3 per cent. The apparent equivalence in time is not explained.

The U.S.A.F.I. *Test of Aural Comprehension*, Form B, was similar to the Lundeberg-Tharp test except for the reduction of the number of items in the phonetic accuracy section (Part I) from 50 to 35, resulting in a maximum of 85 points instead of 100 points for the complete test. Results on this test as a part of the comprehensive examinations from 1945 to 1948 are given in Table 56.

TABLE 55

| Year | N | Mean (Per Cent) |
|------|------|------|
| 1935......... | 100 | 64.0 |
| 1936......... | 91 | 61.0 |
| 1939......... | 117 | 62.3 |
| 1940......... | 94 | 62.3 |

TABLE 56

| Year | N | Mean (Per Cent) |
|------|------|------|
| 1945*........ | 21 | 65.6 |
| 1946......... | 47 | 75.6 |
| 1946*........ | 49 | 70.6 |
| 1947......... | 127 | 66.0 |
| 1948......... | 236 | 56.4 |

* Intensive course, summer quarter.

The 1944 administration was a failure, owing to the operation of a power lawnmower under the windows of the examination hall, and the scores had to be omitted from the final tally; in the 1948 administration, the antics of an overexpressive French examiner nearly ruined the test. Such are some of the hazards of an aural language test! However, on the five administrations given in Table 56, 480 students averaged 66.8 per cent of the maximum number of points, which compares well with the results on the Lundeberg-Tharp test. No norms were published for the U.S.A.F.I. form.

A third set of data was collected by Harold B. Dunkel for the Investigation of the Teaching of a Second Language, an inquiry established at the University of Chicago in 1944 by a grant from the

Rockefeller Foundation and directed by Professor R. W. Tyler. One of the two major purposes of the investigation was to study the effects of applying A.S.T.P. oral-aural and intensive methods to peacetime language instruction in schools and colleges. The influx of veterans in 1946 forced the abandonment of experimentation, and the survey ended.

For purposes of comparison, the investigation's *Lower Level French Aural Comprehension Test*[4] was given to four groups of French 1 students who had (*a*) completed 105 hours of the course and (*b*) taken the *Cooperative French Test* in grammar, vocabulary, and reading at three points in the year, i.e., at 35, 70, and 105 hours.

TABLE 57

| Group | N | Cooperative Test | | I.T.S.L. Aural Test | |
|---|---|---|---|---|---|
| | | Mean | Per-centile | Mean | Decile |
| June, 1945........ | 23 | 77.6 | (99) | 36.1 | (8) |
| June, 1946........ | 13 | 76.5 | (98) | 38.6 | (8) |
| Aug., 1946........ | 13 | 76.5 | (98) | 34.9 | (8) |
| Aug., 1946*...... | 16 | 78.4 | (99) | 44.3 | (10) |
| June, 1945†...... | 8 | 76.5 | (98) | 30.5 | (7) |
| Aug., 1946†...... | 15 | 77.6 | (99) | 34.1 | (8) |

\* All-veteran group.
† With previous experience. Means and percentiles are for one college year.

The total number of cases involved was 88, because of these restrictions. Two of the groups were subdivided statistically, permitting comparison between students with no previous experience, students with previous experience, and an all-veteran group. Both regular and summer intensive courses were represented. Mean scores and percentile ranks on the final Cooperative tests, and mean scores and decile ranking on the I.T.S.L. aural test are shown in Table 57.

The total score norm for one college year on the *Cooperative Advanced French Test* (Form R) is 66.7; for two college years, 76.4. The means for the Chicago groups are equal to, or better than, the national two-year norm. The norm for one college year on the investigation's *Aural French Test*, based on 1,808 students in 21 colleges, was 26.38, which is much less than the lowest mean score for any University of Chicago group tested. The decile rankings for

the several groups were abnormally high. Since the reliability coefficient of the test is .86, these ratings may be assumed as dependable.

The investigators, Agard and Dunkel, commented on the College
performance[5] as follows:

Despite the major emphasis on reading, the consistently high aural scores
demonstrate that aural skill can be a successful by-product of the "extensive-
reading method." Once again the command which these students have of the
high frequency vocabulary and constructions stands them in good stead when
taking the aural tests based on these same counts. Correlation between the
reading and aural skills is generally high as a result, though all the groups are
relatively small and hence the coefficients are subject to considerable sampling
error. French group 1d indicated by * in the above table, which made a higher
aural score than the others, was made up entirely of war veterans, some of
whom had seen service in France or North Africa [p. 153].

For all languages, at instructional levels from one college semester to three
college years, the vast majority of coefficients between the aural and the Cooperative scores fall in the range .30/.60. . . . The usual relation gives little
assurance that aural skill necessarily accompanies reading skill or *vice versa*. He
who teaches reading will not produce students who necessarily understand the
language when spoken; he who teaches aural comprehension will not find his
students automatically developing into competent readers. When both the
scores in the two sorts of skills and their correlation tend to be high (as, for
example, at College G), one finds that a specific reading program has been effectively combined with a specific aural program [p. 158].

### 3. *The Story of the "Cooperatives"*

Between 1934 and 1950, an advanced form (N, O, P, Q, R) of the
*Cooperative French Test* was administered eleven times to French
1A registrants in attendance at the end of the autumn quarter. The
mean scores in reading (R), vocabulary (V), grammar (G), and
total score (T), expressed in *scaled* scores that facilitate comparison,
are set out in Table 58.

The grammar section was omitted in the 1934–37 administrations; total scores are therefore lacking for those years. In 1937–38
the test was not given; that was the year of the reorganization of
the College curriculum. It was omitted also during the war years,
1940–44. In 1947 it was given to a mid-year section of veteran
registrants at the end of the winter quarter. All these groups were
"mixed," containing students with or without previous experience in
French, at study levels ranging from eleventh-grade registrants in

the four-year college to second-year "divisionals" (normally, college Seniors). In 1946 the influx of war veterans and the adoption of a foreign language requirement for the B.A. degree added two new factors of some weight in later results.

The most striking thing about these data is their uniformity over the span of fifteen years. In reading, for example, the range is 54–63, a difference of 9 points; in vocabulary, the range is 63–71, a difference of 8 points. If one considers the changing conditions on the campus of the university and in the world at large, the extreme differences represented in our course personnel in the prewar, war,

TABLE 58

| Year | N | R | V | G | T |
|---|---|---|---|---|---|
| 1934–35..... | 94 | 59.0 | 64.5 | .......... | ......... |
| 1935–36..... | 95 | 58.0 | 66.7 | .......... | ......... |
| 1936–37..... | 73 | 57.3 | 63.0 | .......... | ......... |
| 1938–39..... | 106 | 54.4 | 65.3 | 53.3 | 57.8 |
| 1939–40..... | 116 | 54.0 | 63.6 | 54.2 | 57.9 |
| 1944–45..... | 63 | 56.6 | 66.4 | 50.6 | 58.0 |
| 1945–46..... | 66 | 56.9 | 65.0 | 50.4 | 58.1 |
| 1946–47..... | 135 | 60.2 | 64.1 | 53.0 | 59.7 |
| 1947–48..... | 177 | 60.9 | 71.2 | 54.2 | 63.0 |
| 1947, w...... | 32 | 60.7 | 67.8 | 51.0 | 60.6 |
| 1948–49..... | 156 | 63.0 | 70.2 | 54.4 | 63.7 |
| Total (11) | 1,113 | 58.3 | 66.1 | 52.6 | 59.8 |

and postwar years, the absence of pronounced fluctuations in each of the language aspects tested, and the very definite upward trend of the averages from year to year, one must conclude (as it seems to the author) that French 1A as conducted during that period approximated at least the ideal toward which we had been working since 1920.

Behind the achievement of certain years there are specific causes of which one may be certain, as, for example, the steady level in reading and vocabulary maintained during 1934–37 by the individualized study plan and the use of the West-type readers of the "Chicago French Series," or the peak in the reading and vocabulary means in 1946–49, which was the period of controlled intensive and extensive reading of the *Graded Readers*. The steady rise over the whole period in vocabulary command is no doubt an effect of the gradation of the early reading material and of the emphasis on systematic word study. The fact that the mean achievement in vocabulary (66.1) is in excess of the mean achievement in reading (58.3) is a sign that the 1A student is still preoccupied with words rather than with the longer unit of the sentence. He is concentrating on word stock.

The general upward trend of all the means in 1946–49 can be explained by a combination of causes, such as the presence of a large number of war veterans, who were serious and usually excellent students; a closely integrated program of plateau reading; a higher percentage of upper-level students; and the newly applied system of quarterly examinations. On the other hand, the insignificant differences in the grammar range (4 points) during the period 1938–49 are no doubt due to the same treatment in amount and kind of grammatical instruction (*En Route*) year after year, without change. A much greater range would be undesirable for our main objective.

In French 1A there is not much difference in performance between the students who had had some previous experience with French and those who had had none before entering college. The main superiority of the former is usually in grammar, as the comparison in Table 59 shows.

Of the 552 students represented in this analysis, 344 had had some contact with the language before entering French 1A, and 208 had had none. The group with experience had the advantage of a minimum of two semesters elsewhere *plus* the review training afforded in 1A; yet it averaged only 4.7 points more in reading and 8.2 points in grammar and was no better than the inexperienced group in vocabulary.

Any comparison of the 1A attainment with standard norms involves an unequal matching of time, because the published norms are for years and not for quarters. However, in spite of the disparity in length of exposure, the average performance in 1A was equivalent to the two-year high-school norm in reading (57.7) and in vocabulary (64.8), but it was inferior in grammar by 4.7 points. There was little difference between the respective means for total score. Compared with one-year college norms, the 1A means were close, but not equivalent.

It should be noted that in these and other comparisons with Cooperative norms, all data entering into the comparisons are those reported for "Type I" schools and colleges, which are defined as "pre-professional," the classification being based upon the performance of entering students on the A.C.E. psychological examination. On this test, entering students in the College averaged between .83 and .93 in terms of the national norms.

TABLE 59

| Year | N | R | V | G | T |
|---|---|---|---|---|---|
| | | | A. Without Experience | | |
| 1944–45..... | 23 | 57.4 | 70.0 | 48.3 | 58.9 |
| 1944–45..... | 43 | 55.9 | 66.9 | 49.2 | 57.4 |
| 1945–46..... | 12 | 57.2 | 64.8 | 49.1 | 57.7 |
| 1946–47..... | 70 | 56.8 | 62.7 | 42.8 | 56.4 |
| 1947–48..... | 93 | 59.2 | 65.6 | 52.0 | 59.7 |
| 1948–49..... | 103 | 61.0 | 70.4 | 52.0 | 61.9 |
| Total (6) | 344 | 57.9 | 66.7 | 48.9 | 58.7 |
| | | | B. With Experience | | |
| 1944–45..... | 8 | 59.9 | 65.2 | 56.4 | 60.9 |
| 1944–45..... | 19 | 58.3 | 65.1 | 53.7 | 59.4 |
| 1946–47..... | 65 | 63.6 | 65.5 | 57.2 | 63.0 |
| 1947–48..... | 63 | 65.0 | 66.8 | 59.1 | 64.8 |
| 1948–49..... | 53 | 66.4 | 69.7 | 58.9 | 66.9 |
| Total (5) | 208 | 62.6 | 66.5 | 57.1 | 63.0 |

In French 1B, there have been only eight administrations of the Cooperative tests since 1934, for which there are available records. None were scheduled in 1937–44. As in previous tables, the means shown in Table 60 are *scaled scores* and not raw scores.

Under New College conditions, as explained, the testing of progress from quarter to quarter had its difficulties and uncertainties. That is particularly true of the second quarter of French 1, which explains the smaller number of administrations of the Cooperative tests at that point. The norms for the 621 students for whom scores were tabulated show that the average 1B student made remarkable progress, particularly in reading ability, in which he has a percentile rank of 92 on the basis of one college year. In 1A he had a percentile rank of 29 on the same basis.

The means for reading and vocabulary show an upward progression within a range of 18.2 points, whereas the grammar range is limited to 3.5 points. Any gain in the latter is almost wholly a byproduct of the reading experience. The discrepancy in 1A between

TABLE 60

| Year | N | R | V | G | T |
|---|---|---|---|---|---|
| 1934–35..... | 87 | 70.2 | 73.0 | 57.0 | 67.8 |
| 1935–36..... | 70 | 69.3 | 76.3 | 57.0 | 69.0 |
| 1944–45..... | 54 | 78.2 | 75.9 | 59.2 | 73.6 |
| 1945–46..... | 58 | 78.4 | 78.6 | 57.3 | 73.7 |
| 1946*....... | 30 | 80.2 | 76.0 | 55.4 | 72.8 |
| 1946–47..... | 93 | 81.0 | 74.3 | 53.9 | 72.0 |
| 1947*....... | 27 | 87.5 | 80.1 | 55.4 | 76.3 |
| 1947–48..... | 202 | 75.1 | 76.9 | 56.8 | 71.2 |
| Total (8) | 621 | 77.5 | 76.4 | 56.5 | 72.1 |

* Spring quarter administrations.

TABLE 61

| Course | N | R | V | G | T |
|---|---|---|---|---|---|
| 1A................. | 1,113 | 58.3 | 66.1 | 52.6 | 59.8 |
| 1B................. | 621 | 77.5 | 76.4 | 56.5 | 72.1 |
| Deviates............. | ........ | 19.2 | 10.3 | 3.9 | 12.3 |
| Per cent of gain....... | ........ | 33 | 16 | 7 | 21 |
| Percentile rating*..... | ........ | 92 | 80 | 27 | 71 |

* The P.R. is based on one college year.

the mean scores in reading and vocabulary has disappeared in 1B. The student is moving away from the perception of single speech units to the comprehension of combinations of units. The shift appears more clearly in the comparison between the total group means for 1A and 1B (Table 61).

The high gain in reading (33 per cent) and the lesser gain in vocabulary (16 per cent) have brought the two skills into balance. The grammar gain (7 per cent) is doubtless due to the influence of structural patterns seen and heard many times and in slight degree to the presence of one-unit registrants. Experience proved that unless speech and writing were in the program for 1B, the grammar mean on the Cooperative test fluctuated within narrow limits and stayed at a much lower level than the means for reading and vocabulary. Even in 1C it rarely rose above a scaled score of 59. The skilled reader for whom the speech patterns have become familiar is unaware of structural details.

At the end of 1B, in reading and vocabulary, students without previous experience in French were ahead of the experienced group. In a sampling of 108 cases without experience and 54 cases with experience, the former attained a mean in reading 3.3 points higher than for the latter. The tortoise had caught up with the hare.

A comparison of the 1B means with high-school and college norms at various levels (as in Table 62) indicates that 1B had an equiva-

TABLE 62

| Term | R | V | G | T |
|---|---|---|---|---|
| French 1B............ | 77.5 | 76.4 | 56.5 | 72.1 |
| High school, 2 years.... | 57.7 | 64.8 | 57.3 | 60.8 |
| High school, 3 years.... | 67.3 | 74.6 | 64.9 | 70.8 |
| High school, 4 years.... | 74.5 | 81.3 | 70.4 | 77.9 |
| College, 1 year........ | 63.6 | 69.1 | 62.8 | 66.7 |
| College, 2 years........ | 75.7 | 77.4 | 68.6 | 76.4 |

lence of *three* high-school years or approximately *two* college years, except in grammar. In fact, the 1B mean in reading exceeded the four-year norm for high schools and the second-year norm for colleges. The equivalence with third-year high-school norms becomes even more pronounced if one compares them to the performance of the 108 students who had had no previous experience in French. The latter achieved a mean of 78.6 in reading, 78.3 in vocabulary, 56.0 in grammar, and 73.1 in total score.

The attainment of 1A and 1B on the Cooperative tests raised the question of how to interpret the results obtained by the tests in 1946 and 1947, when they were used as placement examinations for the satisfaction of the College language requirement.[6] Table 63 gives the norms on the Cooperative test for 1A, 1B, and the 1946 and 1947 placements and reveals the question to be a rather serious one.

The 1946 placement group was not duly apprised of the language requirement and was caught off guard. In 1947 the contestants were informed well in advance and were able to review the subject in the summer, as the results for that year seem to indicate.

The 194 high-school graduates who took the 1947 placement test had an average experience of five semesters in French, and 30 per cent of the group averaged six semesters. In recency, 68 per cent had completed their language study in June, three months previous to the placement examination. Their mean scores were midway between the national two-year and three-year norms in reading, vocabulary, grammar, and total score, and therefore matched their average exposure of five semesters. In general intelligence they were a somewhat superior group of students, having a quotient of .92 on the A.C.E. (Thurstone) psychological test.

TABLE 63

| Term | N | R | V | G | T |
|---|---|---|---|---|---|
| French 1A.............. | 1,113 | 58.3 | 66.1 | 52.6 | 59.8 |
| French 1B.............. | 621 | 77.5 | 76.4 | 56.5 | 72.1 |
| Placement, 1946........ | 185 | 59.0 | 63.0 | 44.0 | 56.0 |
| Placement, 1947........ | 194 | 62.0 | 68.0 | 61.0 | 65.0 |
| High school, 2 years, norm | 2,000 | 57.7 | 64.8 | 57.3 | 60.8 |

However, except for a minus deviation in grammar, the achievement of the French 1B group so far surpassed the achievement of the placement group as to indicate for the prospective entrants the likelihood of a high percentage of failure to meet the language requirement, and to make inadvisable placing within 1ABC beyond the second quarter.

Actually, 70 per cent of this group failed in the placement test; 16 per cent were placed in 1B or 1C; and 14 per cent passed and were excused from the language requirement in full.

The test records for 1C, unfortunately, are incomplete. The proximity of the comprehensives in the spring, with "free" periods for reading and review in many subjects, induces such irregularity of attendance that barely a third to a half of a section can be reached for testing at any one time. Also, the best and the poorest students, for quite different reasons, no longer attend class. Table 64 presents all the data available on 12 administrations of the *Cooperative French Test* between 1934 and 1951, involving 716 completions in 1C.

The means in reading range from 76.5 to 90.2, a deviation of 13.7 points; in vocabulary, from 79.0 to 85.5, a difference of 6.5 points; and in grammar, from 55.4 to 66.5, a difference of 11.1 points. The relation between the attainment in reading and the attainment in grammar is very significant, particularly after 1938, when the use of a composition-type grammar was discontinued in 1C and the only grammatical instruction of a formal sort was limited to the use of *En Route* in 1A.

TABLE 64

| Year | N | R | V | G | T |
|------|------|------|------|------|------|
| 1934–35..... | 71 | 76.5 | 79.0 | 59.0 | 75.6 |
| 1935–36..... | 60 | 79.0 | 83.5 | 66.5 | 77.4 |
| 1938–39..... | 80 | 78.6 | 82.1 | 60.5 | 75.6 |
| 1939–40..... | 82 | 77.9 | 84.0 | 58.6 | 76.0 |
| 1944–45..... | 43 | 83.1 | 81.5 | 57.5 | 76.6 |
| 1945–46..... | 49 | 84.9 | 83.7 | 59.9 | 79.0 |
| 1946–47..... | 24 | 90.2 | 80.2 | 59.4 | 79.0 |
| 1946–M..... | 24 | 87.8 | 82.2 | 56.8 | 78.4 |
| 1946–Su..... | 30 | 84.3 | 81.1 | 55.4 | 77.3 |
| 1947–48..... | 135 | 87.4 | 85.5 | 59.3 | 80.1 |
| 1948–Su..... | 32 | 82.3 | 83.5 | 56.8 | 76.4 |
| 1950–51..... | 90 | 79.0 | 80.0 | 57.0 | 74.0 |
| Total (12) | 716 | 82.6 | 82.2 | 58.9 | 77.1 |

The percentile rank of the mean score in reading is 97, on the basis of one college year; in vocabulary, 92; and in total score, 85. These percentiles for mean scores are extremely high. In grammar the percentile rank is 34, slightly higher than for 1B (27). The highest mean total score (in 1947–48) is 80.1, which is at the ninety-second percentile on a one-year basis and at the sixty-fifth percentile on a two-year basis.

When it is recalled that these scores are *averages* and that half the students obtained scores above the indicated norms, then the achievement of French 1, under the conditions that have been described, is almost fantastic. So congested is the distribution of individual scores in 1C in the upper quartile, particularly in reading and vocabulary, that it can be seriously questioned whether the Cooperative tests produced reliable indices of the actual proficiency of the upper 20 per cent of the examinees.

In 1C, as in 1B, those students who had had no previous contact with French on entering the sequence attained equal or higher levels in reading and vocabulary than those with previous experience. In reading, the group with experience achieved a mean score of 84.7, compared to a mean of 84.8 for the group without experience. In vocabulary, the mean for the former was 81.9; for the latter, 83.6. In point of time spent to achieve this equivalence, the group with previous experience was a heavy loser.

It cannot be known exactly how representative of the total enrolment in French 1 these various groups were. For example, in 1947–48, we find that 177 students took the Cooperative test at the end of

TABLE 65

| Group | R | V | G | T |
|---|---|---|---|---|
| French 1A............ | 58.3 | 66.1 | 52.6 | 59.8 |
| French 1B............ | 77.5 | 76.4 | 56.5 | 72.1 |
| French 1C............ | 82.6 | 82.2 | 58.9 | 77.1 |
| 1947 placement........ | 62.0 | 68.0 | 61.0 | 65.0 |
| College, 1 year........ | 63.6 | 69.1 | 62.8 | 66.7 |
| College, 2 years........ | 75.7 | 77.4 | 68.6 | 76.4 |
| High school, 1 year.... | 40.0 | 47.3 | 43.8 | 42.9 |
| High school, 2 years.... | 57.7 | 64.8 | 57.3 | 60.8 |
| High school, 3 years.... | 67.3 | 74.6 | 64.9 | 70.3 |
| High school, 4 years.... | 74.5 | 81.3 | 70.4 | 77.9 |

1A, 202 at the end of 1B, and 97 at the end of 1C. But 236 took the comprehensive examination in June! The question of representation, therefore, is unanswerable.

Table 65 presents in summary form the total group mean scores for 1A, 1B, and 1C; the high-school norms for four years; the college norms for two years; and the 1947 placement norms. All scores are scaled scores, as in preceding tables. Two thousand four hundred and fifty cases furnished the data for French 1ABC; 194 cases for the 1947 placement means; 2,000 cases for the college norms; and 2,500 cases for the high-school norms.

The average achievement in reading, vocabulary, and total score at the end of French 1 reached or surpassed the level for *four* high-school years or *two* college years. In grammar the 1C mean surpassed the second-year high-school norm but fell below the first-year college norm. This deficiency in grammar is a direct result of de-emphasizing speech and writing, just as the high equivalences in reading and vocabulary are the product of the concentration upon reading. The question is one of relative importance and of what is desired.[7]

The rapid progress made in 1B, leading to an average achievement in reading and vocabulary equal to the norms for two college years, suggests a possible use for the third quarter other than for the refinement of reading ability, namely, the cultivation of speech and writing. With half-a-million words of running discourse and thousands of repetitions of speech patterns behind him, a high degree of proficiency might be obtained by even the average student. The experiment would necessitate favorable conditions, careful planning, a long-term run, and special *outillage* for teaching and testing.[8] Such an undertaking belongs more properly in a program of language specialization than in a course of study designed for general education. However, in the long experience of the College French staff with the Reading Method, there has never been a sustained doubt as to the high quality of language use attainable in 1C, were it to be made the principal objective of that course.[9]

## 4. *A Study of French Placements*

Since 1946, when the foreign language requirement for the B.A. degree went into effect, placement examinations in French have been offered for entering students who wished to present that language in satisfaction of the requirements.[10] The ways by which these requirements could be satisfied are explained in the following excerpt from official statements:

Placement is to be determined on the basis of equivalence to performance on the comprehensive examinations in so far as that can be revealed in a short placement test. In order to be excused from a comprehensive examination in any of the following subjects, the student's placement test performance should be equivalent to a C grade on the comprehensive examination. . . .

The placement tests are to be constructed and scored in such a way as to permit the classification of entering students into the following groups: (A) those who have the equivalent of a particular comprehensive examination and will not be required to take that examination; (B) those who have a large proportion of the skills and understandings covered in a particular examination and who may be advised to take that comprehensive examination after less than full attendance at the course; (C) those who may be held only for a certain portion of a course and only for a certain part of the comprehensive, i.e., special art or music; (D) those who should take the full course before taking the comprehensive examination; and (E) those who are likely to fail an examination unless remedial work or some special attention is given. . . . [Only classifications A, B, and D have been used in French.]

Until 1951, the French placement examination consisted of three parts: (1) an advanced form of the *Cooperative French Test*, (2) the U.S.A.F.I. *Aural French* test or an equivalent, and (3) a civilization test of 50 items selected from French 1 comprehensive examinations. The determining factor in final decisions was a comparison between the Cooperative scores and the base line composed of the means in the 1945 administration of that test to registrants in French 1C. In setting the 1945 norms as a standard for comparison, the staff acted in the belief that the norms for that year were representative of normal, average achievement as of the end of the first-year sequence.

Between 1946 and 1952, 1,095 students took the French placement. Of these, 24 per cent (257) were excused from the foreign language requirement, as a consequence; 10 per cent received partial exemption from course requirements but were held to the comprehensive examination; and 66 per cent (722) were held to the full requirement. Of the 10 per cent who received partial exemption, 3 per cent were placed in 1C, 5 per cent in 1B, and 2 per cent were excused from the course but were held to the comprehensive examination.

The high-school applicants were from three levels, namely, eleventh grade (Juniors), twelfth grade (Seniors), and thirteenth grade (graduates). Of the 197 eleventh-grade contestants, 22.6 per cent were excused from the language requirement; of the 130 twelfth-grade contestants, 28 per cent; and of the 442 high-school graduates, 28 per cent. In so far as French attainment is concerned, there seems to be small argument in these data for detaining high-school students beyond the Sophomore year from entering college. As for distinctions between Junior and Senior year-end achievement, there were none; the percentages excused and held were the same for both levels.

Experience in the language varied from one to four years (more, in some transfer cases). In 1946, out of 168 applicants, 18 had studied the language for four years; 67 per cent of the latter were excused from the requirement in full. Forty-two students had studied French for three years; 29 per cent were excused. Eighty-one had studied French for two years; only 4 per cent were excused. None of the 27 students with one year of experience were excused.

In March, 1948, the writer made a study of 267 applicants for admission to the College who had taken the French placement the preceding September, in order to discover what happened to them. Fourteen per cent of the group were excused in full; 6 per cent were recommended for 1B; 10 per cent for 1C; and 70 per cent (187 students) were held to the requirements. Six of the 187 students registered for a language other than French (!), 22 decided not to enter the College, and 36 registered for French 1A in the autumn quarter, 1947. Only 54 per cent of the original 267 examinees could be accounted for; the other 46 per cent were a shadowy "backlog," any portion of which might appear at any time in the future at any point in the College program—with equally uncertain promise of success, having no doubt lost the slight abilities they may have possessed. Delays in the satisfaction of language-arts-type subjects are costly—costly to the student and costly to the school.

In a placement-test situation there are two factors that can be analyzed with relative ease and accuracy, namely, the amount of training received by the examinees and its recency. The kind and the quality of the training, which are of more importance, cannot be reduced to statistics, if learned at all. For the following discussion of training and recency the 273 cases in the 1947 group were subdivided into (1) the group with high-school preparation only and (2) the group with high-school and college training or with college training only.

There were 194 cases of high-school preparation only, ranging from one to eight semesters, inclusive. The average was four and one-half semesters. In this group, 27 were excused from the full requirement; 37 were excused from part of the requirement; and 130 (68 per cent) failed of placement and were held to the full requirement. The percentage distribution of these results, tabulated by semesters of training, is given in Table 66.

The four-semester group represented 47.9 per cent of the total number of cases and contributed 56.1 per cent of the total number of failures, more than all other semester groups combined. Of the 93 cases, one-third had had their training previous to 1946–47, and two-thirds had finished their last French course in June, 1947. Since 74 per cent of the latter failed on placement, the factor of recency seems to have had little positive influence on their performance.

The six-semester group, which constituted 30 per cent of the total number of students of high-school preparation only, contributed 20.8 per cent of its failures. One-third of the 43 students who had completed their French training in June, 1947, were among these cases of failure.

The highest percentage of failure on the placement test (84.6 per cent) was made by the two-semester group, 62 per cent of which had finished their French course in 1947, three months previous to the

TABLE 66

| Semesters | Cases | Per Cent Passed | Per Cent Placed | Per Cent Failed |
|---|---|---|---|---|
| 1........ | 1 | 100.0 | ......... | ......... |
| 2........ | 26 | 11.5 | 3.9 | 84.6 |
| 3........ | 4 | ......... | 25.0 | 75.0 |
| 4........ | 93 | 6.4 | 15.0 | 78.6 |
| 5........ | 3 | ......... | ......... | 100.0 |
| 6........ | 58 | 22.4 | 31.0 | 46.6 |
| 7........ | 3 | 33.3 | 66.7 | ......... |
| 8........ | 6 | 50.0 | 50.0 | ......... |

examination period. Recency certainly had little to do with their performance.

Certain general conclusions can be drawn from the above statements: (1) the recency factor, taken by itself, is of little importance; (2) the length-of-training factor, taken by itself, is more meaningful; (3) the liability of failing diminishes with the increase in the amount of training; (4) two semesters of high-school study, from the standpoint of language proficiency, are a waste of time; and (5) six semesters, plus recency as of the year of entering college, hold the highest promise of success. Furthermore, be it recalled, these conclusions are based upon the performance not of average high-school students but of students for whom the mean intelligence quotient was .92.

In a further attempt to find the relationship between success and recency of training, a fixed amount of training, i.e., four semesters, was kept as a constant factor, and the percentages of failure in that

bracket were computed for each year when the training was completed, from 1938 to 1947. Not only was there no gradation in the
percentages from year to year as one approached 1947, but the 1947
percentage (74.2 per cent) was approximately the same as for 1944
and 1946. In a group having the same amount of training, the
recency of that training had relatively little prognostic value in
respect to placement-test results.

The standards set for the parts of the French placement were
expressed in *raw* scores, as a measure of convenience. On the Cooperative test, a total raw score of 78 "passed"; one of 64 or less
failed. Normally, a score between 65 and 69 placed the student in
1B, whereas a score between 70 and 77 placed either in 1B or in 1C,
or "passed," depending upon the support given by the reading and
vocabulary scores. The intention was to prevent the overweighting
of grammar achievement at the expense of the ability to read in
making the final decisions.

On the U.S.A.F.I. aural test, a raw score of 56, which was 65 per
cent of the maximum number of points, was the lower limit for
passing. On the civilization test, 40 per cent of the maximum number
of points was deemed passing. That absurd standard was all that the
high-school traffic could bear without disaster.

To summarize, the passing grade of C (actually a "low" C),
established by the College for all placement examinations, could be
obtained in the case of French by satisfying three conditions: (1) a
raw total score on an advanced form of the *Cooperative French Test*
of 78, or better (with high R and V scores, the level could drop to
70); (2) a raw score of 56 on the U.S.A.F.I. *Aural French Test;* and
(3) a raw score of 20 on a 50-item civilization test. The standards
for the first two tests were equivalent to established means for
French 1C.[11]

How far did the applicants in 1947 succeed in meeting these
standards? The answer is found in the summary of their mean
scores on the Cooperative (CO) and U.S.A.F.I. tests (Table 67),
expressed in *raw* scores for the latter, and in scaled scores for the
Cooperative test (the U.S.A.F.I. means cannot be scaled). These
norms are for 273 students, of whom 41 had had college, or high-
school and college training in French. It is not likely that this subgroup greatly influenced the attainment for the total group.

The deviations from the average mean scores reported for French 1C are as follows: $-20.6$ points in reading, $-14.2$ points in vocabulary, $+2.1$ points in grammar, and $-12.1$ points in total score. On the U.S.A.F.I. aural test, the deviation is $-11.16$ points. It is not difficult to understand why 70 per cent of the group failed to meet the standards set for the satisfaction of the language requirement on the basis of the placement examination and performance in French 1C. The performance of the placement group did not equal the mean achievement of 1B even, except in *grammar*—the one strong card played by these college aspirants.

Is grammar the one hope for survival of the modern foreign languages in the secondary-school curriculum? It did not save the

TABLE 67

| Part | Mean* | S.D.* | Scaled |
|---|---|---|---|
| CO reading.......... | 17.71 | 10.98 | 62 |
| CO vocabulary....... | 22.10 | 8.90 | 68 |
| CO grammar........ | 14.88 | 10.25 | 61 |
| CO total score....... | 54.69 | .......... | 65 |
| U.S.A.F.I. aural...... | 45.44 | 14.45 | ........ |

\* Raw scores.

classics. And what can be said for the lower fourth of the 1947 group who did not attain a raw score of 4.63 (scaled, 47) in grammar, or (what is even worse) a raw score of 6.73 (scaled, 39) in reading comprehension? How far, Agard and Dunkel ask, can the language teaching profession "contract to deliver linguistic skill . . . to the students who languish in the limbo of those who cannot read nor speak nor comprehend?"[12] And how much longer will school administrators continue to certify language proficiency in lower quartile cases like those described above? Or permit in their programs one-year courses in a foreign language?

This chapter concludes the account of two decades of language achievement in French 1, as expressed in letter grades won on comprehensive examinations; in raw scores obtained on aural tests of high reliability; and in scaled scores for proficiency in reading, vocabulary, and grammar measured by standard tests nationally known and accepted. The instruments of evaluation were scientifically constructed, objective in techniques, reliable, and for the most part valid and were administered and scored by an agency independent of the teaching staff. The results have been summarized, compared, and interpreted. On these results, in large measure, rests the case for the Reading Method.

## CHAPTER X

# PROJECTIONS

## 1. *Backward*

THE preceding pages have dealt factually with cause and effect in relation to the Reading Method. It is now the turn of personal opinion. First, to look back, and then forward.

New life came into the teaching of the modern languages at the beginning of the century with the advent of the Reform movement. The expressed aim of the Reform was "reading ability developed by means of speaking facility."[1] In order to attain this aim, the profession resorted to addition, i.e., more hours, more sections, more years, more claims, and eventually more costs. Most school administrators are more interested in subtraction than in addition when it is a question of foreign language programs. Their feeling in respect to language study, as Curme said, "is a deep conviction that we cannot use it in life." Consequently, they asked the profession for some hard facts to back up the demands. The language profession did not have any. Instead, it offered postulates and spoke passionately of travel benefits, cultural enrichment, literary appreciation, formal disciplines, and the like.

European methodologists and their American disciples lay siege to the secondary-school curriculum with unprecedented energy and vociferousness. The American school system being what it was, language instruction and language teachers were in a confused state by 1914.

"Speaking facility" required more and more time in the curriculum: three years, four years, six years. Only a few of our schools could support such a program. And only a few of our teachers were equipped to teach by the "Direct Method" or could afford the requisite time and money for adequate preparation. Trained by the

grammatical method, thinking in grammatical terms, equipped with automatically controlled grammars, convinced of the reliability of grammatical knowledge as an index of linguistic proficiency, they clung to the grammatical framework of their courses as to a raft in a raging sea. And when the science of grammar and the "art of conversation" had been "mastered" (the verb is in the catalogue statements), only a modicum of the "reading ability" originally proposed as the ultimate aim was possible. There was no longer enough time.

After World War I, school administrators, language teachers, and former language students realized that the time for an accounting had come. In 1924 the Modern Foreign Language Study undertook that accounting.

By the time the last of the Study's eighteen volumes of reports appeared in 1932, language instruction in the secondary schools was in retrogression. Enrolments declined. Teachers became argumentative over values, aims, methods, and precedence. Administrators argued over the place of language study in the curriculum, the budget, and the time schedule. Recriminations passed back and forth. Meantime, the social sciences moved in and took over the relinquished space in the timetable.

The subsequent discussion over "general education" versus "specialized education" led to further retrenchments in the language offerings. The profession, placed on the defensive, babbled about "social competency," appreciation of foreign civilizations, tolerance of foreign points of view, international "reciprocities of appreciation," "democratic competency," "appreciation of leisure," etc., as their language aims, rationalizing in terms of current social psychology. Few teachers were old-fashioned enough to advocate vocally language mastery as the legitimate aim of a language course.

By 1940, foreign language instruction in the secondary schools had shrunk to two years, even to one year in the smaller schools. The latter were looking favorably upon "general language" courses as a more profitable way to spend the time. The recommendations of the Coleman report relative to the limitation of objectives were given little more than lip service; even the gains in the amount of reading were slight. Publishers switched back to old stock materials, photographically and typographically pepped up, and dispensed language, literature, and life in "omnibus" volumes, each sufficient for a year's activity. In the public preference, Spanish moved up on the Good Neighbor bandwagon, and French moved down after the June blitzkrieg. Latin, moribund, intrenched itself behind the Classical League and resigned itself, if necessary, to an honorable demise. The Latin screenings took Spanish or German.

Before World War II was actively over, linguisticians, semanticists, and educationists were in dispute again over the disposal of what was left of second-language learning. Enrolments in French, German, and Latin were nearing the zero point, and language staffs were dispersing and converting to anything that promised security. Military language programs were in the hands of theorists and "intensive language" experts. And then the locust bands of GI postwar students swarmed into the depleted classrooms and saved the day. Language teachers, in a festive and speculative mood, invested in A.S.T.P. stock, asserted once again that the time for change had come, and once again cultivated in their classrooms the nearly forgotten art of conversation. But in the halls of curriculum committees, boards of education, and administrative officers, in city and country high schools, in state universities and privately endowed colleges, East and West, entrance requirements in foreign languages were being done away with and course offerings curtailed or canceled.

Once more, after thirty years of wandering, the language teaching profession, doggedly maintaining that its aim is "reading ability developed by means of speaking facility," ignoring the hard lessons and sage counsel of yesterday, is back on the educational doorstep, clamoring for more time, more hours, more sections—at more costs. And the door is slowly closing.

## 2. Forward[2]

The status of foreign languages in general education has always been peculiarly sensitive to trends, "movements," reforms, new philosophies, international politics, the vagaries of public sentiment, and other disturbances affecting educational polity. In addition, the language teaching profession has the unhappy faculty of calling attention to itself through self-criticism or through domestic jealousies. Fascinated by externals, it has an overwhelming desire to please, while remaining at heart timid and despairingly conservative, forever faithful to the precepts of Donatus. A sense of the unreal has plagued it since its formal entrance into the American school curriculum. This unreality has communicated itself to both teacher and administrator.

The curriculum-makers are frankly puzzled about what to do with foreign languages, and their puzzlement fills the language teacher with unrest and uncertainty as to his future. At the present moment, two things seem certain: one, that foreign language study is touching bottom and, two, that only a rise is possible.

Let no one think that, for the great majority of schools and colleges, the curriculum of tomorrow will not have a foreign language program. That certain educational philosophies in recent years all but rationalized foreign language teaching in our schools out of existence does not matter. It does not matter that total enrolment in foreign languages in our high schools in 1943 was only 18 per cent of the school population (it was 55 per cent in 1922!). Nor is it significant that French, German, and Spanish jockey for position in the curricular sun.

These conditions, like little systems, have their day. They acquire a certain importance in respect to the general problem of the "core" curriculum, but they neither prove nor disprove the value of foreign language instruction in our schools. Circumstances eventually correct them.

Throughout the world, interest in foreign languages is pressing upward in a ferment of reality. People are trying to communicate with other people. A second language is becoming a useful, a desirable, possession. It is being studied, not so much for its disciplines or for college entrance requirements or by order of higher authority as for voluntary communication between one man and another.

For an increasing number of people it is no longer just a labyrinthine process in a school for screening out the educationally unfit. For them, there are no "unit" or "credit" tags tied to it. It is a competency that they want. And when this attitude prevails in the language classrooms, then foreign language instruction will find a permanent and equitable place in the curriculum. That may lead to a language Renaissance.

And if it were to become *useful* as well as ornamental, a whole chain of reactions might be loosened. Textbook publishers would

have to overhaul their stocks again. New approaches to old problems of methods and materials would have to be thought out, new
attitudes taken, new tests devised. Teacher training, so long static
and unrealistic, would have to be changed. Competent staffs would
not be easily found, and many old-line teachers would be unhappy.
There would have to be subject-matter integration, interdepartmental co-operation, and recourse to the conference table. More
than ever before, the language staff would need a blueprint and a
timetable.

This is not a prophecy. It is a contingency.

Beyond the four horizons, at the moment, thousands of Americans
in uniform and a host of others in civilian attire are struggling with
strange words, unaccustomed sounds, odd speech rhythms, and
queer expressions used by peoples of whose existence they were only
dimly aware a few years ago. They are interested in these foreign
languages because they *need* them or because they like the sound of
them or because they are attracted to the idea or the image behind
the symbol. And the symbols, becoming common possessions of
men and women of diverse races, religions, and cultures, become
minute bonds tying them together more closely into the web of
human society.

And then there is the tremendous postwar increase in the inter-
change of students, scholars, official missions, observers, and plain
tourists. The air and water lanes are filled with their comings and
goings. Scholarships, fellowships, subsidies from foundations or from
the national government sustain the flow at a high level. There is
small likelihood of its cessation.

For these unorganized and informal language learners, as well as
for the formal ones, foreign language learning has come to have a
*social* meaning. It is a contribution to international understanding
and good will. And this is a second fundamental change of which
tomorrow's teachers will have to take cognizance.

When American military personnel and civilians return home and
take up their life again in the United States, they will have new
ideas about what constitutes a general education, or secondary
education. They will not be thinking just of themselves. They will
join the veterans of past conflicts in voicing opinions of influence in
shaping educational policies. It seems improbable that they will be

satisfied with the status quo. They will certainly not be satisfied with a long, tedious apprenticeship to formal grammar, or routines of unreal transliteration of unrelated matter, or pointless classroom chatter about childish things. They will not like the slow pace or the course in which little is read and still less is heard.

They will want an assurance of language competency, of courses so planned and executed that, with honest application and a respectable intellectual endowment, a student may be able to convert that assurance into fact. That is a third change that must be made.

The charge of incompetency brought against current language instruction in general is not lightly made. It is not due, of course, to any one cause. Foreign language teaching has shared in the general educational rout of the last two decades. Critics on the sidelines have not been very constructive. Those language teachers who were in contact with the educational policies and the military demands of 1918, and again in 1943, find little solace in the tumultuous years intervening. Language competency is still the exception, rather than the rule.

World disturbances bring to the American public an increasing awareness of the importance of two virtues of ordinary toil, namely, concentration on the job in hand and co-operation with one's fellow-worker. Both are excellent qualities in education.

In the area of language instruction, they constitute a fourth change for tomorrow. The language program must be shorn of futile, though pleasant, pastimes, such as the rattling of Spanish castanets, the singing of "Frère Jacques" on school time, the many amusing distractions to be found in our entertaining textbooks, the exemptions from homework in favor of the athletic field, and diversions conjured up to meet the "happiness" prescription of some "progressive" theory. Language study, at best, is a complicated and difficult activity. It needs all the concentrated effort one can give it, if a real competency is to be acquired. It is not to be turned into a recreation period, unless play is the objective of the course of study.

Furthermore, it must be taken out of its curricular isolation. It is not a subject matter that thrives in a vacuum. If the language course is properly conducted, it deals with both form and substance; it is a blend of subject matter and techniques. Too seldom is attention paid to the first ingredient. That defect must be remedied in the future.

As a social device for the use of man, language should be related to his immediate environment, to his world at large, and to the past as to the present. Its study should have a concern for the history and culture of the people whose mother-tongue it is. But what can be accomplished so long as the pabulum of beginning language courses has its counterpart in the elementary grades? Is a civilization to be found only in "story books"? Has contemporary France no interest for a high-school French student? How can one appreciate this present without some knowledge of the past? The argument is not for "language and area" studies in the A.S.T.P. tradition, but in dilution, in moderation.

But this concern in the foreign language course for other civilizations should include concern for our own. Foreign language elements in English,[3] the contributions of a foreign people to our national history and institutions, the part which that people played in the past (and is still playing) in the formation of our mores and culture— these are legitimate areas in a planned content for a foreign language course. Is it not deplorable, as an example, that universally in our French classes little or no attention is paid to the extensive and important role played by the French in the settlement and Colonial periods of our own history?[4]

The well-integrated language course should reach into other departments, such as art, music, history, English, the social sciences, and the humanities.[5] Why not? It may also call for assistance in its own area, for every foreign language can find something of use in every other. That may mean a unified foreign language staff, like a unified military command, with a round table instead of partitions.

A sound policy needs a good blueprint. The language course needs one. A syllabus or a detailed course outline is like a directional beam; it reduces the hazards of a disastrous landing. The advice may seem trivial, but in the author's experience in educational surveys of various schools, no language department has been encountered that had one. It is paradoxical that a language-arts-type subject should be commonly subjected to science-type methods, and yet not use specifications, plans, and data on its production lines. The blueprint and the proving ground are another change for the future course.

The two-year foreign language course in the secondary school or its one-year college counterpart has not yet fully demonstrated what it may be able to do. Properly planned and executed, it could deliver a substantial competency in one language skill, if not two. More than that would need more time than it now has at its disposal.

Whatever the language course does in the future, it must have reality, usefulness, and a social value, as well as a competency. Co-operative and concentrated effort expended in behalf of attainable objectives will be needed. A working plan and an effective system of inspecting the products will provide insurance against mediocrity and failure. Given these components, tomorrow's foreign language instruction in the schools and colleges of America might achieve what the teachers of 1925 hoped for—and the teachers of 1950 await.[6]

# DEFINITIONS OF EDUCATIONAL TERMS

CORRELATION—When two quantities are so related that the fluctuations in one are in sympathy with the fluctuations in the other, so that an increase or decrease of one is found in connection with an increase or decrease (or inversely) of the other, and the greater the magnitude of the changes in the one, the greater the magnitude of the changes in the other, the quantities are said to be correlated (Bowley). In interpreting correlation, causal relationship is to be avoided; it is a "mathematical expression of the degree of association between the traits, regardless of the factors producing the results" (Holzinger).

Perfect correlation is equal to 1.00. A coefficient of .95 to .99 is rarely found. Symbol: $r$.

DEVIATION—The difference found by subtracting some fixed number, such as the mean or the median of a series of measures, from any item in the series. The *standard deviation* is the square root of the arithmetic mean of the squares of the deviations of the items from the mean of the series. Its symbol is $(\sigma)$, or S.D.; it is also referred to as *sigma*.

MEANS—The sum of a series of measures divided by their number; the mathematical average of a series of measures. It may not respond to an actual measure. It is the most important and generally the most reliable average. Several means can be averaged to form an *average mean;* medians cannot be so averaged. Symbol: $M$ (Holzinger).

MEDIANS—When measures are arranged in order of size, the median is the middle measure or (lacking a middle measure) midway between the two middlemost measures. Half of the individuals in a series are on one side of it, and half on the other (McCall). Symbol: $Md$.

PERCENTILE—A value of the variable below which a given percentage of the frequencies lie in a distribution. The fiftieth percentile is the median, or mid-point; the twenty-fifth and the seventy-fifth percentiles are the lower and upper quartile, respectively. The percentile may divide the series into ten equal parts, called *deciles*. The *percentile rank* of a given score shows what percentage of the students in that particular group achieve scores below that score in the distribution.

QUARTILES—The medians dividing the halves of the distribution into equal parts are known as *quartiles*. Starting with the lower end of the distribution, the median dividing the lower half is known as the *first quartile* $(Q^1)$, whereas the median dividing the upper half of the distribution is known as the *third quartile* ($Q^3$) (Gregory).

RELIABILITY—The degree of accuracy with which a test measures what it really does measure, or its consistency with itself in measuring the same ability at different times. It is a measurement of the amount of confidence that may be placed in a score on the test as a measure of some ability in the student. Symbol: $r$.

VALIDITY—The degree to which a test fulfils the requirement of measuring what it purports to measure. A test is valid when it includes elements or items that are the most important, and excludes those that are not essential.

# NUMBER OF COURSE COMPLETIONS IN FRENCH 1ABC FOR EACH YEAR FROM 1920 TO 1940*

| Year | 1A | 1B | 1C | Total |
|---|---|---|---|---|
| 1920–21........ | 150 | 100 | 84 | 334 |
| 1921–22........ | 152 | 128 | 120 | 400 |
| 1922–23........ | 123 | 125 | 85 | 333 |
| 1923–24........ | 148 | 185 | 90 | 423 |
| 1924–25........ | 128 | 103 | 95 | 326 |
| 1925–26........ | 119 | 99 | 101 | 319 |
| 1926–27........ | 137 | 107 | 76 | 320 |
| 1927–28........ | 143 | 113 | 151 | 407 |
| 1928–29........ | 127 | 107 | 127 | 361 |
| 1929–30........ | 131 | 115 | 176 | 422 |
| 1930–31........ | 122 | 113 | 186 | 421 |
| 1931–32........ | 121 | 108 | 109 | 338 |
| 1932–33........ | 102 | 88 | 100 | 290 |
| 1933–34........ | 134 | 125 | 107 | 366 |
| 1934–35........ | 149 | 122 | 121 | 392 |
| 1935–36........ | 138 | 113 | 110 | 361 |
| 1936–37........ | 124 | 100 | 93 | 317 |
| 1937–38........ | 156 | 128 | 119 | 403 |
| 1938–39........ | 159 | 137 | 119 | 415 |
| 1939–40........ | 134 | 123 | 119 | 376 |
| Total (20)... | 2,491 | 2,339 | 2,288 | 7,329 |

Number of 1C completions   = 2,288
1C completions, 1920–37   = 1,931
1ABC comprehensive scores   = 2,419
Total 1ABC completions   = 7,329
101-G registrations, 1926–40 = 1,009
2ABC completions, 1927–40 = 2,383

* *Notes:* (1) For the period of the Reading Collection Survey (1927–33), there were 2,239 quarter-students. (2) After 1940, completions counted as year-students, since credits were determined by comprehensive examinations. (3) Numbers in the table represent the number of students listed in the instructors' final quarterly reports; they are not initial registrations. (4) From 1920 to 1927, the courses were under the jurisdiction of the School of Education; from 1927 to 1931, they were under the College of Arts, Old Plan; from 1931 onward, they were in the College New Plan.

# STUDENT PERSONAL RECORD CARD
## (1928 Form)*

\* The 1924 and 1926 forms differed from the 1928 form only in arrangement and in the form of the statements. The 1928 form is in current use.

NAME................Classification..........Year...........PERSONAL RECORD  ⌐

Birthplace............................Date of Birth..............Home Address..................

Parentage...........................Health..........Deficient [Hearing] [Sight] [Speech].......

...........................Why are you studying [French] [German] [Spanish]?...................

...........................If you have not studied a foreign language previously, why not?........

...........................If you began the study of a foreign language and then dropped it, state language and reason..................................If you think that language study is unduly difficult for you, state reason.......................................

...........................Check your main interest in language study [Reading—1, 2, 3], [Writing—1, 2, 3] [Speaking—1, 2, 3]. Reason for your choice?...................

...............................................................................

What foreign countries have you visited? Length of stay in each?...................

Do you like or dislike the study of English?...............Favorite English authors?...........

...........................Favorite study?...................

Personal hobbies or interests?...........................What artistic abilities have you?

...........................Do you read [slowly] [moderately] [rapidly] in English? Scholarship...................

### TRAINING

| Subject | Yrs. Studied | Name and Location of School | Grammar Used in First Course | Grade | Units |
|---|---|---|---|---|---|
| French.... | | | | | |
| Spanish... | | | | | |
| German... | | | | | |
| Latin..... | | | | | |

Comment:                              Date Filed:

Knowledge of other languages?.......................Additional texts used in [French] [Spanish] [German]: give author, title, and amount................................................................................

.............................................Extensive (outside) reading in [Fr.] [Sp.] [Ger.]: Amount

..............................pages. Titles..........................................................................................

....................................................................................................................................................

....................................................................................................................................................

Method of instruction: [Direct] [Grammatical] [Compromise] [Home-Study]? Knowledge of phonetics?........................................................................................................................

Instruction given in foreign language?.....................Dictation?.....................Free themes?

.....................Vocabulary?.....................Idioms?.........................................................................

## PROGRAM

| CHECK YEAR AND QUARTER | 19  a.w.sp.s. | 19  a.w.sp.s. | 19  a.w.sp.s. | 19  a.w.sp.s. | 19  a.w.sp.s. |
|---|---|---|---|---|---|
| Courses [1]........ | | | | | |
| "     [2]........ | | | | | |
| "     [3]........ | | | | | |
| Student Activities.. | | | | | |
| Social Activities.... | | | | | |
| Athletic Activities.. | | | | | |
| Employment [wk.-hrs.]........ | | | | | |
| Extramural Activities............ | | | | | |
| Laboratory Periods. | | | | | |
| Gymnasium Periods | | | | | |
| Local Address...... | | | | | |
| Telephone Number. | | | | | |

311

# CLASS ATTENDANCE AND PERSONAL RECORD CARD USED IN FRENCH 1 AND FRENCH 2*

CLASS RECORD

| NAME | | | | | COURSE | 1 | 2 | A | B | C | | YEAR |
|---|---|---|---|---|---|---|---|---|---|---|---|---|

| WEEK | 1 | 2 | 3 | 4 | 5 | 6 | 7 | 8 | 9 | 10 | 11 | SUMMARY |
|---|---|---|---|---|---|---|---|---|---|---|---|---|
| Aural Comprehension..... | | | | | | | | | | | | |
| Composition............ | | | | | | | | | | | | |
| Cultural Information...... | | | | | | | | | | | | |
| Dictation............... | | | | | | | | | | | | |
| Extensive Reading........ | | | | | | | | | | | | |
| Grammar............... | | | | | | | | | | | | |
| Idioms................. | | | | | | | | | | | | |
| Pronunciation........... | | | | | | | | | | | | |
| Reading Comprehension... | | | | | | | | | | | | |
| Verbs.................. | | | | | | | | | | | | |
| Vocabulary............. | | | | | | | | | | | | |
| ..................... | | | | | | | | | | | | |
| ..................... | | | | | | | | | | | | |

* These 3 × 5 ruled forms were used instead of the usual teacher's classbook, to keep a record of test scores, test summaries, attendance, conferences, special assignments, withdrawals, transfers, Cooperative test scores, placement results, quarterly final grade, and the final grade on the comprehensive. The card form facilitated sorting, grouping, checking, and quick and easy reference.

## ATTENDANCE AND PERSONAL RECORD

NAME _____     CLASSIFICATION: COLL. ☐  DIV. ☐  I  II  III  IV

| WEEK | 1 | 2 | 3 | 4 | 5 | 6 | 7 | 8 | 9 | 10 | 11 | COMMENT |
|------|---|---|---|---|---|---|---|---|---|----|----|---------|
| Monday..... | | | | | | | | | | | | |
| Tuesday..... | | | | | | | | | | | | |
| Wednesday.. | | | | | | | | | | | | |
| Thursday.... | | | | | | | | | | | | |
| Friday...... | | | | | | | | | | | | |

Conferences [1]_____[2]_____

Reports_____

Special Assignments_____

Dropped_____Changed to_____

Cooperative Score: Reading [　　] Vocab. [　　] Grammar [　　] Total [　　]

Final Grade [　　]   Placement_____ Quarterly Grade [　　]

APPENDIX V

FRENCH 1 COMPREHENSIVE EXAMINATION, THE UNIVERSITY OF CHICAGO, JUNE 2, 1952.[*]

PASSAGE I

## L'Infirme

Cette aventure m'est arrivée vers 1882.  Je venais de m'installer dans le coin d'un wagon vide, et j'avais refermé la portière,[*] avec l'espérance de rester seul, quand elle se rouvrit brusquement, et j'entendis une voix qui disait:

--Prenez garde, monsieur, nous nous trouvons juste au croisement des lignes; le marche-pied[*] est très haut.

--Ne crains rien, Laurent, je vais prendre les poignées.[*]

Puis une tête apparut coiffée d'un chapeau rond, et deux mains, s'accrochant aux lanières[*] de cuir et de drap suspendues des deux côtés de la portière, hissèrent lentement un gros corps, dont les pieds firent sur le marchepied un bruit de canne frappant le sol.

Or, quand l'homme eut fait entrer son torse dans le compartiment, je vis apparaître, dans l'étoffe flasque[*] du pantalon, le bout peint en noir d'une jambe de bois, qu'un autre pilon[*] pareil suivit bientôt.

Une tête se montra derrière ce voyageur et demanda:

—Vous êtes bien, monsieur?

—Oui, mon garçon.

—Alors, voilà vos paquets et vos béquilles.[*]

Et un domestique, qui avait l'air d'un vieux soldat, monta à son tour, portant en ses bras un tas de choses, enveloppées en des papiers noirs et jaunes, ficelées soigneusement, et les déposa, l'une après l'autre, dans le filet au-dessus de la tête de son maître.  Puis il dit:

--Voilà, monsieur, c'est tout.  Il y en a cinq:  les bonbons, la poupée, le tambour, le fusil et le pâté de foies gras.

—C'est bien, mon garcon.

--Bon voyage, monsieur.

--Merci, Laurent; bonne santé!

L'homme s'en alla en repoussant la porte, et je regardai mon voisin.

Il pouvait avoir trente-cinq ans, bien que ses cheveux fussent presque blancs; il était décoré, moustachu, fort gros, atteint de cette obésité poussive[*] des hommes actifs et forts qu'une infirmité tient immobiles.

Il s'essuya le front, souffla et, me regardant bien en face:

—La fumée vous gêne-t-elle, monsieur?

—Non, monsieur.

---

portière, door (here, of railway carriage); marchepied, step; poignées, handles; lanières, straps; flasques, loose; pilon, wooden leg; béquilles, crutches; poussive, puffing.

[*]The complete form is reproduced here with the exception of the sentence statements read by the examiner for the Audition Test, Part 3.

Cet oeil, cette voix, ce visage, je les connaissais. Mais d'où, de quand? Certes, j'avais rencontré ce garçon-là, je lui avais parlé, je lui avais serré la main. Cela datait de loin, de très loin, c'était perdu dans cette brume où l'esprit semble chercher à tâtons les souvenirs et les poursuit, comme des fantômes fuyants, sans les saisir.

Lui aussi, maintenant, me dévisageait avec la ténacité et la fixité d'un homme qui se rappelle un peu, mais pas tout à fait.

Nos yeux, gênés de ce contact obstiné des regards, se détournèrent; puis, au bout de quelques secondes, attirés de nouveau par la volonté obscure et tenace de la mémoire en travail, ils se rencontrèrent encore, et je dis:

—Mon Dieu, monsieur, au lieu de nous observer à la dérobée pendant une heure, ne vaudrait-il pas mieux chercher ensemble où nous nous sommes connus?

Le voisin répondit avec bonne grâce :

—Vous avez tout à fait raison, monsieur.

Je me nommai:

—Je m'appelle Henry Bonclair, magistrat.

Il hésita quelques secondes; puis, avec ce vague de l'oeil et de la voix qui accompagne les grandes tensions d'esprit:

—Ah! parfaitement, je vous ai rencontré chez les Poincel, autrefois, avant la guerre, voilà douze ans de cela!

—Oui, monsieur . . . Ah! . . . ah! . . . vous êtes le lieutenant Revalière?

—Oui . . . Je fus même le capitaine Revalière jusqu'au jour où j'ai perdu mes pieds . . . tous les deux d'un seul coup, sur le passage d'un boulet.

Et nous nous regardâmes de nouveau, maintenant que nous nous connaissions.

Je me rappelais parfaitement avoir vu ce beau garçon mince qui conduisait les cotillons* avec une furie agile et gracieuse et qu'on avait surnommé, je crois, "la Trombe."* Mais derrière cette image, nettement évoquée, flottait encore quelque chose d'insaisissable, une histoire que j'avais sue et oubliée, une de ces histoires auxquelles on prête une attention bienveillante et courte, et qui ne laissent dans l'esprit qu'une marque presque imperceptible.

Il y avait de l'amour là-dedans. J'en retrouvais la sensation particulière au fond de ma mémoire, mais rien de plus, sensation comparable au fumet* que même pour le nez d'un chien le pied d'un gibier sur le sol.

Peu à peu, cependant, les ombres s'éclaircirent et une figure de jeune fille surgit devant mes yeux. Puis son nom éclata dans ma tête comme un pétard* qui s'allume: Mlle de Mandal. Je me rappelais tout, maintenant. C'était, en effet, une histoire d'amour, mais banale. Cette jeune fille aimait ce jeune homme, lorsque je l'avais rencontré, et on parlait de leur prochain mariage. Il paraissait lui-même très épris, très heureux.

Je levai les yeux vers le filet où tous les paquets apportés par le domestique de mon voisin tremblotaient aux secousses du train, et la voix du serviteur me revint comme s'il finissait à peine de parler.

Il avait dit:

—Voilà, monsieur, c'est tout. Il y en a cinq: les bonbons, la poupée, le tambour, le fusil et le pâté de foies gras.

---

cotillon, a type of dance; Trombe, "Whirlwind"; fumet, scent; pétard, firecracker.

Alors, en une seconde, un roman se composa et se déroula dans ma tête. Il ressemblait d'ailleurs à tous ceux que j'avais lus où, tantôt le jeune homme, tantôt la jeune fille, épouse son fiancé ou sa fiancée après la catastrophe, soit corporelle, soit financière. Donc, cet officier mutilé pendant la guerre avait retrouvé, après la campagne, la jeune fille qui s'était promise à lui; et, tenant son engagement elle s'était donnée.

Je jugeais cela beau, mais simple, comme on juge simples tous les dévouements et tous les dénouements des livres et du théâtre. Il semble toujours, quand on lit, ou quand on écoute, à ces écoles de magnanimité, qu'on se serait sacrifié soi-même avec un plaisir enthousiaste, avec un élan magnifique. Mais on est de fort mauvaise humeur, le lendemain, quand un ami misérable vient vous emprunter quelque argent.

Puis, soudain, une autre supposition, moins poétique et plus réaliste, se substitua à la première. Peut-être s'était-il marié avant la guerre, avant l'épouvantable accident de ce boulet lui coupant les jambes, et avait-elle dû, désolée et résignée, recevoir, soigner, consoler, soutenir ce mari, parti fort et beau, revenu avec les pieds fauchés,* affreux débris voué à l'immobilité, aux colères impuissantes et à l'obésité fatale.

Etait-il heureux ou torturé? Une envie, légère d'abord, puis grandissante, puis irrésistible, me saisit de connaître son histoire, d'en savoir au moins les points principaux, qui me permettraient de deviner ce qu'il ne pourrait pas ou ne voudrait pas me dire.

Je lui parlais, tout en songeant. Nous avions échangé quelques paroles banales; et moi, les yeux levés vers le filet, je pensais: "Il a donc trois enfants: les bonbons sont pour sa femme, la poupée pour sa petite fille, le tambour et le fusil pour ses fils, ce pâté de foies gras pour lui."

Soudain, je lui demandai:

—Vous êtes père, monsieur?

Il répondit:

—Non, monsieur.

Je me sentis soudain confus comme si j'avais commis une grosse inconvenance et je repris:

—Je vous demande pardon. Je l'avais pensé en entendant votre domestique parler de jouets. On entend sans écouter, et on conclut malgré soi.

Il sourit, puis murmura:

—Non, je ne suis même pas marié. J'en suis resté aux préliminaires.

J'eus l'air de me souvenir tout à coup.

—Ah! . . . c'est vrai, vous étiez fiancé, quand je vous ai connu, fiancé avec Mlle de Mandal, je crois.

—Oui, monsieur, votre mémoire est excellente.

J'eus une audace excessive, et j'ajoutai:

—Oui, je crois me rappeler aussi avoir entendu dire que Mlle de Mandal avait épousé monsieur . . . monsieur . . .

Il prononça tranquillement ce nom.

—M. de Fleurel.

—Oui, c'est cela! Oui . . . je me rappelle même, à ce propos, avoir entendu parler de votre blessure.

Je le regardais bien en face, et il rougit.

---

fauchés, cut off.

Sa figure pleine, bouffie,* que l'afflux constant de sang rendait déjà pourpre, se teinta davantage encore.

Il répondit avec vivacité, avec l'ardeur soudaine d'un homme qui plaide une cause perdue d'avance, perdue dans son esprit et dans son coeur, mais qu'il veut gagner devant l'opinion.

—On a tort, monsieur, de prononcer à côté du mien le nom de Mme de Fleurel. Quand je suis revenu de la guerre, sans mes pieds, hélas! je n'aurais jamais accepté, jamais, qu'elle devînt ma femme. Est-ce que c'était possible? Quand on se marie, monsieur, ce n'est pas pour faire parade de générosité: c'est pour vivre, tous les jours, toutes les heures, toutes les minutes, toutes les secondes, à côté d'un homme; et, si cet homme est difforme, comme moi, on se condamne, en l'épousant, à une souffrance qui durera jusqu'à la mort! Oh! je comprends, j'admire tous les sacrifices, tous les dévouements, quand ils ont une limite, mais je n'admets pas le renoncement d'une femme à toute une vie qu'elle espère heureuse, à toutes les joies, à tous les rêves, pour satisfaire l'admiration de la galerie. Quand j'entends sur le plancher de ma chambre le battement de mes pilons et celui de mes béquilles, ce bruit de moulin que je fais à chaque pas, j'ai des exaspérations à étrangler mon serviteur. Croyez-vous qu'on puisse accepter d'une femme de tolérer ce qu'on ne supporte pas soi-même? Et puis, vous imaginez-vous que c'est joli, mes bouts de jambes? . . ."

Il se tut. Que lui dire? Je trouvais qu'il avait raison! Pouvais-je la blâmer, la mépriser, même lui donner tort, à elle? Non. Cependant? Le dénouement conforme à la règle, à la moyenne, à la vérité, à la vraisemblance, ne satisfaisait pas mon appétit poétique. Ces moignons* héroïques appelaient un beau sacrifice qui me manquait, et j'en éprouvais une déception.

Je lui demandai tout à coup:

—Mme de Fleurel a des enfants?

—Oui, une fille et deux garçons. C'est pour eux que je porte ces jouets. Son mari et elle ont été très bons pour moi.

Le train montait la rampe de Saint-Germain. Il passa les tunnels, entra en gare, s'arrêta.

J'allais offrir mon bras pour aider la descente de l'officier mutilé quand deux mains se tendirent vers lui, par la portière ouverte:

—Bonjour! mon cher Revalière.

—Ah! bonjour, Fleurel.

Derrière l'homme, la femme souriait radieuse, encore jolie, envoyant des "bonjour!" de ses doigts gantés. Une petite fille, à côté d'elle, sautillait de joie, et deux garçonnets regardaient avec des yeux avides le tambour et le fusil passant du filet du wagon entre les mains de leur père.

Quand l'infirme fut sur le quai, tous les enfants l'embrassèrent. Puis on se mit en route, et la fillette, par amitié, tenait dans sa petite main la traverse vernie* d'une béquille, comme elle aurait pu tenir, en marchant à son côté, le pouce de son grand ami.

—Guy de Maupassant

1. Le narrateur

    A- avait autrefois connu l'infirme.
    B- n'avait jamais vu l'infirme avant 1882.
    C- avait parfois vu l'infirme après 1870.
    D- avait été témoin de l'accident qui était arrivé au soldat.

2. Le domestique Laurent

    A- devait bientôt être battu par son maître.
    B- fait le voyage avec son maître.
    C- avait probablement été longtemps soldat.
    D- fit la connaissance du narrateur pendant le voyage.

---

bouffie, swollen; moignons, stumps; traverse vernie, polished cross-bar.

3. Le narrateur

    A- explique que c'est dans la brume qu'il faut chercher les fantômes.
    B- compare son esprit à un fantôme.
    C- compare ses souvenirs à des fantômes.
    D- trouve que son esprit saisit immédiatement les fantômes.

4. D'après ses remarques nous pouvons supposer que

    A- l'infirme aime à fumer.
    B- qu'il a été défendu à l'infirme de fumer à cause de son manque d'haleine.
    C- que le narrateur a offert une cigarette à l'infirme.
    D- que le narrateur a accepté une cigarette de la part de l'infirme.

5. Les deux voyageurs

    A- se reconnaissent tout de suite.
    B- s'étaient rencontrés chez des amis qui avaient une fille à marier.
    C- se reconnaissent au bout d'une heure.
    D- s'étaient rencontrés avant la guerre de 1870.

6. Le narrateur

    A- attend une heure avant de faire la remarque qui ouvre la conversation entre les deux hommes.
    B- se sent attiré par la volonté tenace de son compagnon de voyage.
    C- aurait voulu attendre le départ du domestique avant de commencer à parler à l'infirme.
    D- se met à parler à l'infirme pour mettre fin à un silence gênant.

7. Après quelques instants de réflexion le narrateur

    A- comprend que l'infirme est maintenant marié.
    B- devine que Revalière est maintenant capitaine.
    C- parle au domestique qui avait apporté tous les paquets.
    D- se souvient du nom de la jeune fille.

8. Pour expliquer la présence des paquets dans les filets le narrateur suppose <u>d'abord</u>

    A- que Revalière avait, malgré sa difformité, épousé Mlle de Mandal.
    B- que le soldat avait refusé de se marier avant de partir en guerre.
    C- que l'infirme a cinq enfants.
    D- un roman réaliste plutôt que poétique.

9. Le narrateur trouve que

    A- sa première hypothèse n'est guère poétique.
    B- les dénouements des romans et des pièces de théâtre sont souvent d'accord avec la réalité.
    C- le roman et le théâtre mettent les gens en fort mauvaise humeur.
    D- le roman et le théâtre répandent de fausses conceptions de la vie.

10. Le narrateur se montre sceptique envers les romans et les pièces de théâtre qui enseignent la magnanimité parce qu'il

    A- a un ami misérable qui lui emprunte de l'argent.
    B- est de fort mauvaise humeur.
    C- a fait des réflexions sur les expériences de la vie.
    D- a une âme desséchée.

11. L'infirme

    A- prononce en rougissant le nom de son rival pour la main de Mlle de Mandal.
    B- aime mieux ne pas parler de son amour malheureux.
    C- ne refuse pas d'aider la mémoire du narrateur.
    D- prononce toujours ses mots avec tranquillité.

12. L'infirme, en expliquant pourquoi il n'a pas épousé Mlle de Mandal,

    A- se montre incapable de comprendre la beauté morale d'un sacrifice.
    B- se montre avant tout un homme qui aime à gagner "l'admiration de la galerie."
    C- révèle inconsciemment qu'il n'a jamais aimé Mlle de Mandal.
    D- nous dit qu'il n'aime pas voir une jeune fille privée des joies auxquelles elle a droit dans cette vie.

13. Selon Revalière,

    A- l'épouse d'un difforme doit renoncer à bien des plaisirs.
    B- le mariage entre gens difformes a beaucoup de chances de réussir.
    C- la femme ne cherche que la joie dans le mariage.
    D- il faut tout supporter pour satisfaire la galerie.

14. Vers la fin du conte le narrateur devient mécontent

    A- parce que Revalière n'a pas dit toute la vérité.
    B- parce que l'infirme n'a pas su se résigner à son malheur.
    C- parce qu'il trouve Mlle de Mandal condamnable.
    D- parce qu'un dénouement si peu poétique ne le satisfait pas.

15. A la fin du conte

    A- nous comprenons que Revalière est l'ami de Fleurel.
    B- nous voyons qu'une des petites filles a besoin de béquilles.
    C- les enfants reçoivent leurs nouveaux jouets de la main de Revalière.
    D- nous voyons que la petite fille est plus contente que ses frères des cadeaux qu'elle a reçus.

16. Ce qu'il y a d'intéressant dans ce conte, c'est

    A- la révélation progressive du caractère de Revalière et de sa situation.
    B- la peinture minutieuse d'un voyage en chemin de fer.
    C- le récit des sacrifices faits par une fiancée dévouée.
    D- la narration des exploits militaires de Revalière.

- - - - - -

LEAVE ANSWER SPACES 17-30 BLANK

- - - - - -

PASSAGE 2

## Un Secret

Mon âme a son secret, ma vie a son mystère:
Un amour éternel en un moment conçu.
Le mal est sans espoir, aussi j'ai dû le taire,
Et celle qui l'a fait n'en a jamais rien su.

Hélas! j'aurai passé près d'elle inaperçu,
Toujours à ses côtés, et pourtant solitaire,
Et j'aurai jusqu'au bout fait mon temps sur la terre,
N'osant rien demander et n'ayant rien reçu.

Pour elle, quoique Dieu l'ait faite douce et tendre,
Elle ira son chemin, distraite, et sans entendre
Ce murmure d'amour élevé sur ses pas;

A l'austère devoir pieusement fidèle,
Elle dira, lisant ces vers tout remplis d'elle:
"Quelle est donc cette femme?" et ne comprendra pas.

                    —Félix Arvers

31. Arvers dit que

      A- sa femme n'a jamais su combien il l'aimait.
      B- le mystère de sa vie est connu seulement de sa bien-aimée.
      C- il n'a jamais osé avouer son amour à l'objet de ses soupirs.
      D- il souffre d'une maladie organique qui doit bientôt l'emporter.

32. Selon Arvers, la jeune fille en question

      A- n'a jamais fait la connaissance du poète.
      B- est sourde.
      C- se trouve souvent en présence du poète.
      D- a refusé l'amour du poète.

33. L'auteur pense

      A- qu'un jour son poème sera lu par celle qu'il aime.
      B- que son poème rendra immortelle sa bien-aimée.
      C- que l'autre femme est plus intelligente que celle qu'il aime à présent.
      D- que même si elle lit son poème la jeune fille ne saura pas qu'Arvers avait aimée deux femmes à la fois.

34. La jeune fille ne comprendra pas tout à fait le poème d'Arvers parce que

      A- elle sera aveuglée par son amour-propre.
      B- elle sera toujours pieuse.
      C- elle n'a pas le coeur sensible.
      D- elle ne saura pas pour qui Arvers écrivit ce poème.

35. Le poète développe son idée par

      A- deux quatrains qui explique la nature du secret du poète suivis de deux tercets expliquant pourquoi la jeune fille traite les avances du poète avec dédain.
      B- un quatrain qui explique la nature du secret du poète suivi d'un autre quatrain et de deux tercets où le poète explique pourquoi il a fait un long voyage au bout de la terre.
      C- deux quatrains qui insistent sur l'amour du poète, suivis de deux tercets qui révèlent l'ignorance dans laquelle la jeune fille est restée à l'égard de cet amour.
      D- une comparaison entre la profondeur de l'amour qu'il ressent pour la jeune fille et la profondeur de l'ignorance dans laquelle la jeune fille est restée à l'égard de cet amour.

- - - - - - -

LEAVE ANSWER SPACES 36-45 BLANK

- - - - - - -

## PASSAGE 3

Pourquoi les ouvrages de la nature sont-ils si parfaits? c'est que chaque ouvrage est un tout, et qu'elle travaille sur un plan éternel dont elle ne s'écarte jamais; elle prépare en silence les germes de ses productions; elle ébauche,* par un acte unique, la forme primitive de tout être vivant; elle la développe, elle la perfectionne par un mouvement continu et dans un temps prescrit. L'ouvrage étonne; mais c'est l'empreinte divine dont il porte les traits qui doit nous frapper. L'esprit humain ne peut rien créer; il ne produira qu'après avoir été fécondé par l'expérience et la méditation; ses connaissances sont les germes de ses productions: mais s'il imite la nature dans sa marche et dans son travail, s'il s'élève par la contemplation aux vérités les plus sublimes, s'il les réunit, s'il les enchaîne, s'il en forme un tout, un système par la réflexion, il établira sur des fondements inébranlables* des monuments immortels.

C'est faute de plan, c'est pour n'avoir pas assez réfléchi sur son objet, qu'un homme d'esprit se trouve embarrassé, et ne sait par où commencer à écrire. Il aperçoit à la fois un grand nombre d'idées; et comme il ne les a ni comparées ni subordonnées, rien ne le détermine à préférer les unes aux autres; il demeure donc dans la perplexité: mais lorsqu'il se sera fait un plan, lorsqu'une fois il aura rassemblé et mis en ordre toutes les pensées essentielles à son sujet, il s'apercevra aisément de l'instant auquel il doit prendre la plume; il sentira le point de maturité de la production de l'esprit, il sera pressé de la faire éclore*, il n'aura même que du plaisir à écrire: les idées se succéderont aisément, et le style sera naturel et facile; la chaleur naîtra de ce plaisir, se répandra partout, et donnera la vie à chaque expression; tout s'animera de plus en plus, le ton s'élèvera, les objets prendront de la couleur; et le sentiment, se joignant à la lumière, l'augmentera, la portera plus loin, la fera passer de ce que l'on dit à ce que l'on va dire, et le style deviendra intéressant et lumineux.

—Buffon

46. Buffon développe le sujet de ce passage principalement

    A— par une comparaison entre l'empreinte divine et les ouvrages de la nature.
    B— en discutant les restrictions qu'on peut apporter à son opinion.
    C— en établissant un rapport de cause à effet entre l'homme et la nature.
    D— à l'aide de considérations sur les ouvrages de la nature.

47. Selon Buffon une oeuvre littéraire est parfois inférieure aux ouvrages de la nature

    A— parce que l'empreinte divine manque à cette oeuvre.
    B— parce que l'auteur a dépassé les limites du temps prescrit.
    C— parce que l'auteur n'a pas préparé un plan avant de se mettre à composer.
    D— parce que l'auteur n'a pas préparé son oeuvre selon les exigences d'un plan éternel.

48. Buffon trouve que

    A— sans plan il est impossible d'avoir des idées.
    B— le développement d'un plan rendra inutile le recours à l'expérience et à la méditation.
    C— le mérite d'un bon plan est de nous obliger à comparer et à subordonner nos idées.
    D— il est essentiel d'oublier quelques unes de nos idées si nous voulons arriver à perfectionner notre plan.

49. Buffon croit qu'un bon style

    A— ne dépend pas de l'ordonnance de nos idées.
    B— est caractérisé par l'aisance, le mouvement et la couleur.
    C— est plus difficile à trouver qu'un bon plan.
    D— se trouve seulement chez les auteurs qui ont conçu leurs idées avec chaleur et sentiment.

---

ébauche, rough hews; inébranlables, unshakable; éclore, blossom.

50. Buffon semble dire

    A- que l'esprit crée des ouvrages exactement comme la nature.
    B- que la production des oeuvres durables est indépendante des grandes vérités.
    C- qu'il n'y a pas de rapport entre les "vérités sublimes" et le "plan éternel" sur lequel travaille la nature.
    D- que l'esprit, dans sa manière de produire ses ouvrages, se distingue de la nature par une impuissance de créer.

51. Les "germes de ses productions" (ligne 3) dont parle Buffon sont probablement

    A- les principes d'un plan éternel.
    B- des êtres microscopiques.
    C- les principes organisateurs des choses créées.
    D- peu nombreux puisqu'ils sont perfectionnés dans un temps prescrit.

52. Selon Buffon un bon style est le résultat

    A- de la chaleur apportée par l'écrivain dans son travail.
    B- de la puissance qu'a l'écrivain à évoquer des couleurs.
    C- de l'élaboration et de l'emploi d'un plan.
    D- de conceptions intéressantes et lumineuses.

- - - - - - -

PASSAGE 4

De loin, la plage avait l'air d'un long jardin plein de fleurs éclatantes. Sur la grande dune de sable jaune, depuis la jetée jusqu'aux Roches-Noires, les ombrelles de toutes les couleurs, les chapeaux de toutes les formes, les toilettes de toutes les nuances, par groupes devant les cabines, par lignes le long du flot ou dispersés çà et là, ressemblaient vraiment à des bouquets énormes dans une prairie démesurée. Et le bruit confus, proche et lointain des voix égrenées dans l'air léger, les appels, les cris d'enfants qu'on baigne, les rires clairs des femmes faisaient une rumeur continue et douce, mêlée à la brise insensible et qu'on aspirait avec elle.

Pierre marchait au milieu de ces gens, plus perdu, plus séparé d'eux, plus isolé, plus noyé dans sa pensée torturante, que si on l'avait jeté à la mer du pont d'un navire, à cent lieues au large. Il les frôlait, entendait, sans écouter, quelques phrases; et il voyait, sans regarder, les hommes parler aux femmes et les femmes sourire aux hommes.

Mais tout à coup, comme s'il s'éveillait, il les aperçut distinctement; et une haine surgit en lui contre eux, car ils semblaient heureux et contents.

Il allait maintenant, frôlant les groupes, tournant autour, saisi par des pensées nouvelles. Toutes ces toilettes multicolores qui couvraient le sable comme un bouquet, ces étoffes jolies, ces ombrelles voyantes, la grâce factice des tailles emprisonnées, toutes ces inventions ingénieuses de la mode depuis la chaussure mignonne jusqu'au chapeau extravagant, la séduction du geste, de la voix et du sourire, la coquetterie enfin étalée sur cette plage lui apparaissaient soudain comme une immense floraison de la perversité féminine.

—Maupassant

53. Maupassant décrit la plage

    A- à travers les impressions de Pierre, même au début du passage.
    B- en évoquant d'abord ce qu'un observateur aurait pu voir, et ensuite ce qu'il aurait pu entendre.
    C- en commençant par une allusion au jardin qui était tout près.
    D- en attirant l'attention d'abord sur l'état de la mer et ensuite sur la foule humaine.

54. Le bruit qu'on entendait

    A- s'élevait, à en juger par le passage, des hommes, des femmes et des enfants assemblés sur la plage.
    B- diminuait ou croissait par moments, suivant les mouvements de la brise marine.
    C- semblait venir de loin, malgré la proximité de l'observateur (Pierre).
    D- se composait de deux couches: la rumeur de la mer et les voix humaines.

55. D'abord Pierre se promenait

    A- au bord de la mer comme s'il avait l'intention de s'y jeter.
    B- dans la foule sans faire attention à ce qui l'entourait.
    C- au milieu des gens sans regarder les hommes et les femmes qui parlaient de lui.
    D- au milieu de la foule comme il s'était promené sur le pont du navire avant d'arriver.

56. Pierre

    A- s'aperçut sans émotion du fait que tous ces gens étaient satisfaits et heureux.
    B- vit avec une sorte de fureur le bonheur apparent d'un homme et d'une femme.
    C- devint soudain conscient de la scène étalée sur la plage.
    D- quitta la foule parce qu'elle lui était devenue soudain insupportable.

57. Le changement dans l'attitude de Pierre

    A- est dû à un brusque retour de la haine qu'il ressentait depuis quelque temps pour les gens communs.
    B- est dû à un coup soudain qui l'éveilla.
    C- s'explique par le fait qu'il aperçut la foule tout à coup comme de loin.
    D- est présenté comme un phénomène subit et spontané.

58. Les détails qui attirèrent l'attention de Pierre

    A- servirent à chasser l'idée dont il était obsédé depuis quelque temps.
    B- semblent être des détails de coquetterie féminine.
    C- sont nombreux mais exclusivement visuels.
    D- lui inspirèrent des réflexions nouvelles sur la vanité du bonheur humain.

59. Vu dans son ensemble, ce passage

    A- est remarquable pour le manque de détails concrets et pour l'abondance de l'analyse psychologique.
    B- paraît obscur à première vue parce que les transitions sont cachées.
    C- est composé d'une description, suivie d'un rapport des réactions d'une personne à la scène décrite.
    D- est le récit d'un incident où les sentiments bienveillants d'un homme se transforment en haine.

60. L'allusion à la "floraison de la perversité féminine" (dernière ligne du passage)

    A- est une façon de souligner, par un contraste saisissant, l'attitude bienveillante de Pierre envers la foule.
    B- indique que Pierre a reconnu sa femme parmi les personnes assemblées sur la plage.
    C- reprend la comparaison faite au début du passage, tout en la modifiant pour indiquer mieux l'état d'esprit de Pierre.
    D- permet à Maupassant de terminer le passage sur une métaphore inattendue et complètement nouvelle.

61. Mme Roland apprend enfin le résultat des recherches de Pierre lorsqu'elle

    A- entend une conversation entre Pierre et Jean.
    B- trouve et lit le journal de Pierre.
    C- le suit à Trouville.
    D- reçoit une lettre anonyme, venant en réalité de Pierre.

62. Alors Mme Roland

    A- sait qu'elle a bien gardé son secret puisque Pierre s'est trompé sur le caractère de Maréchal.
    B- sent que Jean a mal agi en acceptant l'héritage.
    C- essaie de se justifier auprès de Pierre, sans y réussir d'ailleurs.
    D- n'est pas heureuse, mais ne peut pas regretter vraiment l'épisode avec Maréchal.

63. Le départ de Pierre, qui est en quelque sorte la solution au problème posé par l'action du roman, est rendu possible surtout par les efforts de

    A— Jean.
    B— Mme Rosémilly.
    C— le capitaine Beausire.
    D— Marowsko.

64. Roland, à la fin du roman,

    A— s'oppose obstinément à ce que son fils parte sur le transatlantique.
    B— n'a rien compris au drame qui s'était déroulé chez lui.
    C— commence à mépriser sa femme à cause de sa mauvaise conduite.
    D— finit avec l'aide de Mme Rosémilly par apaiser la tension entre ses deux fils.

- - - - - - -

## PASSAGE 5

La Société est utile et nécessaire à la félicité de l'homme; il ne peut se rendre heureux tout seul; un être faible et rempli de besoins, il exige à tout moment des secours qu'il ne peut se donner à lui-même. Ce n'est qu'à l'aide de ses semblables qu'il se met en état de résister aux coups du sort, et de réparer les maux physiques qu'il est forcé d'éprouver. Encouragé, soutenu par les autres, son industrie se déploie, sa raison s'éclaire, il parvient à combattre le mal moral qui n'est que le fruit de son ignorance et de ses préjugés. En un mot, comme on l'a déjà dit, l'homme est dans la nature l'être le plus utile à l'homme.

Ainsi, n'écoutons point une philosophie découragée qui nous invite à fuir la Société, à renoncer au commerce des humains, à rentrer dans les forêts où vivaient nos premiers pères, pour y disputer comme eux notre subsistance aux bêtes. Quand la chose serait praticable; quand même on pourrait parvenir à faire oublier à des hommes civilisés les idées, les opinions, les habitudes, le bien-être et les commodités de la Vie Sociale; quand même on les réduirait à l'état des brutes dont ils ne différaient que très peu dans l'origine; quand, dis-je, on mettrait en exécution cet étrange système, à moins de dénaturer l'homme, d'anéantir ses facultés, de le priver de ses desirs, de son activité, de sa tendance naturelle à perfectionner son sort, de sa curiosité, de son inconstance; l'homme repasserait successivement par les mêmes états; il ne ferait que recommencer la carrière parcourue par ses ancêtres; et au bout de quelques siècles il se retrouverait au même point où nous le voyons aujourd'hui.

            —Holbach

65. Selon Holbach la vie de société

    A— oblige l'homme à résister aux coups du sort.
    B— n'est pas indispensable au bonheur de l'homme.
    C— est rendue indispensable à cause de la faiblesse de l'homme.
    D— est le résultat d'un contrat social.

66. Selon Holbach

    A— la société a l'inconvénient de faire accroître les besoins de l'homme.
    B— l'homme qui vit en société n'a pas de dangers à craindre.
    C— il devrait y avoir une loi contre les gens qui veulent se faire ermites.
    D— l'homme ne peut longtemps triompher tout seul des difficultés qui l'environnent.

67. D'après ce passage il est possible d'inférer que

    A— les philosophes ne pensaient pas tous comme Holbach.
    B— les philosophes opposés à Holbach avait perdu l'espoir de gagner leur cause.
    C— la Révolution française devait bientôt éclater.
    D— Holbach n'aimait pas la nature.

68. Holbach se déclare l'ennemi des philosophes qui veulent nous faire quitter la vie de société

    A— parce qu'une telle tentative produirait une révolution.
    B— parce qu'il faudrait trop de temps, des siècles, pour prouver laquelle des deux philosophies est la bonne.
    C— sans même se demander si un pareil projet serait praticable.
    D— parce qu'il faudrait, pour réussir dans un tel projet, détruire l'homme.

69. Holbach croit que les hommes, à l'état primitif,

    A— ne se distinguaient guère des animaux.
    B— n'avaient ni désirs ni facultés rationnelles.
    C— étaient dénaturés.
    D— ne voulaient pas se perfectionner.

70. Holbach développe son idée

    A— en montrant que la vie de société est une conséquence de l'ignorance de l'homme.
    B— en montrant comment la vertu diminue avec l'accroissement des rapports sociaux entre les hommes.
    C— par un paragraphe qui insiste sur les causes de la vie de société, suivi d'un deuxième paragraphe qui insiste sur ses effets.
    D— par un paragraphe qui insiste sur la valeur de la vie sociale, suivi d'un autre paragraphe qui explique la futilité de toute tentative qui serait faite pour la détruire.

- - - - - - -

## PASSAGE 6

La liberté n'existe point exclusivement dans la république, où les publicistes des deux derniers siècles l'avaient relégué d'après les publicistes anciens. Les trois divisions du gouvernement, monarchie, aristocratie, démocratie, sont des puérilités de l'école, en ce qui implique la jouissance de la liberté: la liberté peut se trouver dans une de ces formes, comme elle en peut être exclue. Il n'y a qu'une constitution réelle pour tout l'Etat: liberté, n'importe le mode.

La liberté est de droit naturel et non de droit politique. Ainsi qu'on l'a dit fort mal à propos: chaque homme l'a reçue en naissant sous le nom d'indépendance individuelle. Conséquemment, et par dérivation de ces principes, cette liberté existe en portions égales dans les trois formes de gouvernement. Aucun prince, aucune assemblée ne saurait vous donner ce qui ne lui appartient pas, ni vous ravir ce qui est à vous.

D'où il suit encore que la souveraineté n'est ni de droit divin ni de droit populaire: la souveraineté est l'ordre établi par la force, c'est-à-dire par le pouvoir admis dans l'Etat. Le roi est le souverain dans la monarchie, le corps aristocratique dans l'aristocratie, le peuple dans la démocratie. Ces pouvoirs sont inhabiles à communiquer la souveraineté à quelque chose qui n'est pas eux: il n'y a ni roi, ni aristocrate, ni peuple à détrôner.

Ces bases posées, l'historien n'a plus à se passionner pour la forme monarchique ou pour la forme républicaine: dégagé de tout système politique, il n'a ni haine ni amour ou pour les peuples ou pour les rois; il les juge selon les siècles où ils ont vécu, n'appliquant de force à leurs moeurs aucune théorie, ne leur prêtant pas des idées qu'ils n'avaient et ne pouvaient avoir lorsqu'ils étaient tous et ensemble dans un égal état d'enfance, de simplicité et d'ignorance.

                —Chateaubriand

Directions: Translate the preceding passage into correct, idiomatic English. Use the booklet provided for this purpose. **Please write legibly.**

PART II—HISTORY AND CIVILIZATION

Directions: Items 91-115 refer directly or indirectly to certain ones of the passages and
authors in Part I. In certain cases you may wish to look back at the selections. For each
item, blacken the answer space corresponding to the one best completion.

- - - - - - - - - - - -
Leave answer spaces 71-90 blank.
- - - - - - - - - - - -

Items 91-95 refer to Passage 1 above.

91. Maupassant a écrit ce conte

    A- avant la chute de Napoléon III.
    B- avant la naissance de la IIIe république.
    C- après la guerre franco-prussienne.
    D- au temps de la première guerre mondiale.

92. Maupassant est un écrivain

    A- de l'école romantique.
    B- parnassien.
    C- de l'école naturaliste.
    D- symboliste.

93. Maupassant est surtout connu pour

    A- ses contes.
    B- ses essais philosophiques.
    C- sa poésie.
    D- son théâtre.

94. Maupassant est né en Normandie. Cette ancienne province

    A- se trouve dans le Midi, c'est-à-dire, près de la côte basque.
    B- est célèbre pour son cidre, aussi bien que pour ses grandes villes de Rouen et du
       Havre.
    C- est près de la frontière allemande.
    D- est un pays d'oliviers et de mûriers.

95. Un des peintres célèbres qui a été le contemporain de Maupassant s'appelle

    A- Géricault.
    B- David.
    C- Cézanne.
    D- Delacroix.

Items 96-100 refer indirectly to Passage 2 above.

96. Bien avant Arvers, Du Bellay écrivit, lui aussi, des sonnets. Il vécut

    A- au temps de Richelieu.
    B- avant les guerres de religion.
    C- après la publication de l'édit de Nantes.
    D- au temps de Jeanne d'Arc.

97. Du Bellay est surtout connu pour

    A- son théâtre.
    B- ses découvertes d'anciens manuscrits latins.
    C- sa poésie.
    D- sa musique.

98. Du Bellay appartenait au groupe

    A- des symbolistes.
    B- des romantiques.
    C- de la Pléiade.
    D- des Grands Rhétoriqueurs.

99. Le Sonnet eut ses origines en Italie.  L'influence italienne en France, si grande à l'époque de Du Bellay, se fait encore remarquer dans l'oeuvre de son contemporain

    A— Baudelaire.
    B— Bossuet.
    C— Ronsard.
    D— Villehardouin.

100. Du Bellay est né en Anjou, province que traverse la Loire.  Ce fleuve

    A— a sa source en Suisse.
    B— se jette dans la Méditérranée.
    C— coule vers l'est.
    D— se trouve au sud de la Seine.

Items 101-105 refer to Passage 3 above.

101. Buffon a écrit

    A— au temps de Voltaire.
    B— pendant l'époque de Napoléon.
    C— pendant le siècle de Louis XIV.
    D— au temps de Rabelais.

102. Buffon est connu pour

    A— ses romans réalistes.
    B— sa poésie satirique.
    C— son théâtre, où les passions sont finement analysées.
    D— des ouvrages consacrés aux sciences naturelles.

103. Buffon est né en Bourgogne.  Cette partie de la France

    A— est célèbre pour ses vins de Bordeaux.
    B— se trouve dans l'est du pays.
    C— fait partie des provinces d'Alsace et de Lorraine.
    D— se trouve près de l'Espagne.

104. Pendant la Guerre de Cent Ans la Bourgogne fut alliée avec les Anglais contre la France.  Cette guerre eut lieu aux

    A— XIIe et XIIIe siécles.
    B— XIVe et XVe siécles.
    C— XIIIe et XIVe siécles.
    D— XVe et XVIe siécles.

105. Le personnage le plus célèbre de la Guerre de Cent Ans s'appelle

    A— Louis XI.
    B— Richelieu.
    C— Jeanne d'Arc.
    D— Charlemagne.

Items 106-109 refer to Passage 5 above.

106. Holbach, contemporain de Voltaire, a écrit

    A— pendant le règne de Louis XV.
    B— pendant le règne de Louis XIII.
    C— pendant la Révolution.
    D— au début du XIXe siècle.

107. Holbach, par son allusion aux philosophes qui veulent fuir la société, semble viser

    A— Lamartine.
    B— Hugo.
    C— Rousseau.
    D— Chateaubriand.

108. Holbach est né en Allemagne, sur la rive gauche du Rhin. Parmi les rois français qui ont rêvé de faire du Rhin la frontière nord-est de la France, on pourrait nommer Henri IV qui a régné

    A- au début du XVIe siècle.
    B- au début du XVIIe siècle.
    C- au début du XVIIIe siècle.
    D- à la fin du XVIIe siècle.

109. Henri IV est surtout célèbre pour avoir promulgué l'Edit de Nantes. Cet édit eut pour résultat une diminution

    A- de la violence dans la guerre contre Charles V d'Espagne.
    B- des guerres de religion.
    C- du pouvoir des nobles français.
    D- de la persécution des Albigeois.

Items 110-115 refer to _Passage 6_ above.

110. Chateaubriand a surtout écrit

    A- pendant les années qui ont immédiatement précédé la chute de Napoleon III.
    B- à l'époque de Zola et Daudet.
    C- sous Napoleon Ier.
    D- avant la Révolution française.

111. Chateaubriand a beaucoup contribué au développement du

    A- romantisme.
    B- symbolisme.
    C- classicisme.
    D- naturalisme.

112. Chateaubriand est surtout connu pour

    A- sa poésie.
    B- son théâtre.
    C- son traité sur les beautés de la religion chrétienne.
    D- son traité sur l'architecture gothique.

113. Chateaubriand a contribué à la renaissance en France du goût pour les vieilles églises. Le romancier qui a rendu célèbre dans le monde entier la cathédrale de Paris s'appelle

    A- Musset.
    B- Gautier.
    C- Hugo.
    D- Vigny.

114. L'architecture gothique se développa d'abord

    A- dans l'Ile de France.
    B- dans le Midi.
    C- en Picardie.
    D- en Alsace-Lorraine.

115. Plusieurs grand écrivains religieux vécurent au XVIIe siècle. Un des plus célèbres fut

    A- Calvin.
    B- Bossuet.
    C- Descartes.
    D- Boileau.

- - - - - - -

## PART III—AUDITION TEST

Directions: (For items 116-125) The examiner will read a series of statements which are to be considered with reference to the three pictures reproduced below. Blacken the answer space corresponding to the picture to which each statement applies. **If it applies to none of the pictures, blacken space D.**

A

B

C

Example: A droite et à gauche on voit plusieurs arbres.

In this case the correct space to blacken would be A.

Remember that you should blacken space **D** if the statement applies to **none** of the pictures.

# NOTES

*Note:* In footnotes, whenever Roman and Arabic numerals inclosed in brackets, e.g., [II, 174], follow a reference, the Roman numeral indicates the volume number of Coleman's *Analytical Bibliography*, and the Arabic numeral the number of the item which concerns the reference.

## FOREWORD

1. The members of the College French staff since 1920, with their periods of service, are: O. F. Bond (1920——), Robert Winter (1921–23), Durbin Rowland (1923——), Ernest Haden (1928–35), R. C. Trotter (1929–31), Leon P. Smith (1930–35), Lawrence Andrus (1935–39), Sylvain Minault (1940–42), Roger Oake (1945–50), George Playe (1946——), Hugh Davidson (1946——), John Prévost (1949——), Merle Perkins (1950——).

## THE LURE OF LANGUAGE

1. "Language involves an array of intricate problems, especially those concerning the relation of language to personality and thought. In language learning, where the complexities of both language and learning must be handled simultaneously, the problems we confront are usually those which are the most baffling of each field individually; and additional difficulties arise out of the combination" (Harold B. Dunkel, *Second-Language Learning* [Boston: Ginn & Co., 1948], p. 1).

2. C. A. Wheeler, *Enrollment in the Modern Foreign Languages in Secondary Schools and Colleges of the United States* (New York: Macmillan Co., 1928).

3. R. H. Fife and A. Coleman, *An Analytical Bibliography of Modern Language Teaching (1937–1942)*, Vol. III (New York: King's Crown Press, Columbia University, 1949). Vols. I (1927–32) and II (1932–37), by Algernon Coleman, were published by the University of Chicago Press in 1933 and 1938, respectively.

4. *Modern Language Instruction in Canada* ("Publications of the American and Canadian Committees on Modern Languages," Vols. VI and VII [2 vols.; Toronto: University of Toronto Press, 1928]).

5. C. H. Handschin, *Methods of Teaching Modern Languages* (Yonkers-on-Hudson: World Book Co., 1923).

6. R. D. Cole, *Modern Foreign Languages and Their Teaching* (New York: D. Appleton & Co., 1931); revised by J. B. Tharp (1937).

7. T. E. Oliver, *The Modern Language Teacher's Handbook* (Boston: D. C. Heath & Co., 1935).

8. "The scientific emphasis on experimentation, quantifications, exact measurement, and the like may demand a mind set found among only a few of those persons attracted to languages. . . . The language teacher draws back in dismay when he realizes that workers in such varied fields as anthropology, child

development, education, literary criticism, law, linguistics, neurology, philosophy, psychiatry, psychology, semantics, sociology and speech correction . . . are also interested in speech and language" (Dunkel, *op. cit.*, p. 7).

9. O. F. Bond, "A Preliminary Survey of Research and Experimentation in Modern Foreign Language Pedagogy," *Mod. Lang. Jour.*, XVIII (May, 1934), 551–56; also J. B. Tharp, "Second Annual Survey of Research and Experimentation in Modern Foreign Language Teaching," *Mod. Lang. Jour.*, XX (October, 1935), 31–36; and "Third Annual Survey . . . ," *ibid.*, XXI (October, 1936), 36–41.

## CHAPTER I

1. Michael West, *Language in Education* (London: Longmans, Green & Co., 1932).

2. H. C. Morrison, *The Practice of Teaching in the Secondary School* (Chicago: University of Chicago Press, 1926; rev. ed., 1931).

3. Peter Hagboldt, *Language Learning* (Chicago: University of Chicago Press, 1935).

4. Algernon Coleman, *Teaching of Modern Foreign Languages in the United States* (New York: Macmillan Co., 1929).

5. "Learning our students is just as important as teaching them; indeed it is prerequisite to good teaching. It has been suggested that if one-fourth of the energy now devoted to *teaching* were devoted to *learning* our students, the remaining three-fourths would produce ten times the good results now achieved, and would eliminate most of the ills that attend our present half-blind teaching efforts" (Ben D. Wood, *New York Experiments with New Type Modern Language Tests* [New York: Macmillan Co., 1927], p. 99).

6. In the University of Chicago *Announcements*, the first-year French course has been numbered at various times 101, 102, 103; 1, 2, 3, and 1ABC to denote the three quarter courses in the year sequence. To prevent confusion, the present terminology "1ABC" is adopted here and elsewhere in the book.

7. Students with one unit of language credit, e.g., one year of high-school French, normally registered for French 1C; special cases were placed in 1B. These placements changed as the course developed.

8. Vice-president MacIntosh of Haverford College, in *Behind the Academic Curtain* (New York: Harper & Bros., 1948), asserts that 61.1 per cent of college students in institutions over 1,000 fail to complete their course of study, primarily because of academic failure, with financial difficulties, transfer, personal, health, domestic, and other reasons in the order named. He concludes that "the successful end of a college course lies in its beginning."

9. Sixty per cent of the one-year group failed on the placement tests given in the University of Wisconsin in 1931–44, according to F. C. Cheydleur (correspondence, 1947).

10. Dean Ernest H. Wilkins, of the College of Arts, Literature, and Science, in January, 1924, organized twenty-four faculty-student committees "to inaugurate a systematic campaign for the improvement, through faculty-student

cooperation, of the conditions of our undergraduate life and work." The *Report of the Committee on Distribution of Students' Time* appeared in 1925 (Chicago: University of Chicago Press).

11. E. L. Thorndike, *Adult Learning* (New York: Macmillan Co., 1928), p. 269, compares the gains in French studies in two large evening schools in New York City. Taking the age range twenty to twenty-four as the base, he indicates a 59 per cent gain for the fourteen- to sixteen-year range; an 86 per cent gain for the seventeen- to nineteen-year range; an 89 per cent gain for the twenty-five- to twenty-nine-year range, and an 86 per cent gain for those aged thirty or more. He concludes that there is little difference between adults and children in learning and that the trouble is that adults *believe* they cannot learn so well.

## CHAPTER II

1. The 1921 outline was a revision of an untried 1919 outline organized similarly with a phonetic introduction, grammar-for-reading, and practice in aural comprehension, and leading to early intensive and extensive reading, with speech and writing deferred. E. H. Wilkins, in the Preface to his *First Italian Book* (Chicago: University of Chicago Press, 1920), recommended a similar procedure, saying: "In the teaching of a modern foreign language to students who have passed the age of childhood the first several weeks should be devoted exclusively and intensively to enabling them to acquire a good understanding of that language as written and spoken; and that the study of grammar as such, and the endeavor to train students to speak and write the language, should be postponed until a good understanding of the language as written and spoken has been attained. This I believe to be true not only for students who need primarily the ability to understand the language as written, but also for those who desire primarily a practical speaking and writing knowledge" (p. v).

2. Although placement tests have been given since 1931 to new students for the purpose of aiding advisers in counseling, the faculty did not recommend the placing of students in the College program on the basis of proved competence instead of credits until autumn, 1943 (for foreign languages, autumn, 1946) (see Benjamin Bloom and Jane Allison, "Developing a Placement Test Program" in *The Idea and Practice of General Education*, ed. F. Champion Ward [Chicago: University of Chicago Press, 1950], pp. 281–96).

3. So persistent and general is this ignorance of grammatical terminology that the faculty, in 1949, recommended committee publication of a manual "to explain and illustrate the fundamental terms and usages of English grammar" and that all incoming students be required to purchase it. The manual, *Elements of English Grammar*, was published by the University of Chicago Press (1951).

4. The lesson sheets were a revision of the grammatical material in O. F. Bond and Hilda Norman, *Military Manual of Elementary French* (Austin, Texas: E. L. Steck, 1918).

5. See p. 43.

6. They were still viewed officially as registrants in a department of the

University High School, one of the Laboratory Schools of the School of Education.

7. See pp. 125–27.

8. See pp. 12–13.

9. O. F. Bond (chairman) and Robert Winter, in French; John C. Ransmeier and Frederick Hanley, in Spanish.

10. The method used was similar to the presentation of the verb in O. F. Bond, *En Route!* (Boston: D. C. Heath & Co., 1938).

11. By this procedure, the student *won* his freedom from classroom attendance on the basis of his ability to do a high quality of work through individual study. The practice antedates the New Plan policy of granting such freedom as a *general principle*, available to anyone without proof of worthiness.

12. Especially in respect to cultural content and proficiency in speech and writing.

13. See O. F. Bond, "The Modern Languages Taught by Correspondence," *Proceedings of the Ninth Annual Conference of the National University Extension Association* (Milwaukee, 1924).

## CHAPTER III

1. See Reuben Frodin, "Very Simple but Thoroughgoing" in *The Idea and Practice of General Education: An Account of the College of the University of Chicago*, ed. F. Champion Ward (Chicago: University of Chicago Press, 1950), pp. 25–99; also Chauncey S. Boucher, *The Chicago College Plan* (Chicago: University of Chicago Press, 1935); revised by A. J. Brumbaugh (1940).

2. See O. F. Bond, "The Organization and Administration of a First Year French Course at the College Level," in W. C. Reavis, *Studies in Secondary Education*, Vol. II: *University High School* ("Supplementary Educational Monographs," No. 26 [Chicago: University of Chicago Press, 1925]), pp. 177–201.

3. "The greater the number of pages successfully read, the greater are the students' abilities in all other language arts. . . . This is the result of our experience in the Junior College of the University of Chicago, where the ability to read the foreign language intelligently is the primary aim. Altogether independent from each other in the manner and aim of our observations, we came to the same conclusions in different classes and languages, German, French, and Spanish. The best written theme, the best oral expression, the quickest analysis of a difficult sentence structure, always came from the student who had read with great interest and, therefore, intelligently and a great deal" (Peter Hagboldt, "Reading and Its Influence upon Other Language Objectives," *Jahrbuch für deutsche Pädagogik*, 1924).

4. See pp. 12–13.

5. "You would probably succeed in building up an extensive writing vocabulary if you were to treat writing in the same way and in the same spirit and to the same extent that you have the extensive reading" (H. C. Morrison, memorandum, July, 1924).

6. "Mass education is ill-adapted to produce the highest type of personalities. ... The touch of the *individual* teacher is the most potent educational force. It is said that our colleges have not a staff adequate to supply such individualized guidance; I answer that if we are to do our work we shall have to find them. Better a few students well educated than many inadequately trained" (Ernest DeWitt Burton, *The Business of a College* ["Alumni Pamphlets," No. 1 (University of Chicago, 1923)]).

7. "This is, of course, a perfectly natural outcome of American tradition. You take modern language courses in order to get credit and to graduate, but it would be obviously unfair to suggest the use of the foreign language in any practical way whatsoever. ... Perhaps sometime some of the instructors may find that students can read French and German and Spanish" (H. C. Morrison, correspondence, July, 1924).

8. See pp. 61–64.

9. See O. F. Bond, "The Organization and Use of a Departmental Reading Collection in the Modern Languages," *Mod. Lang. Jour.*, IX, No. 8 (May, 1925), 483–88; also A. F. Kuhlman, "Some Implications in the New Plan of the University of Chicago for College Libraries," *Library Quarterly*, III, No. 1 (January, 1933), 21–36.

10. The statement was phrased and proposed to the board by Professor Morrison.

11. See O. F. Bond, "Reading for Language Power," *Mod. Lang. Jour.*, X, No. 7 (April, 1926), 411–26.

12. O. F. Bond, *Introduction to the Study of French* (mimeographed ed., 1924); revised and published by the University of Chicago Press (1926); recast and republished as *En Route!* (Boston: D. C. Heath & Co., 1938).

13. See Peter Hagboldt, "An Experiment on Reading Known Material in Beginners' Classes," *Mod. Lang. Jour.*, IX, No. 6 (March, 1925), 342–54. The experiment was not repeated because the student, left to his own choice, preferred to read original German texts.

14. See p. 71, n. 3.

15. The totals included known material read in German translations, and material read and reread.

16. See pp. 93–95.

17. Cf. H. C. Morrison, *The Practice of Teaching in the Secondary School* (2d ed.; Chicago: University of Chicago Press, 1931): "A rough method of identifying the presence of the adaptation in a reading course is to note when the learner begins to read voluntarily upon exposure to attractive reading material" (p. 472). "... The standard set either by the passing-grade method or by the standardized norm throws us back into a situation in which the adaptation will not be attained except by a casual few" (p. 473). "In the reading of a foreign language, the associated skills which are built up on the basis of the reading adaptation can in general be described as *fluency*" (p. 19). "The adaptation is a unitary thing, and the pupil has either attained it or he has not. ... Skill, on

the other hand, is essentially a variable. . . . Two individuals can differ widely in skill and yet each possess skill" (p. 21).

18. See pp. 84–85, 160–61, 171.

19. Cf. p. 77, n. 11; a complete tabular analysis is given in the article.

20. "Throughout the stage of silent reading, in class, from books, the emphasis is upon much reading rather than upon intensive reading. The teaching problem is to furnish the basis for so much practice with content which has a meaning and appeal of its own that the principle of initial diffuse movements may have full swing, under motivation which originates in interest in the content read" (Morrison, *op. cit.*, p. 496).

21. The survey was made by Durbin Rowland and O. F. Bond. Cf. O. F. Bond, "Junior College Work in Modern Foreign Languages," in W. S. Gray (ed.), *The Junior College Curriculum* (Chicago: University of Chicago Press, 1930), pp. 181–200.

22. Frodin (*op. cit.*, p. 41) reports that in 1923 approximately one hundred graduate students were teaching elementary courses and that the annual turnover in the staff of these courses was 40 per cent.

23. The Study program appeared in March, 1925, as *Bulletin No. 2;* it was later reprinted as Appendix 1, in A. C. Coleman, *The Teaching of Modern Foreign Languages in the United States* (New York: Macmillan Co., 1929). Only a few of the 123 problems listed were investigated by the Study.

24. Cf. "Two American Experiments in Language Teaching. I. The Bond Reading Method," in *Modern Language Instruction in Canada* (Toronto: University of Toronto Press, 1928), I, 490–99.

25. Outlines and details were given to Professor Coleman in May, 1925; he asked Professor Young to try them out at the University of Iowa. This was the first application of our procedures elsewhere. For an account of the Iowa experiments see (1) C. E. Young and G. E. Vander Beke, "An Experiment in Second-Year French," *Mod. Lang. Jour.*, XI (October, 1926), 25–31; (2) C. E. Young and Josephine Daus, "An Experiment in First-Year French," *Mod. Lang. Jour.*, XII, No. 5 (February, 1928), 356–64; (3) Coleman, *op. cit.*, pp. 151–54 [I, 199].

26. Especially chaps. xxiii ("The Language Arts") and xxiv ("Teaching in Foreign Language"), pp. 467–511, which drew upon five years of reportage by members of the Junior College staff.

27. See Peter Hagboldt, *How To Study Modern Languages in College* (Chicago: University of Chicago Press, 1925); also his *How To Study Modern Languages in High School* (Chicago: University of Chicago Press, 1925). These pamphlets were part of the required supplies for the student.

28. See p. 82.

29. "We see the better course and acknowledge that it is the better; we follow the worse. In other words, our vision of right and truth is but a lesson learned. It is difficult to be too confident of the regenerative power of the School in the complex of human affairs, if only the schoolmaster can learn to identify and impart the true learning products, in the place of the daily routine of lessons conned and performance scored" (Morrison, *op. cit.*, p. 62).

30. In June, 1922, the authors of the Los Angeles *Course of Study Monograph* asserted that teaching high-school students to write and speak a foreign language was unjustifiable, that *abundant reading is basic to learning to read,* that reading should begin early and continue (to even ten times the amount then read!), that composition work was of little value in a course with reading ability in view, and that little grammar was needed before beginning to read. These were radical views six years before the Coleman report. However, in the *Course of Study* that followed this declaration, all four language aims were asserted, the class reading was set at 75 pages for the first year, and at 175 pages for the second year, and *mastery* of the grammatical minima for "oral and written use" was prescribed from the first semester on.

31. "From the passing grade to the highest grades awarded, partial performance is accepted and sanctioned as valid performance. Now, even granted that performance is translatable into learning, mastery can certainly not arise out of partial performance. The whole theory, therefore, of necessity eventuates in building up in the developing pupil the conviction that performance is achievement, that very inferior work is acceptable work, and that the most superior performance is still less than full performance. . . . The pupil comes to see any task which he has to do, not as a thing to be accomplished in a finished manner as a matter of course, but rather as an undertaking upon which he will economize effort to the degree which experience has taught him will be accepted. . . . The attitude carried over into adult life means irresponsibility, low standards, and, whenever the social controls become relaxed, lawlessness in a variety of social relations" (Morrison, *op. cit.,* pp. 48–49).

32. See p. 189.

33. "Sustaining motivation, arising out of genuine interest is a very intimate relationship between subject matter and the learner, and it is obviously the only form which can be depended upon as an element of the ultimate learning products, namely, abiding and general intellectual interest and educational self-dependence" (Morrison, *op. cit.,* p. 111).

34. See p. 77, n. 12. In 20 lesson assignments, the grammar, syntax, and phonology necessary for reading were analyzed and drilled, without reference to their active use in speech and writing. The vocabulary was limited to 500 high-frequency words in the Wilkins and Henmon lists.

35. Cf. Robert D. Cole, "Selecting French Readers," *Mod. Lang. Forum,* XVII, No. 2 (April, 1932), 42–45.

36. O. F. Bond, *The Sounds of French* (Chicago: University of Chicago Press, 1925), a *graded* phonetic manual with progressive drills on the separate speech sounds, taken singly, in syllables, and in words. The 34 exercises were recorded on five 12-inch double-disk records by Columbia for the Student Educational Records, Inc., Lakewood, N.J. Subsequently, manual and records were transferred to D. C. Heath & Co., as part of the "Heath-Chicago Series."

37. The project called for a progressive development of the speech and writing skills through the use of "construction patterns," without the use of retranslation or rules of usage. It was postponed until word counts should be

available (1929), and then abandoned for lack of a syntax count (published in 1943).

38. O. F. Bond, *Review Essentials of French Grammar and Composition* (New York: Macmillan Co., 1925). The innovations were (*a*) the limitation of vocabulary and thought content by the use of two short stories (*Deux amis, La dernière classe*) as a basis of examples and exercises and (*b*) a wide choice of drill types, direct and indirect, oral and written, formal and free, providing a needed flexibility for our programs.

39. The first volume of the series was to develop the *physical* and *political* France by combining geography and history and relying heavily on cognates; the second would develop the *personal* France by means of an anthology of fiction and nonfictional passages dealing with French life; and the third, also an anthology, would present French *cultural* contributions in the nineteenth century.

40. "When a child is learning to read a language, he reads and the *reading-book* teaches him. Everything therefore depends on the book; the teacher is a mere master of ceremonies" (Michael West, *Learning To Read a Foreign Language* [London: Longmans, Green & Co., 1926], p. 16).

41. "[The teacher] feels that no text available is worth following in detail. This belief may be sound since few existing texts have been prepared for this sort of use. Publishers are in the business to sell books, and they try to toss sops in the direction of as many potential users as they can. As a result, present texts are often such a hodge-podge that they cannot be followed without ending in chaos" (Harold Dunkel, *Second-Language Learning* [Boston: Ginn & Co., 1948], p. 147).

42. In 1934, the University of Chicago Press made a joint publishing arrangement with D. C. Heath & Co. by which the latter would publish and distribute Press texts in French, Spanish, German, and (lately) Russian under the joint imprint of the "Heath-Chicago Language Series."

43. The *American Council Alpha French, German, and Spanish Tests* (Yonkers-on-Hudson: World Book Co., 1926). V. A. C. Henmon prepared Part I (vocabulary) of the French test; Algernon Coleman, Parts II (grammar) and III (reading); and Marion Trabue, Part IV (composition scales). For an analysis of the tests see V. A. C. Henmon, *Achievement Tests in the Modern Foreign Languages* (New York: Macmillan Co., 1929) [I, 6].

44. Cf. Peter Hagboldt, "Achievement at the End of the Second Quarter, Measured by the A.C. Alpha Test," *German Quarterly*, I, No. 4 (November, 1928), 160–69; and "Achievement after Three Quarters of College German as Measured by the A.C. Alpha Test, Form B," *ibid.*, II, No. 2 (March, 1929), 33–43 [I, 176]. The results led him to consider the A.C. norms as indicative of "depressingly low standards."

45. Cf. M. V. O'Shea, *The Reading of the Modern Foreign Languages* (U.S. Bureau of Education, Bull. XVI [1927]) [I, 550]; also A. Dvorak, "The Prevalence and Utility of the Modern Foreign Language Requirements for the

Master's and Doctor of Philosophy Degrees," in *Studies in Modern Language Teaching* ("Publications of the American and Canadian Committees on Modern Languages," Vol. XVII [New York: Macmillan Co., 1930]), pp. 475–91.

46. "We must learn how to measure education as well as schooling. Useless hurdles must be abandoned. For every doctorate candidate to be required to pass a language examination no longer should be defended in the name of scholarship. . . . Applied to *every* candidate, it is a hurdle which is completely superficial and entirely hypocritical" (Alonzo G. Grace, "From Potsdam to Bonn," *University of Chicago Magazine*, XLIII, No. 3 [December, 1950], 14).

47. ". . . In effect, transfer of learning takes place in so far as the learner perceives similarities of structure or meaning between the new situations and the ones in which he learned the responses" (R. W. Tyler, "The Need for a More Comprehensive Formulation of the Theory of Learning a Second Language," *Mod. Lang. Jour.*, XXXII, No. 8 [December, 1948], 565).

48. "Not once, to the writer's knowledge, has a foreign language department conducted a study to ascertain in how short a time it is possible to develop in the young scholar the ability to use the foreign language as a tool, the need for which is used as a justification for the foreign language requirement in practically every reputable graduate school and college" (Dvorak, *op. cit.*, p. 491). This statement was made in 1930.

49. Made by Émile Stéphan and Hélène Coustenoble, of the University of London. The recordings included selections from the Gospels, *Le Bourgeois gentilhomme*, *L'Avare*, *Cyrano de Bergerac*, *Le Crime de Sylvestre Bonnard*, Hugo, De Musset, Béranger, Voltaire, and La Fontaine.

50. See p. 91, n. 36.

51. See pp. 247 ff. More recent and more elaborate installations are at the Peabody Institute for Teachers, Ohio State University, University of Louisiana, Northwestern University, Cornell College, Purdue University, University of Utah, etc.

52. G. T. Buswell, *A Laboratory Study of the Reading of Modern Foreign Languages* ("Publications of the Modern Language Study," (Vol. II [New York: Macmillan Co., 1927]) [I, 3]; cf. also Coleman, *op. cit.*, pp. 147–51.

53. Michael West, *Bilingualism (with Special Reference to Bengal)* ("Occasional Reports," No. 13 [Calcutta: Government of India Central Publication Branch, 1926]); cf. also M. A. Buchanan and E. D. MacPhee, "An Annotated Bibliography of Modern Language Methodology," in *Modern Language Instruction in Canada*, I, 215–19.

54. "The implications of the term 'direct method' as employed by Professor Buswell . . . are not, in the judgment of the Committee, to be fully identified with those suggested in such professional discussions of method [Jespersen, Kirkman, Walter, Schweitzer] in teaching foreign languages, but rather, for example, with the procedure outlined by Morrison . . . which is summarized as 'learning to read thought content by abundant experience in reading thought content from the beginning'" (Buswell, *op. cit.*, Foreword, p. vi).

55. West, *Learning to Read a Foreign Language*, p. 6; see also West, *Language in Education* (London: Longmans, Green & Co., 1929). Both books offer in condensed form the essential findings of *Bilingualism*.

## CHAPTER IV

1. "Because of the wide range of factors which must be taken into account, language experimentation is extremely difficult and demands the most careful planning and execution. Unfortunately, in practice most experiments are hastily conceived, short-lived, and executed under appalling difficulties" (F. B. Agard and Harold Dunkel, *An Investigation of Second-Language Teaching* [New York: Ginn & Co., 1948], p. 300).

2. See p. 65, n. 1.

3. Cf. Reuben Frodin, "Very Simple but Thoroughgoing," in *The Idea and Practice of General Education: An Account of the College of the University of Chicago*, ed. F. Champion Ward (Chicago: University of Chicago Press, 1950), p. 89, n. 42.

4. The parallelism between these recommendations and those in our reports is explainable by the fact that Superintendent Morrison and Dean Wilkins were the instigators of the commission.

5. In 1927, Junior College students constituted 47 per cent of French 2A, 50 per cent of Spanish 2A, and 80 per cent of German 2A registrants.

6. See p. 36.

7. "There can be no doubt about the necessity of sweeping away, completely and for all time, the time-serving conception which has thus far so largely dominated the organization and administration of modern language instruction. The continuance of this indefensible iniquity would be a crime against both teachers and students. It is the direct cause of many of the worst evils attending modern language work. It puts a premium upon stupidity and laziness, and penalizes intelligence and industry" (Ben D. Wood, *New York Experiments with New Type Modern Language Tests* [New York: Macmillan Co., 1927], p. 102).

8. Cf. Chauncey S. Boucher, *The Chicago College Plan* (Chicago: University of Chicago Press, 1935), pp. 3–7.

9. Cf. *ibid.*, pp. 289–96; also C. S. Boucher, "Readjustments in the Junior College Curriculum at the University of Chicago," in W. S. Gray (ed.), *The Junior College Curriculum* (Chicago: University of Chicago Press, 1930), pp. 170–80; and "The New Plan at the University of Chicago," in W. S. Gray (ed.), *Recent Trends in American Education* (Chicago: University of Chicago Press, 1930), pp. 46–60.

10. "In building an educational institution, one of the things that should be kept in mind is that education is largely a matter of will. If a man is to be educated, he must want to be educated. He cannot be educated against his will. He can be told that if he wants to be educated, there are certain things he must do. But he cannot be forced to be educated. Not much will be accomplished by forcing him to attend classes; nor is it likely that forcing him to attend will do his character as much good as having him see for himself the penalties of failing

to attend voluntarily" (Robert M. Hutchins, *The State of the University: 1929–1949* [privately circulated, September, 1949]).

11. The R grade was counterfeit currency from its invention, as Dean Boucher's memorandum to the College faculty (October 26, 1932) shows: "In some courses effective instruction can be given only with the co-operative participation of students desiring the instruction; in such a course, whenever a student shows a disinclination to co-operate effectively, he may be notified by the instructor that henceforth he will be regarded as a visitor and will be reported R; or, when a student, through lack of adequate preparation or ability, shows himself to be an unreasonable drag upon the progress of the majority who can and do work effectively in a co-operative enterprise, he may be notified by the instructor that henceforth, if he continues to attend, he will be regarded as a visitor, and will be reported R. . . . An instructor is not obligated to devote any more of his time and efforts than he may choose to give to 'visitors.' "

12. See pp. 66 ff.

13. Cf. O. F. Bond, "Junior College Work in Modern Foreign Languages," in Gray, *The Junior College Curriculum*, pp. 181–99; also "A Reading Technique in Elementary Foreign Language Instruction: Structure," *Mod. Lang. Jour.*, XIV, No. 5 (February, 1930), 363–74, and "Results and Implications," *ibid.*, XIV, No. 7 (April, 1930), 532–44.

14. "No method has ever yet been evolved and no book written, nor in the nature of the case is it likely that such ever will be produced, which will enable anybody to follow a routine course in the assurance that certain results must follow" (H. C. Morrison, *The Practice of Teaching in the Secondary School* [1st ed.; Chicago: University of Chicago Press, 1926], p. 221).

15. Only 15 of the 386 registrants in elementary modern language courses in the College in 1932 were studying the foreign language in order to satisfy the College language requirement.

16. "Objectives are the most important variables in teaching and learning because they tend to determine everything else except the characteristics of the student" (Harold B. Dunkel, *Second-Language Learning* [Boston: Ginn & Co., 1948], p. 121).

17. "The efficiency of our higher institutions of learning, in the future, will be dependent not upon the number they eliminate . . . but upon the extent to which they guide students wisely, train them in proper habits of thinking, become interested in their individual abilities and personal welfare, reorganize the materials of instruction, improve their methods of teaching, introduce programs of work adapted to modern society and to the needs of the students" (L. D. Coffman, "Major Problems of the Freshman Year," *Transactions and Proceedings of the National Association of State Universities*, XXII [1927], 42).

18. "The learning process is a series of random movements, hit or miss, in which the hits gradually come to exceed the misses and the latter finally disappear altogether. Sometime during the struggle of hits and misses, a feeling of confidence in language use comes and thenceforth learning is simply a matter of the final elimination of misses, that is to say, the acquisition of skill or facility.

Such is the essence of language-arts learning everywhere" (Morrison, *op. cit.*, p. 481).

19. Cf. Michael West, *Language in Education* (London: Longmans, Green & Co., 1932), pp. 56–60. This principle is known also as "learn to read by reading," "learn to speak by speaking," etc.

20. See p. 91, n. 34.

21. Cf. O. F. Bond, *Introduction to the Study of French* (rev. ed.; Chicago: University of Chicago Press, 1926), pp. 92–101; also *En Route!* (Boston: D. C. Heath & Co., 1938), pp. 93–98.

22. "There is perhaps no part of the field of general education characterized by more inefficiency than that which deals with training in English writing and the learning of foreign languages. It is easy to believe that the chief reason for such inefficiency has been the failure, first, to discriminate between the educational purposes which grammar is well calculated to serve; and, second, to realize that the use of discourse as a means of receiving or expressing thought can be learned only on principles which are wholly unlike those which apply to the acquisition of an understanding of the structure of discourse" (Morrison, *op. cit.* [1st ed.], pp. 216–17).

23. O. F. Bond, *Terre de France* (Chicago: University of Chicago Press, 1928), the first of the three projected cultural readers (cf. above, p. 92, n. 39); it was a condensation of Gallouédec and Maurette's geography of France, followed by an anthology of the political history of the nation.

24. W. B. Pillsbury and C. L. Meader, *The Psychology of Language* (New York: D. Appleton & Co., 1928), pp. 140 ff.

25. "The latter [the grammatical daily-lesson type of approach] attempts to teach a language through the application of science-type principles to a discourse situation. It rarely succeeds and then only in a casual and uneconomical way" (Morrison, *op. cit.*, p. 474).

26. See p. 91, n. 36.

27. "Many people think that a good command of foreign language accent is synonymous with command of the language itself. It does not follow. . . . On the other hand, vocalization seems to be intimately a contribution to the acquisition of language-use sense. Reading probably always involves that subconscious utterance which is sometimes called inner speech and which seems to be bound up fundamentally with the thought process itself" (Morrison, *op. cit.*, p. 494).

28. "The formalist can quickly kill an incipient intellectual interest of this sort by becoming unduly critical as to whether the pupils are 'reading thoroughly.' It is not essential that they should read thoroughly. Thoroughness applies to the actual mastery of reading ability and not to drudgery with exercise work. If they are reading voluntarily what they desire to read, that is quite sufficient. . . . Free reading which is really free gives us the best possible evidence of approaching mastery of the true learning product, because it enables us to observe the behavior of the pupil in an unsupervised and unconstrained situa-

tion. The pupil who is really reading will disclose to the teacher in manifold ways the reality and extent of his reading" (Morrison, *op. cit.*, p. 496).

29. See p. 92, n. 38.

30. Benjamin F. Woodbridge, *La Semeuse* (Chicago: University of Chicago Press, 1928), an anthology of nineteenth-century literature, unsimplified, with exercises in language use.

31. "If a student before graduating from high school or from college could take a newspaper or current scientific, historical, political, or sociological book or magazine and read it readily and understandingly, would he not be encouraged to continue his reading in these fields after graduation? On the other hand, if his reading in school and in college is confined almost wholly to material which is pursued for the purpose of furnishing illustrations or practice in grammatical, rhetorical or literary excellence, is it not probable that after graduation, when he becomes absorbed in current problems, he will abandon his foreign languages and confine his reading to his native tongue?" (M. V. O'Shea, *The Reading of the Modern Foreign Languages* [U.S. Bureau of Education, Bull. XVI (1927)], p. 78) [I, 550].

32. "It is hard for the teacher who is habituated to the grammatical approach to believe that it is at all possible for pupils to understand the meaning of a form unless that form has been practiced in isolation until the pupil has a visual image of its place in the list of its kindred. It is still harder for him to believe that the pupil can manage a meaning expressed, let us say, in Latin indirect discourse, unless he has studied the principles of indirect discourse and then learned to make the application. Nevertheless, the pupil does so in practice, with on the whole less difficulty than his fellow-pupil at the same stage of advancement who has been trained in the grammatical principle involved and who has memorized all the paradigms which he has occasion to use. He does so because he is learning according to the principles which apply to effective learning in this type" (Morrison, *op. cit.*, p. 488).

33. "There should be concurrently two kinds of reading: *intensive*, that is, reading with exact understanding under the strict control of the instructor; *extensive*, that is, reading for content, without such control. The former will develop accuracy and precision; the latter will stimulate interest, alertness, and swift vision, will give the opportunity for a wider range of situations, will train the student in the habit of direct and ready comprehension, develop in him the power of inference, and give him the necessary confidence in himself. The last point is of great importance" (M. S. Pargment, "What Constitutes a Reading Knowledge of a Foreign Language and How Can It Be Acquired," *French Review*, III [December, 1943], 78).

34. Cf. Morrison, *op. cit.*, p. 474.

35. See p. 48.

36. O. F. Bond, *Introduction to the Study of French;* John C. Ransmeier, *A Spanish Recognition Grammar* (1929); and Peter Hagboldt, *A Modern German Grammar: Minimum Essentials Inductively Presented* (1927). All three were published by the University of Chicago Press.

37. Carlos Castillo, *Lecturas introductorias* (Chicago: University of Chicago Press, 1928), a prepared cultural reader dealing with the geography, history, folklore, traditions, and monuments of Spain.

38. Peter Hagboldt, *Inductive Readings in German*, Book I (1928); Book II (1929), both published by the University of Chicago Press. F. W. Kaufmann collaborated on *Book I*. The two volumes presented "an introduction to the spirit of German life and literature."

39. The University of Chicago Press issued three different experimental series of French texts: (1) the "Junior College French Series" (1926–28); (2) the "Chicago French Series" (1929–32); and (3) the "Heath-Chicago Series of Graded French Readers" (1936——).

40. Ernest H. Wilkins and Antonio Marinoni, *L'Italia* (Chicago: University of Chicago Press, 1920). Like all cultural readers, its oversized vocabulary (one-third of the book) was not compensated for by the cognate stock.

41. Cf. *Les Langues modernes* (August–September, 1914); also, "L'Enseignement des langues vivantes par la méthode scientifique," *Bulletin de la Société française de pédagogie* (June, 1927); and his articles in *Mod. Lang. Jour.*, XIV, No. 1 (October, 1929), 1–19; No. 2 (November, 1929), 122–27 [I, 19]. His method is based on his textbook *La Famille Dupont* (1920), reissued by Holt & Co. in 1931.

42. Harold E. Palmer, *The Scientific Study and Teaching of Languages* (London: Harrap & Co., 1917); cf. also *Modern Language Instruction in Canada* (Toronto: University of Toronto Press, 1928), I, 139–40. "Scientific" for Palmer meant a close analysis of problems, a precise nomenclature, and a complicated philological approach to language learning.

43. Ernst Otto, *Methodik und Didaktik des neusprachlichen Unterrichts* (Leipzig: Velhagen & Klasing, 1921; rev. ed., 1925) [I, 96], a scholarly and influential work.

44. George E. Vander Beke, *French Word Book* (New York: Macmillan Co., 1929), a collaboration of 96 school and college French teachers in counting 1,147,748 running words in 85 prose units of fiction, plays, newspapers, and historical and scientific material [I, 17].

45. Frederic D. Cheydleur, *French Idiom List* (New York: Macmillan Co., 1929), the work of 85 collaborators in counting 1,183,000 running words in 87 prose text units, including novels, plays, newspapers, reviews, history, biography, science, philosophy, and religion [I, 16].

46. See pp. 96, n. 53, and 98, n. 55.

47. Harold Palmer, *Report on Research Activities* (Tokyo: Institute for Research in English Teaching, 1929), an attempt to define scientifically a "word" and an "idiom," using a special nomenclature for their classification. In counting words, instead of accepting only frequency, he would make a place for normality, weight, and functional, semantic, stylistic, and phonetic values. Under "weight" he discusses "light" words (simple words with definite meanings) and "heavy" words (having many values, as "get," "will," "go," "away").

48. *Modern Language Instruction in Canada*, I, xliii, Introd.

49. Michael West, *The New Method Readers* (London: Longmans, Green & Co., 1926–30), Books IA, IB, II–IX.

50. Edward L. Thorndike, *The Teacher's Word Book* (New York: Teachers College, Columbia University, 1921; 2d ed., 1927), an alphabetical list, with indexes of range and frequency, of the 10,000 commonest words found in *ca.* 4,565,000 running words in 41 English sources.

51. West took his material from *Robinson Crusoe, The Deerslayer, King Solomon's Mines, Count of Monte-Cristo, Treasure Island,* etc. He gave three reasons for his choices and their use: (1) they act "as an interesting and effective form of revision"; (2) they encourage the student "by demonstrating to him how greatly he has progressed, and what pleasure is to be had from his accomplishment"; and (3) "these books provide valuable practice for increase in fluency and ease of reading. Fluency is the best and only sure preventive of the habit of mental translating." The argument for the use of "plateau" readers has not been better phrased.

52. From 1927 to 1932, to quote West, "what began as a teaching experiment became for a time an enquiry into and an experiment in the construction of teaching materials"; see his *Bilingualism (with Special Reference to Bengal)* ("Occasional Reports," No. 13 [Calcutta: Government of India Central Publication Branch, 1926]), p. 262.

53. Helen M. Eddy, *Beginning French: Training for Reading* (1929), basic inductive-type grammar; Grace Cochran and Helen M. Eddy, *Si nous lisions* (1929), first-semester reader, correlated with *Beginning French,* Lessons I–XV; Grace Cochran and Helen M. Eddy, *Pierrille* (Clarétie) (1929), second-semester reader, correlated with *Beginning French,* Lessons XVI–XXVI; Helen M. Eddy, *French Workbook* (1929), pupil's drillbook to accompany *Beginning French;* Helen M. Eddy, *Progress Tests* (1929), folder of 58 objective progress tests on grammar and 49 tests on pronunciation; Helen M. Eddy, *Training for Reading: Teacher's Manual* (1929–30).

54. See pp. 179 ff.

55. Cf. Robert D. Cole, *Modern Foreign Languages and Their Teaching* (rev. ed.; New York: D. Appleton & Co., 1937), pp. 74–77, 81–92, 112; also Algernon Coleman, *Analytical Bibliography of Modern Language Teaching,* Vol. I (1927–32), items 29–38, and Vol. II (1932–37), *passim;* the main argument centered upon Coleman's recommendation in favor of the reading objective.

56. Cf. Robert A. Hall, "Progress and Reaction in Modern Language Teaching," *Bull. Amer. Assoc. Univ. Professors,* XXI, No. 2 (summer, 1945), refers to the adoption of the reading objective as the "Munich of modern language teaching."

57. Ruth Meade, Grace Cochran, and Helen M. Eddy, *Sans famille* (Malot) (1931), to follow *Beginning French,* Lesson X, and *Si nous lisions,* Lesson X; Allis Pollard, Grace Cochran, and Helen M. Eddy, *L'Abbé Constantin* (Halévy) (1931), to follow *Beginning French,* Lesson XV, and *Si nous lisions,* end; Marguirette Struble and Helen M. Eddy, *Les Trois mousquetaires* (Dumas) (1932), basic reader for third semester; Florence Williams, Grace Cochran, and

Helen M. Eddy, *Madame Thérèse* (Erckmann-Chatrian) (1932), supplementary to follow *Pierrille*.

58. J. D. Haygood, *Les Oberlé* (Bazin) (1936); Louis H. Limper, *Le Petit Chose* (Daudet) (1934); Laura B. Johnson, *Le Livre d'or* (Mme de Witt) (1932); Louise Seibert, *Perrine* (Malot) (1934); L. C. and Clotilde Dahl, *Le Roi des montagnes* (About) (1938).

59. Cochran, Eddy, and Redfield, *Basic French I* (Boston: D. C. Heath & Co., 1936); Eddy, Cochran, Struble, and Williams, *Basic French II* (1940).

60. Grace Cochran, *Avant de lire* (1936).

61. Helen M. Eddy and Marguirette Struble, *Ecrivons* (1940).

62. A. G. Bovée, A. Coleman, H. M. Eddy, R. P. Jameson, and J. B. Tharp, "The Basic French Vocabulary," *Mod. Lang. Jour.*, XVIII (December, 1934), 238–74; reprinted in pamphlet form as "Supplementary Series," No. 2 [II, 543]. The committee was appointed in 1931.

63. West, *Bilingualism*, pp. 304–5.

## CHAPTER V

1. See p. 40. Our recommendations are echoed by Morrison: "If foreign language is in the program, then the library should have an abundance of informational material in the languages taught. Children should be released for free reading whenever opportunity serves, and we shall find many such opportunities. The pupils should have free access to the shelves and not be inhibited by the formalism of the typical library routine. Doubtless this practice will result in the loss of some books but loss can be reduced to a minimum, and the comparatively small annual cost traceable to this item is, after all, a productive cost" (H. C. Morrison, *The Practice of Teaching in the Secondary School* [2d ed.; Chicago: University of Chicago Press, 1931], p. 176).

2. See pp. 46–47.

3. M. Llewellyn Raney, "Junior College and Its Books," *Library Journal*, February 15, 1934; also, "The New College Plan at the University of Chicago and Its Library," *ibid.*, March 1, 1934.

4. A check during eleven days in November and December, 1927, showed 335 withdrawals, or approximately 30 calls per day.

5. One of the most popular lists in our files, integrating French literature and music and current local offerings in opera, recitals, ballet, and radio programs. It lists 50 compositions, 40 of which are based on literary works that are readable and accessible.

6. Prepared by H. D. Gideonse, of the College social science staff (1932).

7. O. F. Bond, *Extensive Reading Report Blanks* (Chicago: University of Chicago Press, 1926); large format: *Language Reading Report Blanks* ("Heath-Chicago French Series" [1930]).

8. Cf. Peter Hagboldt, *How To Study Modern Languages in College* (Chicago: University of Chicago Press, 1925), pp. 13–16.

9. (1) A survey of extensive reading and its effects in two sections of 1ABC and 2AB, 1926–28 (Bond); (2) a check of the calls from the reading collection,

1927-32 (Kaden); (3) an analysis of student reading summary sheets, 1927-32 (Rowland, Bond); and (4) a study of extensive reading by author and title, 1927-32 (Rowland, Bond).

10. Durbin Rowland, "Rate and Quantity in the First Year's Extensive Reading in College French," *Mod. Lang. Jour.*, XIX, No. 3 (December, 1934), 181-86.

11. The 679 entering students in the College in 1931 averaged 218 points (S.D., 62.6) on the A.C.E. (Thurstone) psychological test. A group of 88 who took French 1ABC averaged 221.8 points (S.D., 62.5), which is close to the norm for the total group. The standard median was 164 (S.D., 58.1).

12. Cf. Durbin Rowland, "Some Results of Free Choice in Extensive Reading in French," *Mod. Lang. Jour.*, XX, No. 8 (May, 1936), 471-76. Rowland lists the 50 most popular novels and the 25 most popular plays read and analyzes some of the reasons for the students' choices.

13. *La Science française* (2 vols.; Paris: Larousse, 1915). Each special field of the bibliography is prepared by a prominent French scholar in that field, who also provides a historical introduction to the section. The work was done under the direction of Lucien Poincaré for the Ministère de l'Instruction publique.

14. "The development in the pupil of the capacity for willing sustained application, founded only on the expectation that the subject matter will ultimately yield a sustaining interest, is therefore the foundation of any systematic technique of teaching and learning. It is the starting-point of control technique" (Morrison, *op. cit.*, p. 111).

15. "Every people has its own peculiar thought processes which are faithfully reflected in peculiar forms of expression. The pupil who learns to read and reads a great deal comes to sense these peculiar meanings. To some extent he enters into the spirit of the other people and indeed this is in itself an important educational objective" (Morrison, *op. cit.*, p. 469).

## CHAPTER VI

1. The last three analyses were made by H. D. Baird, E. Mosier, and Leone Cheshire, respectively, members of the staff of the Board of Examiners.

2. The total number of grades is 4,114, which is larger than the number reported by the Bureau of Records, because of the inclusion of grades incurred in University College (downtown) classes.

3. Cheydleur states that, in ten years at the University of Wisconsin, the average number of conditions and fails in French was 17 per cent for the first semester and 11 per cent for the second semester ("The Use of Placement Tests in Modern Languages at the University of Wisconsin," *Mod. Lang. Jour.*, XV, No. 4 [January, 1931], 262-80) [I, 445].

4. Cf. O. F. Bond, "Junior College Work in Modern Foreign Languages," in W. S. Gray, *The Junior College Curriculum* (Chicago: University of Chicago Press, 1929), pp. 181-99.

5. See pp. 82-85.

6. See pp. 107–12.

7. Distributions, norms, and percentile ranks are given for college students in the *Manual of Directions*, pp. 9–12.

8. *American Council French Grammar Test* (selection type), prepared by F. D. Cheydleur (Yonkers-on-Hudson: World Book Co., 1927) [I, 461]; cf. also F. D. Cheydleur, "The Construction and Validation of a French Grammar Test of the Multiple Choice Type," *Jour. Educ. Res.*, XVII, No. 3 (March, 1928), 184–96 [I, 427].

9. The A.C.E. medians for seven college semesters are: vocabulary, 58.7; grammar, 35.9; reading, 22.9. No sixth-semester norms are published. Less than 100 cases are involved in the data.

10. "For some time many language teachers have doubted whether initial reading ability could later be expanded to include aural and oral commands. On the other hand, some proponents of the oral-aural introduction had assumed that these abilities would lead, almost automatically, to satisfactory reading ability. Many parts of our data cast grave doubts on this assumption" (F. B. Agard and Harold Dunkel, *An Investigation of Second-Language Teaching* [New York: Ginn & Co., 1948], p. 296).

11. Fife, in 1925, stated that of 9,169 college Freshmen presenting two years or more of foreign languages for admission, only 38 per cent continued the subject in college (*Germanic Quarterly*, I, 14–15). In 1930, Rice claimed that 80 per cent in California high schools stopped language study with two years. In 1942, Klier reported that 58 per cent of the language pupils in Wisconsin public schools took only *one year;* 27 per cent, two years; 4 per cent, three years. In 1950, Cheydleur, at the University of Wisconsin, stated that 20 per cent stopped at the end of one year in "conversational method" courses, and 24.9 per cent in "traditional method" courses.

12. Cf. Algernon Coleman, *Teaching of Modern Foreign Languages in the United States* (New York: Macmillan Co., 1929), pp. 109–10, 169–70, 232–33, 276–78.

13. See p. 93, n. 44.

14. Henmon reported that 50 per cent of 4,173 high-school students tested by the A.C.E. *Alpha Silent Reading Test* were above or below their classification by a semester or more and added: "The situation in colleges was no better" (V. A. C. Henmon, *Achievement Tests in the Modern Foreign Languages* [New York: Macmillan Co., 1929], p. 146).

15. The A.C. total group median was 164 (S.D. 58.1); for the Chicago group, 1932 Freshmen, the median was 218 (S.D. 62.6).

16. The group median on the Thurstone A.C. test was 221.8 (S.D. 62.5), comparable to the achievement of the total group.

17. See p. 175.

18. Cheydleur, in the group A and group B experiments (see p. 179), reported for one college semester a correlation of .54 between vocabulary and reading.

19. Other admissible explanations, in part, are the nature of the A.C.E. test as a whole, its technique of testing vocabulary in isolation, the inclusion of grammatical variables in the vocabulary section, the admixture of techniques in the functional grammar section, and irregular values for the choices in both sections. It is also possible that, for the fluent reader, grammar is a matter more of vocabulary than of usage and syntax.

20. The 1931 and 1932 personnel in our courses were "Old Plan" entrants, little affected by the reorganization changes.

21. See pp. 163 ff.

22. Dunkel inclines toward the latter opinion, but as a hypothesis in lieu of an anchor test, such as a test in linguistic aptitude. He points out that the first factor by the Thurstone technique generally tends to be a general factor which measures nothing much specifically. Ormiston found a G factor of .762 [III, 70].

23. The zero loading in 1A reading for Factor V is understandable. Grammar in 1A is of the recognition type; in the A.C.E. test it is functional, with completion, mutation, substitution, and multiple-choice techniques, and requires a knowledge of nomenclature differing from that used in 1A.

24. A. Coleman, "Testing Achievement in Modern Languages," *Proceedings of the Ohio State Educational Conference, 1929*, pp. 389–99 [I, 392].

25. Cf. R. D. Cole, "A Plea for More Experimental Work by College Departments of Modern Foreign Languages," *School and Society*, Vol. XXXV (April 9, 1932).

26. Cf. A. Coleman, Lorna Murphy, Alma Prucha, C. E. Young, and G. E. Vander Beke, "The Milwaukee Experiment in Reading," in Algernon Coleman *et al., Experiments and Studies in Modern Language Teaching* (Chicago: University of Chicago Press, 1934), pp. 145–90 [II, 388].

27. The amount was slight, control sections reading 450 pages, and the experimental sections 1,352 pages. The six sections numbered 102 students.

28. Cf. F. D. Cheydleur, "Placement Tests in Foreign Languages at the University of Wisconsin, 1930–1943," *Bull. Univ. Wisconsin*, No. 2470 (November, 1943), pp. 9 ff.

29. See p. 120, n. 53.

30. "From the point of view of set-up, scope, and testing, this project, covering the period from 1927 to 1933, constitutes one of the most valuable contributions on the results of the 'direct' reading method" (F. D. Cheydleur, "Attainment by the Reading Method," in *op. cit.*, p. 104) [II, 387].

31. *Ibid.*, pp. 100–144.

32. Cf. *ibid.*, pp. 108–10, replies to objections raised by the author in 1932.

33. W. H. Shields, supervisor of the Los Angeles experiment, was obliged to cut the program drastically, saying: "The reassignment downward of the Eddy material is significant. With the best of intentions and trials, our teachers find the series outline impossible to accomplish with fairness to pupils in our 40-minute periods" (memo, April 29, 1932). Were there other cases, unknown to Cheydleur?

34. Cf. F. D. Cheydleur, "Criteria of Effective Teaching in Basic French Courses at the University of Wisconsin, 1919–1943," *Bull. Univ. Wisconsin*, No. 2567 (August, 1945), p. 13, table showing effect on grades of the 1930–31 Wisconsin experiment.

35. "Those students who are to study a language for only two years should concentrate on the acquisition of a large vocabulary and a ready comprehension rather than upon a systematic study of the grammar of the language. But for those who intend to master the language an ever-increasing need of grammar develops" (G. A. Rice, "A Study of Achievement in French and Spanish in Junior and Senior High School, with Consideration of Some of the Factors That Condition Achievement," in *Studies in Modern Language Teaching* [New York: Macmillan Co., 1930], p. 462). Rice based his conclusions on the test data for 6,400 pupils in 210 classes in 15 California cities. Mastery of grammar would apply to only 20 per cent, at most [I, 18].

36. "The task [of the College] in brief then is to give a sound general education to those who want nothing more and to give a specific orientation in the divisional field to those planning to enter it, without at the same time ruining their general education by premature specialization" (R. M. Hutchins, "The Reorganization of the University of Chicago," *University of Chicago Record*, XVII, No. 1 [January, 1931], p. 7).

37. It was demonstrated at Stephens College from 1936 to 1940, under the direction of the author, and later at the Lyons Township (Ill.) Junior College, in 1940–42.

38. Cf. Helen M. Eddy, "Training for Reading: Technique," *Mod. Lang. Jour.*, XV, No. 3 (December, 1930), 176–91 [I, 171].

39. Carl C. Cassel, "On apprend à lire," *Clearing House*, VIII, No. 9 (May, 1934), 555–57 [II, 386].

40. Cf. H. E. Ford, "Written Tests as a Measure of Oral Achievement," *Modern Language Instruction in Canada* (2 vols.; Toronto: University of Toronto Press, 1928), II, 837–46. His data show that the written test is nearly as good an indication of oral ability as teacher's grades, since the latter are apparently based upon "ability to translate, functional grammar, and phonetic accuracy."

41. See p. 85, n. 24.

42. Cf. E. C. Hills, "Should Beginner's Courses in French, German, Italian, and Spanish Be Given in College?" *Mod. Lang. Jour.*, XIII, No. 2 (November, 1928), 101–11. Of 85 institutions, the University of Chicago was the only one with a "separate staff, organized independently, and composed entirely or chiefly of trained teachers who give the elementary courses." His approval is qualified.

43. "Elementary language teaching has too often been considered a period of penal servitude to be endured until the instructor has acquired sufficient departmental seniority and reputation to be allowed to teach what he really wants. . . . Few language teachers have made, or been able to make, a career

of studying language learning" (Harold Dunkel, *Second-Language Learning* [Boston: Ginn & Co., 1948], p. 6).

44. See p. 17.

45. Cf. O. F. Bond, "Adapting Instruction in the Modern Languages to Individual Needs," in W. S. Gray, *Provision for the Individual in College Education* (Chicago: University of Chicago Press, 1932) [II, 782, 783].

46. Cf. P. H. Churchman, "How May One Learn To Read?" *Mod. Lang. Jour.*, XXI, No. 5 (February, 1937), 323-32 [II, 429]; also, "Some Aspects of the Reading Emphasis," *Hispania*, XIX, No. 2 (May, 1936), 265-72 [II, 430].

## CHAPTER VII

1. See pp. 65 ff., 100 ff.

2. Cf. C. S. Boucher, *The Chicago College Plan* (Chicago: University of Chicago Press, 1935); revised by A. J. Brumbaugh (1940); also *The Idea and Practice of General Education*, ed. F. Champion Ward (Chicago: University of Chicago Press, 1950).

3. Final approval for granting the degree of B.A. on the completion of the prescribed curriculum was given in April, 1942.

4. See pp. 107 ff.

5. It became necessary, for practical reasons, to limit the administration of comprehensives to June, September, and December.

6. Under present practices, one may advise a student who fails in 1A or 1B not to continue further in the sequence, but one cannot prevent him from doing so. He is free also to essay the comprehensive.

7. In the spring of 1941, there were 106 registrants for 1C, of which 44 were attending class more or less regularly. The shrinkage from 1A in the autumn amounted to 60 per cent of the enrolment. In the June comprehensive, there were 68 applicants, 24 of whom were unknown to the staff. Thirteen examinees failed. The year's total loss was 75 students, or 71 per cent of enrolment—a high price for individual liberty.

8. From the Minutes of the College faculty, June 8, 1951.

9. "That in order to be eligible for the mark 'R' . . . the student must be one who has (*a*) completed at least three quarters of study (registration for courses) in the College, (*b*) passed all comprehensive examinations for which he is assumed to have prepared with the help of the courses taken, and (*c*) registered with his advisor for that mark within the first five weeks of the quarter" (Minutes, College faculty, June 1951).

10. Cf. Boucher, *op. cit.*, pp. 259-73; also R. M. Hutchins, *No Friendly Voice* (Chicago: University of Chicago Press, 1936), pp. 188-97.

11. "Report and Recommendations of the College Curriculum Committee" (March 11, 1933). The faculty sent the report back to committee.

12. Elsie M. Smithies (High School), H. W. Prescott (Division), and O. F. Bond (College).

13. ". . . The conclusion of their work, i.e., the four-year unit will mark the end of formal instruction for most students. They will not go on to the uni-

versity. Nevertheless we must have a curriculum which will, in the main, do as well for those who are going on as those who are not" (R. M. Hutchins, *The Higher Learning in America* [New Haven: Yale University Press, 1936], p. 77).

14. Cf. Daniel Feder and Grace Cochran, "A Study of Individualized Instruction at the College Level," *Mod. Lang. Jour.*, XXI, No. 1 (October, 1936), 23–35 [II, 788, 789].

15. Published under the direction of Ben D. Wood, by the Cooperative Test Service of the American Council on Education, New York. The first French form was issued in 1932.

16. See pp. 93–95.

17. Boucher, *op. cit.*, p. 34.

18. O. F. Bond and John C. Ransmeier, *Syllabus for French 101–106 and Spanish 101–106* (Chicago: University of Chicago Bookstore, 1932).

19. Courses numbered 107, 108, 109, in the Senior College, and higher courses.

20. With the status of "visitor," indicated in quarter reports by the mark "R."

21. See pp. 125 ff.

22. See pp. 104 ff.

23. See p. 194, n. 14; also [II, 789].

24. In March, 1929, and February, 1934, the author addressed the Iowa State Educational Conference on aspects of individualized study applied to language learning. In the interim, he was in correspondence with the Iowa staff.

25. Prepared by Paul Goode, published by the University of Chicago Press, 1931. We used form No. 17.

26. Tutorial speech-and-writing sections during 1933–36, open only to 2AB students, were popular and effective. They combined topical grammar review with cultural information.

27. Joseph A. Landry, *Graded French Word and Idiom Book* (Boston: D. C. Heath & Co., 1938) [III, 302], a service list of the first 4,569 Vander Beke items and 600 Cheydleur items.

28. See p. 120.

29. French 101, 102, and 103 was the official numbering for 1ABC.

30. The statement is more wishful than factual.

CHAPTER VIII

1. See pp. 115 ff.

2. See p. 48.

3. See pp. 119–22.

4. E.g., "Les trois ours," "Les douze mois," "Boum-Boum," and "La Cloche," in *Si nous lisions*.

5. Cf. Harold Palmer's series of French texts for use in the Belgian Congo: *Premier livre de français* (1939); *Deuxième livre* (1940); *Troisième livre* (1950); (with West) *Premier livre de lecture* (1950) (London: Longmans, Green & Co.).

6. Cf. Michael West, *Language in Education* (London: Longmans, Green & Co., 1929; 2d ed., 1932) [I, 103]; this and other points are discussed in detail.

7. The first two classes are "structurals"; the last two are "content" words. Later, West added a fifth classification, i.e., "zonal" ("rice" for the East, "bacon" for the West) (cf. M. West, "Vocabulary Selection," *Yearbook of Education* [London: Evans Bros., 1940]) [III, 288].

8. See p. 190, n. 45.

9. He advocated keeping the students on carefully graded material for a much longer time, to prevent them from forming a habit of "leaping over difficulties . . . and by a faulty inference form (and remain contented with) a completely wrong interpretation of a passage"; and he reflected on "the probable wastage in relearning words met once, but forgotten before they are encountered again." But he admitted that these objections had less application to mature students of college grade (cf. Michael West, "The Problem of 'Weaning' in Reading a Foreign Language," *Mod. Lang. Jour.*, XV, No. 7 [April, 1931], 481–89) [I, 187].

10. The "deceptive" cognate is not the problem in French for the English-speaking student that West feared it would be (cf. pp. 244–45, for cognate use in the *Graded French Readers*).

11. West found the "study-books" stuffy and loaded with literary and syntactical annotations. The "juveniles" he chose did not meet the standards of the English books he had in mind: *Moune et Roby*, *M. Méridien au pays des neiges*, *Le Trésor de M. Toupie*, etc.

12. Michael West, "English as a World Language and the Technique of Teaching It," *New Era*, I (January, 1933), 11–15 [II, 280].

13. The appearance in 1934 of *A Critical Examination of Basic English* (Toronto: University of Toronto Press), by West, Swenson, and others, and "English as a World Language," *American Speech*, Vol. IX, No. 3 (October, 1934), by West, was followed by a conference in New York under the auspices of the Carnegie Corporation to discuss word lists in the teaching of English as a foreign language. Subsequently, Michael West, Harold Palmer, and Laurence Fawcett prepared an "Interim Report on Vocabulary Selection," adopted in the London conference of 1935, and published by P. S. King & Son, as a *General Service List*, in 1936. It is commonly called the "Carnegie Report" [II, 498].

14. Georges Toudouze, *Le petit roi d'Ys*, simplified and edited by Michael West (Chicago: University of Chicago Press, 1934; English edition, London: Oxford University Press, 1935).

15. Edgar Dale, "Familiarity of 8,000 Common Words to Pupils in the Fourth, Sixth, and Eighth Grades" (unpublished; Columbus, Ohio: Bureau of Educational Research, Ohio State University, 1933); the first 2,000 words of Thorndike's list were assumed as known.

16. Elaine Swenson and Michael West, *The Counting of New Words in Textbooks for Teaching Foreign Languages* (Toronto: University of Toronto Press, 1934); the theory and technique of vocabulary control are Swenson's; the rating scales are West's.

17. Privately printed in sheet form, in Toronto. The classified list was in typescript. They were distributed only to workers on projects in Toronto and Chicago.

18. H. E. Palmer and A. S. Hornby, *Thousand-Word English* (London: Harrap & Co., 1937).

19. Edgar Dale, *Bibliography of Vocabulary Studies* (Columbus, Ohio: Bureau of Educational Research, Ohio State University, 1939) [III, 290]; Charles Fries and Eilene Travers, *English Word Lists* (Washington: American Council on Education, 1940) [III, 746]; Herman Bongers, *The History and Principles of Vocabulary Selection* (2 vols.; Woerden, Holland: Wocopi, 1947); A. Coleman, *An Analytical Bibiolgraphy of Modern Language Teaching* (3 vols.) (cf. p. xi, n. 3).

20. F. W. Kaeding, *Haüfigkeitswörterbuch der deutschen Sprache* (Berlin: Steiglitz, 1892); established as an aid in training stenographers, it set the pattern for later word counts.

21. Hayward Keniston, "Common Words in Spanish," *Hispania*, III (March, 1920), 85–96. His *Basic List of Spanish Words and Idioms* (Chicago: University of Chicago Press, 1933) and its revision, *A Standard List of Spanish Words and Idioms* (Boston: D. C. Heath & Co., 1941), are combined lists of the earlier one and those of Cartwright and Buchanan. The *Standard List* is a layering of 3,060 words and 575 idioms. The *Hispania* list was the first to show both range and frequency for a foreign language vocabulary.

22. E. L. Thorndike, *The Teacher's Word Book* (New York: Teachers College, Columbia University, 1921), a 10,000-word list. A *20,000-Word Book* followed in 1932 and (with I. Lorge) a *30,000-Word Book* in 1944. The latter includes the Lorge-Thorndike semantic count of 4.5 million words based on values in the Oxford dictionary.

23. Albert de la Court, *De meest voorkomende Woorden en Woordcombinaties in het Nederlands* (Batavia: Volkslectuur, 1937). In 1939 Gaston Vannes published his *Vocabulaire de néerlandais de base* (Antwerp: Sikkel), which is the De la Court list with French equivalents. De la Court lists 3,296 words, based on a million count.

24. See p. 123, n. 62.

25. Michael West, "Vocabulary Limitation," *Journal of Education*, LXXI, No. 842 (September, 1939), 582–84 [III, 287]. By "downward" he means the number of spelling units; by "sideways," the varieties of meaning for each unit. This dual aspect of a vocabulary word is later called an "L-graph."

26. Harold Palmer, *The Grading and Simplifying of Literary Material* (Tokyo: Institute for Research in English Teaching, 1932), see chap. ii, "A Brief Lexicological Survey," for his definitions.

27. V. A. C. Henmon, *French Word Book* (Madison: Bureau of Educational Research, University of Wisconsin, 1924), frequency list of 9,187 words, based on a count of 400,000 running words. Vander Beke listed the Henmon credits with his own, separately, placing the first 69 items occurring 453 times or more in Part I of his *Word Book*.

28. Of the Vander Beke first 1,000 words, 13.8 per cent were not used in the basic first-year readers. Furthermore, cognates were not counted (444 in *Pierrille*) nor a number of specific story-telling words (49 in *Pierrille*).

29. The 10,000-word book was preferred to the later list, which includes items from the Horn, Pressey, Curtis, Powers, and Classical League counts.

30. See p. 233, n. 15.

31. The main theme of his suggestions was to make the derivative idea a systematic principle in establishing a truly "basic" list. Some of his suggestions were accepted by J. B. Tharp in his revised *Basic French Vocabulary* (New York: Henry Holt & Co., 1939).

32. Cf. Vander Beke, *French Word Book* (New York: Macmillan Co., 1929), pp. 13–14. The correlation coefficient diminishes markedly for every 250 words, e.g., first 250 words, .71; second 250 words, .34; fourth 250 words, .07. West concludes that "the actual relationship between range and frequency has yet to be discovered" (*Definition Vocabulary* [Toronto: University of Toronto Press, 1935], p. 23).

33. H. E. Ford and R. K. Hicks, of the University of Toronto, compiled a "basic" French vocabulary by comparing the ranking of the first 500 words in the Vander Beke list by range and by frequency, with supplements of words slightly below either level. They used the list in preparing the *New French Reader* (New York: Henry Holt & Co., 1930).

34. Ernest Haden, Leon Smith, and Lawrence Andrus, of the College staff; and Dorothy McCann, of the London (Canada) Central Collegiate Institute.

35. Michael West and O. F. Bond, *A Grouped-Frequency French Word List* (Chicago: University of Chicago Press, 1939) [III, 320]. Part I ranks 2,049 "units" of 4,579 words, or 78 per cent of the 6,136 entries in the Vander Beke *French Word Book*. No word or group with a total credit of less than 26 is listed. Part II is an alphabetical arrangement to serve as an index. The principle of grouping frequencies of root words and derivatives was applied by B. Q. Morgan in his *German Frequency Word Book* (New York: Macmillan Co., 1929); by De la Court, *op. cit.*; and Bongers in the *K-L-M-English List* (see p. 246, n. 49).

36. *The Deerslayer* and *The Cloister and the Hearth* (cf. West, *Learning To Speak a Foreign Language* [London: Longmans, Green & Co., 1933], pp. 59–88), method of reducing the vocabulary [II, 384].

37. Michael West and James Endicott, *The New Method English Dictionary* (London: Longmans, Green & Co., 1935), approximately 24,000 items defined within a vocabulary of 1,490 words (final revision of the initial definition list of 1,779 words). Cf. West, *Definition Vocabulary*, for their methods of compilation and vocabulary reduction [II, 551].

38. The "prereading" part used deduction, inference, French-in-English devices, comic strips, cognates, "ask-and-answer" based on line drawings, identification of objects in "agglomerate" drawings, "look-see" and "head-tail-and-across" puzzles. The story part used fore-vocabularies for the sections, emphasized derivatives, affixes, and English elements, and introduced grammar only as needed in the story. Ninety-two per cent of the vocabulary was in the

West-Bond grouped-frequency word list; all but 45 words, in the minimum adequate vocabulary list; and 90 per cent, within the 1A/2C ratings in the *Basic French Vocabulary* (1934 list). In addition, all words were measured for their "learning burden" by the West scales.

39. The series originally proposed to West in 1932, but displaced by vocabulary studies and *L'Île mystérieuse,* was not undertaken until 1936, when the writer, in order to test the effectiveness of MAV, retold Dumas's *Le vaillant petit tailleur* as *Sept-d'un-coup* (Book I), the first step in a reading "staircase" of 20 readers, in two series (O. F. Bond *et al., Graded French Readers* [("Heath-Chicago Series") Boston: D. C. Heath & Co., 1936–52]).

40. The variables, listed separately by Vander Beke in Part II of the *French Word Book,* are: *trois, quatre, cinq, six, sept, huit, neuf; quel, quelle, quels, quelles; ton, ta, tes; ici, là; eux, ceci, cela, ça, quoi, lequel* (all forms).

41. *Dantès* (Book I, alternate) is told in 5,800 running words, with a new word density of 29, a learning burden of noncognate words (237), which is 91 per cent within MAV (excluding Henmon variables) and which constitutes only 43 per cent of the total vocabulary, and a cognate content of 317 words, or 57 per cent of the total.

42. The first five readers are issued in single-volume form under the title *Première étape;* the second five, under the title *Deuxième étape.*

43. Cf. Harold Dunkel, *Second-Language Learning* (Boston: Ginn & Co., 1948), p. 155.

44. In the Bengali-English experiments, West used a density of 60, or 17 new words per thousand running words. There was no cognate element present. For English-speaking students learning French, West thought that a density of 30 (33 per thousand) would be a "minimum rate for new words." Limper found that 60 per cent of the words beyond the first 500 in the *French Word Book* are cognates.

45. H. E. Palmer, *On Learning To Read Foreign Languages* (Tokyo: Institute for Research in English Teaching, 1932), p. 37.

46. John F. Miller, "A Vocabulary Study of Ten French Reading Texts Based on the Vander Beke French Word Book" (unpublished Master's thesis, University of Iowa, 1931) [I, 257].

47. It furnished 48 per cent of the 3,423 different words, including a separate count of semantic extensions, used in the complete series.

48. Of the 1,109 noncognate words introduced in Books I–V of the alternate series, 923, or 83 per cent, are within the MAV.

49. Bongers' *K-L-M List* consists of three separate zones of 1,000 words each, based upon a combination of the following word lists: Thorndike (20,000), Fawcett-Maki (6,000), Palmer's "Second Interim Report" (3,000), "Carnegie Report" (3,000), and Palmer-Hornby's *Thousand-Word English.* The *K-L-M List* was found to be adequate (97.48 per cent) by comparative analytical methods, using ten English works (such as *The Good Earth; Good-bye, Mr. Chips; Wuthering Heights; Tale of Two Cities; Black Beauty*), in amounts of 1,000 words each. Coverage claimed for the K-zone (first 1,000) is 89.46 per cent.

50. Yet the French press (November, 1951) announced the appointment of the Finno-Ugric scholar, M. Sauvageot, and the philologist, M. Gougenheim, in a UNESCO-sponsored project to draw up a list "qui comportera environ *un millier de mots* ... pour former une langue française de base," for propaganda purposes, the list to be ready within one year. According to plans as reported, their source will be "des dialogues courants enregistrés sur disques: dialogues d'hommes d'affaires, d'ouvriers étrangers, etc."

51. See p. 43.

52. See pp. 95 ff.

53. The Cornell laboratory is said to have cost $20,000, granted by the Gray Research and Development Co.; the audio-visual laboratory at Purdue, reportedly $15,000.

54. See p. 91, n. 36.

55. Currently in use are three records by Pierre Delattre: *French Speech Habits* (New York: Henry Holt & Co.).

56. Cf. Dunkel, *op. cit.*, p. 156.

57. Distributed by Henry Holt & Co., under the title of *Spoken French*.

58. See pp. 223 ff.

59. These records are in the *Anthologie sonore* (The Gramophone Shop, Inc., 18 E. 48th St., New York), a comprehensive collection of recordings, directed originally by Dr. Kurt Sachs, illustrating the history of music from the eleventh through the eighteenth century.

60. "The great difficulty with audio-visual aids is that they have usually not been adequately integrated with the work of the course. . . . They are a potential ally whose services are largely neglected" (Dunkel, *op. cit.*, p. 299).

61. The 35-mm. film strip and slides in color or black and white are promising sources (cf. Franco-American Audio-visual Distribution Center's publications, *Present-Day France* and *The French Heritage* [New York, 1951]).

62. Cf. R. W. Tyler, "The Need for a More Comprehensive Formulation of Theory of Learning a Second Language," *Mod. Lang. Jour.*, XXXII, No. 8 (December, 1948), 566.

63. Cf. Agard and Dunkel, *An Investigation of Second-Language Teaching* (Boston: Ginn & Co., 1948), p. 11.

64. "Teachers often begrudge the time demanded by an adequate program of tests. Believing that students come to class to be taught and not to be tested and being acutely aware of the few hours available for language teaching, they hate to spare a moment for testing or experimentation. But, since it is at least theoretically questionable how well spent teaching time will be in view of our present ignorance, this frugality is short-sighted" (Dunkel, *op. cit.*, p. 170).

65. Progress tests have been used since 1920; achievement tests since 1925; comprehensive examinations since 1946; and placement tests, officially, since 1947.

66. "The teacher who has . . . the fundamental objective in view all the time adjusts instruction, course content, and assimilative practice to the end in view. He tests with reference to the end, studies defects in the learning process,

and corrects them with the objective in mind. . . . This is the essence of direct teaching" (H. C. Morrison, *The Practice of Teaching in the Secondary School* [Chicago: University of Chicago Press, 1926; rev. ed., 1931], p. 470).

67. See the outline, pp. 220–22, for the place of each test and the explanation of the text abbreviations. In the table, *m.c.* refers to "multiple-choice"; *T-F*, to "true-false"; and *s.c.* to "sentence-completion."

68. For examples of test procedures see *Language Comprehensive Examinations: Sample Questions* (University of Chicago Bookstore, 1948) and *Description of Language Reading Examinations for Higher Degrees* (1950; issued by the University Examiners).

69. Cf. J. M. and R. C. Stalnaker, "Chance *vs.* Selected Distractors in a Vocabulary Test," *Jour. Educ. Psychology* (March, 1935), pp. 161–68. They conclude that "selected distractors were found to be marked to a significantly greater extent than were chance distractors . . . for items of each difficulty level measured."

70. See pp. 205 ff.

71. Cf. Ernest Haden and J. M. Stalnaker, "A New Type of Comprehensive Foreign Language Test," *Mod. Lang. Jour.*, XIX, No. 2 (December, 1934), 81–92 [II, 843], a technique borrowed from the French 2 comprehensives.

72. Cf. C. H. Judd, *Psychology of High School Subjects* (rev. ed.; Boston: Ginn & Co., 1927), p. 239; also H. R. Huse, *Psychology of Foreign Language Study* (Chapel Hill: University of North Carolina Press, 1931), p. 213. The two views are divergent, Judd advocating learning in context, and Huse supporting the memorization of word pairs. Cf. West, *Learning To Speak a Foreign Language*, p. 35, for a denial of the validity of the Huse experiments.

73. J. M. Stalnaker and William Kurath, "A Comparison of Two Types of Foreign Language Vocabulary Test," *Jour. Educ. Psychology*, XXVI, No. 6 (September, 1935), 435–42 [II, 853].

74. *The United States Armed Forces Institute Subject Examinations in the Foreign Languages at the High School and College Levels* (Chicago: Examinations Staff, 6010 Dorchester Ave., 1947).

75. Cf. F. B. Agard and Harold Dunkel, *An Investigation of Second-Language Teaching* (New York: Ginn & Co., 1948), pp. 42 ff.

76. Cf. R. D. Cole, *Modern Foreign Languages and Their Teaching* (New York: D. Appleton-Century Co., 1931; rev. ed., 1937), pp. 346–47.

77. Louise Seibert and Ben D. Wood, *Columbia Research Bureau Aural French Test* (Yonkers-on-Hudson: World Book Co., 1930).

78. Line drawings were used in the Seibert-Wood *Aural Test.* Cf. the audition test section of the 1952 form of the French 1 Comprehensive Examination, Appendix V, p. 315.

## CHAPTER IX

1. Comparison with the table for 1920–31 (Table 21, p. 153) shows that the reduction of wastage (through failure) under the Old Plan did not continue under the New Plan.

2. Harold Palmer and H. Vere Redman, *This Language Learning Business* (Yonkers-on-Hudson: World Book Co., 1932), the Palmerian doctrine of "language as speech," set in Socratic dialogue form, with a summary dismissal of other theories [II, 264].

3. O. K. Lundeberg and J. B. Tharp, *Lundeberg-Tharp Audition Test in French* (privately printed, 1929); cf. R. D. Cole, *Modern Foreign Languages and Their Teaching* (New York: Appleton-Century, 1931; rev. ed., 1937), pp. 343–46 [I, 470].

4. Cf. F. B. Agard and Harold Dunkel, *An Investigation of Second-Language Teaching* (Boston: Ginn & Co., 1948), pp. 41–55, describes the "Lower Level French" form. It was administered by phonograph recordings in order to minimize the subjective element encountered in the usual examiner.

5. Cf. *ibid.*, pp. 151–54 and 323.

6. See p. 276.

7. "If it is desirable to give the learner that independent critical command of the language which grammar implies, then let us organize a course in the essentials of grammar and offer it to pupils who have attained the reading adaptation" (H. C. Morrison, *The Practice of Teaching in the Secondary School* [Chicago: University of Chicago Press, 1926; rev. ed., 1931], p. 476).

8. Cf. Agard and Dunkel, *op. cit.*, pp. 279–301.

9. Cf. Roger Oake and George Playe, "The College Course in French: A Proposal," *Mod. Lang. Jour.*, XXXV, No. 3 (March, 1951), 204–9; possibilities of continuation study after 1ABC.

10. Cf. *The Placement Test Program of the College* (University of Chicago official bulletin).

11. See p. 290.

12. Agard and Dunkel, *op. cit.*, p. 295.

## CHAPTER X

1. Carl A. Krause, *The Direct Method in Modern Languages* (New York: Charles Scribner's Sons, 1916), p. 65.

2. "In education it is too often forgotten that the essence of experimentation is that final decision is reserved until the experiment is complete" (R. M. Hutchins, Inaugural Address [1929]).

3. "Half the beauty and power of our own speech is lost, unseen and unusable, to those who know no other language. To know only one's native speech is to be caught in a cage, condemned to limited vision and incomplete understanding" (*Report on the Curriculum* [University of Oregon, 1951]).

4. Cf. Detroit Institute of Arts, *The French in America: 1520–1880* (Detroit, 1951), catalogue of the special exhibition on the occasion of the two hundred and fiftieth anniversary of the founding of Detroit. See also Hélène and Robert Fouré, *Souvenirs français en Amérique* (Boston: Ginn & Co., 1940).

5. "As in the case of English and Mathematics, it would seem that the work in foreign language can and should be related closely to the context which a re-

quired curriculum in general education supplies" (F. C. Ward, "Languages," in *The Idea and Practice of General Education*, ed. F. Champion Ward [Chicago: University of Chicago Press, 1950], p. 214).

6. Radical changes in the status of modern foreign language instruction in our common schools are being proposed as this book goes to press. Cf. the address of E. J. McGrath, U.S. Commissioner of Education, presented at the Conference on the Role of Foreign Languages in American Schools, held in Washington, D.C., January 15 and 16, 1953 (reprinted, Boston: D. C. Heath & Co., 1953).

# INDEX

Absenteeism, 18–19, 51, 192–93

Achievement tests; *see* Tests

Activities of college students, investigation into, 12–13

Admission: to the College, 51–52; credit, for one unit of foreign language, 47–49

Advisers, board of official, 103

Agard, F. B., 283, 297

Age, influence of, in second-language learning, 22

American Council on Education *Alpha French Tests:* administration of, 109, 112, 151, 155–56, 195; attainment of "straight continuants" on, 157, 166–67, 170–71; results obtained on, analysis of, 161–72; tryouts of, 92–93

*Analytical Bibliography of Modern Language Teaching,* 4

Andrus, Lawrence, 258, 261, 264

Armed Services Training Program, tryout in French 1 of materials for, 195–96

Arvin, N. C., 189

Attainment in French 1: superiority of, investigation into causes of, 168–70; surveys of, 151–72; *see also* First-year French

Attendance in class: form for recording, 312–13; importance of, in foreign language courses, 198; statement concerning, in 1941 *Syllabus,* 211; *see also* Absenteeism; College of the University of Chicago

Audio-visual aids, 246–53

Audition room, equipment and plan of our, 247–50; *see also* Phonetics

*Audition Test in French* (Lundeberg-Tharp), 280

Aural comprehension: indirect evidence of proficiency in, 158; investigation into degree of, obtained in French 1, 282–83; results on standard tests of, 280–83; techniques used in testing, 270–75; *see also* Comprehensive examinations; Outline; Placement examinations; Syllabus; Tests

Baird, H. D., 157, 159, 160

*Bilingualism* (West), 96–98, 118

Board of examiners, 103

Boucher, C. S., 101, 104, 195–96

Buchanan, M. A., 237

Bulletin boards, 213

Bush, S. H., 190

Buswell, G. T., 96–98

Cassell, C. L., 186

Certification, based on learning products, 101–2

Cheshire, Leone, 172–76

Cheydleur, F. D., 181–87, 190

"Chicago French Series," experimental use of, outside Chicago, 182–83; *see also* Graded readers

Chronological order of subject matter in French 1, changes in, 41

Churchman, P. H., 190

Cochran, Grace, 181

Cognates: correlation between Thorndike's ranking of, and familiarity to tenth-grade pupils, 236; inferribility of, West's experiment in, 235–36; use of, in Bond's *Graded French Readers,* 245

Cole, R. D., 4, 190

Coleman, A. C., 4, 7, 33–34, 85, 93

College of the University of Chicago, the: Four-Year Plan of, 191, 193–94; "New Plan" of, 103; Two-Year Plan of, 191–93

"Commission on the Future of the Colleges," 100

Completions in French 1 and French 2, summary of, 309

Composition: accuracy in, importance of, 198; free, experiment with, 69

Comprehensive examinations: adoption of, 103; analysis of, for French 1, 254–75; aural proficiency in, results of measuring, 280–81; correlation of parts in, 262, 267–71, 274; grades obtained on, 268, 278–80; grammar items in, distribution of, 255; inclusion of cultural and comparative items in reading section of, 270, 272–74; inclusion of known material in reading section of, 270–73; omission of vocabulary section in, 271, 273–74; reading section of, contribution of, to total score of, 267; rules and procedures for, 276–77; specifications of, 255–60, 263–67, 269–73; specimen copy of 1952 form of, 315–30; "split," 195; students taking French 1, number and

361

distribution of, by year and course, 137, 139–41; diversity in, exemplified in field of art, 145–46; evaluation of, in computing final grades, 81, 86; as factor in language attainment, 175–76; first use of, in French 1A, 49, 50; forms for reporting, 56, 129, 198, 212; highest-ranking titles in, by amounts read, 141–42; how to get students to do, 189; individualizing of, 211; investigation into, basis of, 136; judging student's choice of, 148; minimum requirements for, experiment to determine, 58–59; nature and amount of, early in our experiment, 71, 75, 77–78, 89–90, 111; nonfictional works read in, commonest, 144, 145; norms for French 1ABC straight continuants, 140; personal choice in selecting material for, 147; progressive increase in amount of, effect of, upon grades, 83, 154; quarterly shifts in nature of, reasons for, 144–45; range distribution of amounts read in, 140–41; reaching individual student through, 198; reading maturity of French 1 students revealed in survey of, 146; removing requirements in, result of, 81; surveys of, in French 1ABC, 133–46; taste in selecting material for, question of, 148; techniques of reporting on, 56–57, 129–32; unbalanced programs in, problem of, 148; values of, 147–50; vocabulary-building through, 55; as voluntary activity in French 1A, 77–79, 90, 109; see also Outline; Reading; Syllabus

Factor analysis: intercorrelations in, of achievement in French 1ABC, 173–74; interpretation of results of, of French 1ABC, 174–76; materials and procedures used in, of French 1ABC, 172, 173

Failure: causes of, in French and Spanish 1ABC, 17–24; reduction of, by administrative changes, 25–26; request for mid-quarter reports on cases of, 30; see also Comprehensive examinations; Continuation study; First-year French; Grades; Instructor's reports; Placement examinations

Feder, Daniel, 202, 209

Ficken, C. E., 187

Fife, Robert H., 3

Final reports; see Instructor's reports

First trial course (1920–21): attainment in, 29, 31, 36; conclusions from, 32; continuation data on, 36–37; materials used in, 29, 31, 32; methods used in, 29, 30, 31, 32; objectives of, 28, 30, 32; outline for French 1, resulting from, 35; plan of, 28; rate of failure in, 37; recommendations in reports of, 30, 36, 102; registration and grades in 29, 31, 32; restrictions on, 33–34; shrinkage in, 37; testing program in, 35

First-year French (1ABC): accrediting of, 33, 211; arrangement of quarter-courses in, 216; compression of, into "capsule" course, 196; conditions affecting experimentation in, 27–28, 66–67; as elective, 193–94; as foundation course, 106; objectives of, 69, 213; organization of, 107–13; supplementary activities in, 209; as terminal course, 106, 194; test coverage in first quarter of, 255; training in first quarter of, importance of, 176; as validating course, 105

Ford and Hicks, 237

Foreign language study: aims of, in general education, 300; educational policy toward, influences affecting, 301–2; integration of, into curriculum, 305; interest in, 2, 301–3; place of, in Four-Year College, 193–94; preferences in, student, 14–17; reasons for, 14–16; tool and social values of, 303–4; see also Second-language learning

Foreign language teaching: competency as product of, 302–4; concentration on essentials in, 304; condition of, in last 50 years, 299–301; cultural information as concern of, 92, 305; grammar in, dominance of, 300; problems in, for investigation, 48; research into, 3–5, 177; status of, 301–6; syllabi and outlines in, need of, 305

Forms: for class attendance and study record, 312–13; for reporting extensive reading, 129–32; for student personal records, 310–11

Four-Year College, program of foreign language courses in, 104; see also College of the University of Chicago

French 101G (301); see Requirements

*French Word Book* (Vander Beke): publication of, 118; value and use of, in constructing minimum vocabulary, 233–41, 245

German, end of experiment in, 192; see also Hagboldt

Graded readers: achievement in French 1A through use of, 284–85; advantages and disadvantages of our, 228–29; "Chicago French Series" of, 119–24, 228–29; co-operation of West in plan-